MW00995673

Crypto-Finance, Law and Regulation

Crypto-Finance, Law and Regulation investigates whether crypto-finance will cause a paradigm shift in regulation from a centralised model to a model based on distributed consensus.

This book explores the emergence of a decentralised and disintermediated crypto-market and investigates the way in which it can transform the financial markets. It examines three components of the financial market – technology, finance and the law – and shows how their interrelationship dictates the structure of a crypto-market. It focuses on regulators' enforcement policies and their jurisdiction over crypto-finance operators and participants. The book also discusses the latest developments in crypto-finance, and the advantages and disadvantages of cryptocurrency as an alternative payment product. It also investigates how such a decentralised crypto-finance system can provide access to finance, promote a shared economy and allow access to justice.

By exploring the law, regulation and governance of crypto-finance from a national, regional and global viewpoint, the book provides a fascinating and comprehensive overview of this important topic and will appeal to students, scholars and practitioners interested in regulation, finance and the law.

Joseph Lee is a Reader in law in the School of Law at the University of Manchester, UK.

Routledge Research in Finance and Banking Law

For more information about this series, please visit: www.routledge.com/Routledge
-Research-in-Finance-and-Banking-Law/book-series/FINANCIALLAW

Crypto-Finance, Law and Regulation

Governing an Emerging Ecosystem

Joseph Lee

Routledge
Taylor & Francis Group

LONDON AND NEW YORK

First published 2022
by Routledge
2 Park Square, Milton Park, Abingdon, Oxon OX14 4RN

and by Routledge
605 Third Avenue, New York, NY 10158

Routledge is an imprint of the Taylor & Francis Group, an informa business

© 2022 Joseph Lee

British Library Cataloguing-in-Publication Data
A catalogue record for this book is available from the British Library

Library of Congress Cataloging-in-Publication Data
Names: Lee, Joseph (Law teacher), author.
Title: Crypto-finance, law and regulation : governing an emerging ecosystem / Joseph Lee.
Description: Abingdon, Oxon ; New York, NY : Routledge, 2022. |
Series: Routledge research in finance and banking law | Includes bibliographical references and index.
Identifiers: LCCN 2021041190 | ISBN 9780367086619 (hardback) |
ISBN 9781032211565 (paperback) | ISBN 9780429023613 (ebook)
Subjects: LCSH: Cryptocurrencies--Law and legislation.
Classification: LCC K4433 .L44 2022 | DDC 343/.032--dc23
LC record available at https://lccn.loc.gov/2021041190

ISBN: 978-0-367-08661-9 (hbk)
ISBN: 978-1-032-21156-5 (pbk)
ISBN: 978-0-429-02361-3 (ebk)

DOI: 10.4324/9780429023613

Typeset in Times New Roman
by Deanta Global Publishing Services, Chennai, India

To my parents and to the memory of my grandparents

Contents

Preface

I started working on this crypto-finance project in 2015, after I purchased my first crypto-asset, Bitcoin, with 10,000 Japanese Yen in Ginza district in Tokyo. I used it to pay for a plate of sushi. I then began to explore the possibility of using technology to connect stock markets and set up a research network on exchange interconnections that was founded by the British Academy. In 2016, a seminar was convened to examine the possibility of using a distributed ledger technology as an infrastructure for accessing finance and investing, overcoming geographical constraints. Alas, the technology limitations, as well as legal and regulatory restrictions, have shown that crypto-finance is in many respects incompatible with the current financial markets' operations and governance. I then began to consider whether crypto-finance can be developed in parallel to the incumbent financial markets, to increase financial inclusion and as a model for a shared economy.

Over the course of these years, I have met with researchers, practitioners and policy makers in finance and fintech industries who have provided me with invaluable guidance and feedback at various seminars and research engagement events that I have organised. Some of these events were funded by the UK Economic and Social Research Council. I would like to thank the following persons who have helped me during the course of this project, by providing institutional access and personal support: Mr Yuzo Kano of BitFlyer, Japan; Ms Diana Chan of EuroCCP; Dr Jochen Dürr of SIX Switzerland; Mr Ian Cornwall of FESE (Federation of European Securities Exchanges); Professor Andrea Sironi of Borsa Italiana; Dr Huang Nai-Kuan of the Taiwan Stock Exchange; Mr James Freis of Market Integrity Solutions LLC; Mr Matthias Bauer-Langgartner of the UK Financial Conduct Authority; Dr Migual Vaz of Börse Stuttgart; Mr Keith Bear of Cambridge Alternative Finance; Professor Ge Jianqiu of Fudan University China; Mr Ted Sheils of HSBC; Ms Praoporn Senanarong of the Securities Exchange Commission, Thailand; Sir William Blair, former Judge in charge of the Commercial Court of England and Wales; Mr Hans van der Loo; and Ambassador David Yung-lo Lin. I also would like to thank my research assistants: Dr Yonghui Bao, Ms Vere Marie Khan and Mr Florian Lheureux for their diligence and patience. I also would like to thank my family: Gary, a computer engineer in California, for some introductory lessons on the semi-conductor industry; Dora, a civil engineer in NY City, for her view on sustainable smart cities; and my nieces and nephews, Kashiwa, Ine, Hiro, Kaya and Amy for being my sounding board. And finally, I have lost all the Bitcoin I purchased in Tokyo, long before I completed this book project.

Joseph Lee
10 September 2021
London, UK

Figures

1 Introduction

Crypto-finance is an anti-establishment movement that has emerged as a response to current financial markets that are intermediated and overcentralised. It has been said that the rise of cryptocurrencies such as Bitcoin is a response to dissatisfaction with the excessive risk-taking of financial intermediaries that led to the financial crisis, and the use by governments of quantitative easing as a remedial measure to bail out failing financial institutions. Blockchain-based crypto-finance has developed through the initial coin offering (ICO) market which aims to create a peer-to-peer platform for financing projects. It also addresses the current gaps in financing in the centralised markets provided by stock exchanges and the intermediated private equity market. As crypto-finance has developed, a number of concepts have been introduced that are unknown in traditional markets. Crypto-assets, cryptocurrency, ICO and security token offering, peer-to-peer project financing and the consensus-based regulatory model are all unfamiliar to the current financial markets. Privately issued cryptocurrency is unfamiliar to both users and regulators who are accustomed to relying on currency issued by central banks for payment, investment and as a monetary tool to manage the economy.

Some products such as crypto-vouchers and rewards-based investments are now used on blockchain-based crowdfunding platforms in a way that creates confusion among financial regulators, who are not clear about their jurisdiction, the legal nature of the products and the technology involved in the transactions. Regulators have attempted to bring ICO platforms into the existing regulatory regime for securities and it is possible to use the current securities framework to help understand ICO activity on the blockchain space and to identify risks. However, attempting to use the existing regime to exercise regulatory control of the innovative new market can have a negative impact on its development when the aim is to address structural problems in the financing gap and the lack of opportunity in a shared economy. The cross-border nature of the internet means that crypto-finance can be used by individuals in all corners of the world, and has the potential to transcend the existing financial markets. Yet we also need to use the current legal and regulatory frameworks as we analyse the components of the markets and their inter-relationships to devise an optimal governance model. There are many examples of the way the crypto-market challenges conventional understanding of the functions of the financial market, the proprietary nature of

DOI: 10.4324/9780429023613-1

financial instruments, and the concept of law and justice. This means that we need to clarify the nature and purpose of the crypto-market so that policies, laws and governance models can be developed to ensure stability, safety, transparency and fairness. Technology, finance and the law are all essential components of the crypto-market that together define its concept, structure and dynamics.

Technology

This book examines the technology used to facilitate transactions in the different crypto-markets, including distributed ledger technologies, the blockchain, smart contract, encryption technologies and artificial intelligence. It also discusses how combinations of these technologies can support different crypto-markets, including the cryptocurrency market, the ICO market, the securities tokens offerings market, financial advisory services and the blockchain-based peer-to-peer energy trading platform. In addition, it explores how technology can be used in supervision, as legal technology and as regulatory technology on the crypto-market to provide governance. The aim of the discussion is not to provide detailed explanation of the design of each kind of technology, but to show how they can be embedded in the crypto-financial market to bring transformative effects. Many financial regulators adopt a neutral approach to technology where it is seen as neither good nor bad, so it is important to discuss the functions of technology in the context of finance to see how its transformative effect might operate. By using this approach, we can assess the benefits and risks that technology brings to the financial market and provide a sound basis for legal and regulatory intervention.

Finance

Like technology, finance is also a neutral activity and financial markets can be forces for good as well as evil. So it is important to divide the current financial markets into different sectors such as payment markets, trading spaces, advisory services and peer-to-peer energy trading platforms, to see how technology may be used in each segment or sector. Combinations of the various technologies can result in greater efficiency and efficacy, but they also bring risk. The main function of the financial market is to act as an intermediary between entrepreneurs' projects and investors' finance and in this way they distribute both profit and risk. There are various ways of managing this distribution through the design of different financial products but the financial crisis has shown that financial intermediaries have themselves been taking on the role of investors by partaking in both profits and risks. There were no effective rules in place to control the level of profits gained or to mitigate risk. In the recent crisis, there were such large defaults in the market that institutions were unable to absorb the consequences and states needed to step in to bail them out. In this situation, the financial intermediaries broke the chain that is needed to support a healthy economy. Because states had to bail out the intermediaries and inject more cash into the economy, the legitimacy of the state as the guardian of financial stability was threatened.

If the crypto-market is to provide a solution to structural problems in the current financial markets, it should not only provide potential remedial action to crises that arise, but also act as a catalyst for a socio-economic transformation. The hope is that the crypto-market can transform the financial market by democratising it.

As the industry develops, the crypto-market can play a role not only in finance but also in laying down the conditions for socio-economic transformation by providing access to finance, a shared economy and justice. Because of this, it is important to decide what kind of financial markets the crypto-market should support. It might be that using technology can enhance the efficiency of the market, but this single benefit might be disproportionate to the investment needed to create the necessary infrastructure. In this book, I discuss some new financing markets including cryptocurrency, initial coin offering, securities token offering, algorithm-driven execution and advisory services and the peer-to-peer energy trading platform, to show how disintermediated and decentralised markets can give control to entrepreneurs and investors. In addition, I also discuss what roles financial intermediaries and the state should play in distributing profits and risk through a renewed governance model in this virtual space.

Law

Law therefore plays an essential role in the development of technology in financial markets. Regulators need to understand and approve any technology proposed and must consider both whether it is safe to use and whether it complies with regulatory objectives. For Fintech, policy makers and regulators can apply risk-based regulation and leave the participants to negotiate their intended outcomes. However, the crypto-market has a stated outcome of bringing transformative effects so is it appropriate there to continue to use risk-based regulation or should the law play a more active role in promoting the crypto-market's aims? The intended outcome is relevant to the design of the governance framework and in identifying gaps in the application of current regulation to a particular crypto-market. Clarity about the intended outcome can also help to determine whether property law or relational law should apply to a particular transaction. When the crypto-market is combined with another utility market such as the retail energy market, the combination alters the key purpose of the market. The legal framework and regulatory regime should then be designed to facilitate that new regime, promoting sustainability in this example.

Data governance in the crypto-market

Data and data governance have not been extensively explored in the literature of financial law and regulation. The crypto-market generates large quantities of data, which can be used to transform socio-economic conditions and improve living standards. The current centralised and intermediated market prevents smaller investors and individual entrepreneurs from accessing critical data for raising finance, identifying suitable investment targets or monitoring the risk of their investment. Centralised market infrastructures such as central banks, exchanges, clearing houses and settlement institutions possess and control large amounts of transaction data that are used by financial intermediaries and states to provide services and monitor risk as well as to develop new products, services, projects and policies. But they are also in a position to restrict access to data, charge fees for access or exchange data for benefits with third parties. If the crypto-market is to democratise information and give individuals control, data must be shared with them. Financial intermediaries also collect critical data as required by financial regulators in order to fulfil their risk management obligations. Yet at the same time, data in their possession can enable them to provide further projects and services for the market. What is more, financial intermediaries have super computers that can process data and obtain information more quickly than is possible for individuals. The fundamental role of financial intermediaries is to bring together projects and investors, but with the advantage of privileged access to data, they can themselves act as entrepreneurs and investors rather than simply providing intermediary services. For instance, a bank's client database allows it to develop an asset management business which in turn helps it to develop securities services that also enhance M&A business advisory services. Without resetting the goals for digital finance, market foreclosure and unfair market practices can exacerbate the structural problems caused by intermediation and centralisation.

Three components

Therefore, this book examines three components of the financial market – technology, finance and the law – and shows how their interrelationship dictates the structure of a crypto-market. Technology is an enabler and can drive improvement to social-economic conditions but it can also be used to foreclose the financial market, deprive an individual of wealth and enable state surveillance of citizens. The financial market can be a means of promoting social benefit and prosperity by facilitating the exchange of goods and services. However, it can also play a role in supporting imperialism, colonisation, financial crisis and war. The financial market should provide stable, safe and fair conditions for all its participants: infrastructure providers, intermediary firms, entrepreneurs and investors. And along with these stakeholders, there are others who benefit from the activity of financial markets such as regulators, the government and market service providers. If the aim of the financial market is not clearly defined and innovation continues without a sense of purpose, the financial market can become a space for gaming where the drive for profit leads to excessive risk-taking without accountability. In this regard, technology can help realise the purpose of the financial market and help participants achieve their aims but the purpose and goals of the market need to be agreed upon by stakeholders. Participants can agree to create a casino without a sense of purpose aside from financial gain if they wish to, but if something with a higher ideal is intended, a social contract needs to be agreed that specifies the market's objectives. Based on this, it is possible to develop new principles for a financial market that set out the conditions for socio-economic transformation.

2 Distributed ledger technologies in capital markets

Introduction

In this chapter, I will explain how blockchain technology can be implemented on the current capital markets and identify the relevant risks and the possible governance solutions needed.

Blockchain is one of the algorithmic technologies and distributed ledger technologies (DLTs), as illustrated in Figure 2.1. It is a register containing information shared, recorded and replicated among nodes[1] that has been successfully applied to the creation of cryptocurrencies – value units of transactions on the blockchain ecosystem – such as Bitcoin and Ethereum.[2] Bitcoin and Ethereum are two types of cryptocurrency built on blockchain technology. They are token-based and traded on exchanges, such as on Coinbase.com, a currency exchange brokering between digital assets – a cryptocurrency or reference to a record of the ownership of an asset on a blockchain – and fiat currencies. It should be noted that there is a distinction between public/permission-less networks (public chain) like Bitcoin and Ethereum and the private permissions world (private chain) where only permitted nodes can participate in the network. Public/permission-less ledgers are open to everyone to contribute data to the ledger and cannot be owned. Private and permissioned ledgers may have one or many owners, and only they can add records and verify the contents of the ledger. The successful usage of blockchain in cryptocurrency, which transforms the internet information to

---

1 Nodes refer to the device participating in the peer-to-peer network by running a blockchain client software and relaying information (transactions and blocks).
2 The Economist, 'The Promise of the Blockchain: The Trust Machine' (31 October 2015) www .economist.com/news/leaders/21677198-technology-behind-bitcoin-could-transform-how-econ-omy-works-trust-machine. [Accessed 06 November 2017]; Philip Boucher, European Parliamentary Research Service, 'How Blockchain Technology Could Change Our Lives' (February 2017) http://www.europarl.europa.eu/RegData/etudes/IDAN/2017/581948/EPRS_IDA(2017)581948 _EN.pdf; Saman Adhami, Giancarlo Giudici, and Stefano Martinazzi, 'Why Do Businesses Go Crypto? An Empirical Analysis of Initial Coin Offerings' (20 October 2017). Available at SSRN: https://ssrn.com/abstract=3046209; Satoshi Nakamoto, 'Bitcoin: A Peer-to-Peer Electronic Cash System' (2008) available at: https://bitcoin.org/bitcoin.pdf.

DOI: 10.4324/9780429023613-2

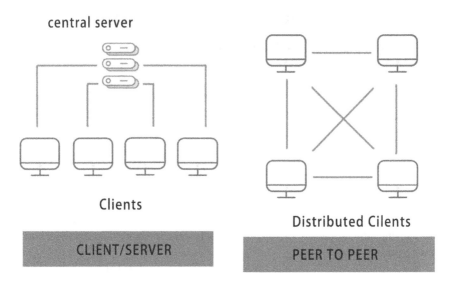

central server

Clients

Distributed Cilents

CLIENT/SERVER

PEER TO PEER

Figure 2.1 Central and distributed models

internet value,[3] has promoted interest in applying it to capital markets – mainly securities trading.[4] This is because such blockchain technology can be modified to incorporate rules, smart contract, digital signatures and other tools such as Artificial Intelligence[5] to make contracts and financial transactions safer and more cost-effective.[6]

Some people are sceptical of such a use in capital markets and have discounted securities trading with blockchain as mere hype, presented as a replacement for all the other technologies as a solution for all the problems in the financial industries.[7] As the blockchain network will need to use shared technology, some financial institutions have also pulled out from this development in

---

3 See Chapter 5 on cryptocurrency. Dan Tapscott and Alex Tapscott, *How the Technology Behind Bitcoin Is Changing Money, Business, and the World* (Penguin Publishing Group 2016).

4 Trevor Kiviat, 'Beyond Bitcoin: Issues in Regulating Blockchain Transactions' (2016) 65 *Duke Law Journal* 65; Philipp Paech, 'Securities, Intermediation and the Blockchain: An Inevitable Choice between Liquidity and Legal Certainty' (2016) 21(4) *Uniform Law Review* 612–639; and Taketoshi Mori, 'Financial Technology: Blockchain and Securities Settlement' (2016) 8(3) *Journal of Securities Operations & Custody* 208–227.

5 See Chapter 7 on artificial intelligence.

6 Digital Asset Holdings, a US blockchain startup, is building business applications and market structure systems based on the distributed ledger, such as working with exchanges and post-trade providers i.e. Depository Trust & Clearing Corp., which provides settlement and clearing services.

7 Paul Michelman, 'Seeing Beyond the Blockchain Hype: The Potential for Blockchain to Transform How Organizations Produce and Capture Value is Very Real, But so are the Challenges to Its Broad Implementation' (2017) 58(4) *MIT Sloan Management Review* 17–19.

order to develop their own blockchain initiatives.[8] Nevertheless, major securities regulators have begun to look into relevant regulatory issues.[9] Some jurisdictions have also passed laws to increase their regulatory capabilities in dealing with any risks that arise once blockchain moves beyond the proof-of-concept stage.[10] In the UK, the Financial Conduct Authority (FCA) has set up an innovation hub and started a legislative process. This is in addition to having created the regulatory sandbox currently in place for addressing the application of blockchain in the financial services sector,[11] for instance in the exchange traded fund (ETF) and future markets, such as BTC (Bitcoin futures)[12] as an asset in conventional financial markets.[13] At the EU level, the European Securities and Market Authority (ESMA) has also begun a consultation process on the use of blockchain in capital markets.[14] In the US, the state of Delaware has also passed the first blockchain legislation, putting itself at the forefront of company law.[15] In Asia, China was becoming the largest market for cryptocurrency trade, with 17 cryptocurrency exchanges, until the issuance of a public notice by the Bank of China, China's banking regulator, in September 2017 caused many exchanges to suspend their trades.[16] This suggests two observations: first, that China has the technical infrastructure to create a model such as Ant Blockchain architecture,

---

8 Goldman Sachs, Santander, and JP Morgan have left the blockchain consortium R 3. Bailey McCann, 'For Banks, 2017 Is Shaping Up to Be the Year of Blockchain' (2016) December, *Institutional Investor*.

9 FCA Discussion Paper: Discussion Paper on Distributed Ledger Technology, DP17/3; IOSCO Research Report on Financial Technologies (Fintech), February 2017; ESMA Discussion Paper on the Distributed Ledger Technology Applied to Securities Markets, 2 June 2016 | ESMA/2016/773 RF.

10 Randolph Robinson, 'The New Digital Wild West: Regulating the Explosion of Initial Coin Offerings' (1 September 2017). University of Denver Legal Studies Research Paper No. 17–41. Available at SSRN: https://ssrn.com/abstract=3087541.

11 See FCA, Distributed Ledger Technology: Feedback Statement on the Discussion Paper 17/03, www.fca.org.uk/publication/feedback/fs17-04.pdf.

12 Paul Vigna, 'Bitcoin Futures May Be Coming, But a Bitcoin ETF Is No Lock; SEC's Opposition to Bitcoin ETF Proposals Suggests Bitcoin Futures Would Need to Build Up a Trading History Before an ETF Can Be Approved' *Wall Street Journal* (Online) (New York, 01 November 2017).

13 FCA, Regulatory sandbox, November 2015.

14 Philipp Hacker and Chris Thomale, 'Crypto-Securities Regulation: ICOs, Token Sales and Cryptocurrencies under EU Financial Law' (22 November 2017). Available at SSRN: https://ssrn.com/abstract=3075820; EU securities markets regulator ESMA also highlights ICO risks for investors and firms www.esma.europa.eu/press-news/esma-news/esma-highlights-ico-risks-investors-and-firms.

15 Andrea Tinianow, 'Delaware Blockchain Initiative: Transforming the Foundational Infrastructure of Corporate Finance' (2017) Delaware Blockchain Initiative and Caitlin Long, Symbiont, on Thursday, March 16, 2017, Harvard Law School Forum on Corporate Governance and Financial Regulation.   https://corpgov.law.harvard.edu/2017/03/16/delaware-blockchain-initiative-transforming-the-foundational-infrastructure-of-corporate-finance/.

16 'China's Bitcoin Market Alive and Well as Traders Defy Crackdown: Activity Moves to Peer-to-Peer Exchanges and Messenger Apps after Beijing's Order to Close Exchanges Earlier This Month' (29 September 2017) *South China Morning Post*, www.scmp.com/news/china/money-wealth/article/2113401/chinas-bitcoin-market-alive-and-well-traders-defy-crackdown.

WeBank's syndicate loan reconciliation and Wanda Blockchain architecture different from those used in the more advanced securities trading markets; and second, that the regulation of crypto-finance, such as an initial coin offering (ICO), is forthcoming in China.[17]

With the implementation of blockchain in cryptocurrency, new laws are being introduced in some jurisdictions,[18] regulators' preparatory work is underway,[19] and there is investment in this sector.[20] Blockchain thus seems to be a promising innovation that will revolutionise capital market structure, or at least have some impact on the post-trade segment of the securities trade.[21] It should be noted that DLTs are not a new technology and that blockchain has already been used to create peer-to-peer networks,[22] mainly in file-sharing in the entertainment industry. However, this technology has not taken off to become widely used in other areas because the central servers have to become more powerful and sophisticated in order to cope with massive data flows. As the central servers became more powerful, centralisation was then reinforced in many trades.[23] In capital markets, centralisation has allowed exchanges to process trading data and information.[24] Small capital holders will need to rely on financial intermediaries to participate in the securities trade. Hence, centralised market operators and financial intermediaries have become the bridge between businesses and capital providers. As the distribution channels have become multi-layered, as shown in Figure 2.2, in order to manage the risk, the distance between small capital holders and businesses has widened, thus making trading and investment costlier for small capital holders and placing increasing restrictions on the ability of small businesses to raise and access capital. Because blockchain is built on a distributed network, it has the potential to challenge market practices surrounding centralisation and the

17 Huasheng Zhu and Zach Zhizhong Zhou, 'Analysis and Outlook of Applications of Blockchain Technology to Equity Crowdfunding in China' (2016) 2(1) *Financial Innovation* 1–11.
18 Andrea Tinianow, 'Delaware Blockchain Initiative: Transforming the Foundational Infrastructure of Corporate Finance' (2017) Delaware Blockchain Initiative and Caitlin Long, Symbiont, on Thursday, March 16, 2017, Harvard Law School Forum on Corporate Governance and Financial Regulation https://corpgov.law.harvard.edu/2017/03/16/delaware-blockchain-initiative-transforming-the-foundational-infrastructure-of-corporate-finance/.
19 FCA, FCA Discussion Paper: Discussion Paper on Distributed Ledger Technology, DP17/3; ESMA, Discussion Paper on the Distributed Ledger Technology Applied to Securities Markets, 2 June 2016. ESMA/2016/773 RF; IOSCO Research Report on Financial Technologies (Fintech), February 2017.
20 VC Blockchain Investments Approach $300 million in H1 2016 as Banks Lead Deployments, M2 Presswire; Coventry [Coventry] 12 Sep 2016.
21 Euroclear and Oliver Wyman, 'Blockchain in Capital Markets: The Prize and the Journey' (February 2016), www.dltmarket.com/docs/BlockchainInCapitalMarkets-ThePrizeAndTheJourney.pdf.
22 See Satoshi whitepaper, available at: http://nakamotoinstitute.org/bitcoin/.
23 Manuela Geranio, *Evolution of the Exchange Industry: from Dealers' Clubs to Multinational Companies* (Switzerland, Springer International Publishing 2016).
24 Jane Winn, 'The Impact of the Internet on US Regulation of Securities Markets' (1997) 2 *Yearbook of International Financial and Economic Law* 409–426.

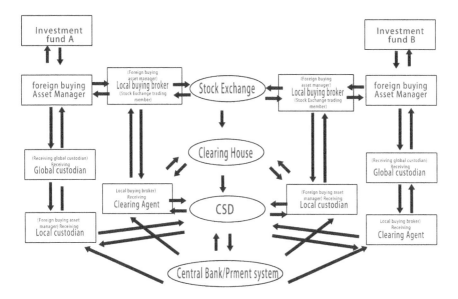

Figure 2.2 Capital market infrastructure

facilitation of intermediation. It may also challenge the surrounding regulation, which is based on a centralised model.[25] It may also bring a safe market ecosystem as highly centralised systems present a high cost single point of failure. They may be vulnerable to cyber-attack and the data is often out of sync, out of date or simply inaccurate.[26] The current environment has many books of records at multiple levels in the hierarchy, and at its simplest, DLT can mean that just one distributed ledger, with suitable permission, can replace this hierarchy. If this is to happen, a suitable governance – i.e. regulatory framework – will need to be in place to ensure the interests of the owners of the network i.e. the participants and the broader interests of society.[27]

25 Gerard Hertig and Ruben Lee, 'Four Predictions about the Future of EU Securities Regulation' (2003) 3(2) *Journal of Corporate Law Studies* 359–378.
26 Government Office for Science, 'Distributed Ledger Technology Beyond Block Chain' 2016, p. 6. Available at: www.gov.uk/government/uploads/system/uploads/attachment_data/file/492972/gs -16-1-distributed-ledger-technology.pdf.
27 Philipp Paech, 'The Governance of Blockchain Financial Networks' (2017) 80(6) *Modern Law Review* 1073–1110.

The structure of distributed ledger technology in the capital market

For securities to be traded on the DLT network,[28] its structure must have two layers: the DLT network and the encoded smart contract. The latter is a set of conditions recorded as code on a distributed ledger and executed automatically by a computing system into which the security and the rules that apply to it are encoded.[29] There will be different nodes in the DLT network, and each one keeps a record of all (or a subset defined by policy) the transactions that occur on the network. For regulatory reasons and others such as tax,[30] not all nodes can view all the transactions, so the blockchain fabric will typically allow only parties to a transaction to see the transaction: other nodes may provide consent but not see the transaction itself. This is how Hyperledger Fabric and R3 Corda both work – by creating platforms through private networks for transferring digital assets among them.[31]

The network is maintained by all the nodes based on a consensus model (community consensus, or protocol consensus) rather than by a single entity. Each node will keep data files and, collectively, they will maintain the network (or on a premise if the participants elect it to run their node).[32] Unlike a centralised system, which is usually maintained by a single entity – such as the exchange – which has its own data centre, there will be no single data centre that keeps the data safe and authenticates the transactions. It should be noted that a blockchain network can be public or private. In a public chain, permission is not required to participate, thus creating a permission-less network with potentially anonymous participants. In a

---

28 Som Shekhar Singh, 'How Blockchain Will Change the Way You Trade in Stock Markets' (15 January 2018) *The Economic Times*, available at: https://economictimes.indiatimes.com/markets/stocks/news/how-blockchain-will-change-the-way-you-trade-in-stock-markets/articleshow /62161610.cms; See also M. Kalderon, F. Snagg and C. Harrop, 'Distributed Ledgers: A Future in Financial Services?' (2016) 31 *Journal of International Banking Law and Regulation* 243, 247.

29 G. W. Peters and E. Panayi, 'Understanding Modern Banking Ledgers through Blockchain Technologies: Future of Transaction Processing and Smart Contracts on the Internet of Money' Working Paper, 18 November 2015 at https://papers.ssrn.com/sol3/Papers.cfm?abstract_id=2692487, 3 (unless otherwise stated, all URLs were last accessed 30 November 2016).

30 M. Kalderon, F. Snagg and C. Harrop, 'Distributed Ledgers: A Future in Financial Services?' (2016) 31 *Journal of International Banking Law and Regulation* 243, 247; Tom Bell, 'Copyrights, Privacy, and the Blockchain' (2016) 42(2) *Ohio Northern University Law Review* 439–470; Belgian tax authorities investigate foreign cryptocurrency exchanges to find Belgian citizens who are required to pay 33% tax on their gains through crypto-trade. 2 March 2018. www.rtl.be/info /belgique/economie/vous-investissez-dans-le-bitcoin-ou-une-autre-cryptomonnaie-attention-le -fisc-pourrait-vous-reserver-une-mauvaise-surprise-1000481.aspx.

31 Hyperledger is to create a platform through the distributed database recording digital events with the batch of transactions timestamped to form a blockchain network. R3 also has an innovation that is the blockchain-based shared-ledger computer software platform known as Concord which allows companies to run high-scale financial applications on permissioned networks across organizations.

32 In Fabric and Corda, there is, though, a central entity to sequence transactions onto the ledger: in fabric the ordering service; in corda the notary.

private chain, the participants can decide who should participate in the network, and participants are known. In a permission-less model, how things operate on the network will be governed by a consensus of the network participants. Whereas in a private chain, rules can be set by the participants (also a consensus model) or by a commonly trusted third party. In other words, the public chain will bring about a more decentralised and disintermediated system than the private chain. A private chain,[33] if adopted by exchanges and other financial intermediaries, can continue the centralised market model but with improved functionality, but it offers non-incumbent operators the opportunity to provide services in this environment.

For the securities trade to gain synergy, an auto-executable smart contract, into which a security (e.g. a share) is encoded, will be used on the DLT network.[34] A smart contract is a pre-written computer code that can be triggered by events, resulting in ledger updates. A smart contract can be seen as a digitised vending machine,[35] which is running according to the pre-written rules. Smart contracts will reduce the cost of transactions in various corporate actions, such as voting and the distribution of dividends.[36] However, in such a network, i.e. one without a centralised system, one must ensure that transactions are genuine and not made by a malicious third party, particularly if such transactions are to take place on an open network (public chain) as opposed to a closed network (private chain). Hence, encryption technology is required to authenticate a transaction, i.e. a transaction in which A transfers 100 shares in Company Q to B.

The question is, therefore, how would smart contract technology affect centralised market practices[37] and would it reduce the need for financial intermediaries such as share services?[38] Second, how would encryption technology displace certain trusted third parties, such as the Certificate Authority (CA) and securities custodians, from centralised market practices? I will first discuss the mechanisms of smart contract and encryption technology and explore their utilities in capital

33 In ESMA blockchain review, it is the view that private chains are likely to be the basis of DLT progression in regulated markets. See Discussion Paper on the Distributed Ledger Technology Applied to Securities Markets, 2 June 2016 | ESMA/2016/773 RF.
34 Reggie O'Shields, 'Smart Contracts: Legal Agreements for the Blockchain' (2017) 21 *North Carolina Banking Institute* 177–194; Alexander Savelyev, 'Contract Law 2.0: Smart Contracts as the Beginning of the End of Classic Contract Law' (2017) 26(2) *Information & Communications Technology Law* 116–134.
35 Nick Szabo, 'Formalizing and Securing Relationships on Public Networks' (1997) 2 First Monday http://firstmonday.org/ojs/index.php/fm/article/view/548/469.
36 Alexander Savelyev, 'Contract Law 2.0: Smart Contracts as the Beginning of the End of Classic Contract Law' (2017) 26(2) *Information & Communications Technology Law* 116–134.
37 Thomais Kotta Kyriakou, 'Harmonizing Corporate Actions for the Achievement of a Capital Markets Union: An Analysis of the Shareholders' Rights Directive, the Green Paper Building a Capital Markets Union and TARGET2-Securities' (2017) 14(3) *European Company Law* 121–126.
38 David Larcker, Allan McCall and Gaizka Ormazabal, 'Outsourcing Shareholder Voting to Proxy Advisory Firms' (2015) 58(1) *Journal of Law & Economics* 173–204; Paul Rose, 'The Corporate Governance Industry' (2007) 32(4) *Journal of Corporation Law* 887–926; Laura Noonan, 'Citi Develops Online Shareholder Voting System' *Financial Times* (13 November 2017), www.ft.com/content/31140600-c619-11e7-a1d2-6786f39ef675.

markets on the DLT network. After discussing how DLTs will affect the life cycle of trades, I will then discuss the pertinent legal issues and challenges.

Smart contracts and investor protection

If activities that take place using blockchain technology are to achieve their intended effects, smart contracts must be used to facilitate the securities trade on the network.[39] For instance, a share can be encoded into a smart contract, which will be automatically executed upon the occasion of an event occurring. For example, when there is a general meeting to decide certain issues, an investor will receive notices and votes according to the shares they hold on the blockchain network; when declared, dividends will be distributed automatically to the investors' cash (or other cryptocurrencies) account; when there is a new issuance of shares, those shares will be allocated automatically to those investors who exercised their pre-emption rights.

To give an example of how a smart contract can operate, imagine that a smart contract can trigger the removal of a director. The contract will contain the following essential clauses: 1) a shareholder can propose an action, i.e. the removal of a director; 2) other shareholders can join the proposal; 3) once the shares have reached a pre-set number, such as 5% of the total shares, a meeting will be called for shareholders to cast their votes; 4) the director will be removed if more than 50% of the votes cast are in favour of removing the director. For example, if a shareholder, Alice, thinks a director is in breach of duty or is unfit to lead the company, she can go through the following steps: step 1: she sends a message to the smart contract to propose a vote; step 2: another shareholder, Bill, also sends the proposal in a second message to the smart contract within one day, triggering a vote on the issue; step 3: shareholders send a message to vote in favour or against the proposal; step 4: once the votes in favour exceed 50 per cent of the votes cast, the removal of the director will be authorised.

However, when and how a corporate action can be triggered still requires human judgement – in the illustrative case above, judgement of whether a director should be removed. A smart contract will not automatically trigger a corporate action: both human and legal judgement are required. In a corporate action such as the removal of a director, notice must be given to the director in question and shareholders will need to decide which director or directors are to be eligible to vote. Shareholders may also need to state why the director is to be removed. If the reason is simply "we don't like you," then the director may be entitled to compensation. However, if the reason is that there has been a breach of duty (not just a breach of rules), the director will not be entitled to compensation. If the reason pertains to "breach of duty," shareholders may also be entitled to "rectify" the

---

39 Mark Giancaspro, 'Is a "Smart Contract" Really a Smart Idea? Insights from a Legal Perspective' (2017) 33 *Computer Law & Security Review* 825–835.

wrong and hence forgive the director. This is a general law that may also need to be written into the smart contract if it is to be used by a UK company.[40]

If a smart contract is set to be triggered automatically when a certain event occurs, a director may be wrongly removed and such an act will render the company liable to pay damages to the director. In a different scenario, a company can call a general meeting to authorise an action if the company's assets fall below a certain threshold[41] and in this case, the smart contract would not be able to detect that the event has happened. Detection of the event will be performed by an external "oracle service." At a stage when oracle services are still in the development stage, if the smart contract wrongly triggers an event that leads to auto-execution of share transfers, the investors can suffer irreparable damage.[42]

Predicted deployment in the capital market

Stock exchanges play a vital role in the capital market by facilitating listing (issuing), trading, clearing and in some cases settlement. They provide an efficient alternative financing mechanism to bank loans[43] or private equity financing.[44] Centralisation is key to the success of this financing mechanism,[45] as it enables the creation of larger capital pools and provides integrated trading services. The major risk of decentralisation is liquidity fragmentation,[46] and it will exacerbate the fragmentation problem that blue chip companies already face.[47] The hope is that blockchain will be guided by a more peer-to-peer model, connecting businesses and investors. The question is, therefore, what type of peer-to-peer model

---

40 Thomais Kyriakou, 'Harmonizing Corporate Actions for the Achievement of a Capital Markets Union: An Analysis of the Shareholders' Rights Directive, the Green Paper Building a Capital Markets Union and TARGET2-Securities' (2017) 14(3) *European Company Law* 121–126.

41 This resembles the written resolution used in private companies under Companies Act 2006, s 288–300. However, such resolution cannot be used to remove company directors.

42 'Bitcoin Divides to Rule: The Crypto-Currency's Split into Two Versions may be Followed by Others' (2017) The Economist, www.economist.com/news/business-and-finance/21725747 -crypto-currencys-split-two-versions-may-be-followed-others-bitcoin.

43 Public markets provide enhanced visibility which is a factor that most European CFOs consider a benefit of going public. See Franck Bancel and Usha Mitto, 'Why Do European Firms Go Public?' (2009) 15(4) *European Financial Management* 844–884.

44 In time of financial crisis, stock markets also provide an exit option for private equity firms. See Emil Plagborg-Møller and Morten Holm, 'IPO or SBO?: The Increasing Importance of Operational Performance for Private Equity Exits Following the Global Financial Crisis of 2007–08' (2017) 29(1) *Journal of Applied Corporate Finance* 115–121.

45 The degree of centralisation can also affect transaction costs in securities trade. See Jean-François Gajewski and Carole Gresse, 'Centralised Order Books versus Hybrid Order Books: A Paired Comparison of Trading Costs on NSC (Euronext Paris) and SETS (London Stock Exchange)' (2007) 31(9) *Journal of Banking & Finance* 2906–2924.

46 Yet, some argue that this depends how distribution happens and distribution does not necessarily mean that liquidity is distributed.

47 Peter Gomber, Satchit Sagade, Erik Theissen, Moritz Christian Weber and Christian Westheide, 'Competition between Equity Markets: A Review of the Consolidation versus Fragmentation Debate' (2017) 31(3) *Journal of Economic Surveys* 792–814.

will there be with blockchain? And, will such a model be more efficient or more distributed (fairer) than the existing centralised model?

Listing and issuing

DLT is said to be able to bring about the democratisation of the financial market through a peer-to-peer network that will break through the current centralised capital market model, which is channelled to capital holders by financial inter-mediaries. This model is perceived to impose too high a cost on businesses and investors, especially SMEs and retail investors. As a result, few investors partici-pate directly in securities trades or exercise their governance rights in the com-panies in which they invested. Additionally, businesses find that access to capital is obstructed by a very high regulatory threshold aimed at investor protection, as well as by the lack of support from intermediaries, in terms of interest in making their trades. Furthermore, the underwriting cost is high, which has the effect of dissuading businesses from using the capital market as a way of raising funds. Because the investment environment is perceived as unfriendly to small capital holders, the potential of DLT to bring about decentralisation and disintermedia-tion has spurred some financial innovations, such as the ICO, which relies on blockchain to raise capital.[48] The use of DLT as the infrastructure for crowdfund-ing platforms and investor protection will be discussed in Chapter 8.

Initial coin offering (ICO) – public/private split

An ICO involves a business issuing "tokens" to investors on the open chain to raise cash, cryptocurrency or a mixture of both. The token represents an "interest" that the investors have in the investee business.[49] There is a set of rights attached to the token that the token holders can exercise against the investee business. Initial coin offerings, therefore, have various parallels with Initial Public Offerings, private placement of securities or crowd sales.[50] ICOs have attracted much regulatory attention and action. For instance, the Securities Exchange Commission (SEC) of the US, in the case of the decentralised autonomous organisation (DAO) hack,

48 Jonathan Rohr and Aaron Wright 'Blockchain-Based Token Sales, Initial Coin Offerings, and the Democratization of Public Capital Markets' (4 October 2017). Cardozo Legal Studies Research Paper No. 527; University of Tennessee Legal Studies Research Paper No. 338. Available at SSRN: https://ssrn.com/abstract=3048104; Philipp Paech, 'Securities, Intermediation and the Blockchain: An Inevitable Choice between Liquidity and Legal Certainty' (2016) 21(4) *Uniform Law Review* 612–639.
49 Monetary Authority of Singapore, 'A Guide to Digital Token Offerings' 14 November 2017, www.mas.gov.sg/~/media/MAS/Regulations%20and%20Financial%20Stability/Regulations%20Guidance%20and%20Licensing/Securities%20Futures%20and%20Fund%20Management/Regulations%20Guidance%20and%20Licensing/Guidelines/A%20Guide%20to%20Digital%20Token%20Offerings%20%2014%20Nov%202017.pdf.
50 Financial Conduct Authority, 'Discussion Paper DP17/3 on Distributed Ledger Technology (DLT)' (April 2017) www.fca.org.uk/publication/discussion/dp17-03.pdf.

decided that the DAO tokens were securities, according to the Howey test, which determines whether something can be considered a security under US securities acts following a 1946 decision of the Supreme Court of the United States.[51] China[52] and South Korea have banned ICOs; the UK,[53] Hong Kong and Singapore[54] are taking a "wait-and-see" approach but have issued a risk warning to investors; France has launched a public consultation process[55] and has introduced a law on the transfer of property in securities on the blockchain network.[56]

The SEC's treatment of ICOs is based on the notion that such a method of capital-raising outside the exchanges circumvents the transparency and disclosure regime aimed at protecting the investor.[57] The issuance of a token, as a type of crypto-security, is not *per se* illegal[58] and indeed the state of Delaware has provided a legal basis for crypto-security enabled by smart contracts transposed on the blockchain. That is to say that DLT can be used by businesses to raise capital under proper legal and regulatory frameworks, thus offering a way to provide a legal basis for an ICO token. The token can be legally recognised on a *sui generis* basis, as though it were a share. The rights attached to a token should also be regulated so as to provide confidence in this kind of crypto-security and also in the working of the ICOs as a legitimate aspect of crypto-finance. The regulatory framework and legal protection, equivalent to those offered to shareholders

51 'SEC Issues Investigative Report Concluding DAO Tokens, a Digital Asset, Were Securities. U.S. Securities Laws May Apply to Offers, Sales, and Trading of Interests in Virtual Organizations' SEC Press Release, published 25/07/2017. Available at: www.sec.gov/news/press-release/2017 -131.

52 'Central Bank of the People's Bank of China PBC Office of Industry and Information Technology Administration of Industry and Commerce China Banking Regulatory Commission China Securities Regulatory Commission CBIRC Notice on Preventing Financing Risk of Tokens Issue' (Translated from Chinese, published 04/09/2017, available at: www.circ.gov.cn/web/site0/tab6554 /info4080736.htm.

53 Financial Conduct Authority, 'Consumer Warning about the Risks of Initial Coin Offerings ("ICOs")'. Published 12/09/2017, available at: www.fca.org.uk/news/statements/initial-coin -offerings.

54 Monetary Authority of Singapore, 'MAS Clarifies Regulatory Position on the Offer of Digital Tokens in Singapore' Published 01/08/2017, available at: www.mas.gov.sg/News-and-Publica-tions/Media-Releases/2017/MAS-clarifies-regulatory-position-on-the-offer-of-digital-tokens-in -Singapore.aspx.

55 The French financial markets regulatory, AMF, publishes a discussion paper on Initial Coin Offerings and initiates its UNICORN programme www.amf-france.org/en_US/Actualites/Commu-niques-de-presse/AMF/annee-2017?docId=workspace%3A%2F%2FSpacesStore%2F5097c770 -e3f7-40bb-81ce-db2c95e7bdae.

56 France, the first among European countries, introduces law regarding the transfer of property in securities on the blockchain network. www.legifrance.gouv.fr/affichTexte.do?cidTexte=JOR FTEXT000036171908.

57 Christoph Jentzsch, 'Decentralized Autonomous Organization to Automate Governance' White Paper 2016, available at: https://download.slock.it/public/DAO/WhitePaper.pdf.

58 Securities and Exchange Commission 'Report of Investigation Pursuant to Section 21(a) of the Securities Exchange Act of 1934: The DAO' Published 25/07/2017, available at: www.sec.gov/ litigation/investreport/34-81207.pdf.

in an IPO, should also be offered to investors in an ICO. Whether a more or less onerous transparency regime should be applied to ICOs will depend on the policy objective and on other safeguards provided by the operators. Although ICOs do not go through cryptocurrency exchange operators, this does not mean that those operators or other financial institutions cannot set up a platform to facilitate ICOs in order to confer legal status on the platform, legal status as a regulated market or as an organised market to help start-ups or SMEs to raise capital.[59]

Book-building process

One possible application of DLTs in the IPO, as a regulatory technology (EegTec), is in the area of the book-building process, where DLTs can increase transparency and fair dealing in the IPO process. The current practice involves a stage in an IPO where the investment bank (the underwriter) can allocate shares at a certain price to buy-side investors, such as brokers. How the price is set and to whom shares will be allocated are not transparent.[60] That is to say that the underwriter can decide, at its own discretion, to whom shares should be allocated, at what volume and at what price. This can create potential conflicts of interest and unfairness, especially if the shares are considered to be highly desirable.[61] For example, underwriters may allocate shares to brokers who will trade those shares on a certain trading venue[62] and to whom the shares have been allocated before the IPO may be known to the market. Using DLT in the book-building process within the IPO can help give a higher degree of transparency to the allocation of shares, minimise potential conflicts of interest and increase fair dealing in the market.[63] The use of DLT will involve the lead underwriter inviting brokers and investors to a private chain network.[64] A smart contract detailing the rights and obligations will be designed by the lead underwriter. The smart contract will also specify the book-building volume, the price and the allocation rules. The brokers and investors will submit their bids specifying the volume of the share desired at

59 Oscar Williams-Grut, 'Crypto Exchanges are Charging Up to $1 Million per ICO to List Tokens: 'It's Pure Capitalism' Business Insider, 12 March 2018. http://uk.businessinsider.com/cryptocurrency-exchanges-listing-tokens-cost-fees-ico-2018-3.
60 Ann Sherman, 'IPOs and Long-Term Relationships: An Advantage of Book Building Sherman' (2000) 13(3) *Review of Financial Studies* 697–714.
61 See Manuela Geranio, Camilla Mazzoli and Fabrizio Palmucci, 'The Effects of Affiliations on the Initial Public Offering Pricing' (2017) 51 *International Review of Economics and Finance* 295–313.
62 Financial Conduct Authority, Investment and Corporate Banking Market Study, (2016) Final report, MS15/1.3 www.fca.org.uk/publication/market-studies/ms15-1-3-final-report.pdf.
63 Financial Conduct Authority, Investment and Corporate Banking Market Study, (2016) Final report, MS15/1.3 www.fca.org.uk/publication/market-studies/ms15-1-3-final-report.pdf.
64 Private chain is favoured by some regulators. See European Central Bank, 'The Potential Impact of DLTs on Securities Post-Trading Harmonisation and on the Wider EU Financial Market Integration' (2017) www.ecb.europa.eu/paym/intro/governance/shared/pdf/201709_dlt_impact_on_harmonisation_and_integration.pdf.

a particular price. Once the lead underwriter determines the price based on the bid information, the shares will be automatically allocated according to the bids and rules of the smart contract. The investors and brokers will be notified of the allocations, and the information on the allocations will be recorded on the distributed ledgers. Banks can also join the network in order to provide payment guarantees and facilitate payment transfers. In this way, DLT can act as an *ex ante* measure to regulate conflicts of interest as well as other market misconduct, such as insider dealing and market manipulation of the IPO. Using book-building in this private chain is a type of regulation technology (RegTech) – technologies that facilitate the delivery of regulatory requirements –[65] for the IPO.

Trading

One of the public utilities performed by the stock exchange and the trading venue is price discovery.[66] That is, through trading on the secondary market, the prices of securities can best reflect their value. Without such a trading mechanism, it would be difficult for investors, especially retail investors, to appreciate the value of companies. For this reason, the securities trade needs the support of financial intermediaries,[67] if it is not to lose visibility in the marketplace and lead to reduced interest in securities trading on the part of investors. The efficiency of such a trading mechanism is attributed to the matching engine (a central server) provided either by the exchange or the trading venue. The more sophisticated this matching engine is, the more trades it can process. It can also process trades in milliseconds in order to support the strategies used by high frequency traders (HFTs).[68]

What will happen to the trading segment given the potential of DLT to decentralise trade? DLT is able to facilitate peer-to-peer trades without the centralised market system operated by the exchanges and the trading venues. So, the question is not whether DLT can facilitate securities trades, but rather whether it can achieve the same function as the centralised market system in terms of price discovery,[69]

65 FCA, 'Call for Input: Supporting the Development and Adoption of RegTech' (2015) www.fca.org.uk/publication/call-for-input/regtech-call-for-input.pdf.
66 Benjamin Clapham and Kai Zimmermann, 'Price Discovery and Convergence in Fragmented Securities Markets' (2016) 12(4) *International Journal of Managerial Finance* 381–407.
67 Amber Anand and Avanidhar Subrahmanyam, 'Information and the Intermediary: Are Market Intermediaries Informed Traders in Electronic Markets?' (2008) 43(1) *Journal of Financial & Quantitative Analysis* 1–28.
68 Viktor Manahov and Robert Hudson, 'The Implications of High-Frequency Trading on Market Efficiency and Price Discovery' (2014) 21(16) *Applied Economics Letters* 1148–1151; Kristin Johnson, 'Regulating Innovation: High Frequency Trading in Dark Pools' (2017) 42(4) *Journal of Corporation Law* 833–886.
69 Bank for International Settlement, 'The Implications of Electronic Trading in Financial Markets' (2001) www.bis.org/publ/cgfs16.pdf; David Lawton, Price: the cornerstone of markets, Speech by Director of Markets of the FCA at the International Capital Market Association (ICMA) Capital Market Lecture Series 2014 on Monday 3 February 2014 www.fca.org.uk/news/speeches/price-cornerstone-markets.

liquidity,[70] and maintaining market integrity against market misconduct,[71] such as insider dealing and market manipulation.[72] In the securities trade market, investors will take different trading positions – long or short – depending on their views of the future market. It is this long–short dynamic that brings about the function of price discovery. Trading on the DLT network will make shorting a security an impossible task because stock-lending will not be possible.[73] Although, in some cases, shorting securities might destabilise the market and the economy in times of financial crisis, short-selling can also be a legitimate investment strategy. DLT can also reduce the level of liquidity caused by the latency problem. Speed is a critical element for brokers who execute orders for their clients. Latency is the reason why there is no interconnected trading venue between the London Stock Exchange and the Borsa Italiana, even though both markets used the same IT system (applications from the Millennium subsidiary of LSEG) for trading.[74] The Milan-based traders felt that they would be put at a disadvantage compared to the London-based traders because the server (the matching engine) would be based in London. Hence, the latency of DLT can cause unfair competition between traders. Furthermore, without a centralised market system, i.e. a regulated market,[75] or a more organised market such as a multilateral trading facility[76] or organised

70 Liquidity refers to the degree to which a market allows assets to be bought and sold without affecting the asset's price. For stock exchanges, lower liquidity tends to result in a more volatile market (especially when there are block trades and there is a huge spread between bid price and ask price), and it causes prices to change more drastically; whereas higher liquidity creates a less volatile market, and prices do not fluctuate as significantly. Evangelos Benos, Richard Payne and Michalis Vasios, 'Centralized Trading, Transparency and Interest Rate Swap Market Liquidity: Evidence from the Implementation of the Dodd-Frank Act' (January 2016), Bank of England Working Paper No. 580 www.bankofengland.co.uk/working-paper/2016/centralized-trading-transparency-and-interest-rate-swap-market-liquidity-evidence-from-the.

71 Oscar Williams-Grut, 'Market Manipulation 101: Wolf of Wall Street-Style "Pump and Dump" Scams Plague Cryptocurrency Markets' (14 November 2017), *Business Insider*, http://uk.businessinsider.com/ico-cryptocurrency-pump-and-dump-telegram-2017-11.

72 Jay Clayton, 'Governance and Transparency at the Commission and in Our Markets' Chairman of SEC Remarks at the PLI 49th Annual Institute on Securities Regulation, 8 November 2017 www.sec.gov/news/speech/speech-clayton-2017-11-08.

73 Some argue that it is possible to undertake stock borrowing and short-selling on DLTs.

74 Joseph Lee, 'Synergies, Risks and the Regulation of Stock Exchange Interconnection' (2017) 11(2) *Masaryk University Journal of Law and Technology* 291–322. https://doi.org/10.5817/MUJLT2017-2-5.

75 A regulated market is a multilateral system operated by a market operator, which brings together or facilitates the bringing together of multiple third-party buying and selling interests in financial instruments. The list of RMs currently includes the London Stock Exchange Main Market.

76 Article 4(15) of MiFID II. An MTF is a multilateral system, operated by an investment firm or a market operator, which brings together multiple third-party buying and selling interests in financial instruments.

trading facilities,[77] market misconduct will be more difficult to detect and regulate.[78] Under the current system, each trade can be linked to a particular investor. However, on a DLT, especially on an open chain network, trades will be made anonymously due to the technology of encryption.[79] This can create a major challenge to law enforcement agencies in their investigation and prevention of market misconduct and crime, such as money laundering.[80] In terms of market safety, a circuit breaker cannot be implemented to create market stability for trades conducted on an open chain network.

Some suggest that DLT can be used for trading in certain venues, such as over-the-counter for large-volume trade and for certain traders, for instance in dark pools. This can potentially reduce the non-transparency of dark pools, in which the parties do not need to make pre-trade disclosures about the price and volume of their securities trades. However, trades in dark pools still require speed. Even if the parties use the private chain network to trade, DLT can be used as a RegTech only if it can overcome the latency problem.

Clearing

The central counterparty (CCP) is an important liquidity provider as well as an important risk management provider to securities traders.[81] It provides the function of netting which, through the legal technique of novation, reduces multiple trades (buying and selling) into one single position.[82] The netted position improves efficiency in the settlement segment performed by the central securities depositories (CSDs), where a transfer of securities against payment is not required upon each trade that takes place on a trading platform. This improves trading efficiency and allows more trades to be placed for the purpose of price discovery.[83]

---

77 Article 4(1)(23) of MiFID II. An OTF is a multilateral system which is not a regulated market or an MTF and in which multiple third-party buying and selling interests in bonds, structured finance products, emission allowances or derivatives are able to interact in the system in a way that results in a contract in accordance with Title II of MiFID II. Equity cannot be traded on OTFs.

78 Kristin Johnson, 'Regulating Innovation: High Frequency Trading in Dark Pools' (2017) 42(4) *Journal of Corporation Law* 833–886.

79 Jan Henrik Ziegeldorf, Roman Matzutt, Martin Henze, Fred Grossmann and Klaus Wehrle, 'Secure and Anonymous Decentralized Bitcoin Mixing' (2018) 80 *Future Generation Computer Systems* 448–466. https://doi.org/10.1016/j.future.2016.05.018.

80 Mark Carney, 'The Future of Money' Speech by Governor of Bank of England (2018), 9. www.bankofengland.co.uk/-/media/boe/files/speech/2018/the-future-of-money-speech-by-mark-carney.pdf?la=en&hash=A51E1C8E90BDD3D071A8D6B4F8C1566E7AC91418.

81 Jo Braithwaite and David Murphy, 'Central Counterparties (CCPs) and the Law of Default Management' (2017) 17(2) *Journal of Corporate Law Studies* 291–325. DOI: 10.1080/14735970.2016.1254448.

82 European Central Bank, Standards for Securities Clearing and Settlement in the European Union, September 2005 www.ecb.europa.eu/pub/pdf/other/escb-cesr-standardssecurities2004en.pdf?46d 110f6ad9e1ea050fa1de9b47a372d.

83 Viktor Manahov and Robert Hudson, 'The Implications of High-Frequency Trading on Market Efficiency and Price Discovery' (2014) 21(16) *Applied Economics Letters* 1148–1151.

The better the quality of the price discovery mechanism, the more informed the investor's decision making. Second, the CCP provides risk management, whereby it will use its defence mechanism to resolve the problem of one party's default in a trade.[84] Such resolution will usually involve the CCP "stepping into" the defaulting party's position to ensure a smooth trade. This can prevent a blockage in the trading system.

How will the blockchain network change the CCP's function in the complete life cycle of the securities trade? The blockchain network, a peer-to-peer network, will facilitate securities trade among different network nodes. Smart contracts can be used to execute transactions, i.e. auto-execution of securities and payment transfers. The blockchain network and smart contract will result in a new trading model where securities trading and securities transfers can take place simultaneously, as opposed to the current practice whereby a securities transfer takes place two days after the trade (T+2).[85] If the current practice of delivery- versus-payment (DVP) is to be followed,[86] funds will need to be in place before the trade can take place – i.e. there must be pre-funded trades. This scenario can contrast with the current trading and clearing arrangement where the CCP provides the funding (partial financing) in the trade for the traders. That is, the trader does not need to have the full amount of funding in its payment account before it can place a trade. However, the CCP can require the collateral and collect margins according to the risk of the trader. In other words, a trader can engage in a securities trade with a value that exceeds the funding the trader has placed in this cash account. With the blockchain network and smart contract, CCP will lose its functions as a liquidity provider[87] and a risk management mechanism. Hence, removing CCP from the trading cycle will not improve trade efficiency or price-discovery efficiency. There may be fewer trades on the platform, as the funding requirement will reduce trades and result in reduced liquidity. The reduced liquidity can affect the critical function of price discovery performed by the exchanges or other trading platforms. Furthermore, trading on the DLT with T instant rather than T+X would increase difficulty in execution, resulting in execution blockage.[88] This will reduce trading at the exchanges and, consequentially, affect their revenue. As exchanges

84 EuroCCP Risk Management Overview, 7 March 2018 https://euroccp.com/document/euroccp-risk-management-overview/.

85 Regulation (EU) No 909/2014 of the European Parliament and of the Council of 23 July 2014 on improving securities settlement in the European Union and on central securities depositories (CSDR). The CSDR requires that the settlement date for transactions, the date on which the assets have to be transferred to the owed party, must be no later than the second business day after the trade takes place (T+2 requirement).

86 IOSCO Recommendations for Securities Settlement Systems, 2001, www.iosco.org/library/pubdocs/pdf/IOSCOPD123.pdf.

87 Froukelien Wendt, 'Central Counterparties: Addressing their Too Important to Fail Nature' IMF Working Paper, January 2015 www.imf.org/external/pubs/ft/wp/2015/wp1521.pdf.

88 Diana Chan, 'Moving from T+2 to T-instant: Blockchain Distributed Ledger Technology could Cut the Costs and Complexity of Post-Trade Processing' *Financial News*, 28 September 2015 www.fnlondon.com/articles/blockchain-moving-from-tplus2-to-t-instant-20151002.

have fixed costs for maintaining their infrastructure and other compliance costs, they will increase trading fees which will be borne by the end-investors.

However, DLT can also facilitate the transfer of collateral to the benefit of the CCPs. As the collateral posted by the clearing members can only be transferred during the opening time of the central securities depositories (CSDs), CCPs need to collect the collateral of their members from a CSD during its opening time.[89] Currently, a European CCP would need to collect collateral of their members against their trading risk during the non-opening time of the European CSD from a US CSD. If DLT can continue allowing collateral to be transferred after the opening time of the CSD, this can potentially increase the efficiency of CCP's risk management function. The question is whether transfers of such collateral on the DLT during the non-opening time of the CSD will be legally recognised and whether such transfer on the DLT will be the same as transfers between accounts by the CSD.

Settlement

The industry's view seems to suggest that the benefit of DLTs lies in the post-trade segment,[90] particularly the settlement of securities.[91] Blockchain will improve efficiency to securities settlements by reducing the settlement time from the current T+2 to T+0, meaning that blockchain can provide almost real-time settlement.[92] How this will be achieved with blockchain has not been detailed and tested, although some of the exchange operators have partnered with tech companies to experiment on selected un-listed companies on a permission-based chain ("private chain"). Therefore, it is reasonable to assume that it is possible to carry this out – be it on an open chain ("permission less-based chain" or "public chain") or a private chain – to achieve the intended outcome of T+0. The benefits the DLT can offer are not unquestionable in terms of their impact on price discovery, participation in the market and the objective of democratising the financial market.

Most contemporary modern financial markets use a central securities depository (CSD) to settle securities trades based on the delivery-versus-payment system ("the DVP system"), where securities are transferred in the centralised ledgers maintained by the CSD against transfers of payment maintained by a bank (i.e. a

---

89 European Central Bank, 'The Potential Impact of DLTs on Securities Post-Trading Harmonisation and on the Wider EU Financial Market Integration' (2017) www.ecb.europa.eu/paym/intro/governance/shared/pdf/201709_dlt_impact_on_harmonisation_and_integration.pdf.

90 Andrea Pinna Wiebe Ruttenberg, 'Distributed Ledger Technologies in Securities Post-Trading: Revolution or Evolution?' European Central Bank, Occasional Paper Series No. 172, April 2016 www.ecb.europa.eu/pub/pdf/scpops/ecbop172.en.pdf.

91 EuroClear and Slaughter and May, Blockchain Settlement: Regulation, Innovation and Application, November 2016, www.swift.com/file/34341/download?token=qqx60Nus

92 Hong Kong Exchanges and Clearing Limited (HKEX) introduced realtime DvP for northbound stock connect trading – its mutual market access programmes with the Shanghai and Shenzhen stock exchanges – in November 2017. Realtime DvP is expected to be used by institutional investors. www.hkex.com.hk/news/news-release/2017/1711062news?sc_lang=en.

central bank). CSDs may or may not legally hold the securities – which are ben-
eficially owned by the end-investors – in the ledgers they electronically maintain,
depending on the law under which the CSD operates. If the CSD is to be replaced
by DLT, how is the default risk of settlements to be mitigated and who can guarantee the ownership of securities?

Mitigating default risk

Settlement efficiency is achieved by the CSD netting all the trades – setting off
trades between parties such as members of the CSD (normally investment banks)
– rather than making a transfer for each trade.[93] The current settlement time is two
days after the trade ("T+2"),[94] and this time period allows securities traded on
different venues and markets to be settled with sufficient time. This also allows
members of the CSD, usually the investment banks and brokers, sufficient time
to consolidate the information on the trades within their organisation and for that
information to be given to the CSD to effect transactions on the centralised ledgers.[95] This can mitigate the default risk that is more likely to arise in a market
system operating on a same-day settlement basis ("T+0"). If the purpose of the
DLT is to bring about a settlement system of T+0, default risk may increase and
can cause a blockage in the trading system, as one trade depends on another successful trade. In addition, there are markets that operate on a T+0 basis without
the use of DLT, such as China and Hong Kong.[96] Thus, if the financial participants
in a market can agree to operate on a T+0 basis, this can be achieved without the
assistance of DLTs. The current T+2 model benefits certain intermediaries who
can utilise the cash realised from the sale of securities. The removal of the centralised ledgers system performed by the CSD will reduce settlement efficiency
by netting multiple transactions into one single position. Furthermore, CSDs can
perform functions ancillary to settlement facilities, such as custodian services and
security gate-keeping. These functions, and the way in which DLT can be used to
realise efficiency and benefits, will be discussed in the following sections.

93 The Giovannini Group, Second Report on EU Clearing and Settlement Arrangements, April 2003
   http://ec.europa.eu/internal_market/financial-markets/docs/clearing/second_giovannini_report_en
   .pdf.
94 Article 5, EU Central Securities Depository Regulation (CSDR).
95 Boston Consulting Group, 'Cost Benefit Analysis of Shortening the Settlement Cycle' 2012 Com-
   missioned by The Depository Trust and Clearing Corporation.
96 Hong Kong Exchanges and Clearing Limited (HKEX) introduced realtime DvP for northbound
   stock connect trading – its mutual market access programmes with the Shanghai and Shenzhen
   stock exchanges – in November 2017. Realtime DvP is expected to be used by institutional investors. www.hkex.com.hk/news/news-release/2017/1711062news?sc_lang=en.

Custodian services

As CSDs maintain a centralised ledger system that records the ownership of securities, they can also act as managers of these securities by holding them for the benefit of the end-investors.[97] In the UK, the CSD does not act as a securities custodian, but rather as a notary of the securities, recording the ownership of the securities held by members.[98] The financial intermediaries, who are members of the CSD, hold the securities in trust for their immediate clients (who are not necessarily the end-investors). Under the current model of securities intermediation, the identities of the end-investors – even the domestic ones – are difficult to ascertain. This can make it difficult to enforce the law against market misconduct, such as money laundering, market abuse and tax evasion. DLT is potentially a regulatory technology (RegTech) that increases the level of transparency in securities trading. However, such a guarantee of transparency can only be achieved through a private chain – a permission-based chain – whereby a trusted third party will act as an authentication authority. The authentication authority will provide the public key infrastructure that prevents fraudulent transactions, i.e. forged transactions. While on the private chain, participants may wish to maintain a certain level of privacy so as to prevent others from knowing their trading positions/strategies as well as their individual personal wealth. At the same time, personal data may need to be made available for law enforcement purposes.[99] The authentication authority will be able to act in such a way that both protects personal data against data theft and protects market integrity against misconduct.

A decentralised network

The blockchain network can potentially revolutionise market practice in securities trading, which is essentially a centralised model, be it an exchange, an organised trading platform or an alternative trading platform. In these centralised trading platforms, trade orders will be matched centrally, netted by a central counterparty (CCP) and settled by a central securities depository (CSD). Decentralisation by DLT means that these operators or their functions could be made redundant. Consequentially, systemic risk, market conduct risk and operational risk would be left unmanaged. The markets will become fragmented on the open chain. It is not certain whether the capital market, when on the DLT, will increase competition, as seen in the rise of the alternative trading platforms. The peer-to-peer

97 Diana Chan, Florence Fontan, Simonetta Rosati and Daniela Russo, 'The Securities Custody Industry' European Central Bank Occasional Paper 68, 2007. www.ecb.europa.eu/pub/pdf/scpops /ecbocp68.pdf?5ff757225862fdd1894d8dab08815b19.
98 Madeleine Yates and Gerald Montagu, *The Law of Global Custody: Legal Risk Management in Securities Investment and Collateral* (4th edn Bloomsbury Professional 2013) 243–286.
99 Matthias Berberich and Malgorzata Steiner, 'Blockchain Technology and the GDPR – How to Reconcile Privacy and Distributed Ledgers' (2016) 2(3) *European Data Protection Law Review* 422–426.

model does not promise more liquidity, ensuring the price-discovery function of the market. This model can also lead to a higher cost for the investor seeking to exit the company or the market. Because a CCP will not perform its netting function, the market on the DLT will operate on a pre-funded basis, losing the function of an open market. Furthermore, the nodes on the open chain will act independently in keeping the ledgers. It will take approximately 20 minutes to update the ledgers on the chain. Because the nodes will be based on different locations around the world, it will be more difficult to coordinate their actions in dealing with market shocks and other instances of market turbulence, such as Black Swan events. When securities trades happen without coordinated action, there will be mismatches in trade, as some nodes may validate a trade without an update on the ledgers. This can lead to systemic problems on the capital market.[100]

Market conduct risk will be difficult to control. Capital market rules have been designed to protect investors and ensure fair dealings. The rules relate to such matters as conflicts of interest,[101] insider dealing, market manipulation,[102] disclosure[103] and transparency regimes.[104] These essential rules apply to listing, issuing, trading, clearing and settlement. For listing, the prospectus regime applies to ensure that the issuing companies pass a certain quality control threshold to protect the investor. The exchanges and other intermediaries, such as underwriters, financial analysts and lawyers in the IPO, all act as critical capital market gatekeepers. On the DLT, especially on an open chain, the location of the issuing entity will be difficult to ascertain. Yet, the issuing of the securities can still reach investors who have access to the nodes on the chain. Yet, there will be reduced or no protection for investors. For trading, because trades will be made on an encrypted basis, no disclosure of information will be made to the market. Pre-trade and post-trade disclosure about price and volume need to be made for trades on regulated markets. This is to ensure that investors obtain the best price available. Without this

100 Bank for International Settlement, 'Distributed Ledger Technology in Payment, Clearing and Settlement: An Analytical Framework' (2017) www.bis.org/cpmi/publ/d157.pdf.
101 G. Ferrarini and N. Moloney, 'Reshaping Order Execution in the EU and the Role of Interest Groups: From MiFID I to MiFID II' (2012) 13(4) *European Business Organization Law Review* 557–597.
102 Council Directive 2003/6/EC on insider dealing and market manipulation; Regulation (EU) No 596/2014 of the European Parliament and of the Council of 16 April 2014 on market abuse.
103 Directive 2003/71/EC of the European Parliament and of the Council of 4 November 2003 on the Prospectus to be Published when Securities are Offered to the Public or Admitted to Trading and Amending Directive 2001/34/EC. Official Journal of the European Union 31 December. Available from: http://data.europa.eu/eli/dir/2003/71/oj.
104 Directive 2013/50/EU of the European Parliament and of the Council of 22 October 2013 amending Directive 2004/109/EC of the European Parliament and of the Council on the harmonisation of transparency requirements in relation to information about issuers whose securities are admitted to trading on a regulated market, Directive 2003/71/EC of the European Parliament and of the Council on the prospectus to be published when securities are offered to the public or admitted to trading and Commission Directive 2007/14/EC laying down detailed rules for the implementation of certain provisions of Directive 2004/109/EC. Official Journal of the European Union 6 November.

information, the prices of the securities offered will be easily manipulated. For trades on DLT, the investor who loses out through price manipulation will have no access to regulatory assistance to obtain compensation. This can be seen in the LIBOR scandal, where pricing could be manipulated because there was no regulatory oversight. For clearing, the CCP performs critical risk management functions for the capital market, and DLT will cause the decentralisation of this risk management function. The current regulatory regime at the EU level shows the risks of CCP's operations in the areas of interoperability, transfer of open interest and third country supervision. If each node on the chain is also to perform such risk management functions, recovery and resolution will be a challenging task, as coordination will be more difficult. For settlement, if the DLT can make delivery-versus-payment (DVP) instantaneous, the question that arises is when, under the law, is settlement recognised? As there will be a time lag between the actual transaction and the validation of the settlement on the nodes, such a time lag represents a risk. Because transactions on the chain are encrypted, trades will be made on the basis of anonymity. In other words, it would be difficult to trace fraudulent transactions. Although settled transactions are not reversible under the current law and market practices, there are exceptions to such irrevocability. One of which is the case of fraudulent transactions. Trades recorded on DLT cannot be easily reversed, as they are immutable. This can lead to the "hard fork" problem, as seen on the Ethereum platform – a cryptocurrency trade platform. When nodes on the platform cannot agree on whether fraudulent trades can be reversed, two parallel systems can be created as a result. If a "hard fork" occurs in the securities trade, it can cause a company's securities to be doubled and traded on two systems. Furthermore, because the trades will be encrypted and the transactions enabled by the use of public and private keys, if the investor loses the private key, they will not be able to recover the assets. If the system is subjected to cyber-attacks,[105] there will be no guarantee of recovery of the investor's assets.

A disintermediated network imagined

Other than exchanges, clearing houses (CCPs), CSDs and custodian banks, there are also brokers, banks and asset managers who intermediate securities trades in the investment world. Without their functionality, cross-border trades and cross-border investment would not be possible in trade across different centralised markets. If DLT created a decentralised market space, the functions of financial intermediaries would be redundant. Brokers would no longer need to execute orders for their clients. Custodian banks would no longer need to hold securities for their clients. Asset management would not be required to create an investment scheme with a portfolio

---

105 Major bitcoin exchanges hit by cyberattacks as record rally makes them a target, see www.cnbc .com/2017/06/14/major-bitcoin-exchanges-hit-by-cyberattacks-as-record-rally-makes-them-a -target.html.

to facilitate cross-border investment to meet the needs of international investors.[106] Proxy advisors and shareholder services would not be in demand, as investors would be able to exercise their own voting rights on the blockchain. The issuing company would be able to know who holds its securities and how much they hold. This information could help the company facilitate corporate actions such as voting rights and other economic entitlements. The peer-to-peer blockchain network has the potential to achieve shareholder transparency and to reduce the cost and risk of intermediated securities. The international central securities depositories (ICSDs) that currently facilitate securities trades at cross-border level would be unnecessary. As a result, discussions about the insolvency of an intermediary and the effect of that insolvency on the rights and entitlements of the end-investor would be redundant.[107]

How to regulate trades on DLT: a consensus model or a private chain?

A consensus model

With the blockchain network, each node will act as a data node and all the nodes will form a network of data centres. Participants maintain the integrity of the ledger by reaching a consensus about its state – the accuracy of a ledger – by using the consensus algorithm. That is the algorithm for mutually approving a distributed ledger using Proof of Work and Proof of Stake. It is difficult to know which law will govern and which regulator will have enforcement power over activities and transactions that occur over the network.[108] If there is a risk of cyber-attack, which relates to cyber-security, the state has a role in ensuring safety over the network (the territorial governance). The state may use criminal law to deter cyber-attacks and may use its sovereign power to cooperate with other state entities in ensuring security at the cross-border level. There are other areas where state intervention – as opposed to self-regulation of network participants – is justified. These may include market abuse, data protection and competition law.

Assume that network participants were able to make their own rules to ensure market safety, stability and investor protection (to ensure participant confidence),

---

106 With the invention of Robo-advisors – which use algorithms to recommend a portfolio of funds based on an investor's answers to an online questionnaire – the asset management role as advisor will be gradually diminished. See Aliya Ram and Robin Wigglesworth, 'When Silicon Valley Came to Wall Street: Mainstream Asset Managers Have Begun Using Big Data and Machine Learning' *Financial Times* (London, 30 October 2017) 6; Also see Ian Hunt and Chris Mills, 'Distributed Ledger Technology – An Emerging Consensus on the Buy-Side' The Alternative Investment Management Association (AIMA) Research Report, 2018 www.aima.org/uploads/assets/uploaded/dd2326bb-b9ed-4be2-b5b905e29d3dfa63.pdf.

107 Luc Thevenoz, 'Intermediated Securities, Legal Risk, and the International Harmonization of Commercial Law' (2008) 13(2) *Stanford Journal of Law, Business & Finance* 384–452.

108 Gabrielle Patrick and Anurag Bana, 'Rule of Law Versus Rule of Code: A Blockchain Driven Legal World' (November 2017), available at: www.ibanet.org/Document/Default.aspx?DocumentUid=https://.

the participants would need to decide 1) who is allowed to join the network; 2) the level of transparency in the network; and 3) how disputes are to be resolved.[109] It is submitted that even a consensus-based network blockchain would need regulation. The question is, therefore, who should regulate and what is to be regulated?[110]

It is submitted that a public–private regulatory collaboration would be the best model to provide the network with rules, adjudication and enforcement.[111] There is nothing new about such a collaborative model. Indeed, there are many areas where such a collaborative regulatory model provides the basis of governance.[112] What may be emerging or shifting is the line of demarcation between state and private regulation.[113] With distributed ledgers connecting between nodes that are based in different jurisdictions, traditional conflict-of-law rules may not, without further development, be applicable to incidents that occur over the network.[114] For instance, which law should be applicable to the transfer of securities in such a distributed ledger network?[115] Since there are different laws across different jurisdictions, the legal status of smart contracts would need to be clarified by introducing a standard that will facilitate compliance issues such as privacy requirement and anti-money laundering control and allow for a life-cycle management of smart contracts.

The need for a trusted third party – authentication and identification management

It has been said that blockchain has the potential to replace a system that requires a trusted third party with a system that is itself a trusted model. This statement is based on two essential premises: decentralisation and disintermediation. Currently, the trust system is built on a centralised system in which the exchanges, CCPs and CSDs will ensure operational safety. A certification authority, which acts as an intermediary between traders and exchanges, authenticates trade orders (proves

109 Pietro Ortolani, 'Self-Enforcing Online Dispute Resolution: Lessons from Bitcoin' (2016) 36 *Oxford Journal of Legal Studies* 595, 608.
110 Elizabeth Sara Ross, 'Nobody Puts Blockchain in a Corner: The Disruptive Role of Blockchain Technology in the Financial Services Industry and Current Regulatory Issues' (2017) 25(2) *Catholic University Journal of Law and Technology* 353–386
111 Dominique Custos and John Reitz, 'Public-Private Partnerships' (2010) 58 *American Journal of Comparative Law* 555–584.
112 Julia Black, 'Enrolling Actors in Regulatory Processes: Examples from UK Financial Services Regulation' (2003) *Public Law* 63–91.
113 Carla Reyes, Nizan Geslevich Packin and Benjamin Edwards, 'Distributed Governance' (2017) 59 *William & Mary Law Review* 1–32.
114 World Economic Forum, 'Realizing the Potential of Blockchain: A Multistakeholder Approach to the Stewardship of Blockchain and Cryptocurrencies' White Paper, June 2017 www3.weforum.org/docs/WEF_Realizing_Potential_Blockchain.pdf.
115 This is one of the risks in ICO as the UK Financial Regulator may not have jurisdiction over transactions over DLTs. See Financial Conduct Authority, 'Consumer Warning about the Risks of Initial Coin Offerings ("ICOs")'. Published 12/09/2017, available at: www.fca.org.uk/news/statements/initial-coin-offerings.

you are who you say you are).[116] The CCP acts as a trusted third party that will step into a default trade, and the CSDs can authenticate the record of securities ownership. Instead of such a centralised trust system, blockchain hopes to bring about a distributed trust system whereby trust is maintained by all the participants (the nodes) through a consensus model. In this distributed trust system, as opposed to a centralised trust system maintained by a third party, authentication will be based on algorithms. In effect, records cannot be tampered with (or be nearly tamper-proof) and fraudulent transactions cannot be made without putting in a substantial amount of time and energy, thus making such fraudulent activities not cost-effective. However, to maximise the power of distributed ledgers, there will need to be interoperability of authentication which, in turn, will require, at international level, agreements about data interoperability, policy interoperability and the effective implementation of international standards. Leaving this question aside, there are a number of issues that blockchain technology has not yet managed to address, including the prevention of money laundering, identity theft, violation of data protection laws, the problem of settlement finality, the hard fork problem, recovery and resolution, and cyber security issues. It is submitted that mechanisms will need to be developed to map blockchain transactions to individual users and entities in a secure manner. Furthermore, credentials on the blockchain will need to be stored and aligned to a sidechain (off blockchain) to be carried out by trusted third parties.

Risk of fraud and money laundering

On the blockchain network, transactions can be made anonymously because participants can use "Private Key Cryptography" and "Public Key Cryptography" to make transactions. Although the transactions are transparent on the shared ledgers, the person who initiates the transaction will not be traceable. In a de-centralised network where each node can facilitate securities trading, using the system to launder the money would be more easily facilitated compared to the present system, where the intermediary can act as a gatekeeper under Know Your Customer (KYC) rules.[117] Bitcoin trades have demonstrated that there are "dark web" trading sites,[118] known as the Silk Road,[119] which associates with criminal transactions,[120] so standards will need to be developed to ensure that the confidentiality, integrity

---

116 Scott Shackelford and Steve Myers, 'Block-by-Block: Leveraging the Power of Blockchain Technology to Build Trust and Promote Cyber Peace' (2017) 19 *Yale Journal of Law and Technology* 334–388.

117 However, DLT, if designed properly, can also be used as RegTech to perform the duty of KYC.

118 Michael Chertoff, 'A Public Policy Perspective of the Dark Web' (2016) 2(1) *Journal of Cyber Policy* 26–38. https://doi.org/10.1080/23738871.2017.1298643.

119 Andrew Norry, 'The History of Silk Road: A Tale of Drugs, Extortion & Bitcoin' Blockonomi 29 November 2017. https://blockonomi.com/history-of-silk-road/.

120 James Ball, Charles Arthur and Adam Gabbatt, 'FBI Claims Largest Bitcoin Seizure after Arrest of Alleged Silk Road Founder' *The Guardian* (London, October 2013) www.theguardian.com/technology/2013/oct/02/alleged-silk-road-website-founder-arrested-bitcoin.

and availability of users and entities are maintained.[121] Compliance with money laundering and Know Your Customer (KYC) requirements will need to be embedded.[122] This will also include standardising electronic KYC processes.[123]

Risk of public and private key infrastructure: loss of assets

In the blockchain network, there will be no central body (or trusted third party) to authenticate transactions and safeguard the information/data. Instead, there will be hyper-ledgers distributed among participants. To transmit, authenticate and access information, both public keys and private keys will be used. Public keys will be used to encrypt documents/messages and private keys to decrypt them.[124]

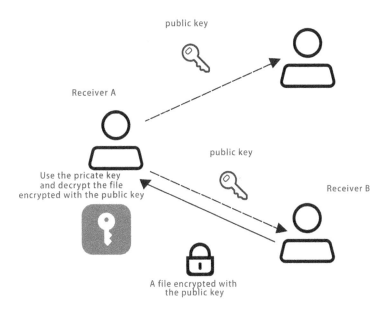

Figure 2.3 Mechanism of public key cryptography

121 Inside Bitcoins, 'Blockchain Identity: Solving the Global Identification Crisis' (27 September 2015). https://insidebitcoins.com/news/blockchain-identity-solving-the-global-identification-crisis/35028.
122 Neepa Patel, 'Blockchain KYC/AML Utilities for International Payments: A Regulatory Solution for Anti-Money Laundering and Financial Inclusion?' R 3 Report, 6 November 2017 www.r3.com/wp-content/uploads/2018/02/blockchain_kyc_aml_utilities_R3.pdf.
123 International Telecommunication Union, 'Successful Use of Security Standards' ITU-T Technical Report, 7 September 2016. www.itu.int/dms_pub/itu-t/opb/tut/T-TUT-SEC-2016-PDF-E.pdf.
124 Public key cryptography, IMB Knowledge Center www.ibm.com/support/knowledgecenter/en/SSB23S_1.1.0.14/gtps7/s7pkey.htm. What is public-key cryptography? A look at the encryption algorithm and its security benefits, GlobalSign, www.globalsign.com/en/ssl-information-center/what-is-public-key-cryptography/.

For instance, as illustrated in Figure 2.3,[125] if A wants to send a message to B, A needs to use a private key to encrypt the message and only A's public key can decrypt it. A can send B a public key to authenticate the message (i.e. to confirm the message is from A). However, if the parties lose these keys or allow others to access them – causing theft – they would lose assets as a result, and it would be impossible to recover those assets.

One world, one internet and the network effect (fork problem)

As seen in the cryptocurrency world, disagreement between participants can lead to a break-up of the network that causes a "fork."[126] A fork involves splitting the path of a blockchain by invalidating transactions confirmed by nodes that have not been upgraded to the new version of the protocol software.[127] This is illustrated in Figure 2.4. A hard fork can be implemented to correct important security risks found in older versions of the software, to add new functionality or to reverse transactions. This can also be a major risk for capital markets that use DLTs. For instance, Company X has 100 shares on Blockchain 1. When a fork occurs, Blockchain 2 will also have 100 shares of Company X (the mirror image of Company X's shares on Blockchain 1), with the same shareholders. Because there will be no central registration of the company's shares, e.g. Companies House in the UK, the fork problem can create duplicate shares which may confuse shareholders, markets and companies. When there is a corporate action, instead of one vote, a shareholder will get two. A gets one vote on Blockchain 1 and one vote on Blockchain 2. When shareholders sell their shares to others on different chains, this can cause major disruption to corporate governance that is currently built on shareholder action. A can sell shares of Company X to B on Blockchain 1 and A can sell to C on Blockchain 2. In other words, a share that was owned by A before the fork is now owned by B on Blockchain 1 and C on Blockchain 2. This creates a problem: who has the voting rights recognised by Company X and by law? There is a need to implement interoperability – allowing transfer of messages and assets across the blockchain. Furthermore, there is a need to incorporate interoperability between different blockchain networks and to non-blockchain networks. In other words, a global approach to data governance is critical in addition to technical interoperability between different blockchains.

125 Nomura Research Institute, Survey on Blockchain Technologies and Related Services FY2015 Report. Available at www.meti.go.jp/english/press/2016/pdf/0531_01f.pdf.
126 J. I. Wong and I. Karr, 'Everything You Need to Know about the Ethereum "Hard Fork"' Quartz 18 July 2016 at http://qz.com/730004/everything-you-need-to-know-about-the-ethereumhard -fork/; 'A Crypto-Currency Civil War. Making Bitcoin Work Better: A Compromise Over the Currency's Future May Not Last' *The Economist* (29th July 2017). www.economist.com/news/ finance-and-economics/21725598-compromise-over-currencys-future-may-not-last-making-bit-coin-work-better.
127 Nomura Research Institute, Survey on Blockchain Technologies and Related Services, 11. FY2015 Report. Available at www.meti.go.jp/english/press/2016/pdf/0531_01f.pdf.

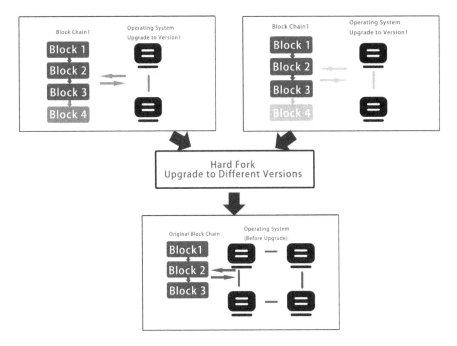

Figure 2.4 A hard fork

Recovery and resolution

Financial institutions need to have a recovery and resolution regime in order to continue their business in times of crisis.[128] For instance, in the event of a major attack or extraordinary event such as flash crashes, exchanges must be able to take measures to secure their operations and maintain market safety. It is said that distributed ledgers are inherently harder to attack because instead of a single database, there are multiple shared copies of the same database, so a cyber-attack would have to attack all the copies simultaneously to be success-ful.[129] However, some argue that centralised systems will have better recovery and resolution capabilities. According to this argument, in a de-centralised and distributed system where there are several nodes – several exchanges and many more banks – the coordination required to design a business continuity plan

128 The EU Recovery and Resolution Directive (RRD) 2014/59/EU of The European Parliament and of The Council, under which financial institutions are required to prepare and regularly update recovery plans that set out the measures they would take to restore their financial position following a significant deterioration.
129 Government Office for Science, 'Distributed Ledger Technology Beyond Block Chain' 2016, 6. Available at: www.gov.uk/government/uploads/system/uploads/attachment_data/file/492972/gs-16-1-distributed-ledger-technology.pdf.

would be more difficult to achieve, and it would be more difficult to take action at the time of an attack, for instance due to software bug or loophole. On the other hand, one may also argue that the blockchain network is itself a recovery and resolution regime. Because blockchain is a distributed ledger network, it would be more difficult for an attacker to launch a successful attack, which would require that a majority of nodes be affected. This is a contentious issue, and we must wait and see how DLTs evolve. Yet, one should also consider how blockchain participants would be protected from joint liability if adoption of blockchain is to be increased.[130]

Conclusion

DLTs have the potential to transform the conduct of public and private sector organisations particularly in areas of highly regulated industry with increased private–public governance partnership.[131] The benefits of DLTs to the capital market are premised on decentralisation and disintermediation. However, a careful examination of the life cycle of the securities trade shows that decentralisation and disintermediation would not bring about the intended benefits for the current capital markets – i.e. lowering the costs of securities trading, facilitating more peer-to-peer trade at the domestic or cross-border level and enabling more access to capital for SME enterprises. That is not to say that DLTs, in their current form, cannot be used to correct some of the market failures by making trades more transparent, the system more secure, and, at the same time, making the system more cost-efficient for the participants. In this sense, DLTs can be a regulation technology (RegTech) – that uses technical code (software and protocols) to assure compliance with legal code (rules consisting of legal obligations), and, in so doing, reduces the costs of legal compliance.[132] Yet this would still require trusted third parties to maintain the DLT's network in order to mitigate market and operational risks and act as *de facto* regulators. Furthermore, the term "distributed" is used to describe the effect to the blockchain network, but it does not denote that there is no overall controlling authority or owner. There are various distributed ledger models, with different degrees of centralisation and different types of access control, to suit different business needs. The question is,

130 Dirk Zetzsche, Ross Buckley and Douglas Arner, 'The Distributed Liability of Distributed Ledgers: Legal Risks of Blockchain' (13 August 2017). University of Illinois Law Review, 2017–2018, Forthcoming; University of Luxembourg Law Working Paper No. 007/2017; Center for Business & Corporate Law (CBC) Working Paper 002/2017; University of Hong Kong Faculty of Law Research Paper No. 2017/020; UNSW Law Research Paper No. 52; European Banking Institute Working Paper Series 14. Available at SSRN: https://ssrn.com/abstract=3018214 or http://dx.doi.org/10.2139/ssrn.3018214.
131 Julia Black, 'Paradoxes and Failures: "New Governance" Techniques and the Financial Crisis' (2012) 75(6) *Modern Law Review* 1037–1063.
132 Government Office for Science 'FinTech Futures: The UK as a World Leader in Financial Technologies' 2015. Available at: www.gov.uk/government/uploads/system/uploads/attachment_data/file/413095/gs-15-3-fintech-futures.pdf.

therefore, who should act as the trusted third parties – governments, incumbent financial market infrastructure operators, banks, technology companies or the new FinTech companies? As DLTs will operate at the cross-border level, how is the governance of such networks, akin to the internet world, to be coordinated at a transnational level?

3 Crypto-assets law and regulation

Introduction

In the last chapter, I discussed the possible infrastructural implementations of DLT on the capital markets and I have highlighted how securities can be tokenised and how smart contracts can be used to embody certain rights in the securities. In this chapter, I will put forward ways in which "things" traded on the blockchain network can gain legal recognition and the difficulties of using the current legal framework to capture them.

Discussion about the way in which crypto-assets can or should be classified in law, otherwise known as legal taxonomy (LT),[1] has made a significant contribution to the development of an infrastructure for crypto-finance and of its regulation.[2] Legal taxonomy clarifies what crypto-assets are in law so that stakeholders and participants in this developing system can understand how to use them to

---

1 Emily Sherwin, 'Legal Taxonomy' (2009) 15 *Legal Theory* 25, 54; Jens Lausen, 'Regulating Initial Coin Offerings? A Taxonomy of Crypto-Assets' (Research Paper, Association for Information Systems, Stockholm & Uppsala, Sweden, 2019), http://aisel.aisnet.org.ecis2019_rp/26; Rafael Delfin, 'A General Taxonomy for Cryptographic Assets' https://assets.ctfassets.net/sdlntm3tthp6/6mq u1HTdBKG46Q6iqa26uE/df09eaf16935053c99c8fcdce658c7ae/General_Taxonomy_for_Cryptographic_Assets.pdf, accessed 05 July 2020.

2 'Cryptoasset Promotions: Consultation' (HM Treasury, July 2020) https://assets.publishing.service .gov.uk/government/uploads/system/uploads/attachment_data/file/902891/Cryptoasset_promotions_consultation.pdf, accessed 22 July 2020; Lin Lin and Dora Neo, 'Alternative Investments in the Tech Era' (2020) 2020(1) *Singapore Journal of Legal Studies* 1–3. Apolline Blandin et al., 'Global Cryptoasset Regulatory Landscape Study' (University of Cambridge Faculty of Law Research Paper No. 23/2019), www.jbs.cam.ac.uk/fileadmin/user_upload/research/centres/alternative-finance/downloads/2019-04-ccaf-global-cryptoasset-regulatory-landscape-study.pdf; 'Global Digital Finance: Code of Conduct – Taxonomy for Cryptographic Assets' www.gdf.io/wp-content/uploads/2018/10/0010_GDF_Taxonomy-for-Cryptographic-Assets_Proof-V2-260719.pdf, accessed 05 July 2020.

DOI: 10.4324/9780429023613-3

catalyse socio-economic transformation,[3] how to monetise them,[4] how to mitigate risks[5] and how to regulate the way the system is used.[6]

Previous research has shown that lack of either legal certainty or regulatory intervention can lead to the downfall of a sector,[7] whether mature or developing. The value fluctuation of unstable coins markets, such as the Bitcoin market, demonstrates that both legal certainty and regulatory intervention are needed for stable market construction.[8] As supervision has been developed sector by sector in most jurisdictions,[9] legal taxonomy also helps determine which regulator has oversight over dealings in any particular asset.[10] The regulator applies existing laws or develops new ones to bring the asset in question under its regulatory purview.[11] In private law, legal taxonomy directs how parties negotiate contracts

3 Robby Houben et al., 'Cryptocurrencies and Blockchain: Legal Context and Implications for Financial Crime, Money Laundering and Tax Evasion' (Research Paper, Policy Department for Economic, Scientific and Quality of Life Policies, European Parliament, 2018).

4 Edmund Mokhtarian and Alexander Lindgren, 'Rise of the Crypto Hedge Fund: Operational Issues and Best Practices for an Emergent Investment Industry' (2018) 23 *Stanford Journal of Law, Business & Finance* 112, 158; 'Money's Past and Fintech's Future: Wildcat Crypto, the Digital Dollar, and Citizen Central' (2019) 2 *Stanford Journal of Blockchain Law & Policy* 1, 11.

5 'Regulatory Challenges and Risks for Central Bank Digital Currency' (Regulatory Requirements and Economic Impact Working Group, International Telecommunication Union, 2019), www.itu .int/en/ITU-T/focusgroups/dfc/Documents/DFC-O-006_Report%20on%20Regulatory%20Challenges%20and%20Risks%20for%20Central%20Bank%20Digital%20Currency.pdf, accessed 05 July 2020.

6 'Cryptoassets Taskforce: Final Report' (UK HM Treasury et al., 2018), https://assets.publishing. service.gov.uk/government/uploads/system/uploads/attachment_data/file/752070/cryptoassets_ taskforce_ final_report_final_web.pdf; 'Guidance of Cryptoassets' (FCA Consultation Paper 19/3, 2019); 'Report with Advice for the European Commission on Crypto-Assets' (European Banking Authority, 2019), https://eba.europa.eu/sites/default/documents/files/documents/10180/2545547 /67493daa-85a8-4429-aa91-e9a5ed880684/EBA%20Report%20on%20crypto%20assets.pdf ?retry=1; Norman Chan, 'Keynote Speech at Treasury Markets Summit 2018 on Crypto-Assets and Money' (Hong Kong Monetary Authority 2018) www.hkma.gov.hk/eng/news-and-media/speeches /2018/09/20180921-1/; 'Conceptual Framework for the Potential Regulation of Virtual Asset Trading Platform Operates' (Securities and Futures Commission of Hong Kong, 2018) www.sfc.hk/ web/EN/files/ER/PDF/App%202_%20Conceptual%20framework%20for%20VA%20tra; 'Notice on Precautions Against the Risks of Bitcoins' (People's Bank of China, 2013) www.miit.gov.cn/ n1146295/n1652858/n1652930/ n3757016/c3762245/content.html, accessed 10 July 2020.

7 Tara Mandjee, 'Bitcoin, Its Legal Classification and Its Regulatory Framework' (2016) 15 *Journal of Business and Securities Law* 158, 211.

8 Joseph Lee and Lheureux Florian, 'A Regulatory Framework for Cryptocurrency' (2020) 31(3) *European Business Law Review* 423–446.

9 International Monetary Fund, 'Evaluating Financial Sector Supervision: Banking, Insurance and Securities Markets', in *Financial Sector Assessment: A Handbook* (International Monetary Fund 2005).

10 Iris H-Y Chiu, 'Pathways to European Policy and Regulation in the Crypto-Economy' (2019) *European Journal of Risk Regulation* 738, 765.

11 Johannes Ehrentraud et al., 'Policy Responses to Fintech: A Cross-Country Overview', (Financial Stability Institute on Policy Implementation No. 23, 2020); Hong Kong: A New Regulatory Approach for Cryptocurrencies, www.dataguidance.com/opinion/hong-kong-new-regulatory -approach-cryptocurrencies; David Lee et al., *Handbook of Blockchain, Digital Finance, and*

for transactions and how lawyers draft documents to provide evidence of their negotiations.[12] Their subsequent actions, including execution, reporting, registration and compliance, will depend on terms embedded in the contract, and these are based on the legal taxonomy of the assets and the regulatory framework that applies to them.[13] For insolvency practitioners and creditors, the legal taxonomy of assets will determine how to safeguard their interest (*ex ante* protection), and also how to assert claims in assets during reorganisation and insolvency proceedings (*ex post* protection).[14]

As new concepts of law and regulation have emerged in this area, software developers have begun to work with lawyers to create smart technologies that link the different functions.[15] Automation can increase the efficiency of the crypto-market as well as monetising new products and services[16] that are generated by, for example, Big Data.[17] Legal taxonomy provides the ground rules within which IT engineers and lawyers can design new hardware and software systems. If the market is recognised as a legal construct,[18] legal taxonomy will also determine how stakeholders congregate to create a market for assets, whether physically in a place such as Lloyd's in London,[19] digitally such as on the London Stock Exchange,[20] or virtually such as on blockchain for cryptocurrency.[21] As a consequence, there are legal implications for the way the market is defined in financial law as well as in competition law.

Crypto systems are aimed at creating a boundary-free[22] regional and global space where stakeholders can benefit from the internet's high-speed transmission

---

Inclusion (1st edn, Elsevier 2018) *Vol 1: Cryptocurrency, Fintech, InsurTech, and Regulation* & *Vol 2: ChinaTech, Mobile Security, and Distributed Ledger.*

12 Carol Goforth, 'The Lawyer's Cryptionary: A Resource for Talking to Clients about Crypto-Trans-actions' (2019) 1 *Campbell Law Review* 47, 122; Rainer Kulms, 'Blockchain: Private Law Matters' (2020) *Singapore Journal of Legal Studies* 63, 89.

13 Carla Reyes, '(Un)Corporate Crypto-Governance' (2020) 88 *Fordham Law Review* 1875, 1922.

14 Janis Sarra and Louise Gullifer, 'Crypto-Claimants and Bitcoin Bankruptcy: Challenges for Recognition and Realization' 2019 (2) *International Insolvency Review* 233, 272.

15 O. Bolotaeva et al., 'The Legal Nature of Cryptocurrency' (IOP Conference Series: Earth and Environmental Science, 2019), https://iopscience.iop.org/article/10.1088/1755-1315/272/3/032166/pdf, accessed 05 July 2020.

16 Emmanuelle Ganne, *Can Blockchain Revolutionise International Trade?* (Word Trade Organisation 2018), www.wto.org/english/res_e/booksp_e/blockchainrev18_e.pdf, accessed 05 July 2020.

17 Albert Opher, Alex Chou, Andrew Onda and Krishna Sounderrajan, 'The Rise of the Data Economy: Driving Value through Internet of Things Data Monetisation: A Perspective for Chief Digital Officers and Chief Technology Officers' (2016) www.ibm.com/downloads/cas/4JROLDQ7, accessed 07 December 2020.

18 Justin Desautels-Stein, 'The Market as a Legal Concept' (2012) 60 *Buffalo Law Review* 387, 492.

19 Frederick Martin, *The History of Lloyd's and of Marine Insurance in Great Britain* (London: Mac-Millan, 2004).

20 Ranald Michie, *The London Stock Exchange: A History* (Oxford: OUP 2003).

21 Joseph Lee and Florian Lheureux, 'A Regulatory Framework for Cryptocurrency' (2020) *European Law Review*, forthcoming.

22 Garrick Hileman and Michel Rauchs, 'Global Cryptocurrency Benchmarking Study' (Cambridge Centre for Alternative Finance, 2019), www.jbs.cam.ac.uk/fileadmin/user_upload/research/cen-

of data;[23] in other words, a virtual world.[24] Crypto-finance facilitates the creation of this universal Crypto-Republic.[25] Under the "law matters" theory,[26] an international standard for the legal taxonomy of crypto-assets can reduce confusion and conflict,[27] and increase competition by developing a rule-based level playing field.[28] Taking current legal and regulatory rules and using them by analogy and extension to support the construction of the crypto-market can be efficient, but to do so without considering the targeted functions and operational matters will stifle development.[29] The rules that are currently in place were not originally designed to regulate crypto-functions.

This chapter will assess the functions and operation of some crypto-assets that are either already on the market[30] or have been proposed,[31] by looking at attempts to regulate them and discussing regulatory attitudes and policy directions. The main crypto-assets to be analysed against both laws and regulations include exchange tokens (payment tokens), security tokens (asset tokens), utility tokens, fund tokens, commodity tokens, title tokens and hybrid tokens.[32] There are

tres/alternative-finance/downloads/2017-04-20-global-cryptocurrency-benchmarking-study.pdf, accessed 06 July 2020.

23 Marco Iansiti and Karim Lakhani, 'The Truth about Blockchain' (2017) Harvard Business Review, https://hbr.org/2017/01/the-truth-about-blockchain, accessed 06 July 2020.

24 Robert Hoogendoorm, 'Virtual Worlds: The Next Frontier for Businesses' https://dappradar.com/blog/virtual-worlds-the-next-frontier-for-businesses, accessed 06 July 2020.

25 Thad Kousser and Matthew McCubbins, 'Social Choice, Crypto-Initiatives, and Policymaking by Direct Democracy' (2005) 78 *Southern California Law Review* 949, 984.

26 Michael Gilbert, 'Does Law Matter? Theory and Evidence from Single-Subject Adjudication' (2011) 40 *Journal of Legal Studies* 333, 365.

27 OECD, 'The Tokenisation of Assets and Potential Implications for Financial Markets' (OECD Blockchain Policy Series, 2020), www.oecd.org/finance/The-Tokenisation-of-Assets-and-Potential-Implications-for-Financial-Markets.pdf, accessed 06 July 2020; Michael Ng, 'Choice of Law for Property Issues regarding Bitcoin under English Law' (2019) 15 *Journal of Private International Law* 315, 338.

28 'Investigating the Impact of Global Stablecoins' (G7 Working Group on Stablecoins October 2019), www.bis.org/cpmi/publ/d187.pdf, accessed 06 July 2020.

29 Apolline Blandin et al., 'Global Cryptoasset Regulatory Landscape Study' (University of Cambridge Faculty of Law Research Paper No. 23/2019) www.jbs.cam.ac.uk/fileadmin/user_upload/research/centres/alternative-finance/downloads/2019-04-ccaf-global-cryptoasset-regulatory-landscape-study.pdf, accessed 06 July 2020.

30 Ibid; Brianne Smith, 'The Life-Cycle and Character of Crypto-Assets: A Framework for Regulation and Investor Protection' (2019) 19 *Journal of Accounting and Finance* 156, 168.

31 Satoshi Nakamoto, 'Bitcoin: A Peer-to-Peer Electronic Cash System' www.bitcoin.com/bitcoin .pdf, accessed 06 July 2020; Dominic Worner et al., 'The Bitcoin Ecosystem: Disruption Beyond Financial Services?' (European Conference on Information Systems, 2016); FCA, 'Guidance on Cryptoassets' (Consultation Paper 19/3, January 2019).

32 Robby Houben and Alexander Snyers, 'Crypto-Assets: Key Developments, Regulatory Concerns and Responses' (Study requested by the ECON Committee, European Parliament), www.europarl .europa.eu/RegData/etudes/STUD/2020/648779/IPOL_STU(2020)648779_EN.pdf, accessed 06 July 2020; Securities and Markets Stakeholder Group, European Securities and Markets Authority, 'Own Initiative Report on Initial Coin Offerings and Crypto-Assets' (Securities and Markets Stakeholder Group, European Securities and Markets Authority 2018) www.esma.europa.eu/sites

also variations within a single token class. For instance, while share tokens and debt tokens are subsets of security tokens, they should not be treated in the same way, using the same rules, in contexts such as issuance or insolvency. The overall aim is to discover whether legal taxonomy and regulatory intervention can help in the construction of the emerging crypto-asset market with the goal of creating a boundary-free virtual Crypto-Republic.

Payment tokens

Payment tokens such as Bitcoin and Ether, also termed exchange tokens, are used as a method of payment and may be either unstable or stable.[33] Unstable tokens are not linked to any particular asset class recognised by the law and are created through the protocols of the "mining" process.[34] An unstable token is an intangible, virtual object that can be used for payment as if it were gold or silver in the past.[35] There is no specific value affixed to this intangible object,[36] unlike fiat money or digital money, both of which have a set value. The value of a payment token is determined by supply and demand in the market and as a result, its price is variable with no stable benchmark to measure its intrinsic value.[37] As payment tokens are not issued by a central bank or a central authority, and there is no defined measure to stabilise their intrinsic value, stabilisation depends on what the participants in the consensus system (the nodes) decide.[38] This can include revision of the original protocols used to create the tokens, which leads to the problem of "forking" with the opportunity for market manipulation at the expense of anybody unable to participate meaningfully in the revision of the original protocols.[39] To counter the instability of unstable payment tokens, some stable coins have emerged, notable among them being LIBRA, which intends to issue tokens

---

/default/files/library/esma22-106-1338_smsg_advice_-_report_on_icos_and_crypto-assets.pdf, accessed 06 July 2020.

33 G7 Working Group on Stablecoins, 'Investing the Impact of Global Stablecoins' (G7 Working Group on Stablecoins 2019) www.bis.org/cpmi/publ/d187.pdf, accessed 07 July 2020.

34 Joseph Lee and Florian Lheureux, 'A Regulatory Framework for Cryptocurrency' (2020) *European Law Review*.

35 Chia Ling Koh, 'The Rise of e-Money and Virtual Currencies: Re-discovering the Meaning of Money from a Legal Perspective' (Osborne Clarke, 2018) www.osborneclarke.com/wp-content/uploads/2018/07/The-rise-of-e-Money-and-virtual-currencies.pdf, accessed 07 July 2020.

36 PWC, 'Cryptographic Assets and Related Transactions: Accounting Considerations under IFRS' (Research Report 2019).

37 EY, 'The Valuation of Crypto-Assets: Minds Made for Shaping Financial Services' (2018) https://assets.ey.com/content/dam/ey-sites/ey-com/en_gl/topics/emeia-financial-services/ey-the-valuation-of-crypto-assets.pdf, accessed 07 July 2020.

38 G7 Working Group on Stablecoins, 'Investing the Impact of Global Stablecoins' (G7 Working Group on Stablecoins 2019) www.bis.org/cpmi/publ/d187.pdf, accessed 07 July 2020.

39 Vitalik Buterin, 'Decentralised Protocol Monetisation and Forks' (2014) https://blog.ethereum.org/2014/04/30/decentralized-protocol-monetization-and-forks/, accessed 07 July 2020.

linked to underlying assets that can be used for payment within the network.[40] The aim is to stabilise the value of the issued tokens, possibly with a fixed price, so that people who purchase them with fiat currencies, use them as payment or receive them as payments or gifts, would have some protection against fluctuations in value. However, as in other fiat currencies, payment tokens can also be used for purposes other than payment. They can be purchased as an investment by some-one expecting the value to go up or to earn interest/dividends when in the custody of intermediaries such as exchanges or banks. They can also be used as a method of transmitting value, though not in retail payment transactions by consumers, for large payments between entities or in investment. This ability is most likely to be used to facilitate exchanges in criminal activity, particularly if the tokens and the trading space are ungoverned.[41]

Current legal taxonomy and regulatory approaches to payment tokens remain sectoral rather than systematic. They are a taxable asset recognised as a "unit of account" by the UK tax authority.[42] However, it is not clear how the UK tax authority intends to treat them in law, for instance, whether payment tokens can be held in trust and are capable of being passed down from the settler to the ulti-mate beneficiaries, or how tax rates can be applied to payment tokens that have no face value and a fluctuating intrinsic value.[43] A decision is needed on how legal taxonomy applies to crypto-assets. Whatever that decision is, the revenue authori-ties will have a keen interest in levying taxes on them, as a receipt of payment, an investment or a gift, either legal or illegal.[44] The tax authorities can levy taxes on gains that originate from money laundering, market abuse, insider dealing or bribes.

As payment tokens have been used to facilitate exchanges associated with crime, money-laundering laws are necessary in order to cut off financing chan-nels for activities such as the drug trade along the Silk Road.[45] In this context, money-laundering law has been the first set of laws to recognise the legal status

40 The Libra Association Members, 'Libra White Paper' (2020) https://libra.org/en-US/white-paper/, accessed 07 July 2020.
41 Public-Private Analytic Exchange Programme, 'Risk and Vulnerabilities of Virtual Currency: Cryptocurrency as a Payment Method' (2017) www.dni.gov/files/PE/Documents/9—2017-AEP _Risks-and-Vulnerabilities-of-Virtual-Currency.pdf, accessed 07 July 2020.
42 HM Revenue & Customs, 'Cryptoassets: Tax for Individuals' (Policy Paper of HM Revenue & Customs, 2019) www.gov.uk/government/publications/tax-on-cryptoassets/cryptoassets-for-indi-viduals, accessed 07 July 2020.
43 Ibid.
44 Peter Chapman and Laura Douglas, 'The Virtual Currency Regulation in the United Kingdom' in Michael Sackheim and Nathan Howell (eds), *The Virtual Currency Regulation Review* (The Law Reviews 2018) 310, 329.
45 David Adler, 'Silk Road: The Dark Side of Cryptocurrency' (2018) *Fordham Journal of Corpo-rate and Financial Law*, https://news.law.fordham.edu/jcfl/2018/02/21/silk-road-the-dark-side-of -cryptocurrency/, accessed 07 July 2020.

of crypto-assets as money.[46] However, payment tokens are still not systematically recognised as money; Bitcoin, for instance, is not considered to be money in the Sale of Goods Act 1979.[47] When Bitcoin and similar tokens are treated as money, there are two implications. First, since the law is targeted at money laundering, Bitcoin and other similar tokens are included within the parameters of anti-money-laundering regulations.[48] Second, it implies that the definition of money used by the anti-money-laundering law is not limited to payment tokens and may be extended to other tokens such as hybrid tokens.

The UK Payment Systems Regulator (PSR), which regulates credit card payments and digital third-party payment providers, does not issue guidance on how payment tokens are to be treated and recognised.[49] There is no reason why payment systems should not have the ability to process payment tokens and be subject to the oversight of the PSR. Although the market operations of payment tokens are different from those of fiat currency and e-money,[50] bringing processing payment tokens under the PSR would enhance the ability of operators to manage risk and promote innovation.[51]

The Information Commissioner's Office, the UK's data protection regulator, also has jurisdiction over payment tokens when they contain personal information. The software design of payment tokens contains information about their origination in blocks on the DLT system, which means that personal information could be revealed.[52] Current encryption technology may not be effective in preventing violations of data protection and privacy.[53]

The discussion above shows that although regulators have begun to exert jurisdiction over payment tokens, they do not take a common approach to LT. The way they share or divide their regulatory oversight largely relies on Memoranda

---

46 Peter Chapman and Laura Douglas, 'The Virtual Currency Regulation in the United Kingdom' in Michael Sackheim and Nathan Howell (eds), *The Virtual Currency Regulation Review* (The Law Reviews 2018) 310, 329.

47 Laurie Korpi and Yasmine Dong, 'Unrivalled Insight into Global Digital Payments Regulation' (2015) https://gamblingcompliance.com/sites/gamblingcompliance.com/files/attachments/page/PaymentsCompliance%20-%20Payments%20Lawyer%20June%202015.pdf, accessed 06 July 2020.

48 Ibid.

49 Chapter 15, 'Guidance on the Scope of the Payment Services Regulations' of PERG Handbook (2017) www.handbook.fca.org.uk/handbook/PERG/15.pdf, accessed 07 July 2020.

50 Digital Watch Observatory, *Cryptocurrencies* (2020) https://dig.watch/issues/cryptocurrencies, accessed 07 July 2020.

51 FCA, 'Innovation in UK Consumer Electronic Payments: A Collaborative Study by Ofcom and the Payment Systems Regulator' (2014), www.fca.org.uk/publication/research/ofcom-psr-joint-study.pdf, accessed 07 July 2020.

52 thinkBLOCKtank, 'The Regulation of Token in Europe: National Legal & Regulatory Frameworks in Select European Countries' (2019), http://thinkblocktank.org/wp-content/uploads/2019/08/thinkBLOCKtank-Token-Regulation-Paper-v1.0-Part-C.pdf, accessed 06 July 2020.

53 PrivSec Report, 'Preventing Data Breaches and Assisting GDPR Compliance Using Encryption' (2017) https://gdpr.report/news/2017/12/21/preventing-data-breaches-assisting-gdpr-compliance-using-encryption/, accessed 06 July 2020.

of Understanding to avoid potential legal, organisational or operational conflicts in this sectoral regulatory sphere.[54] It is likely that payment tokens will continue to be regulated in this way and that a single regulator will not be able to determine the legal status of payment tokens and claim exclusive oversight. The way in which international regulators will coordinate will depend on how assets are legally classified (LT).[55] More detailed discussion will be given in Chapter 5 on crypto-currency.

Utility tokens

Utility tokens allow their holders to access products and services either currently or in the future.[56] They are issued by an individual, an entity or an association, and in this they differ from payment tokens that have their origin in the "mining" process according to a pre-designed protocol. Payment tokens have no fixed face value, but utility tokens have a value that is linked to particular products (two meals or three smart technology applications, for example) or services (three hours of legal services, a training course or purchase of clean energy). They are similar to vouchers or membership cards. A voucher can be redeemed for goods (a book) and for services (seeing a film or using the gym). The terms and conditions of these vouchers usually make their transferability restricted and time limited.[57] When issuers become defunct due to bankruptcy, insolvency or project failure, voucher holders do not have access to asset pools and are unlikely to have any significant monetary claim.[58] However, some vouchers can be transferable,[59] lack a time limit and are even redeemable for multiple goods and services provided by those other than the issuers. If such vouchers are tokenised, they are then similar to payment tokens.

Some membership cards allow their holders to access goods and services.[60] For example, members might access unlimited film viewings at home, gym facilities or benefits provided by golf clubs. When these membership cards are tokenised, they become utility tokens that enable the token holders – individuals or entities – to have access to the utilities provided by the issuer or other third-party partners. Some systems allow membership cards to be sold, even on the open market, and

54 Dax Hansen and Sarah Howland, 'Digital Currencies: International Actions and Regulations' (2020) www.perkinscoie.com/en/news-insights/digital-currencies-international-actions-and-regulations.html, accessed 06 July 2020.
55 Apolline Blandin et al., 'Global Cryptoasset Regulatory Landscape Study' (University of Cambridge Faculty of Law Research Paper No. 23/2019).
56 FCA, 'Guidance on Cryptoassets' (FCA Consultation Paper 19/3, 2019).
57 Ibid.
58 Gareth Malna and Sarah Kenshall, Chapter 25, in Thomas Frick (ed), *The Financial Technology Law Review* (2nd edn, The Law Reviews 2019).
59 Michael Junemann and Johannes Wirtz, 'ICO: Legal Classification of Tokens: Part 4 – Utility Tokens' (2019) www.twobirds.com/en/news/articles/2019/global/ico-legal-classification-of-tokens-utility-token, accessed 07 July 2020.
60 FCA, 'Guidance on Cryptoassets', (FCA Consultation Paper 19/3, 2019).

some even allow participation in the decision-making process of the associated business, for example, a golf club.[61] Some membership cards only allow membership to pass to the next-of-kin; others give cardholders priority in the purchase of goods or services at favourable rates, and with further cumulative benefits (the more you use the more benefits you get).

Because of this variety, defining the legal taxonomy of utility tokens is problematic. They can be a transferable or non-transferable voucher (contract), a payment method, a negotiable instrument (a forward contract for commodities or services) or a unit of investment. They can be taxable assets, be used for facilitating criminal proceeds or be used by financial services and other sectors to provide advice. They can also contain personal information. A regulatory model that is built on Memoranda of Understanding between the various regulatory bodies can assist regulation and avoid conflict. However, if utility tokens become redeemable for multiple goods and services, and there are entities managing these tokens as well as facilitating the redeeming services, such as loyalty points, a regulatory task force is needed to consider consumer protection since there is no specific regulatory entity with responsibility for consumer protection in access to utilities.[62]

Asset tokens

Asset tokens, also known as security tokens, represent underlying assets such as shares, bonds (debt), commodities, units of investment and rights to deal in those assets, such as options and futures.[63] They are issued by entities such as companies, but also by an individual or an association of individuals or entities.[64] If security tokens were treated as securities, it would bring them into the current legal and regulatory framework and securities law would apply to the whole security trading cycle: issuing, trading, clearing and settlement. The current securities law covers the operations of the securities market. It recognises primary and secondary markets, and divides market players into infrastructure providers, issuers, intermediaries, institutional and retail investors, and domestic and foreign participants.[65] Securities law broadly divides into the prudential aspect of regulation with a focus on the systemic aspect, and the conduct aspect with a focus on market integrity, investor protection, consumer protection and market competitiveness.[66]

61 Ibid.
62 Deloitte, 'Making Blockchain Real for Customer Loyalty Rewards Programmes' www.finextra .com/finextra-downloads/newsdocs/us-fsi-making-blockchain-real-for-loyalty-rewards-programs .pdf, accessed 07 July 2020.
63 Deloitte, 'Are Token Assets the Securities of Tomorrow?' (2019) www2.deloitte.com/content/ dam/Deloitte/lu/Documents/technology/lu-token-assets-securities-tomorrow.pdf, accessed 08 July 2020.
64 Ibid.
65 Baker McKenzie, 'Global Financial Services Regulatory Guide' (2016) www.bakermckenzie .com/-/media/files/insight/publications/2016/07/guide_global_fsrguide_2017.pdf?la=en, accessed 07 July 2020.
66 Ibid.

In addition to securities law, company law governs the internal affairs of a corporate organisation.[67] The major issues arising are capital maintenance for investor protection, particularly minority shareholders and outside creditors, governance of the organisation such as the decision-making process and the right to obtain redress, reorganisation, and dissolution of the organisation and dispute resolution.[68] Modern company law accommodates various types of companies, from closely held companies to publicly listed companies. Specific regimes have been created within the company law framework to service companies with different objectives and functions.[69] The aim is to ensure, on the one hand, that capital can continue to be aggregated efficiently through the collective effort of promoters, directors, shareholders, employees and creditors, and, on the other hand, that benefits can be shared equitably among them.[70] New methods, processes and markets have been developed to facilitate the aggregation of capital, including private placement,[71] direct listing,[72] initial public offering,[73] private equity[74] and the newly emerged securities token offering (STO).[75] To ensure that benefits are shared equitably, various mechanisms have been introduced such as minority shareholder protection in closely held companies to corporate governance of listed and quoted companies. Beside these mechanisms, the takeover market has been developed as a way to monitor corporate performance rather than as a way to share the benefits of the company, mainly through the sale of the control premium to the bidders.[76]

67 Deborah DeMott, 'Perspectives on Choice of Law for Corporate Internal Affairs' (1985) 45 *Law and Contemporary Problems* 161, 198.
68 Neal Watson and Beliz McKenzie, 'Shareholders' Right in Private and Public Companies in the UK (England and Wales)' (2019) uk.practicallaw.thomsonreuters.com/5-613-3685?transitionType=Default&contextData=(sc.Default)&firstPage=true, accessed 07 July 2020.
69 Harvard Law School Forum, 'Principles of Corporate Governance' (Harvard Law School Forum on Corporate Governance 2016) https://corpgov.law.harvard.edu/2016/09/08/principles-of-corporate-governance/, accessed 07 July 2020.
70 Paul Davies, 'The Board of Directors: Composition, Structure, Duties and Powers' (Company Law Reform in OECD Countries: A Comparative Outlook of Current Trends, 2000).
71 Andrew Baum, 'The Future of Real Estate Initiative' (Said Business School, University of Oxford 2020) www.sbs.ox.ac.uk/sites/default/files/2020-01/Tokenisation%20Report.pdf, accessed 07 July 2020.
72 Ran Ben-Tzur and James Evans, 'The Rise of Direct Listings: Understanding the Trend, Separating Fact from Fiction' (2019), https://ncfacanada.org/the-rise-of-direct-listings-understanding-the-trend-separating-fact-from-fiction/, accessed 07 July 2020.
73 Ryan Zullo, 'Can Tokenisation Fix the Secondary IPO Market?' (2020), www.eisneramper.com/tokenization-secondary-ipo-catalyst-0420/, accessed 07 July 2020.
74 'The Tokenisation of Financial Market Securities – What's Next?' (in Research Report by Greenwich Associates: 'Security Tokens: Cryptonite for Stock Certificates' 2019) www.r3.com/wp-content/uploads/2019/10/R3.Tokenization.Financial.Market.Securities.Oct2019.pdf, accessed 07 July 2020.
75 Deloitte, 'Are Token Assets the Securities of Tomorrow?' (2019) www2.deloitte.com/content/dam/Deloitte/lu/Documents/technology/lu-token-assets-securities-tomorrow.pdf, accessed 07 July 2020.
76 David Kershaw, *Principles of Takeover Regulation* (1st edn, Oxford University Press 2018) 44.

Including security tokens under the company law framework poses a manageable legal risk for uncertainty but the problem is whether it would defeat the purpose of issuing asset tokens,[77] namely to ensure efficient capital aggregation and equitable sharing of benefits. In many STO projects[78], security tokens are offered on the open market to anyone who can access the internet; issue and purchase do not need the traditional financial intermediaries.[79] However, under the current company law framework, only certain companies can issue securities to the general public,[80] needing, for example, a clean three-year trading record.[81] Furthermore, the corporate governance rules in company law and the Corporate Governance Code place significant burdens on issuers who are often not able to afford the expense of governance services such as legal, compliance and auditing costs.[82] Although "Code as law"[83] seems to be able to mitigate some of these costs through automation,[84] many areas would still require human intervention, especially where cognitive judgement is required to interpret rules that are based on policy objectives or where there are different acts to be balanced against one another.[85] The reason that STO is attractive to legitimate businesses is its ability to reach the entire internet community without infrastructure obstacles or national boundaries.[86] Bringing them under the current company law framework would compromise this benefit. As an example, the US's Howey test, when applied to DAO (an STO project), would prevent development in security token finance and encourage underground STO markets.[87] While many countries have created a

---

77 'Initial Coin Offerings: Issues of Legal Uncertainty Report' (2019) www.comsuregroup.com/news/initial-coin-offerings-issues-of-legal-uncertainty-report-initial-coin-offerings-30-july-2019/, accessed 09 July 2020; Ross Buckley et al., 'TechRisk' 2020 (1) *Singapore Journal of Legal Studies* 35.

78 See Chapter 6.

79 Jovan Ilic, 'Security Token Offerings: What Are They, and Where Are They Going in 2019?' (2019) https://medium.com/mvp-workshop/security-token-offerings-sto-what-are-they-and-where-are-they-going-in-2019-cc075aea6313, accessed 07 July 2020.

80 S 755 of Companies Act 2006 provides that 'a private company limited by shares or limited by guarantee and having a share capital must not; (a) offer to the public any securities of the company, or (b) allot or agree to allot any securities of the company with a view to their being offered to the public'.

81 LR 6.3.1R, FCA.

82 OECD, 'Risk Management and Corporate Governance' (2014) www.oecd.org/daf/ca/risk-management-corporate-governance.pdf, accessed 07 July 2020.

83 See Chapter 11.

84 Gabrielle Patrick and Anurag Bana, 'Rule of Law Versus Rule of Code: A Blockchain-Driven Legal World' (IBA Legal Policy & Research Unit Legal Paper, 2017).

85 Smart Contract Alliance, 'Smart Contracts: Is the Law Ready?' (Smart Contract Whitepaper, Smart Contract Alliance, 2018), https://lowellmilkeninstitute.law.ucla.edu/wp-content/uploads/2018/08/Smart-Contracts-Whitepaper.pdf, accessed 07 July 2020.

86 Deloitte, 'Are Token Assets the Securities of Tomorrow?' (2019), www2.deloitte.com/content/dam/Deloitte/lu/Documents/technology/lu-token-assets-securities-tomorrow.pdf, accessed 07 July 2020.

87 Lennart Ante and Ingo Fiedler, 'Cheap Signals in Security Token Offerings' (Blockchain Research Lab Working Paper Series No. 1, 2019), www.blockchainresearchlab.org/wp-content/uploads

specific legal and regulatory regime for STO and have provided trading platforms for the investment community, none has been successful.

It is time to reconsider the current legal, regulatory and market infrastructures for security tokens. How do they function? Can they change as required by developments in the market? Who has authority to create the law and to control its development? In particular, since the current legal and regulatory framework is the result of regulatory capture, to what extent are participants in today's security tokens market able to influence the law? A detailed analysis of the STO market will be presented in Chapter 6.

Title tokens

There are legal and evidential documents that represent or certify an underlying asset or class of assets.[88] When they are tokenised, they become title tokens. What differentiates them from security tokens is that the title is not recognised as a security such as a land title,[89] documentary title (e.g. a bill of lading),[90] or the title to an artwork. There are also intra-organisational titles that represent workload (hours of work), entitlements (right to receive training courses) or the right to inherent contractual relationships (leader in a direct-selling group). Some of these titles can easily be brought into the current legal framework without the need to introduce a new regime; an example of this is the land title in real property law. Tokenising land titles and moving conveyancing on to a DLT platform can improve the transparency of land ownership and its history,[91] and can reduce intermediary fees such as estate agency and legal fees. It can also improve the efficiency of tax collection by the revenue authorities in levying stamp duty.

Documentary titles such as bills of lading can be accommodated in the sale of goods and carriage of goods laws.[92] This can improve transparency, reduce fraud and remove the legal uncertainty of goods in transit. It can also increase

/2019/07/Cheap-Signals-in-Security-Token-Offerings-BRL-Series-No.-1-update3.pdf, accessed 07 July 2020.

88 Law Commission, 'Electronic Execution of Documents' (Policy Paper of the Law Commission No. 386, 2019), https://s3-eu-west-2.amazonaws.com/lawcom-prod-storage-11jsxou24uy7q/uploads/2019/09/Electronic-Execution-Report.pdf, accessed 07 July 2020.

89 Michael Junemann and Johannes Wirtz, 'ICO: Legal Classification of Tokens: Part 2 – Security Token' (2019), www.twobirds.com/en/news/articles/2019/global/ico-legal-classification-of-tokens-2, accessed 09 July 2020.

90 Marek Dubovec, 'The Problems and Possibilities for Using Electronic Bill of Lading as Collateral' (2006) 23 *Arizona Journal of International and Comparative Law* 437.

91 Nan Liu et al., 'A Critical Review of Distributed Ledger Technology and Its Applications in Real Estate' (2020), www.rics.org/globalassets/rics-website/media/knowledge/research/research-reports/rics0077-001-distributed-ledger-technology-review-report–final.pdf, accessed 08 July 2020.

92 Caslav Pejovic, 'Documents of Title in Carriage of Goods by Sea' (2001) *Journal of Business Law* 461.

the ability of traders to obtain finance from banks through letters of credit.[93] The legal certainty provided by tokenised documentary titles in goods can increase the willingness of banks to remit finance more quickly, and the fees charged by banks can be lower since the risk of legal uncertainty is reduced. Tokenising legal or documentary titles would not pose technical problems in either a centralised or a partly decentralised system, but there would be issues of data protection, privacy protection (including financial privacy) and commercial secrecy protection.[94] The biggest legal challenge is how to transfer the legal interest in the underlying assets of title tokens. The transfer of security tokens, which are recognised as assets, involves registration of interest in distributed ledgers through crediting and debiting, while effecting registration relies on using public and private keys. However, for documentary title transactions, the possession of the titles may or may not be evidence of ownership in the underlying property. For instance, in an international contract for the sale of goods, property passes to the seller from the buyer irrespective of the possession of the bill of lading (the documentary title) if it is a free-on-board contract.[95] In a cost-insurance-freight contract,[96] the transfer of title tokens to a bank (providing the letter of credit) would be necessary for the bank to remit finance, but the bank does not own the goods despite holding the title tokens. The critical question is how transfer of interest in goods can be effected within trade finance market practice, while decoupling it from possession of the title. Market structure and practice may need to be rebuilt if trades based on title tokens are to be made on a DLT network.

For title tokens to represent goods in bulk is legally problematic. Goods in bulk are likely to be split up as they are sold, thus passing from single to multiple ownership with the implication that the tokens need to be similarly subdivided or reissued in order that the new owners can demonstrate their ownership of a component of the original bulk.[97] Without such evidence of a property interest, the buyers may not be able to sell on their new acquisition or to make a claim in insolvency proceedings.

Even for specific goods,[98] tokenised titles can represent a challenge to the market. In the art market where goods are individual and often unique, there is no single legal registration system to evidence ownership. Tokenised titles representing artworks would mean that possession of the artwork itself, such as a painting, is not *prima facie* evidence of owning the property. A good-faith purchaser may not

---

93 Friederike Niepmann and Tim Schmidt-Eisenlohr, 'International Trade, Risk, and the Role of Banks' (Federal Reserve Bank of New York Staff Reports No. 633, 2014).

94 ICO, 'Anonymisation: Managing Data Protection Risk – Code of Practice' https://ico.org.uk/media/1061/anonymisation-code.pdf, accessed 08 July 2020.

95 Martin Davis, 'Delivery and the Passing of Risk' (Oxford Scholarship Online, 2014).

96 Ibid.

97 'Sale of Goods Forming Part of a Bulk' (The Law Commission and The Scottish Law Commission No. 215/145, 1965).

98 Vlad Burilov, 'Regulation of Crypto Tokens and Initial Coin Offerings in the EU' 2019 (6) *European Journal of Comparative Law and Governance* 146, 186.

acquire the legal title in the painting without showing possession of the tokenised title, and, unlike land registration, the purchaser may not know where to find the token holder if there is no centralised system.[99] Furthermore, market practices in the sale of artwork would also need to change, because the shaking of hands in the gallery or the fall of the hammer at an auction would not enable the proprietary interest in the artwork to pass to the buyer because only the transfer of the tokenised title would amount to *prima facie* evidence of such a transfer.

Within an organisation or an association, there may be rules designed to allocate workload and control, and this allocation can be assignable and transferable within the organisation or association. Assigned work and its ownership can be further assigned to others, as in industry's practice of outsourcing. In work that is shared between organisations, a tokenised title representing hours of work (a utility) can demonstrate how the total working hours in a project will be distributed and the hours can be traded among the organisations.[100] The control relationship, if control is to be recognised as a valuable thing or asset, can also be tokenised and assigned. For instance, shareholder agreement on how control is to be exercised or membership agreement on who will be the next controller within the group can be tokenised to show how the control title will be passed. This will doubtlessly raise further legal questions on the transferability, assignability and the ability to delegate these controls (rights and/or duties) as well as public policy issues that give rise to issues of morality, utility and freedom.[101]

It is unlikely a single regulator will be given complete oversight of tokenised titles as they are components of totally different markets ranging from the sale of crude oil to the sale of modern artwork, and from shareholders' to workers' agreements on control.

Commodity tokens

Commodity tokens can represent underlying commodities, such as raw materials, agricultural products or clean energy.[102] In some commodity trades the underlying commodities are securitised with the securities mostly being options and futures – contractual instruments that represent a right to purchase or sell the underlying commodities at a pre-determined price and at a specific time in the future. They do not involve directly securitising a particular asset or an identifiable quantity

---

99 Josias Dewey et al., *Blockchain & Cryptocurrency Regulation* (1st edn, Global Legal Insights 2019)   www.acc.com/sites/default/files/resources/vl/membersonly/Article/1489775_1.pdf, accessed 08 July 2020.

100 Dachs Bernhard, 'The Impact of New Technologies on the Labour Market and the Social Economy' (MPRA Paper 90519, University of Munich 2017).

101 Josias Dewey et al., *Blockchain & Cryptocurrency Regulation* (1st edn, Global Legal Insights 2019).

102 AAX Academy, 'Tokenising Commodities: It's Possible, But Should We?' (2020) https://academy.aax.com/en/tokenizing-commodities-its-possible-but-should-we/, accessed 08 July 2020.

of asset.[103] Trade in other types of commodity involves setting up funds such as Exchange-Traded-Funds,[104] Hedge Funds or Private Equity Funds.[105] When tokenised, the units of investment in these funds can be classified as asset tokens which may be traded in the same way as other security tokens.[106] This means that commodity tokens are not tokenised titles in the underlying asset or commodity, and do not represent the title in the goods in the market practice and in law. Currently, commodity markets are organised as multilateral trading platforms with their own specific market rules.[107] They are only accessible to institutional investors through trading market members; retail investors do not participate directly. Commodity trades are used not only to purchase the underlying commodity goods but also to hedge against the risk of market volatility.[108] In addition, traders, clearing houses and settlement entities may be involved in trading in order to mitigate default risk, enhance legal certainty and provide liquidity. For instance, default in a settlement would be covered by clearing houses.[109] The types of market described above for trading title tokens are mostly bilateral rather than multilateral and even an auction house, which could be seen as an organised market, is not a multilateral trading platform in the way that commodity markets operate. Failure to deliver goods could result in the award of damages or other remedies by a court or by some other dispute settlement mechanisms.

In law, commodity tokens do not represent the specific titles of goods nor a specifically defined bulk of goods, unlike title tokens. Commodity tokens do not confer ownership of goods or goods in bulk to their holders. This affects contractual claims where there has been default in the delivery of the underlying goods, and also claims in priority in insolvency proceedings,[110] as well as other market rules attached to the tokens. The current commodity trades regulators are likely to continue to oversee tokenised commodity trades, but whether the commodity

103 OECD, 'The Tokenisation of Assets and Potential Implications for Financial Markets' (2020) www.oecd.org/finance/The-Tokenisation-of-Assets-and-Potential-Implications-for-Financial-Markets.pdf, accessed 08 July 2020.
104 Adam Marszk and Ewa Lechman, *Exchange-Traded Funds in Europe* (1st edn, Academic Press 2019).
105 Anne Jansen et al., 'Hedge Funds and Financial Market Dynamics' (Occasional Papers of the IMF 1998).
106 Deloitte, 'Are Token Assets the Securities of Tomorrow?' (2019) www2.deloitte.com/content/dam/Deloitte/lu/Documents/technology/lu-token-assets-securities-tomorrow.pdf, accessed 08 July 2020.
107 European Commission, 'Review of the Markets in Financial Instruments Directive' (European Commission 2011), https://ec.europa.eu/commission/presscorner/detail/en/MEMO_11_716, accessed 08 July 2020.
108 Deloitte, 'Commodity Price Risk Management: A Manual of Helping Commodity Price Risk for Corporates' (2018), www2.deloitte.com/content/dam/Deloitte/in/Documents/risk/in-risk-over-view-of-commodity-noexp.PDF, accessed 08 July 2020.
109 Ibid.
110 INSOL International, 'Cryptocurrency and Its Impact on Insolvency and Restructuring' (INSOL Special Report, 2019).

markets regulator should also have jurisdiction over inter-exchangeable tokenised commodities such as computing power or electricity should be examined further.

Hybrid tokens and convertible tokens

Using current legal taxonomy to define the nature of a token may mean that some elements in the token are not covered by conventional legal definitions, and they may also limit its true functionality. The issuers of a token can design it in a way that includes a number of functions and create, for example, a hybrid token that acts both as a payment token and as a utility token.[111] One of the functions of the token might be convertibility – its conversion to another type of token. For instance, a share token issued by a company might be converted into a bond token, or a payment token into a utility token that can then be converted back to a payment token, or a title token could be converted to a payment token, such as Token Equity Convertible (TEC). For example, *SynchroLife Limited*, a subsidiary of Japanese restaurant *SNS Ginkan*, fundraised by offering convertible equities, which allow investors to exchange the equities in the future for their tokens named SynchroGoin.[112] This means that there is a difference between a hybrid token and a convertible token. The former entitles its holders to a specific range of benefits and rights, and also confers liabilities. The latter turns one type of token into another without renegotiating the terms attached to it, without going through an exchange, and without receiving it as a result of a dispute resolution mechanism. Convertibility is embedded in the original design,[113] so when it could be converted, as well as how and what it might be converted into, would need to be pre-agreed by the parties and pre-determined in the design. This is not the same as the concept of automation in a smart contract which enables issuers to buy back tokenised shares when a certain condition has been triggered,[114] resulting in the tokenised shares being returned to the issuing companies, and payment (or payment tokens) remitted to the original share token holders. Convertibility is something quite different.

111 Thijs Maas, 'Why Hybrid Tokens are Superior to Utility Tokens: Comparing Utility Tokens, Security Tokens and Hybrid Tokens' (2019), https://medium.com/hackernoon/hybrid-tokens-are-superior-to-utility-tokens-heres-why-3bec287c465, accessed 09 July 2020.

112 S. Nishimura, 'A New Way to Fundraise? – Token Equity Convertible' (2018), https://medium.com/@vcinsights/a-new-way-to-fundraise-token-equity-convertible-tec-7d3c987e520e, accessed 09 July 2020.

113 PwC, 'Cryptographic Assets and Related Transactions: Accounting Considerations under IFRS' (2019), www.pwc.com/gx/en/audit-services/ifrs/publications/ifrs-16/cryptographic-assets-related-transactions-accounting-considerations-ifrs-pwc-in-depth.pdf, accessed 09 July 2020.

114 Joseph Lee, 'Smart Contracts for Securities Transaction on the DLT Platform (Blockchain): Legal Obstacles and Regulatory Challenges' (2020), https://papers.ssrn.com/sol3/papers.cfm?abstract_id=3523317, accessed 09 July 2020.

There are several benefits associated with convertible tokens. For instance, an insurance token[115] might be converted into a utility voucher, such as a medical voucher or a hotel voucher, when a flight is delayed. A title token representing a worker's hours of work in an organisation might be converted into a utility voucher for clean-energy electricity, or a tokenised green bond. Such convertibility can bypass the need to convert tokens into fiat money through a currency exchange, hence saving costs, and also avoid the need to convert them into payment tokens. Yet, if different token operators were to be linked, the degree of convertibility could be enhanced, thereby bypassing the need to trade them in an open market for the purpose of converting them and eliminating the cost of using intermediaries. The legal imperative is to ensure that all the parties understand convertibility as set out in the contract, and that the event triggering convertibility can be accurately defined in law.[116]

No regulator has yet devised a plan to supervise hybrid tokens or considered the possibility of accepting convertible tokens on the markets. The more likely scenario is that regulators will assert jurisdiction when they perceive that a token contains an element that falls under its regulatory parameter. This situation is likely to create regulatory conflict and competition and it may be that in certain areas, regulators lack the capacity to understand the markets or the ability to resolve disputes.

Innovation

Law and regulation are critical elements in the development of a market. A mature market is a legal construct but also has a heavily embedded regulatory system. The law defines the products and services that the market is constructed on, for instance the stock market, the insurance market, the commodity market or the energy trading market. Often the markets are supported by technical systems and processes; they have physical buildings and legally defined participants such as issuers, traders, institutional investors and consumers. Regulations can bridge legal gaps, enhance enforcement or even foreclose the market in the case of protectionist regulations. In a developing market which is not yet saturated, there are many competing interests and potential markets. Law can help categorise the market, define the scope of private behaviours, and provide the basis for evolution either through doctrinal development that gives legal status to market elements or through legal transplant to replicate an existing market structure.[117] In a mature market with their own legal and regulatory infrastructures already in existence,

115 Peter Temperley, 'Using Crypto Tokens in Insurance' (2018), https://medium.com/@peter.temperley/using-crypto-tokens-in-insurance-7125ccb090eb, accessed 09 July 2020.
116 Robby Houben et al., 'Cryptocurrencies and Blockchain: Legal Context and Implications for Financial Crime, Money Laundering and Tax Evasion' (Research Paper, Policy Department for Economic, Scientific and Quality of Life Policies, European Parliament, 2018).
117 Alan Watson, 'Legal Transplants and European Private Law' (2000) 4.4 *Electronic Journal of Comparative Law*, (December 2000), www.ejcl.org/ejcl/44/44-2.html; Rainer Kulms, 'Block-

developing markets need to select appropriate legal and regulatory systems that both suit their intended function and confer competitive advantage.[118] For example, stock markets compete with bond markets and tech companies compete with other retail companies. Newcomers need to differentiate themselves from existing markets in order to compete with them, and their participants must engage in regulatory capture[119] in order to break away, grow and eventually compete successfully. To win the hearts and minds of current participants in the market, they must demonstrate the benefits of engagement in their new market and win on efficiency (more economical) and efficacy (better results). They will need to create a space for regulatory arbitrage[120] where activities prohibited in existing markets can be launched in a new space. New and old markets will engage in regulatory competition at sectoral, regional or international levels, and such competition can result in a race to either the top or the bottom.[121]

What we have witnessed in the development of crypto-asset markets is a breaking away from the traditional thinking that a market is a legal construct in which the aim of regulation is to promote the market.[122] Participants of the crypto-market do not want to be constrained by traditional norms of the main legal systems (either common law or civil law) and do not wish the state to continue acting as a regulator.[123] The borderless nature of the internet and the appeal of anonymity allow a new "legal and regulatory escape."[124] The hope is that a space, which is not held back by existing legal doctrines and regulatory ethos, can increase access to goods and services. This explains why it is difficult to capture the nature of a cryptocurrency such as Bitcoin while there is an apparent parallel between an

---

chain: Private Law Matters' (2020) *Singapore Journal of Legal Studies* 63, 89, accessed 31 August 2021.

118 Competition & Market Authority, 'Regulation and Competition: A Review of the Evidence' (Competition & Market Authority, 2020) https://assets.publishing.service.gov.uk/government /uploads/system/uploads/attachment_data/file/857024/Regulation_and_Competition_report_- _web_version.pdf, accessed 09 July 2020.

119 Ibid.

120 Ibid.

121 OECD, 'Striking the Right Balance between Competition and Regulation: The Key is Learning from Our Mistakes' (APEC-OECD Co-operative Initiative on Regulatory Reform: Third Workshop Jeju Island, Korea 16–17, 2002), www.oecd.org/regreform/2503205.pdf, accessed 09 July 2020.

122 FCA, 'Guidance on Cryptoassets: Feedback and Final Guidance to CP 19/3', (Policy Statement 19/22, 2019), www.fca.org.uk/publication/policy/ps19-22.pdf, accessed 09 July 2020.

123 Rain Xie, 'Why China Had to Ban Cryptocurrency but the U.S. Did Not: A Comparative Analysis of Regulations on Crypto-Markets between the U.S. and China' (2019) (2) *Washington University Global Studies Law Review* 457, 492; Emmanuelle Ganne, 'Can Blockchain Revolutionise International Trade?' (World Trade Organisation 2018) www.wto.org/english/res_e/booksp_e/ blockchainrev18_e.pdf, accessed 05 July 2020.

124 Sophia Qasir, 'Anonymity in Cyberspace: Judicial and Legislative Regulations' (2013) (81) *Fordham Law Review* 3651, 3691.

initial public offering (IPO) and an initial coin offering (ICO).[125] When traditional legal doctrines prove unable to capture the essence of a new type of token, it is termed a hybrid token and the existence of hybrid tokens challenges conventional legal thinking on the definition of goods, securities, ownership titles and other intangibles such as intellectual property.

The nature of the DLT as a consensus network challenges conventional legal doctrines on contract law and the public law concept of social contract.[126] The way the current global regulatory system has developed is the result of activity over many years by the more advanced economies, and it operates to their agenda and in their self-interest. This has led to mistrust by those who feel that "the establishment" is holding back development and preventing innovation. The regulatory ethos of the crypto-market as a decentralised, consensual and constantly evolving system is seen as a more desirable space for new ways of exchange, communication and living (a virtual life). It is not hard to understand why critics, including myself,[127] immediately cast doubt on the legitimacy, legality, morality and governance of this new form of republic with its promises of total democracy, transparency and freedom. In political terms, the new republic is a response to the frustration of current global governance in the hands of major international powers.[128] One of the results of such global governance is the concentration of resources in the hands of a few powerful nations and entities.[129] This also includes a concentration of capital through globalised financial systems that are furthered by major central banks, by financial exchanges, by circles of institutional investors and the regulatory powers they have taken upon themselves.[130] Placing this Crypto-Republic under the current system of global governance would reduce citizens' ability to innovate, grow and eventually compete.

The emerging tool of code as law[131] is not an attempt to break away from conventional law and regulation; instead, it incorporates laws into smart technologies and uses those technologies to police the market in a system of surveillance capitalism. Experimenting with new regulatory systems as an innovative tool is aimed neither at displacing the current regulatory framework nor at substituting

---

125 Barbara Jones et al, *The Evolution of Token Offerings and Regulation: From ICO to STO* (Westlaw 2019).

126 Telecommunication Standardisation Sector of ITU, 'Distributed Ledger Technology Regulatory Framework' (Telecommunication Standardisation Sector of ITU, Technical Report 2019).

127 Joseph Lee and Lheureux Florian, 'A Regulatory Framework for Cryptocurrency' (2020) *European Business Law Review*, forthcoming.

128 Kelly Buckley, 'Crypto Revolution: Bitcoin, Cryptocurrency and the Future of Money' (Southbank Investment Research 2019).

129 Emmanuelle Ganne, 'Can Blockchain Revolutionise International Trade?' (World Trade Organisation 2018), www.wto.org/english/res_e/booksp_e/blockchainrev18_e.pdf, accessed 05 July 2020.

130 Ibid.

131 Primavera De Filippi and Samer Hassan, 'Blockchain Technology as a Regulatory Technology: From Code is Law to Law is Code' (2016), https://firstmonday.org/ojs/index.php/fm/article/view/7113/5657, accessed 09 July 2020.

for current legal doctrines. This code as law innovation is more likely to affect organisational structures by moving from human intervention to machine learning and execution.[132] A new form of social contract is required. That social contract should be the basis for the creation of a new Crypto-Republic where assets are created, owned and shared differently from the way they are in "our world." In Chapter 10, I will discuss how such a Crypto-Republic concept can be realised in a sustainable community project under the peer-to-peer energy trading platform model.

Conclusion

This chapter has discussed how current legal taxonomy (classification) can help define crypto-assets by looking at the function, participants and operation of market structures. The way in which tokens are named can be very different from the way that the law defines them now or in the future, and the way they are regulated can help clarify their legal status. However, a token's definition that is recognised by one regulator is not necessarily shared by other regulatory agencies or by the courts. The legal fluidity of crypto-assets creates legal confusion. As a result, creating a coherent legal and regulatory framework, either through the application of legal analogy or by extending the current regulatory framework, becomes a challenging task.

The current classification of crypto-assets into payment, utility, security, title, commodity and hybrid tokens is based on their function, the perceptions of market participants and regulatory attitudes towards them. Legal doctrines such as contract and property can help define, or provide a basis for clarification of, rights and obligations as well as the methods of and implications for their transfer and assignment. Statutory definitions of money, insurance, security and units of investment can also provide such a basis. Yet, some crypto-assets are hard to define, so new approaches need to be created to support their development.

Using current legal and regulatory frameworks for crypto-finance may not transform the economy or the market because they have evolved as mechanisms to support the *status quo* in the current financial markets. Extending existing systems to include crypto-assets would merely perpetuate the dominance of existing interests by another form of regulatory capture. A new crypto-asset market structure cannot be created without introducing new laws and rules and this requires the establishment of a new social contract for governance based on new legal doctrines that transcend "contract" and "property." A new regulatory form and ethos should be devised because code as law, RegTech or LegalTech indoctrinated by the current legal and regulatory frameworks are unlikely to generate a true transformation of the market.

---

132 Darrell West and John Allen, 'How Artificial Intelligence is Transforming the World' (2018), www.brookings.edu/research/how-artificial-intelligence-is-transforming-the-world/, accessed 09 July 2020.

4 Smart contracts and financial transactions: practice, risk and governance

Introduction

In Chapter 2, I briefly discussed how smart contracts, in a technical sense, can be used when implementing the DLT on the capital markets, in particular for automating corporate actions. In Chapter 3, I also discussed the process of tokenising securities that can be traded on the blockchain network. Both the process of tokenisation and automation such as trading on the blockchain network will need to rely on the technology of smart contracts. In this chapter, I will discuss the concept of smart contracts both in the technological sense and in the legal sense.

The benefits of using smart contracts to facilitate securities/interests transfers (trading) on distributed ledger technology (DLT) platforms have been presented by Fintech developers and financial institutions.[1] The main benefits are DLT's technological ability to bring about decentralisation and disintermediation which are the main characteristics of peer-to-peer trading platforms that can reduce transaction costs for users as well as for financial systems as a whole.[2] In addition to these main features, smart contracts (essentially, computer programmes) that facilitate the trading platform on the DLT will also be able to record all the transactions on the system securely, thus making every activity transparent and immutable (tamper-proof).[3] As a result, it would be difficult for parties on the platforms to dispute the factual existence of transactions. Automation is another function on the DLT platform that smart contracts can deliver, thus reducing the time and

---

1 R. T. Svikhart, 'Blockchain's Big Hurdle' (2017–2018) 70 *Stanford Law Review* 100, 101; Michael Crosby, Nachiappan, Pradan Pattanayak, Sanjeev Verma and Vignesh Kalyanaraman, 'Blockchain Technology: Beyond Bitcoin' (2016) 2 *Applied Innovation Review, Berkeley* 6–19, 8.
2 Alex Tapscott and Don Tapscott, 'How Blockchain Is Changing Finance' (*Harvard Business Review*, 01 March 2017) https://hbr.org/2017/03/how-blockchain-is-changing-finance, accessed 11 July 2019; See also Franklin Allen and Anthony M. Santomero, 'What do Financial Intermediaries Do?' (2001) 25(2) *Journal of Banking and Finance* 271, 273; E Micheler, 'Custody Chains and Asset Values: Why Crypto-Securities Are Worth Contemplating' (2015) 74(3) *Cambridge Law Journal* 505, 507; OECD, 'Initial Coin Offerings (ICOs) for SME Financing' (2019), p. 47. Available at: www.oecd.org/finance/initial-coin-offerings-for-sme-financing.htm.
3 Joseph J. Bambara and Paul R. Allen, *Blockchain* (1st edn, McGraw-Hill Education, 2018).

DOI: 10.4324/9780429023613-4

resources needed to enforce contracts, transfer securities or assign interests.[4] The combination of the functions of smart contracts and the DLT therefore enables peer-to-peer transactions to be realised more securely and efficiently.[5]

While smart contracts and DLT platforms have not yet been successfully or widely used by the general public to transfer security interests such as shares or debts,[6] smart contracts have already been used by some exchanges to automate securities transactions – notably through using their centralised match-engine to deal with multiple securities transactions.[7] Using a smart contract on the DLT platform to facilitate peer-to-peer securities transactions is technically feasible[8] but the issue is how to ensure that the system is safe to operate and legally certain enough that it can be offered to the general public (both individual retail investors and consumers) without the need for relying on professional intermediaries.[9] Using smart contracts on the DLT network to facilitate peer-to-peer securities transfers raises a number of legal issues.[10] First, how is the legal nature of the "interest" encoded on the smart contract defined;[11] second, how is the smart contract compatible with the principles of contract law;[12] third, how is the interest in the securities deemed delivered and perfected and the transaction settled;[13] and

---

4 Diana Chan, 'Moving from T+2 to T-Instant: Blockchain Distributed Ledger Technology Could Cut the Costs and Complexity of Post-Trade Processing' (Financial News, 28 September 2015), www.fnlondon.com/articles/blockchain-moving-from-tplus2-to-t-instant-20151002.

5 Andrea Pinna and Wiebe Ruttenberg, 'Distributed Ledger Technologies in Securities Post-Trading: Revolution or Evolution?' (ECB Occasional Paper Series No 172, 2016) 18, www.ecb.europa.eu/pub/pdf/scpops/ecbop172.en.pdf.

6 Eric Wall and Gustaf Malm, 'Using Blockchain Technology and Smart Contracts to Create a Distributed Securities Depository (Department of Electrical and Information Technology Lund University, 29 June 2016) 39.

7 A Non-Custodial Smart Contract Exchange, available at: https://dolomite.io/assets/Dolomite -Technical-Whitepaper.pdf.

8 K. Silverberg, C. French and D. Ferenzy, 'Getting Smart: Contracts on the Blockchain' (2016) Institute of International Finance 2, www.iif.com/publication/research-note/getting-smart-con-tracts-blockchain.

9 European Securities and Markets Authority (ESMA), Report: The Distributed Ledger Technology Applied to Securities Markets (2017) para 3.1.9; Oliver Wyman, 'Blockchain in Capital Markets: The Prize and the Journey' (Euroclear Research Paper, 2016) 10, www.oliverwyman.com/content /dam/oliver-wyman/global/en/2016/feb/BlockChain-In-Capital-Markets.pdf>; European Securities and Markets Authority (ESMA) released statements to warn firms involved ICO process and investors. Available at: www.esma.europa.eu/press-news/esma-news/esma-highlights-ico-risks -investors-and-firms.

10 L. Gullifer, 'Chapter 1 - Ownership of Securities' in L. Gullifer, J. Payne (eds), *Intermediated Securities: Legal Problems and Practical Issues* (Hart Publishing 2010) 15.

11 Mateja Durovic and Andre Janssen, 'Formation of Smart Contracts under Contract Law' in Larry A. DiMatteo, Michel Cannarsa and Cristina Poncibo (eds), *Smart Contracts, Blockchain Technology and Digital Platforms* (Cambridge University Press, October 2019), available at: www.cambridge.org/core/books/cambridge-handbook-of-smart-contracts-blockchain-technol-ogy-and-digital-platforms/contract-law-and-smart-contracts/FDBB3AB93D16CF94867BBFB 05B5AF04C/core-reader#.

12 Ibid.

13 Ibid.

fourth, how can issues relating to conflict of laws be resolved in the areas of regulatory oversight, dispute resolution and consumer/investor protection.[14]

The legal status of the underlying asset

Financial instruments such as shares, bonds, money and derivatives can be encoded into a smart contract which is simply a set of computer codes.[15] The smart contract can be created to represent the tokenised interests i.e. a tokenised share or tokenised currency (stablecoins).[16] In other words, the smart contract is a dematerialised certificate that proves the interest that is attached to the underlying asset, such as a share or a debt instrument.[17] It should be noted that some smart contracts appear to be an "asset," however, they may not be legally recognised.[18] For instance, issuing unstable coins on public chains is considered to be a means of payment but is not legal tender.[19] Cryptocurrencies such as Bitcoin and Ether fall within this category.[20] Since the underlying "asset" for unstable coins is difficult to define,[21] the smart contract is unlikely to be recognised as a certificate or a negotiable instrument that is capable of being disposed of i.e. transfer of the interest by the parties. Hence, the smart contract can be used as a certificate to support the underlying interest that is capable of being legally defined, such as share interest (securities) or debt interest.[22] Securities interests are then encoded to a smart contract. This is similar to the process of share dematerialisation in which the certificate of a securities interest is digitised (virtualised).[23] The process

14 Giovannini Group, European Commission, Directorate-General for Economic and Financial Affairs, Second Report on EU Clearing and Settlement Arrangements (Directorate-General for Economic and Financial Affairs, European Commission) section 2, page 12.

15 Philipp Paech, 'The Governance of Blockchain Financial Networks' (2017) 80 *The Modern Law Review* 1082; Riccardo De Caria, 'The Legal Meaning of Smart Contracts' (2018) 26 *European Review of Private Law* 735; Lauren Henry Scholz, 'Algorithmic Contracts' (2017) 20 *Stanford Technology Law Review* 128, 135.

16 Mendelson, Michael, 'From Initial Coin Offerings to Security Tokens: A U.S. Federal Securities Law Analysis' (2019) 22(1) *Stanford Technology Law Review* 76.

17 Marek Dubovec, *The Law of Securities, Commodities and Bank Accounts: The Rights of Account Holders* (Edward Elgar Publishing, 2014) 57.

18 Financial Conduct Authority, 'Guidance on Cryptoassets' on 23 January 2019, p. 20. Available at: www.fca.org.uk/publications/consultation-papers/cp19-3-guidance-cryptoassets.

19 Investigating the Impact of Global Stablecoins, (A Report by the G7 Working Group on Stablecoins, October 2019), available at: www.bis.org/cpmi/publ/d187.pdf

20 Pierluigi Cuccuru, 'Beyond Bitcoin: An Early Overview on Smart Contracts' (2017) 25 *International Journal of Law and Information Technology* 188; Seijas, Thompson and McAdams, 'Scripting Smart Contracts for Distributed Ledger Technology' (2017) *IACR Cryptology ePrint Archive*.

21 Iris H-Y Chiu, 'Decoupling Tokens from Trading: Reaching Beyond Investment Regulation for Regulatory Policy in Initial Coin Offerings' (2018) 3 *International Business Law Journal* 265–287.

22 Smart Contracts and Legal Enforceability, (Cardozo Blockchain Project, Research Report No. 2, October 2018), available at: https://cardozo.yu.edu/sites/default/files/Smart%20Contracts %20Report%20%232_0.pdf.

23 Phoebus L. Athanassiou, 'DLTs, Blockchain and Distributed Ledgers: Scope, Definitions and Headline Legal and Regulatory Issues' (Chapter Two), in *Digital Innovation in Financial Services: Legal Challenges and Regulatory Policy Issues* (Wolters Kluwer, November 2017).

for encoding the interest into smart contracts to be issued on the DLT network is called tokenisation.[24] The process does not affect the legal nature of the underlying asset – share, debt (bond) and derivatives. Even if the securities interests are encoded into a smart contract, the interests represented by the smart contract are not necessarily of a contractual nature. A smart contract, containing a set of computer codes, may contain securities interests but may also contain other contractual terms relating to the number of shares to be transferred, the price and the date of such a transfer (i.e. a purchase/transfer agreement). In other words, a smart contract may need to be treated as a combination of multiple legal instruments such as a share along with its share purchase agreement.[25]

Another legal challenge arises when the smart contract encodes an "intangible asset" that has no clear legal recognition, such as the unstable coins on a public chain (i.e. Bitcoin), or has ambiguous legal status, such as utility vouchers that would enable holders to receive benefits realised by future projects.[26] The legal nature of unstable coins (cryptocurrency) such as Bitcoin and Ether is still unclear.[27] Even though cryptocurrency has been recognised as a "currency" for the purpose of enforcing anti-money laundering law or anti-tax evasion law, it is still not legal tender as far as English law is concerned.[28] Hence, it is not clear whether using unstable coins (Bitcoins) as a means of payment for a contract for the sale of goods would be covered under the UK Sale of Goods Act 1979 which provides a set of pre-determined rules for the parties and protection to consumers. However, some unstable coins or units of account capable of storing value, could be a legally recognised consideration under English law and, in this case, a contract concluded with unstable coins could be legally enforced.[29]

Where the underlying asset is a utility voucher (token) that links to a future project which may realise benefits, its legal nature will depend on the legal nature of the benefits to be realised, such as receiving rental income on a real estate property or being able to use facilities on that property such as the golf course. The property could be held jointly in trust by the holders of the token, or by a company in which the token holders are shareholders, or by a limited liability partnership (LLP) in which token holders are partners, or by a trust scheme in which token

24 Martin Rupp, Tokenisation in Banking and Financial Services, available at: www.cryptomathic .com/news-events/blog/tokenization-in-banking-and-financial-services.
25 M. Staples et al., Risks and Opportunities for Systems Using Blockchain and Smart Contracts (Data 61 CSIRO, May 2017).
26 Investigating the Impact of Global Stablecoins, (A Report by the G7 Working Group on Stablecoins, October 2019), available at: www.bis.org/cpmi/publ/d187.pdf.
27 Robby Houben and Alexander Snyers, *Cryptocurrencies and Blockchain: Legal Context and Implications for Financial Crime, Money Laundering and Tax Evasion* (Policy Department for Economic, Scientific and Quality of Life Policies, European Parliament, July 2018).
28 Regulation of Cryptocurrency Around the World, available at www.loc.gov/law/help/cryptocurrency/world-survey.php.
29 Regulatory Approaches to Cryptoassets in Selected Jurisdictions (April 2019), available at: www .loc.gov/law/help/cryptoassets/cryptoasset-regulation.pdf.

holders are the ultimate beneficiaries. Hence, the legal nature of the tokenised utility voucher would depend on the investment vehicle used.[30]

The risk of contractual invalidity and its management

Scholars have been attempting to fit smart contracts into traditional contract law principles.[31] A smart contract, a set of computer codes, may contain more than one contract.[32] For instance, a smart contract can encode a debt instrument (bond) as well as a contract to purchase the debt instrument; smart contracts are being used in online commercial activities such booking train tickets;[33] they have also been used by traders on stock exchanges to buy and sell securities; high frequency traders (HFTs) use smart contracts (computer codes) to "negotiate" (placing and cancelling orders) and execute transactions.[34] The emerging legal problem of using smart contracts to trade is that the DLT network (i.e. blockchain network) is potentially open to the general public.[35] While stock exchanges are membership-based centralised trading platforms, the decentralised and disintermediated DLT platforms can potentially be accessed by anybody.[36] Hence, the risk of default in the chain of transactions in automated DLT platforms cannot be mitigated as they would be by clearing institutions which are only accessible to professional members.[37]

There are a number of legal factors that can cause a contract to be null and void, to be rescinded and to be unenforceable, but these outcomes are difficult

30 David Uzsoki, 'Tokenisation of Infrastructure: A Blockchain-Based Solution to Financing Sustainable Infrastructure' (International Institute for Sustainable Development January 2019).

31 S. A Kalamsyah, A. M. Barmawi and M. Arzaki, 'Digital Contract using Block Chaining and Elliptic Curve Based Digital Signature' (2018), *6th International Conference on Information and Communication Technology*, 435–440, 435; Amelia Rawls, 'Contract Formation in An Internet Age' (2009) 10 *The Columbia Science and Technology Law Review* 200–231, 201; Maren K. Woebbeking, 'The Impact of Smart Contracts on Traditional Concepts of Contract Law' (2019) 10 *Journal of Intellectual Property, Information Technology and Electronic Commerce Law* 106–113, 106; Kevin Werbach and Nicolas Cornell, 'Contracts Ex Machina' (2017) 67 *Duke Law Review* 368; Larry A. Dimatteo and Cristina Poncibó, 'Quandary of Smart Contracts and Remedies: The Role of Contract Law and Self-Help Remedies' (2018) 26 *European Review of Private Law* 813.

32 Primavera De Filippi and Aaron Wright, *Blockchain and the Law: The Rule of Code*, (1st edn, Harvard University Press 2018) 23; Mark Giancaspro, 'Is a "Smart Contract" Really A Smart Idea? Insights from A Legal Perspective', (2017) 33 *Computer Law & Security Review* 825–835, 826.

33 *Thornton v Shoe Lane Parking Ltd* (1971) 2 QB 163; *Software Solutions Partners Ltd, R (on the application of) v HM Customs & Excise* (2007) EWHC 971.

34 High Frequency Trading: The Application of Advanced Trading Technology in the European Market Place, (AFM, November 2010).

35 P. Cartwright, 'Understanding and Protecting Vulnerable Financial Consumers' (2015) 38 *Journal of Consumer Policy* 119.

36 Distributed Ledger Technology (DLT) and Blockchain, (Fin Tech Note No. 1, World Bank Group, 2017), available at: http://documents.worldbank.org/curated/en/177911513714062215/pdf /122140-WP-PUBLIC-Distributed-Ledger-Technology-and-Blockchain-Fintech-Notes.pdf.

37 Louise Gullifer and Roy Good, *Good on Legal Problems of Credit and Security* (Louise Gullifer tr, 5th edn, Sweet & Maxwell 2013) [6-07].

to implement by smart contracts on the DLT platform.[38] A breach of term might not entitle the innocent party to repudiate the contract – terminating his or her side of the obligation – if the smart contract automatically transfers the tokenised interest to a third party.[39] Even if the consequences of a breach of such a term can be properly encoded into the smart contract, for example by a liquidated damage clause, other consequences of stopping the transfer of the securities in question could cause serious traction in the trading system.[40]

There are legal factors that can cause a default in the chain of transactions. On a DLT platform, an underage person, who does not have the legal capacity (capacity) to execute transactions,[41] may have access to the trading platform and begin dealing in tokenised securities or interests.[42] If material information was not properly presented to the user, as a result of such a misrepresentation, the user is entitled to rescind the contract (misrepresentation). There is also a great risk that people using a smart contract do not have a good understanding of what it entails. For instance, they may not appreciate that pressing the "click" button on the screen will trigger a transfer of shares to a third party at a particular price with reference to a benchmark and this may give rise to a mistake in contract where there is no meeting of minds (mistake).[43] When the validity of the contract is successfully challenged, the smart contract may cause the securities transferred (not fungible) to third parties to be re-vested to innocent parties.

Computer science is not capable of producing smart contracts that transpose the legal terms accurately, without mistakes (no bugs) into a set of computer codes (errors in coding).[44] When contract terms are wrongly interpreted, or mistakenly drafted with grammatical or spelling mistakes,[45] judges or arbitrators can correct the terms and attempt to interpret them in such a way that they meet the original intentions of the parties.[46] However, in a DLT trading platform facilitated by smart contracts, parties may not be able to rely on judges or other human beings

---

38 Blockchain and Cryptocurrency Regulation 2020: 13 Legal Issues Surrounding the Use Smart Contracts, (GLI, 2019), available at: www.globallegalinsights.com/practice-areas/blockchain -laws-and-regulations/13-legal-issues-surrounding-the-use-of-smart-contracts.
39 Kevin Werbach and Nicolas Cornell, 'Contracts Ex Machina' (2017) 67 *Duke Law Review* 340.
40 Ibid.
41 *Chapple v Cooper* (1844) 13 M & W 252; 153 ER 105.
42 Ewan McKendrick, *Contract Law* (12th edn, Palgrave 2017) 311; Unless there is a digital identification system to ensure the capacity of the person, the automation of the smart contracts can render the trading system unworkable.
43 Ewan McKendrick, *Contract Law: Text, Cases and Materials* (6th edn, OUP 2014) ch 16; *Cundy v Lindsay* (1878) 3 App Cas 459; *Shogun Finance Ltd v Hudson* [2003] UKHL 62.
44 Phoebus Athanassiou, 'Impact of Digital Innovation on the Processing of Electronic Payments and Contracting: An Overview of Legal Risks' (European Central Bank Legal Working Paper Series, No. 16, October 2017).
45 Jeremy M. Sklaroff, 'Smart Contracts and the Cost of Inflexibility' (2017) 166 *University of Pennsylvania Law Review* 292.
46 Kristian Lauslahti et al., 'Expanding the Platform: Smart Contracts as Boundary Resources', in A Smedlund et al. (eds), *Collaborative Value Co-Creation in the Platform Economy* (Transnational Systems Sciences 2018).

in tribunals to remedy human mistakes.[47] The computer programmes will not be able to "correct" the mistakes in coding, and the effect can be both systematic (causing a computer glitch in the transaction)[48] as well as systemic (causing a serious traction in the chain of transactions).[49] The risk of mistake is amplified when vague terms such as "reasonable," "good faith" or "frustrating event" are coded into a smart contract.[50] Even when using advanced natural language processing (NLP) to define these terms based on legal precedents,[51] there is a substantial risk that parties may not agree with an outcome delivered by algorithms. The codes in smart contracts would need to be able to suspend the automation function until the parties decide how such disputes will be resolved. It is not possible in a contract for parties to waive their right to have the disputes resolved through a dispute mechanism.[52] It is also questionable whether the outcome of an NLP "decision" would be legally recognised as a dispute resolution.[53]

CCP in a DLT market?

In a DLT securities trading platform facilitated by smart contracts, there is a need to have a central counterparty (CCP) that stands in the middle of all the transactions.[54] This central counterparty would perform the function of a contractual guarantee to mitigate risks but not that of a netting agent to increase the efficiency of the trades.[55] This CCP would need to certify that the smart contracts used are securely coded and that they are compliant with relevant laws and regulations. When the CCP acts as a guarantor to the transactions, transfers of the securities and the corresponding funds would continue uninterrupted. Any dispute among the parties would need to be raised with the CCP which would then act as a

---

47 Steffen Wettig and Eberhard Zehendner, 'A Legal Analysis of Human and Electronic Agents' (2004) 12 *Artificial Intelligence and Law* 111–135, 121.

48 European Securities and Markets Authority (ESMA), 'Report: The Distributed Ledger Technology Applied to Securities Markets' (2017) para 5.36.

49 Philipp Maume and Mathias Fromberger, 'Regulations of Initial Coin Offerings: Reconciling U.S. and E.U. Securities Laws' (2019) 19(2) *Chicago Journal of International Law* 548–585.

50 Wulf A. Kaal and Craig Calcaterra, 'Crypto Transaction Dispute Resolution' (2017) 73(1) *Business Lawyer* 109–152.

51 J. G. Allen, 'Wrapped and Stacked: "Smart Contracts" and the Interaction of Natural and Formal Language' (2018) 14 *European Review of Contract Law* 307–343, 313.

52 Kevin Webach, 'Trust, But Verify: Why the Blockchain Needs The Law' (2019) 33 *Berkeley Technology Law Journal* 487–550, 516; But also see Charles Clark, 'The Answer To The Machine Is The Machine', in Bernt Hugenholtz (eds), *The Future of Copyright in a Digital Environment: Proceedings of the Royal Academy Colloquium* (The Hague: Kluwer Law International 1996) 139–145, 139.

53 Joseph Raz, *The Authority of Law: Essays on Law and Morality,* (Oxford University Press 2011) 164; John Finnis, *Natural Law and Natural Rights* (2nd edn, Oxford University Press 2011) 6–8.

54 Andrea Pinna and Wiebe Rettenberg, 'Distributed Ledger Technologies in Securities Post-Trading: Revolution or Evolution?' (European Central Bank Occasional Paper Series No. 172, April 2016).

55 Steven L. Schwarcz and Joanna Benjamin, 'Intermediary Risk in the Indirect Holding System for Securities' (2002) 12 *Duke Journal of Comparative & International Law* 309, 310.

mediator or adjudicator. Any compensation for damages would need to be made outside the trading system. For instance, the users could claim mistaken transactions because of the problem of "fat fingers."[56] The parties may not allow the transactions of the securities to be rewound, but the fund could be returned.[57] The CCP needs to design a system where consumers can be protected from mistakes caused by "fat fingers." It might be that margins should be collected from the users and used to cover mistakes of this kind. This would also allow the CCP to vet users and assess their risks based on their attributes and previous behaviour on the blockchain.[58] The CCP could provide risk scores on the users which will affect the collateral and margins to be required of them.[59]

Delivery and perfecting tokenised interest

How can a securities transaction be settled on a DLT platform? In other words, how can a tokenised security be delivered, or tokenised interest perfected, in a decentralised DLT platform? In a centralised securities settlement system, securities are delivered through digital transfers.[60] Delivery takes place when the transferee's security account is credited with the amount transferred, and the transferor's security account is then debited with the amount transferred.[61] The same effect of crediting and debiting will be shown on the accounts of the participants on the decentralised blockchain trading platform.[62] The users use "public keys" and "private keys" as the encryption technology to make transactions on the platform.[63] The public key represents the account number known to the network and the private key is the password that enables participants to access and

56 'The Future of Computer Trading in Financial Markets: An International Perspective' (Final Project Report, Government Office for Science, October 2012).
57 Scott A. McKinney, Rachel Landy and Rachel Wilka, 'Smart Contracts, Blockchain, and the Next Frontier of Transactional Law' (2018) 13 *Washington Journal of Law, Technology & Arts* 329.
58 'Blockchain: Opportunities for Private Enterprises in Emerging Markets' (Working Paper, Second and Expanded Edition, IFC, January 2019).
59 Marc Pilkington, 'Blockchain Technology: Principles and Applications' in F. Xavier Olleros and Majlinda Zhegu (eds), *Research Handbook on Digital Transformations* (Edward Elgar 2016) 228.
60 David C. Donald, 'Chapter 50 - Securities Settlement Systems' in Gerard Caprio, Douglas W. Arner, Thorsten Beck, Charles W. Calomiris, Larry Neal and Nicolas Veron (eds), *Handbook of Key Global Financial Markets, Institutions, and Infrastructure* (San Diego, CA: Academic Press, 2013).
61 'Bank of International Settlements (BIS), Delivery versus Payment Report in Securities Settlement Systems' (Reports prepared by the Committee on Payments and Settlement Systems of the central banks of the Group of Ten countries, Basel, 1992) para 2.3.
62 Slaughter and May, Euroclear, 'Blockchain Settlement: Regulation, Innovation and Application – Regulatory and Legal Aspects Related to the Use of Distributed Ledger Technology in Post-Trade Settlement' (2016) 18, www.euroclear.com/newsandinsights/en/Format/Whitepapers-Reports/BlockchainSettlement.html.
63 G. Zyskind and Oz Nathan, 'Decentralising Privacy: Using Blockchain to Protect Personal Data (IEEE Security and Privacy Workshops, 21 May 2015, https://ieeexplore.ieee.org/document/7163223/.

transfer assets in the account.[64] The major difference between the blockchain-based platform with centralised delivery versus the payment securities settlement system is that the users of the blockchain-based platform can make the delivery of the tokenised securities and the perfection of the tokenised interest without the intervention of a centralised settlement body.[65] That is to say that the delivery can be done on a peer-to-peer basis. The public and private keys – the encryption technology – are the main tools to prevent the cyber risk of hacking into this peer-to-peer system in order to tamper with the messages in a way that can distort transactions.[66] The legal question is at what time is the settlement deemed made? Is the delivery deemed made: 1) when the transferor sends a transaction message to the transferee using the keys, or 2) when the transferee receives the message using the keys to access the account? Parties on the chain may agree to use the English "postal rule" whereby the delivery is made when the transferor sends the transaction message.[67] Since transactions on the blockchain network are "transparent" and cannot be tampered with, it would not be difficult to prove that messages have been sent or received.[68] Users on the blockchain should appreciate that a transaction is deemed settled – the tokenised security being delivered or the tokenised interest perfected – when the transferor sends the message and not when the transferee receives it. It could be the case that the settlement is made when the parties agree to the transfer by clicking the button.

This system does pose a significant risk. This is because there is a time lag, approximately 15 minutes, in updating all the accounts (nodes) on the blockchain network.[69] Therefore, it is likely that within this time lag no further transactions can be made with regard to the particular tokenised securities. If there is a blackout or system failure before all the nodes have updated the information, the risk is with the transferee. This may present an unjustified risk to the transferee, even though they have been made aware of such a risk. So the CCP should also act as the settlement guarantee so that when there is a blackout or system failure, the transferee's fund will not be affected, despite not having the account credited with the amount of securities. This means that the CCP will have access to the users' accounts on their requests in order to guarantee that the transferee does not take on this counterparty risk.[70] The transferees may not be able to receive economic

64 Riley Svikhart, 'Blockchain's Big Hurdle' (2017) 70 *Stanford Law Review* 100–111.
65 David Donald, 'From Block Lords to Blockchain: How Securities Dealers Make Markets' (2018) 44(1) *Journal of Corporation Law* 29–64.
66 'Encryption: Everything You Need to Know about Cryptography' (Crysberry, June 2019), available at: https://crysberry.com/encryption-everything-you-need-to-know-about-cryptography/.
67 Gabrielle Patrick and Anurag Bana, 'Rule of Law Versus Rule of Code: A Blockchain-Driven Legal World' (IBA Legal Policy and Research Unite Legal Paper, November 2017).
68 George S. Geis, 'Traceable Shares and Corporate Law' (2018) 113 *Northwestern University Law Review* 227.
69 Matthew F. Dixon et al., 'Blockchain Analytics for Intraday Financial Risk Modeling' (2019) 1 *Digital Finance* 67–89.
70 'Implementing Derivatives Clearing on Distributed Ledger Technology Platforms' (FinTech Futures, November 2017), available at: www.fintechfutures.com/2017/11/implementing-derivatives-clearing-on-distributed-ledger-technology-platforms/.

benefits or other entitlements such as voting rights during this period. As a smart contract can automate the distribution of economic benefits such as dividends, and other entitlements such as voting rights attached to the tokenised securities or interests, there must be a system to ensure that the accrued interests and rights are allocated to the transferee during this window period.[71]

Hence, there must be a system to ensure that the accrued interests and rights are allocated to the transferee during this window period. In addition, certain corporate communications could be made during this period such as corporate notices to call a general meeting for votes to be cast. However, it could happen that during this window period, communications could be lost as the issuers (companies) do not have an updated list of the holders of tokenised securities.

Jurisdiction and the choice of law

The determination of governing law and jurisdiction poses a major problem to tokenised securities trading on the decentralised and disintermediated blockchain.[72] In the case of centralised trading venues such as exchanges, the governing law for trading securities can be different from that for settlement.[73] Furthermore, what governs the benefits of tokenised securities, such as voting rights and economic entitlements, can be different from the governing laws for trading and settlement.[74]

Decentralisation makes determination of the location of the trading venue and settlement place problematic.[75] Trading venues, such as those operated by regulated exchanges, normally require their members (the intermediaries) to choose the governing law required by the trading rules of the venue (platform) to govern their trades, regardless of which jurisdiction members are based in. Since members are professional traders, consumer protection law, which can override the choice of law, does not apply to their trades on these regulated markets. On a blockchain network, even though the participants may agree on a governing law

---

71 Charles W. Mooney, 'Beyond Intermediation: A New (FinTech) Model for Securities Holding Infrastructures' (Penn Law: Legal Scholarship Repository, October 2019).

72 Available at: https://ec.europa.eu/info/finance-consultations-2017-securities-and-claims_en. This consultation has since given rise to a Proposal for a Regulation on the law applicable to the third-party effects of assignments of claims, available at: https://ec.europa.eu/info/law/better-regulation /initiative/184489/attachment/090166e5b927bdfb_en.

73 Giovannini Group, European Commission, Directorate-General for Economic and Financial Affairs, 'Cross-border Clearing and Settlement Arrangements in the European Union' (Directorate-General for Economic and Financial Affairs, European Commission, 2002) section 2, page 18; See also Joseph Lee, 'Equity Clearing and Settlement Models in the UK and Taiwan: Market Stability and Investor Protection Perspectives' in Chang-fa Lo & Nigel Li (eds) *Economics, Law and Institutions in Asia Pacific* (Springer 2016) 423–444.

74 P. Paech, 'Securities, Intermediation and the Blockchain – An Inevitable Choice Between Liquidity and Legal Certainty?' (2016) 21 *Uniform Law Review* 612, 635.

75 Javier Sebastian Cermeno, 'Blockchain in Financial Services: Regulatory Landscape and Future Challenges for its Commercial Application' (2016) Banco Bilbao Vizcaya Argentina Working Paper No. 16/20, 16, www.smallake.kr/wp-content/uploads/2017/01/WP_16-20.pdf.

for trading (as if done over the counter),[76] it is likely that the participants will be treated as consumers in the eyes of the law of the jurisdiction in which the participants (nodes or accounts) are based. Designing a smart contract that is compliant with all the laws of whatever jurisdiction the participants are based in is a challenging task. For instance, some sophisticated traders could use discriminatory algorithms to automate trades with the consumer participants, to the detriment of those consumers. If these transactions are deemed illegal, such illegality will distort trade flows. I will discuss how such discriminatory practices can be made in more detail in Chapter 8 on investor protection on the DLT-based crowdfunding platforms.

The governing law for the settlement of tokenised securities or interests affects the rules on the delivery of securities and on the perfection of interests. It also affects enforcement against the property interests of the participants.[77] For instance, insolvency proceedings can be brought against participants to recover securities they own, or confiscation proceedings can be brought against participants based on anti-money laundering law. However, since the accounts are collectively maintained by the nodes in the blockchain network, the *lex situs* rule may not be applicable.[78] This is because the accounts are distributed rather than centralised as they would be if maintained by a central securities depository (CSD). A contractual approach may not work either. If a participant is treated as a consumer, the consumer law of the country will override the chosen governing law. Furthermore, control of the tokenised assets is based on access to the public and private keys (the wallet).[79] The participants might be mobile and use the keys to make each transaction in different jurisdictions.[80] Unlike bank deposit accounts or securities accounts, enforcement against property will depend on the location of the accounts rather than the person.[81] In a decentralised system, the rule may have instead to be based on the location of the person at a particular time (or possibly when an enforcement was to be made) rather than the location of the account because the person who possesses the keys (password) to the accounts (wallet)

76 Luca Enriques and Tobias H. Troger, 'Issuer Choice in Europe' (2008) 67(3) *Cambridge Law Journal* 521–559.
77 K. Takahashi 'Implications of the Blockchain Technology for the UNICTRAL Works' 17, available at: www.uncitral.org/pdf/english/congress/Papers_for_Programme/30-TAKAHASHI-Implications_of_the_Blockchain_Technology_and_UNCITRAL_works.pdf.
78 Convention on the Law Applicable to Certain Rights in Respect of Securities held with an Intermediary (Hague Securities of 17 June 2008 on the law applicable to contractual obligations (Rome I), available at: http://eur-lex.europa.eu/legal-content/en/ALL/?uri=CELEX%3A32008R0593.
79 Wulf A. Kaal and Craig Calcaterra, 'Crypto Transaction Dispute Resolution' (2017) 73 *Business Lawyer* 109, 111.
80 G. Gabison, 'Policy Considerations for the Blockchain Technology Public and Private Applications' (2016) 19(3) *SMU Science & Technology Law Review* 327, 329.
81 Directive 2002/47/EC of the European Parliament and of the Council on Financial Collateral Arrangements (Financial Collateral Directive) [2002] art 9(1).

is able to dispose of the property.[82] It might be that a trusted third party also has access to the keys, and in that case, proceedings would be against the third party. Unless there is a requirement to be registered in a particular jurisdiction, the third party could be a mobile virtual entity without a centralised office, thus rendering the *lex situs* rule inapplicable.

The law governing economic benefits and other entitlements of tokenised securities or interests will be governed by the law in which the issuers are based (*lex societatis*).[83] It is likely that the issuers will not be a registered legal entity, but a decentralised project such as the DAO (Decentralised Autonomous Organisation).[84] This will present a major risk as there will be no gatekeepers to control the quality of the "listing" of the tokens on the platform.[85] This may prompt regulators around the world to assert jurisdiction over these tokenised securities and interests.

Exercising regulatory oversight will also be significantly challenging because, with a decentralised and distributed network, it is difficult for a single country to claim regulatory oversight over the activities on the platform.[86] As can be seen in securities trading, five jurisdictions can potentially claim to have a regulatory oversight: the jurisdiction of the entities issuing the tokenised securities or interest; the jurisdiction of listing and issuing (i.e. the listing authority);[87] the jurisdiction of trading; the jurisdiction of clearing; and the jurisdiction of settlement. The jurisdiction that has the power to enforce market conduct rules, and thus to prevent market manipulation and insider dealing, is vital for maintaining market integrity and investor protection.[88] Currently, the *lex situs* rule – the place of the trading venue – determines which jurisdiction has oversight.[89] However, on the distributed blockchain network, it is both technologically difficult to determine the physical place of the trading venue, and legally difficult to determine the legal seat of the venue.[90] The current approach to determine the regulatory oversight over the trading venue is based on the legal seat of the trading venue regardless of

82 P. Paech, 'Securities, Intermediation and the Blockchain – An Inevitable Choice Between Liquidity and Legal Certainty?' (2016) 21 *Uniform Law Review* 612, 635.

83 Dicey, Morris and Collins, *The Conflict of Laws*, vol. 2 (15th edn, Sweet & Maxwell 2012) 22–40.

84 SEC report 'Framework for "Investment Contract" Analysis of Digital Assets', available at: https://www.sec.gov/litigation/investreport/34-81207.pdf.

85 Vladislav Burilov, 'Utility Token Offerings and Crypto Exchange Listings: How Regulation Can Help?' (The International Conference 'Blockchain, Public Trust, Law and Governance', University of Groningen, November 2018).

86 Pierre Schammo, 'Regulating Transatlantic Stock Exchanges' (2008) 57(4) *International & Comparative Law Quarterly* 827–862.

87 Joseph Lee, 'Synergies, Risks and the Regulation of Stock Exchange Interconnection' (2017) 11(2) *Masaryk University Journal of Law and Technology* 291.

88 Lev Bromberg, George Gilligan and Ian Ramsay, 'Financial Market Manipulation and Insider Trading: An International Study of Enforcement Approaches' (2017) 8 *Journal of Business Law* 652–679.

89 Joanna Benjamin, 'Determining the Situs of Interests in Immobilised Securities' (1998) 47(4) *International & Comparative Law Quarterly* 923–934.

90 Michael Bridge, 'The Proprietary Aspects of Assignment and Choice of Law' (2009) 125 *Law Quarterly Review* 671–698.

the location of the data centre, the machine engine, the traders or the order book. If this is to continue to be the approach to determine regulatory jurisdiction, the blockchain network will need to choose a legal seat for the purposes of regulatory oversight.[91] That is to say that the network may technically be decentralised, but its legal headquarters are based in a single jurisdiction. In other words, governance will need to be legally centralised. This will require the network to have a registered office in a specified country. However, even if this jurisdiction issue is resolved, practical issues of enforcement remain problematic. How can the regulators, such as the UK FCA or the US SEC, require all the nodes to comply with their market conduct rules such as their respective market abuse regimes?[92] As mentioned, current trading venues and, especially settlement systems, are membership-based. Hence, it is straightforward for regulators and trading venue operators to supervise trading members. However, on the blockchain network, participants are based in different jurisdictions, and even if the regulator has the technological means to impose sanctions digitally, such as suspending the nodes and transferring tokenised securities/interests to a regulator's wallet (a method of confiscation), enforcement against persons (imprisonment for insider dealing and market manipulation) and against non-crypto-assets (fiat currencies) would be difficult.[93] This would require other jurisdictions to recognise that the regulator has the regulatory oversight in order to provide enforcement assistance such as arrest, extradition and seizure of documents and assets.[94]

Suspension of trading activities

Regulators have the power to suspend the trading of securities on a platform.[95] They may do so to prevent systemic risk, to protect investors or to maintain market integrity. For instance, regulators can: suspend securities trades to prevent a flash crash;[96] suspend trades when investors are being manipulated by discriminatory

91 John Salmon and Gordon Myers, 'Blockchain and Associated Legal Issues for Emerging Markets' (International Finance Corporation Note 63, January 2019); also see Chapter 2 Blockchain Technology's Opportunities and Challenges in Michael Casey et al, 'The Impact of Blockchain Technology on Finance: A Catalyst for Change: Geneva Reports on the World Economy' 21.

92 William B. Haseltine, 'International Regulation of Securities Markets: Interaction between United States and Foreign Laws' (1987) 36(2) *International & Comparative Law Quarterly* 307–328.

93 Hans Jochen Scholl and Manuel Pedro Rodriguez Bolivar, 'Regulation as Both Enabler of Technology Use and Global Competitive Tool: The Gibraltar Case' (2019) 3 *Government Information Quarterly* 601–613.

94 Trevor Hartley, 'Jurisdiction in Conflict of Laws – Disclosure, Third-Party Debt and Freezing Orders' (2010) 126 *Law Quarterly Review* 194–221.

95 Chapter 5 (Suspending, Cancelling and Restoring Listing and Reverse Takeovers: All Securities), Listing Rules, available at: https://www.handbook.fca.org.uk/handbook/LR/5.pdf.

96 'The Future of Computer Trading in Financial Markets' (Government Office for Science Working Paper 11/1276, 2011).

algorithms;[97] or suspend trades when there are suspected insider dealings.[98] Even if the platform has its registered legal seat in the UK, and the UK regulators therefore have regulatory oversight, due to the fact that the blockchain network is supported by distributed nodes, possibly through "cloud" technology,[99] the regulators in the UK may not have the technical capability to shut down the whole network.[100] That is to say, even if the nodes based in the UK are not trading the securities, participants of nodes based outside the UK can continue using smart contracts to automate trade in securities on a peer-to-peer basis, without following the UK regulators' instructions. Cooperation between international regulators would therefore be critical to regulatory supervision in the crypto-finance sphere.

Impact of smart contracts on other businesses

Securities lending

The current securities trading system is intermediated through a number of entities – custodian banks, securities banks and brokers.[101] Under this system, securities (i.e. shares) can be loaned for the purposes of short-selling, pledging for cash and collateral management.[102] On the blockchain network, it would be difficult to lend securities. There are two reasons for this. First, securities borrowing is normally done by hedge funds which use it to short-sell securities.[103] Hedge funds borrow securities with a high market price and sell them immediately back to the market to gain cash at that high price. They then buy the securities back at a lower price (betting on their price going down) and return them to the lender.[104] In these movements, hedge funds can make high financial gains. Information on stock lending activities is publicly available, but the market does not know whether the sellers own the securities or if they are on loan. On the blockchain platform, it would be difficult for hedge funds to use this trading strategy, since

---

97 Danny Busch, 'MiFID II: Regulating High Frequency Trading, Other Forms of Algorithmic Trading and Direct Electronic Market Access' 2016 (10) *Law and Financial Market Review* 72–84.

98 Ibid.

99 Simanta Shekhar Sarmah, 'Application of Blockchain in Cloud Computing' 2019 (8) *International Journal of Innovative Technology and Exploring Engineering* 4698–4704.

100 Brant Carson, Giulio Romanelli, Patricia Walsh, and Askhat Zhumaev, 'Blockchain beyond the Hype: What is the Strategic Business Value?' Available at: www.mckinsey.com/business-functions/mckinsey-digital/our-insights/blockchain-beyond-the-hype-what-is-the-strategic-business-value.

101 S. Ann Becker and Robert E. Niebuhr, *Cases on Technology Innovation: Entrepreneurial Successes and Pitfalls* (Hershey New York, 2010) 295.

102 'Securities Lending Transactions: Market Development and Implications' (Working Paper, Technical Committee of the International Organisation of Securities Commissions and Committee on Payment and Settlement Systems, July 1999).

103 Dmitriy Muravyev et al, 'Understanding Returns to Short Selling Using Option-Implied Stock Borrowing Fees', available at SSRN: https://papers.ssrn.com/sol3/papers.cfm?abstract_id=2851560.

104 Ibid.

borrowing tokenised securities from distributed participants would be more costly and slower, even if it were technically possible.[105] Furthermore, hedge funds may not wish to disclose their short-selling activities to the market, nor to reveal the owner of, the number of and the price paid for the borrowed securities. They may lose this advantage when smart contracts are used to facilitate trading, since the price, time and amount that will trigger the automation will need to be pre-set in the algorithms.[106] This will allow the market to have knowledge about the event before it is triggered. This will cause the market participants to "game."

The second question is whether securities borrowing is technologically possible. Under the current model, custodian banks are the platforms for borrowing and lending securities.[107] Since the securities are on loan for only a short time, it does not lead to disputes about economic benefits and other entitlements. Legally speaking, the holder of the securities will receive the economic benefits or exercise the entitlements on behalf of the actual or legal owners.[108] In reality, the legal structure that ensures that the actual owners are entitled to any economic benefits and legal entitlements is more complicated than this. In the UK, the trust model is used in which custodian banks hold the securities in trust for the clients at the next level of the investment chain.[109] In Germany, the agency model is used in which custodian banks hold the securities acting as an agent of the clients at the next level.[110] However, when securities are on loan, the legal relationship will depend on the terms of the loan agreement.[111] According to the agreement provided by the London Stock Exchange,[112] when securities are on loan to hedge funds, the hedge funds will hold these securities as legal owners. In other words, they will be entitled to receive the economic benefits and to exercise voting rights and other corporate actions, and they will need to account to the lenders for any economic benefits, such as generated income.[113] How voting rights should be exercised will

105 Jeremy M. Sklaroff, 'Smart Contracts and the Cost of Inflexibility' (2018) Prize Winning Papers 9. https://scholarship.law.upenn.edu/prize_papers/9.
106 'Understanding Algorithmic Decision-Making: Opportunities and Challenges' (Working Paper of the Panel for the Future of Science and Technology, European Parliament, March 2019).
107 'Global Custodians Advance Peer-to-Peer Initiatives for Securities Lending', available at: http://posttrade360.com/news-in-the-world/global-custodians-advance-peer-to-peer-initiatives-for-securities-lending/.
108 Neal Watson and Beliz McKenzie, 'Shareholders' Rights in Private and Public companies in the UK', available at: uk.practicallaw.thomsonreuters.com/5-613-3685?transitionType=Default&contextData=(sc.Default)&firstPage=true.
109 'The Custody Services of Banks' (The Clearing House, July 2013), available at: www.davispolk.com/files/20160728_tch_white_paper_the_custody_services_of_banks.pdf.
110 Diana Chan, Florence Fontan, Simonetta Rosati and Daniela Russo, 'The Securities Custody Industry' (Occasional Paper Series No. 68, European Central Bank, August 2007).
111 Andrew Evans and Philip Abbott, 'Margin Lending: A Brief Introduction' (Fieldfisher, June 2014), available at: www.fieldfisher.com/en/insights/margin-lending-a-brief-introduction.
112 Global Master Securities Lending Agreement provided by the London Stock Exchange, available at: www.londonstockexchange.com/traders-and-brokers/rules-regulations/formsagreements/global-lending-agreement.pdf.
113 Ibid.

depend on negotiation between the two parties and how corporate actions should be exercised will also depend on the contract. These contractual terms will need to be encoded into smart contracts that will automate both the terms of the tokenised securities lending agreement and the transfers and re-transfers of tokenised securities. As a result, automated distribution of income from the tokenised securities will need to be re-directed (re-programmed) to the beneficial owners under the securities lending agreement. Furthermore, transferring the loaned tokenised securities back to the lender will be technically difficult, because tokenised securities are not "fungible" (inter-changeable) so it is not possible to automate the return of the securities if the third party (who is not bound by the tokenised securities lending) does not wish to transfer them. An off-chain platform will be required to continue such a mechanism for lending securities and this is important for collateral management.[114]

Proxy business

Proxy voting enables a person who is not the legal owner of securities to cast votes exercising governance rights.[115] Under the current system, a legal owner can appoint a proxy to cast votes, using the corporate proxy form.[116] Smart contracts can facilitate this by encoding a proxy form into the tokenised securities so that the votes can be "transferred" to the nodes (accounts) of the proxies, according to the instructions given by the proxy forms in the smart contract.[117] However, such proxy votes can only be transferred by the legal owner of the securities. In other words, once tokenised securities have been transferred to another legal owner, the associated proxy forms will be invalid unless the transferees of the tokenised securities are aware that a proxy has been appointed to cast votes on his or her behalf. Otherwise, the proxy votes may be deemed invalid because they were cast without the consent of the legal owners.[118] Therefore, when tokenised securities are transferred, such a proxy arrangement must be made known to the transferees before the transfer. Furthermore, the legal owners are entitled to revoke a proxy (termination of proxy's authority) so the smart contract must enable the legal owners to do so and notify the issuing company.[119] However, on a peer-to-peer platform,

114 'The Potential Impact of DLTs on Securities Post-Trading Harmonisation and on the Wider EU Financial Market Integration' (Working Paper, Advisory Group on Market Infrastructure for Securities and Collateral, European Central Bank, September 2017).

115 David C. Donald, 'Heart of Darkness: The Problem at the Core of the U.S. Proxy System and its Solution' (2011) 6 *Virginia Law & Business Review* 41; David Yermack, 'Corporate Governance and Blockchains' (2017) 21 *Review of Finance* 7. https://doi.org/10.1093/rof/rfw074 at 24.

116 Dirk Zetzsche, 'Shareholder Passivity, Cross-Border Voting and the Shareholder Rights Directive' (2008) 8 *Journal of Corporate Law Studies* 289.

117 Vice Chancellor J. Travis Laster, 'The Block Chain Plunger: Using Technology to Clean Up Proxy Plumbing and Take Back the Vote', Council of Institutional Investors (Sept. 2016), http://www.cii.org/files/09_29_16_laster_remarks.pdf.

118 s 330(3), 2006 CA.

119 s 330 CA 2006.

intermediaries on the proxy votes chain will be less relevant since the participants will be able to cast their votes directly.[120] If the voting system is facilitated directly by a smart contract rather than through intermediaries, changes of votes and last-minute vote submissions would be more efficiently managed than that under the current system.[121] Yet, proxy advisory services may continue to exist since the participants may not have the time or resources to understand all the voting issues. Advisory services will need to focus on individual participants rather than institutional investors. While individual investors can take more control of voting issues, advisory services can provide instructions (advice) to individual investors,[122] and the votes can be automated by smart contracts. For instance, individual investors can indicate how their votes should be cast on director's pay by linking their votes to an advisory service. The instructions of the advisory services will automate the votes of investors with smart contracts. Individual investors could even change the way they wish to vote by switching to another advisory service.

Policy recommendations

What does a smart contract entail?

Smart contracts are computer codes that can perform whatever action the participants agree to with tokenised securities or interests over the blockchain network. In this decentralised and disintermediated platform, trading of tokenised securities or interests can be a simple way to achieve the peer-to-peer goal. However, the computer codes may contain several legal elements such as property rights, and a number of contractual obligations which the participants may not be aware of or are easily confused about, and this poses a major risk to market safety. Hence, even though this method of peer-to-peer trading is simpler and apparently more efficient than the current system, participants will need to be aware of the legal risks of using this platform. They need to understand the legal nature of the tokenised securities or interests, the legal risks involved in contract and consumer protection law, and appreciate the implications of the encryption keys for transaction settlement. They will also need to comply with the market conduct rules on the platform such as market manipulation and insider dealing rules. They will also need to be aware of other securities market practices such as securities lending and proxy voting in order to safeguard their interests.

---

120 David Donald, 'From Block Lords to Blockchain: How Securities Dealers Make Markets' (2018) 44(1) *Journal of Corporation Law* 29–64.

121 Philip Boucher, 'How Blockchain Technology Could Change Our Lives: In-Depth Analysis' (European Parliamentary Research Service PE 581.948, February 2017).

122 Ibid.

How would the automated element be compatible with the contract law?

With smart contracts, transfers of tokenised securities or interests are automated according to pre-set parameters or more advanced algorithms such as AI. However, several elements in contract law can potentially make such contracts invalid, void, rescinded or unenforceable. This risk is amplified when participants are treated as consumers who are then entitled to a higher level of legal protection. Virtual dealing over the blockchain platform also requires a stronger level of proof of identify in order to ensure that people trading on the platform have the legal capacity to do so. This may involve using digital identification, such as personal biometric data, for the purpose of authentication and this calls for stronger personal data protection law and a robust data management system on the blockchain platform. Furthermore, errors in the coding of contracts bring a major risk of rendering transactions invalid. Since automation is the essence of the system, the question arises as to whether trades facilitated by smart contracts can be technically halted without causing the system to fail, and whether mistaken transactions caused by errors in coding can be legally remedied. Smart contracts should be vetted by trusted parties to make sure that they are not confusing, compliant with contract principles, correctly coded for use on the platform and that legal remedies are available outside the system. Even if transactions cannot be reversed, damages should be given to innocent parties.

How would automation between different contracts coordinate?

In traditional securities trading models, there are several layers with a chain of intermediaries to facilitate transactions. These intermediaries have their own arrangements to manage the risk caused by any default in the chain. Furthermore, the membership-based model for each layer of the trading cycle (trading, clearing and settlement) removes the risk of misunderstanding and of default as internal rules for the members at each layer of the trading cycle ensure standardisation. Trades over the blockchain platform facilitated by smart contracts to achieve peer-to-peer trading do not use intermediaries. Therefore, the system needs to be able to coordinate different smart contracts in order to provide efficiency through automation. For instance, how can a new resolution passed to allow pre-emption rights in the securities be implemented in related smart contracts? Would trades be automatically halted if a party challenges the validity of the contract? How could settled trades be rewound if the transaction was held to be fraudulent? How can securities lending and proxy voting be implemented? Risk management entities would need to take up some of the default risks as they do in the current securities trading system and they may also collect margins and collateral based on an individual's risk scores. They should also be responsible for certifying the safety of the smart contracts used, and for ensuring that they are legally compliant and correctly coded.

How can a workable solution be constructed to deal with conflict of laws issues?

Conflict of laws problems has already caused a major problem to the integration of securities markets. The legal status of the securities, their issuance, trading, clearing and settlement can be subject to different laws. In some areas, parties can decide the governing law and jurisdiction but there may be competition between different jurisdictions. On a peer-to-peer platform, since participants are likely to be consumers, this will allow consumer protection claims to override other contractual agreements. National regulators will also want to have a regulatory oversight of the activities. There should be an internationally agreed approach to conflict of laws issues, that takes into account the peer-to-peer nature of the platform and the automation function of its smart contracts. This situation is unprecedented, so national regulators need to agree on regulatory cooperation to provide assistance in prevention, investigation and enforcement. Even if the platform is decentralised, regulatory oversight will continue to be centralised unless regulators can develop a framework to share it, especially if actions will be required against persons and assets outside the country.

Major changes to securities businesses (resistance, recalibration or transformation)

Disintermediation will affect some trade practices in which intermediaries are the major provider, such as securities lending and proxy voting. Since securities will be distributed across the nodes, custodian banks and some central securities depositories (CSDs) will no longer be able to loan securities. Losing this business may prompt resistance from the securities custodian industry against migrating current trades to the blockchain platform. The securities lending business could be re-calibrated so that, for instance, securities lending business providers may allow owners of securities to "bank" their securities with them using a digital "wallet." This will require the business providers to provide financial benefits to the securities owners, and hence allow owners to share benefits made through securities lending. It might also be the case that a smart contract enables "securities lending" on a peer-to-peer basis with all the subsequent actions automated. Since this will be done on a peer-to-peer basis on the blockchain, the algorithms can detect who wants the borrowed securities, why they want them, how they are using them and what amount for what price. This can increase market transparency and reduce the opaqueness of the market that some currently rely on to short-sell securities for dubious purposes.

Conclusion

This chapter discusses how smart contracts can be used for securities transactions on the DLT network. First, it discusses the legal nature of tokenised securities (crypto-assets) encoded into smart contracts and emphasises that the legal basis of the underlying assets will continue to govern the rights of holders of crypto-assets. The legal basis of some crypto-assets, such as cryptocurrency, remains obscure while that of others, such as tokenised vouchers, requires further investigation to determine the legal structure of the investment. Smart contracts can be involved in different processes in the securities trading cycle. Transfers of tokenised securities will have contract law implications and there are several factors in contract law that can disrupt the flow of securities trading. Errors in coding contracts into smart contracts can cause both systemic and systematic failures so the introduction of a central counterparty system (CCP) is proposed to mitigate these risks. The CCP would have two functions: ensuring the safety of the smart contracts used and managing default risks. It may need to conduct risk assessments on the participants and to collect margins from them as part of its management of risk.

Second, the paper discusses how conflict of laws issues can affect market safety on the platform and affect regulatory oversight. There are difficulties for both market surveillance and the enforcement proceedings involved in a potentially cross-border securities trading platform, so it is likely that a legal seat will be required for the platform operators, despite the fact that the platform is technologically accessible to parties outside the jurisdiction. There should be a way to exercise jurisdiction against a person outside the jurisdiction and against the proceeds of that person.

Third, the paper discusses how the platform will affect current market practices such as securities lending and proxy voting. Despite the range of potential problems identified, there are also positive effects for individual investors. For instance, individual investors can share benefits from the securities lending businesses. Individual voting decisions about corporate affairs can be more efficiently implemented if proxy advisory services can advise individual investors directly, and advisory services can provide oracle services to the smart contracts (smart votes) in order to automate individual voting.

5 Regulatory objectives for cryptocurrency systems: unstable coins, stable coins and state-backed cryptocurrency

Introduction

Many aspects of crypto-finance are currently under discussion,[1] such as initial coin offering,[2] security token offering, distributed autonomous organisation and non-fungible tokens, but cryptocurrency is the most hotly debated among them.[3] Currently, it is also the most used and most traded crypto-finance on the open market. There are hundreds of cryptocurrencies traded on exchanges that can convert fiat currencies into cryptocurrencies and vice versa. Some cryptocurrency exchanges are also listed on major stock exchanges, such as Coinbase on Nasdaq. The emergence of cryptocurrencies, such as Bitcoin and Ether, is a direct response to the inequality brought about by the current centralised and intermediated financial markets where a few international global currencies dominate cross-border trading and are handled by major multinational banks, from trade finance to clearing services.[4] Cryptocurrency is a new payment system that is consensus-based and is not controlled by governments. It is regarded by some as a solution to the current disparity between countries in their wealth, economic development and political power, but it is not difficult to see why concerns have been raised by some central bankers, and why international banks have resisted accepting

---

1 Joseph Lee and Florian Lheureux, 'A Regulatory Framework for Cryptocurrency' (2020) 313 *European Business Law Review* 423, 446.
2 Philipp Hacker and Chris Thomale, 'Crypto-Securities Regulation: ICOs, Token Sales and Cryptocurrencies under EU Financial Law' (2018) 15 *European Company and Financial Law Review* 645–696. Available at SSRN: https://ssrn.com/abstract=3075820 or http://dx.doi.org/10.2139/ssrn.3075820.
3 A. Blandin, A. S. Cloots, H. Hussain, M. Rauchs, R. Saleuddin, J. G. Allen, et al., *Global Cryptoasset Regulatory Landscape Study* (Cambridge: Cambridge Centre for Alternative Finance, 2019); FS Board – Basel: Financial Stability Board, *Crypto-Asset Markets Potential Channels for Future Financial Stability Implications* (2018); FCA, *PS 19/22: Guidance on Cryptoassets Feedback and Final Guidance to CP 19/3* (2019).
4 Marco Lichtfous, Vivek Yadav and Valentina Fratino, 'Can Blockchain Accelerate Financial Inclusion Globally?' (Inside Magazine 2018).

DOI: 10.4324/9780429023613-5

cryptocurrency as a credible and legitimate financial system.[5] Regulators, government institutions,[6] private entities[7] and users have all begun to express their diverse views on cryptocurrencies and have started taking strategic measures to hedge their positions against this emerging system[8]. The cryptocurrency market is no longer a marginalised space for financial speculators and for illicit activities such as money laundering and tax evasion. With private institutions making significant investments in cryptocurrencies, both existing examples such as Bitcoin and Ether or those newly developed such as Diem,[9] regulators have at the same time started issuing policy papers on the risks to consumers and on regulatory approaches. Some governments have also launched projects to build state-backed digital currencies in response to the rise of public chain-based cryptocurrencies such as Bitcoin.[10] As an example, the Chinese government has introduced its own Digital Currency Electronic Payment system to compete with other cryptocurrencies as well as to internationalise the Chinese fiat currency,[11] the Renminbi. Following this Chinese Central Bank initiative,[12] private consortia have launched stable coin projects to rival both unstable coin systems on the public chain such as Bitcoin and state-backed digital currencies.[13] One example of such a private project is Facebook's Libra (now called Diem).[14] Not surprisingly, the European

5 Adrea Shalal and Christian Kraemer, 'G7 Finance Officials Back Need to Regulate Digital Currencies: Treasury' *Reuteurs.com* (London, December 7 2020), www.reuters.com/article/g7-digital/g7 -finance-officials-backneed-to-regulate-digital-currencies-treasury-idUSKBN28H1Y6. Accessed 03 January 2021.
6 Congressional Research Service, 'Cryptocurrencies: The Economics of Money and Selected Policy Issues' (2018) 20.
7 EUR-LEX, 'Proposal for a Regulation of the European Parliament and of the Council on Markets in Crypto-Assets, and Amending Directive (EU) 2019/1937', https://eur-lex.europa.eu/legalcontent/EN/TXT/?uri=CELEX%3A52020PC0593. Accessed 03 January 2021.
8 Financial Conduct Authority, *Guidance on Cryptoassets*, www.fca.org.uk/publications/consultation-papers/cp19-3-guidance-cryptoassets (accessed 15 March 2019).
9 Diem 'Libre White Paper v2.0, From Libra Association Members' (April 2020), DIEM.COM, p.   1,   https://wp.diem.com/en-US/wp-content/uploads/sites/23/2020/04/Libra_WhitePaperV2 _April2020.pdf. Accessed 03 January 2020 [hereinafter LIBRA WHITEPAPER 2.0].
10 Shan Wei and Clara Lewis, 'When Central Bank Digital Currency and Libra Meet: In the Same Boat or on Different Paths?' (2020) 35(10) *Journal of International Banking Law and Regulation* 393–409.
11 Jemma Xu and Dan Prudhomme, 'China's Digital Currency Revolution and Implications for Global Business Strategy' (2020) *London School of Economics Business Review*. DOI: 10.13140/ RG.2.2.18819.94240.
12 Rain Xie, 'Why China Had to Ban Cryptocurrency but the U.S. Did Not: A Comparative Analysis of Regulations on Crypto-Markets between the U.S. and China' (2019) 18 *Washington University Global Studies Law Review*.
13 'Inside China's Drive For Digital Currency Dominance' (Fortune, 2021) https://fortune.com/2020 /08/10/china-digital-currency-electronic-yuan-bitcoin-cryptocurrency/. Accessed 03 January 2021.
14 Bruhl Volker, 'LIBRA – A Differentiated View on Facebook's Virtual Currency Project' (CFS Working Paper Series No. 633, 2019).

Central Bank has issued a warning on this type of cryptocurrency system and has begun its own research on central bank digital currencies.

This chapter investigates three types of cryptocurrency system: unstable coin systems on the public chain, stable coin systems on the private chain and state-backed cryptocurrency systems. It assesses the extent to which each of them can promote access to finance by focusing on four regulatory objectives: value stability, market integrity, consumer protection and fairness, and security against theft. These four objectives form the initial basis for analysing whether a cryptocurrency system can give users sufficient confidence for them to access this emerging financial system (a discussion on data governance is covered in Chapter 9). First, Bitcoin is used as an example of an unstable coin system on the public chain to examine its ability to provide access to finance. The risks involved in this system are pointed out along with a discussion about whether stable coins, such as Diem,[15] can mitigate them. State-backed digital currency (as a type of state-backed cryptocurrency) is then used to highlight further pros and cons of decentralised cryptocurrency systems such as Bitcoin and Diem, and to analyse whether it provides a better solution for users.

At the time of writing, none of these cryptocurrency systems has been recognised as legal tender, and none has been widely used by any state agency as either a means of payment or an investment instrument.[16] However, as their success depends on state support to give them legal status and to coordinate stakeholders through a regulatory framework, there is a degree of competition between cryptocurrency systems and a state's own services in the form of fiat currency.[17] As states can make laws that affect a cryptocurrency's development while at the same time providing vital infrastructure for it, there is a degree of regulatory capture. States may regulate the market to serve their own interests.[18]

15　Mehrsa Baradaran, 'Facebook's Cryptocurrency Won't Help the Poor Access Banks. Here's What Would', The Washington Post, PostEverything, Perspective (29 October 2019), www.washington-post.com/outlook/2019/10/29/facebooks-cryptocurrency-wont-help-poor-access-banksheres-what -would/. Accessed 03 January 2020.

16　Bank of England, *The Future of Money* – Speech by Mark Carney, www.bankofengland.co.uk /speech/2018/mark-carney-speech-to-the-inaugural-scottish-economics-conference (accessed 17 March 2019); G20, *Communiqué – Finance Ministers and Central Bank Governors*, www.mof .go.jp/english/international_policy/convention/g20/20180722.htm (accessed 17 March 2019); In France, crypto-assets are neither regarded as a currency nor considered a means of payment by the Banque de France. See Banque de France, *Les dangers liés au développement des monnaies virtuelles : l'exemple du Bitcoin (The Dangers of the Development of Virtual Currencies: The Bitcoin Example)*, https://publications.banque-france.fr/sites/default/files/medias/documents/focus -10_2013-12-05_fr.pdf (accessed 18 March 2019).

17　Thibault Schrepel, 'Libra: A Concentrate of "Blockchain Antitrust"' (2019–2020) 118 *Michigan Law Review Online* 160.

18　Martin Arnold, 'ECB Executive Highlights Risks of Digital Currencies like Facebook's Libra' (London, 9 November 2020), https://www.ft.com/content/518a94cf-91e2-4e9f-bca8-5f29693340e7. Accessed 03 January 2021.

The systems and processes of cryptocurrency

Distributed ledger technology: decentralisation and disintermediation

Unstable coin systems

Cryptocurrency is a financial system built on blockchain technology, a type of distributed ledger technology.[19] Each block in a distributed network contains transactional information and is then chained to the previous block of information, in order to create records of transactions.[20] In this network of transactions, a financial system is created where information is shared among the network participants (the nodes) and is immutable.[21] There are different types of blockchain, each with different functions, benefits and risks: public chains, private chains and hybrid chains. In a public chain network, users simply download software and use its protocols to make transactions as "network clients."[22] In a private chain network, only permitted participants are able to use the network and to record transaction information.[23] The protocols are set by the participants, and permission is required to join the network, to maintain it, to share information and to add information. In some cases, participants may be able to alter the information. Hybrid chain networks vary in what they allow participants to do; in some cases, participants can make transactions by adding information to the database while not having the right to view all the information.

The infrastructure that Bitcoin uses is that of a public chain network in which anyone can participate and make transactions by simply downloading the software and using its protocols to add information to the chain.[24] Participants solve mathematical puzzles, the so-called "proof-of-work" (PoW),[25] and are then allowed to act as "mining nodes" which maintain the network and add information to it.[26]

---

19 O. Cann, 'These are the Top 10 Emerging Technologies of 2016' www.weforum.org/agenda/2016
    /06/top-10-emerging-technologies-2016/ (accessed 15 March 2019); K. Panetta, 'Gartner's Top
    10 Strategic Technology Trends for 2017' www.gartner.com/smarterwithgartner/gartners-top-10
    -technology-trends-2017/ (accessed 15 March 2019).
20 UK Government Office for Science, 'Distributed Ledger Technology: Beyond Blockchain' (2016).
21 Advait Deshpande, Katherine Stewart, Louise Lepetit and Salil Gunashekar, 'Distributed Ledger
    Technologies/Blockchain: Challenges, Opportunities and the Prospects for Standards', British
    Standards Institution 1 (2017).
22 World Bank Group, 'Distributed Ledger Technology (DLT) and Blockchain' http://documents
    .worldbank.org/curated/en/177911513714062215/pdf/122140-WP-PUBLIC-DistributedLedger
    -Technology-and-Blockchain-Fintech-Notes.pdf (accessed 17 March 2019).
23 Dominique Guegan, 'The Digital World: II – Alternatives to the Bitcoin Blockchain?' (2018)
    16 *Documents de Travail du Centre d'Economie de la Sorbonne* 2; Dominique Guegan, 'Public
    Blockchain versus Private Blockchain' (2017) 20 *Documents de Travail du Centre d'Economie de
    la Sorbonne* 3–4.
24 Richard Caetano, *Learning Bitcoin* (Packt Publishing Ltd, 2015).
25 Michael Crosby et al., 'Blockchain Technology Beyond Bitcoin' (2015) Sutardja Center for Entre-
    preneurship & Technology Technical Report 10.
26 Merlinda Andoni et al., 'Blockchain Technology in the Energy Sector: A Systematic Review of
    Challenges and Opportunities' (2019) 100 *Renewable and Sustainable Energy Reviews* 146.

They obtain coins as a reward for performing the mining node function. Because Bitcoin operates on a public chain network and permission is not required to join it, everyone with relevant IT equipment and knowledge can join this crypto-finance market, work as a mining node, make transactions on the system and view the transaction information. There is no legal or physical barrier to entry.[27] Transactions are made simply by using two types of crypto-graphic keys: a public key and a private key.[28] A public key is essentially a user's public address which is known to everyone on the network and allows assets to be moved between users. A private key is a user's password which is required to send transaction messages to a receiver in order to add information to the network. This effects a transaction and records it on the network's database just as clearing banks effect financial transactions between banks by providing what is, in effect, a transaction messaging service. The use of a crypto-graphic key avoids double-spending,[29] a problem that previous digital currencies were prone to; the use of these two crypto-graphic keys prevents someone from copying coins and spending them twice.

The design of the protocols does not require users to validate their identity when they join the network, so they can participate in the Bitcoin system anonymously. This is attractive for users who wish to conceal their identity and may be seen as privacy-enhancing technology that confers legal protection on financial privacy. In some countries, cryptocurrency exchanges may be legally obliged to validate a user's identity before an account is opened and transactions made. However, it is possible for users to make transactions in such a jurisdiction without going through the regulated cryptocurrency exchanges if they do not need to convert cryptocurrency into fiat currency, or vice versa, and they then use it as a medium to transfer a payment out of the jurisdiction. As the coins are "mined" according to the protocols of the software, there is no central bank or other government institution involved in deciding the number of coins to be issued or withdrawn from the system.

Stable coin systems

In order to mitigate the risks associated with unstable coin systems on the permission-less public chain, and to compete with them, stable coin systems have been developed. Some but not all stable coin systems rely on privately developed blockchain networks in which only permitted members can act as a node to maintain the network, to add blocks of information to the chain, to view the

---

27 Rainer Böhme, Nicolas Christin, Benjamin Edelman and Tyler Moore, 'Bitcoin: Economics, Technology, and Governance' (2015) 29(2) *Journal of Economic Perspectives* 225.
28 Andreas M. Antonopoulos, *Keys, Addresses in Mastering Bitcoin: Unlocking Digital Crypto-Currencies* (O'Reilly, 2014).
29 Kevin V. Tu and Michael W. Meredith, 'Rethinking Virtual Currency Regulation in the Bitcoin Age' (2015) 90 *Washington Law Review* 279.

information on the system's database or to modify information recorded in the database.[30] The network can be maintained by a consortium, either as a partnership or a legal entity such as Diem or R3.[31] The Swift system is an example of such a chain. It is becoming common in private blockchains for the operator in charge to be officially appointed in charge of the technical platforms that support blockchain.[32]

The consortium or some decision-making body within it can decide the system's processes and governance with regard to the issuance of stable coins. Issuance can be based on a reserve of different kinds of stable assets such as currencies, government bonds, asset management funds or other asset classes such as oil or gold. Since it is a permission-based network, there is a difference here in the relationship between the nodes and the normal users of the coins in the system. The nodes perform infrastructure support to maintain the network while users mainly use the coins as a means of payment or investment without having the right to add information to the network or to view the information on it. Since the issuance of coins is decided by an entity or an association, coins cannot be "mined" by the nodes of the network. In a private chain network, real identity is required of permissioned network members, so while the nodes cannot remain anonymous, it is still possible for users who are not nodes to make and receive payments without revealing their identity. However, some private chain stable coin networks, such as Diem, propose to require users to show their real identity in order to make transactions.

Diem makes a useful example to take as a model. It is widely accepted that cryptocurrencies such as Bitcoin are characterised as assets with high volatility and greater risks. A potential solution for these disadvantages is for global commercial giants to back up cryptocurrencies in the way that fiat currencies are supported by governments.[33] Diem, developed by Facebook, is aiming to achieve this goal.[34] Blockchain technology has been applied in constructing Diem and the Diem Association plans to provide backing from a global network of commercial

30 Karl Wüst and Arthur Gervais, *Do You Need a Blockchain?* (Zurich: ETH, London: Imperial College, 2018).

31 L. Hobbs, 'Facebook's Libra: The Social Media Giant's Pursuit of Global Financial Inclusion' (2020) North Carolina Banking Institute 24.

32 Vitalik Buterin, 'On Public and Private Blockchains' https://blog.ethereum.org/2015/08/07/on -public-and-private-blockchains/ (accessed 18 March 2019). See also Jean Bacon, Johan David Michels, Christopher Millard and Jatinder Singh, 'Blockchain Demystified: A Technical and Legal Introduction to Distributed and Centralised Ledgers' (2018) 25(1) *Richmond Journal of Law & Technology*.

33 Robby Houben and Alexander Snyers, 'Cryptocurrencies and Blockchain: Legal Context and Implications for Financial Crime, Money Laundering and Tax Evasion' (Study of European Parliament 2018) www.europarl.europa.eu/cmsdata/150761/TAX3%20Study%20on%20cryptocurren-cies%20and%20blockchain.pdf. Accessed 29 June 2021.

34 Libra Association, 'An Introduction to Libra' (2019) https://sls.gmu.edu/pfrt/wp-content/uploads/sites/54/2020/02/LibraWhitePaper_en_US-Rev0723.pdf. Accessed 27 June 2021.

giants in the expectation of attracting billions of users.[35] As a decentralised network, validation of Diem by network users and consensus among them are essential. However, allowing validation and reaching consensus among the billions of users who are trading simultaneously on the network poses a huge challenge to the capacity of the process of validation for transactions.[36] In other words, there is a conflict between scale and speed. As discussed in Chapter 2, the permissionless blockchain is slow as it involves unrequired computations to reach consensus on the network.[37] A permissioned operating model would not only promote efficient transaction, but also avoid sacrificing governance by the network organiser.[38] Diem grants validation authority to the Diem Association, which allows Diem to operate on a permissioned blockchain. In addition, unlike the operation of some unstable coins on the public chain such as Bitcoin, Diem's demand is related to the exchange rate between fiat currencies, which corrects the high volatility character of cryptocurrencies. Low volatility assets, such as fiat currencies including the USD and Euro, will be stored as Diem reserve.[39] Confidence about security is also essential for attracting users to Diem. Novi, a digital wallet that was introduced in 2020, allows Diem holders to save and spend Diem.[40] Furthermore, Novi can be connected to Diem users' credit cards.[41] Novi is expected to be an independent body from Facebook and is currently registered as a subsidiary of Facebook.[42] Diem is aiming to increase access to finance in developing countries and to facilitate transactions globally and, according to the Diem Association, its reserves will be used to cover the costs of the Diem system as well as reducing transaction fees and paying dividends to investors.[43] The Diem Association has the ambition to increase financial inclusion in underdeveloped regions and facilitate global transactions to increase access to finance, but the requirements of anti-money laundering and counter-terrorist financing requirements will need

35 Jahja Rrustemi and Nils Tuchschmid, 'Facebook's Digital Currency Venture "Diem": The New Frontier ... or a Galaxy Far, Far Away?' (2020) 10(12) *Technology Innovation Management Review* 19, 30.

36 Ibid.

37 101 Blockchains, 'Permissioned VS Permissionless Blockchains' (2020) https://101blockchains .com/permissioned-vs-permissionless-blockchains/. Accessed 29 June 2021.

38 101 Blockchains, 'Introduction to Permissioned Blockchains' (2019) https://101blockchains.com/ permissioned-blockchain/. Accessed 29 June 2021.

39 Christian Catalini and Joshua Gan, 'Some Simple Economics of the Blockchain' (National Bureau of Economic Research Working Paper 22952, 2019) www.nber.org/papers/w22952. Accessed 27 June 2021.

40 Diem Association, 'Economics and the Reserve' (2020) www.diem.com/en-us/economics-and-the -reserve/#overview. Accessed 29 June 2021.

41 Novi, 'A Connected Wallet for a Connected World' (2021) www.novi.com/. Accessed 30 June 2021.

42 Ibid.

43 Diem Association, 'Economics and the Reserve' (2020) www.diem.com/en-us/economics-and-the -reserve/#overview. Accessed 29 June 2021.

to be in place in the Diem system.[44] The system should ensure that the assets in a Novi wallet are not used for illegal purposes. Even in a blockchain environment, this process is costly and time-consuming.[45]

State-backed cryptocurrency systems

Little information is available about proposed state-backed cryptocurrencies, but it is expected that they are most likely to use the private chain network system for their infrastructure.[46] The network will be maintained either by the state or by a public–private partnership led and controlled by the state. The issuance of state-backed cryptocurrencies will not depend on coins being issued as a reward through the mining process, as in the Bitcoin system, but will depend on decisions by the state or its central bank in a similar way to the issuance of fiat currency. It is likely that the network will be maintained by a number of nodes with the capacity to add blocks of information and share information in the system's database. A possible model is for a number of central banks to form a consortium, perhaps with private banks joining the network to form a public–private partnership. It is not known whether there are plans for private entities, such as merchants or social media groups, to join such a state-backed network or to allow them to share in decision making. It is unlikely that ordinary users would be able to participate as a node to share or add information or to take part in decisions concerning governance or the issuance of coins.

It is useful here to present a mode that uses the system developed by the Chinese government. China's National Digital Currency, digital currency and electronic payments (DCEP), is the first central bank digital currency in the world.[47] DCEP applied blockchain technology and cryptographic technology, aiming to enhance the circulation of the RMB and to promote its progress as a global currency similar to the USD.[48] According to China's Central Bank, the function of DCEP is exactly the same as paper money, despite its digital form.[49]

---

44 Jahja Rrustemi and Nils Tuchschmid, 'Facebook's Digital Currency Venture "Diem": The New Frontier … or a Galaxy Far, Far Away?' (2020) 10(12) *Technology Innovation Management Review* 19, 30.

45 Ibid.

46 Codruta Boar, Henry Holden and Amber Wadsworth, 'Impending Arrival – A Sequel to the Survey on Central Bank Digital Currency' Bank for International Settlements, BIS Papers No 107, E42, E58, 033 (January 2020) p. 3, www.bis.org/publ/bppdf/bispap107.pdf. Accessed 03 January 2020.

47 Boxmining, 'China's National Digital Currency DCEP/CBDC Overview' (2021) https://boxmining.com/dcep/#:~:text=What%20is%20DCEP%3F,Bank%20of%20China%20(PBoC), accessed 30 June 2021.

48 Christopher McNally, 'The DCEP: Developing the Globe's First Major Central Bank Digital Currency' (2020) www.chinausfocus.com/finance-economy/the-dcep-developing-the-globes-first-major-central-bank-digital-currency. Accessed 30 June 2021.

49 South China Morning Post, 'What is China's Sovereign Digital Currency' (2020) www.scmp.com/economy/china-economy/article/3083952/what-chinas-cryptocurrency-sovereign-digital-currency-and-why. Accessed 30 June 2021.

DCEP can be circulated without internet connections because of its distributed character. Offline transactions can be recorded and backed up to each node once the network is reconnected. By contrast, electronic payment systems such as Alipay and WeChat Pay, are third-party payment systems, which merely provide a platform for users to make payments by transferring money into accounts created on the platform. The platform serves as a guarantee to ensure the completion of the transaction but in these systems, third-party payments do not replace paper currency. DCEP, by contrast, aims to replace paper currency completely. But if DCEP totally replaces paper currency, third-party payment systems need to co-exist with it because central banks cannot provide a payment guarantee for DCEP users in the way that third-party payment systems do. DCEP differs from distributed and anonymous network cryptocurrencies, such as Bitcoin, because, although DCEP is based on blockchain technology, it is in essence a centralised system. Since the Chinese Central Bank issues the digital currency, comprehensive details of its circulation can easily be traced. However, the quantity of issuance is still decided by the central bank, even if DCEP replaces paper currency, and in this regard, it is similar to cryptocurrencies such as Bitcoin or Diem.

Because DCEP transactions are traceable, bribes made on using the system are easily detected. The system also enhances macro-control of the economy by the government since all transaction data, and hence the state of supply and demand in different sectors, are easily shown by using algorithms.[50] In the financial market, introduction of DCEP can also enhance the governance of currency speculation and the control of systemic risk. For instance, short selling can be prohibited through restricting the DCEP account of market participants. But at the same time, government control of transaction data through the traceability function of DCEP may lead to issues of data protection.

Value stability

A system that does not provide stable value to its instruments and commodities cannot gain the necessary confidence to attract users or to function financially. International trade has been dominated by currencies that are perceived to be stable such as US dollars, Japanese Yen and the Euro. Even for currency investment, stable currencies such as British Stirling, the Swiss Franc and the Japanese Yen are preferred by the asset management market, particularly for hedging purposes. Emerging currencies in international trade such the Chinese RMB, though they are eager to be accepted as international currencies for trade and investment, are also pegged to stable currencies such as the US dollar to stabilise their value. Although value fluctuation may be unavoidable in a financial market controlled by supply and demand, when the objective of a means of payment is to increase

---

50 Daan de Jonge and Max de Jonge, 'China and Digital Currency Electronic Payment (DCEP): Channelling Innovation' (2019) https://theasiadialogue.com/2019/05/09/china-and-digital-currency-electronic-payment-dcep-channelling-innovation/. Accessed 01 July 2021.

access to finance, its stability is vital. Value stability should be the main regulatory objective for a cryptocurrency system.

Unstable coin systems

The history of unstable coins is one of rapid and sharp changes in their value, both rises and falls. Bitcoin is the best-known example and there are a number of reasons for rises in its value.[51]

First, it is a means of payment favoured by users in developing countries which do not have stable currencies or access to stable currencies. When Bitcoin is perceived as more stable than their local currency, it is preferable for them to hold it as an asset and to use it as a payment medium, especially when purchasing goods and services on e-commerce platforms. Second, Bitcoin provides the opportunity for users in countries that do not have payment services (currency exchanges, third party payment services or digital payment services) to make international transactions and to purchase goods or services on a foreign internet platform as well as participating in crowdfunding platforms to obtain future goods and services. Third, it allows financial investors to use the unstable coins as a hedging tool against fluctuations in value of fiat currencies, especially when central banks use quantitative easing to increase the money supply with a resulting fall in the value of the fiat currency. Some investors use derivatives to trade on unstable coins, causing their value to rise sharply.[52] This was the reason that the FCA decided to make derivative contracts of cryptocurrency illegal and unenforceable in order to protect retail investors from high volatility and risks.[53] Well-known entrepreneurs, such as Elon Musk, and banks, such as Citibank and BlackRock have started to support Bitcoin which has validated it as a legitimate investment, if not yet as a means of payment. Their support, either through direct investment in the systems or by facilitating token trades based on the system, also sends a strong message to the financial market that Bitcoin is a legitimate payment method for the future as well as an international currency for trades and services. Japan has recognised Bitcoin as a legal tender, enabling Bitcoin to be used as an official form of payment to pay a public or private debt or meet a financial obligation.[54] Such legal recognition pushed Bitcoin prices up by 2% in 24 hours and increased the price globally by 160% for the next two months.[55]

---

51 Chairman Ben S. Bernanke, 'Stabilizing the Financial Markets and the Economy', www.federal-reserve.gov/newsevents/speech/bernanke20081015a.htm (accessed 22 September 2019).

52 Neil Gandal and Hanna Halaburda, 'Working Paper: Competition in the Cryptocurrency Market' (2014) 33 *Bank of Canada Working Paper* 15.

53 FCA, 'FCA Proposes Ban on Sale of Crypto-Derivatives to Retail Consumers', www.fca.org.uk/news/press-releases/fca-proposes-ban-sale-crypto-derivatives-retail-consumers (accessed 19 November 2019).

54 Marta Gonzalez, 'Blockchain in Japan' (EU-Japan Centre for Industrial Cooperation, 2018).

55 Ibid. at 31.

On the other hand, Bitcoin has been used to facilitate illicit and illegal criminal activities such as money laundering, tax evasion, fraud and terrorist financing. Because the supply of Bitcoin is limited by its protocols, continued demand for it by criminals has caused it to rise in value on the open market. The value of Bitcoin also depends on the miners' willingness to continue mining coins to maintain the network and to continue adding blocks of information. Mining is expensive as it requires equipment and consumes energy, so its continuation depends on the fees that miners can charge and users' willingness to pay.

On the demand side, a variety of factors affect the value of unstable coins.[56] Some investors may bet on it becoming legal tender and accepted for international payments. Since stable fiat currencies can become unstable as central banks change their monetary policy, unstable coins could become a hedging tool for investors against loss of currency value, but also for users in a country whose currency is pegged to the fiat currency. Since many stable coin systems are being developed, including state-backed systems, cryptocurrency stakeholders may expect competition in the market between unstable, stable and state-backed cryptocurrency systems. If so, unstable coins would have an advantage over the others for their anonymity (or privacy), their limited supply and their peer-to-peer function without the need to use middlemen. It is also possible that unstable coins could become more stable than other fiat currencies because limited supply is designed into their system. Once all the coins have been mined, there could be a shortage of coins in the system. Regulators might be tempted to ban trade in unstable coins or to prohibit them from being used as a payment, but if there is strong market demand, a legal ban may not cause a fall in value. The question for regulators should therefore be whether there is a benefit in stabilising unstable coins, such as Bitcoin, whether they should intervene to help stabilisation and if so, how?[57]

Stable coin systems

Stable coin systems are linked to stable assets. A reserve can be created through a basket of stable assets including stable fiat currencies, stable treasury bonds (government debt) and other stable funds that invest in stable assets.[58] Users can convert fiat currencies into stable coins and, by doing so, those in a country with an unstable fiat currency will be able to use stable coins to purchase goods and services on e-platforms that accept stable coins as a means of payment. Individual

---

56 See Joseph Lee and Florian Lheureux, 'A Regulatory Framework for Cryptocurrency' 2020 (31) 3 *European Business Law Review* 423, 446.

57 Michal Polasik, Anna Piotrowska, Radoslaw Kotkowski and Tomasz Piotr Wisniewski, 'Price Fluctuations and the Use of Bitcoin: An Empirical Inquiry' (2015) 20(1) *International Journal of Electronic Commerce* 9, 49.

58 D. Zetzsche, R. Buckley and D. Arner, 'Regulating Libra: The Transformative Potential of Facebook's Cryptocurrency and Possible Regulatory Responses' (2019) 47 *University of New South Wales Faculty of Law Research Series* 11.

investors, who may not have access to international currency exchange services to obtain stable currencies, or do not have sufficient funds to purchase them and would like to use stable currencies as a hedge, may purchase stable coins for investment purposes. International traders who do not have access to stable fait currencies, due to local regulatory restrictions, can use stable coins as a means of payment to engage in trade. The strategy used by a stable coin system can be the opposite to that of an unstable system, particularly when investors use unstable coins to hedge against the value fluctuations of stable currencies. As mentioned, investment in unstable coins can be a no-confidence vote against stable fiat currencies such as US dollars because of a state's "out-of-control" money supply. The trade in unstable coins, especially in the derivative markets, may make stable fiat currencies unstable and affect the value of stable coins that use them as a reserve. Once stable coins are on the market, they can also be subject to market trading mechanisms, and their price can be quoted on open markets, including derivatives markets. Furthermore, derivatives can also be created based on stable coins – either to stabilise or de-stabilise them.[59] They can be subject to short-selling strategies, depending on the expectations of the market. The fact that a cryptocurrency is linked to a number of stable assets does not make it immune from value volatility. Many fiat currencies of developing countries are linked to the stable fiat currencies of developed countries, but such pegging strategies do not necessarily make their currencies more stable internally. For instance, when a developed country uses quantitative easing, developing countries whose currency is linked may need to increase the amount of their fiat currency in circulation and as a result, may not be able to control domestic inflation. Central banks which use this strategy to maintain their exchange rate can be accused of currency manipulation.

Stable coins can be linked to stable commodities such as gold. However, the price of precious metals is also subject to market trading mechanisms and can lead to value changes. When stable coins are accessed by users in a remote country, the government of that country may not be able to stabilise the value of the coins or offer protective measures for users. This can create a situation where users cannot hold their government to account for value changes. Governance and accountability are particularly important when a cryptocurrency system aims to provide access to finance and to help bring about socio-economic transformation.

State-backed cryptocurrency systems

If crypto-graphic technology is used, state-backed digital or cryptocurrency can be the most stable coin system of the three types because it is linked to the state's own fiat currency. For instance, the Chinese DCEP is stabilised in value because it is linked to the Chinese RMB. A state-backed cryptocurrency can also be linked

---

59 See Joseph Lee and Florian Lheureux, 'A Regulatory Framework for Cryptocurrency' 2020 (31)3 *European Business Law Review* 423, 446.

to a particular commodity that the country owns such as gold, oil or other types of energy, as long as the value is stable. The risk to the value of the cryptocurrency is then similar to that of a fiat currency. But what limits the number of coins to be issued? In a fiat currency system, governments may increase money supply in order to solve financial crises such as a "credit crunch" and, paradoxically, this is the reason why investors and those who use the currency as a means of payment continue to have confidence in the system. However, in a state-backed cryptocurrency, if the number of coins is limited and no more can be produced once the limit has been reached, and then there is heavy demand for it due to a "credit crunch," a black market can be created for the coins. Similarly, investors may dump the digital currency and cause the state to buy its currency back. This is another source of volatility in the market.

The rise of cryptocurrencies such as Bitcoin prompts questions about the cycle of a currency: how it is created, how it is distributed, what its value can be measured against and when it can be withdrawn from circulation. Looking at the three types of cryptocurrency system, it is apparent that there is no single way to stabilise the value of a cryptocurrency, let alone a fiat currency. Experience from the time the US dollar was de-coupled from the gold reserves in the 1960s up to the currency pegging strategy adopted today by many developing countries, shows that it may not be possible to create a single global currency that suits the needs of every different economy. However, if cryptocurrency aims to protect those who use it for cross-border transactions, especially for smaller scale trading, value stability should be the primary objective in its design along with a governance framework that enables it to provide access to finance.

Soft and hard forks as a major risk to financial stability

Soft and hard[60] forks in cryptocurrency represent a major risk to financial stability and consumer protection. A soft fork is a modification of the blockchain protocol that is compatible with the older version of the blockchain.[61] In this case, the old validated blocks remain compatible with the new and stricter rules. Miners and nodes do not need to join the upgraded version of the blockchain to get access to the system's user base and transactional traffic.[62] A hard fork is a major modification of the protocol that can revise any aspect of the code and whose new rules are not compatible with previous ones.[63] Given the protocol's distributed nature, such

---

60 Jeffery Atik and George Gerro, 'Hard Forks on the Bitcoin Blockchain: Reversible Exit, Continuing Voice' (2018) 1 *Stanford Journal of Blockchain Law & Policy* 29.

61 Henri Arslanian and Fabrice Fischer, *The Future of Finance: The Impact of FinTech, AI, and Crypto on Financial Services* (Springer, 2019).

62 Bruno Biais, Christophe Bisière, Matthieu Bouvard and Catherine Casamatta, 'The Blockchain Folk Theorem' (TSE Working Papers, 2018).

63 A. Zamyatin, N. Stifter, A. Judmayer, P. Schindler, E. Weippl and W. J. Knottenbelt, *A Wild Velvet Fork Appears! Inclusive Blockchain Protocol Changes in Practice* (London: Imperial College; Austria: SBA Research, 2018).

modification must be incorporated into the software code held individually by each node. To ensure the effectiveness of the hard fork, a majority of nodes must adopt it. If some of the miners and nodes refuse the update, then two blockchains will exist in parallel, resulting in two different cryptocurrencies.[64] The newly-created branch keeps the same blocks as the main blockchain prior to the hard fork, but will then create its own separate block history.[65] Thus, each person who had owned cryptocurrency before the hard fork will have the same amount in the new updated cryptocurrency.[66] Well-known hard forks include Bitcoin Cash (BCH), from Bitcoin, or Ethereum Classic (ETC), from Ethereum.[67] Consumers who purchase the coins may not appreciate the risks of forks, nor know how to update the software protocols in order to safeguard their coins.

Market integrity

Unstable coin systems

Many cryptocurrencies have been used for illicit and illegal purposes, such as money laundering, tax evasion, fraud and terrorist financing.[68] They can also be used to avoid trade sanctions, since some cryptocurrencies do not rely on financial intermediaries such as clearing banks to process transactions.[69] One of the reasons that some cryptocurrencies can be used for these purposes is anonymity. Users do not need to use their real identity to make transactions and it is only when they convert the cryptocurrency into a fiat currency in a regulated cryptocurrency exchange that their identity may be required. An example of how the law might be circumvented is as follows. A requires B to send an amount of cryptocurrency to A for some illegal substance. A then sends an amount of cryptocurrency to C and

64 Jean Bacon, Johan David Michels, Christopher Millard and Jatinder Singh, 'Blockchain Demystified: A Technical and Legal Introduction to Distributed and Centralised Ledgers' (2018) 25(1) *Richmond Journal of Law & Technology*.

65 Christopher Natoli, Jiangshan Yu, Vincent Gramoli and Paulo Esteves-Verissimo, 'Deconstructing Blockchains: A Comprehensive Survey on Consensus, Membership and Structure', arXiv:1908.08316, https://arxiv.org/pdf/1908.08316.pdf (accessed 30 August 2019).

66 Robby Houben and Alexander Snyers, 'Study Requested by the TAX3 Committee: Cryptocurrencies and Blockchain – Legal Context and Implications for Financial Crime, Money Laundering and Tax Evasion' (2018). Available at: www.europarl.europa.eu/cmsdata/150761/TAX3%20Study%20on%20cryptocurrencies%20and%20blockchain.pdf.

67 Lawrence J. Trautman, 'Bitcoin, Virtual Currencies, and the Struggle of Law and Regulation to Keep Pace' (2018) 102 *Marquette Law Review* 496; Danhui Xu, 'Free Money, But Not Tax-Free: A Proposal for the Tax Treatment of Cryptocurrency Hard Forks' (2018) 87 *Fordham Law Review* 2698; A. K. M. Najmul Islam, Matti Mäntymäki and Marja Turunen, 'Why do Blockchains Split? An Actor-Network Perspective on Bitcoin Splits' (2019) 148 *Technological Forecasting and Social Change*.

68 R. E. Kadyrov and I. V. Prokhorov, 'Regulating Cryptocurrencies: New Challenges to Economic Security and Problems Created by Individuals Involved in the Schemes of Laundering Cryptocurrencies-Generated Profits' (2018) *Moscow Engineering Physics Institute* 2.

69 Raphael Auer and Stijn Claessens, 'Regulating Cryptocurrencies: Assessing Market Reactions' (2018) *BIS Quarterly Review* 52

D in exchange for fiat currency, without going through a regulated cryptocurrency exchange. C and D then make legitimate trades with E and F on a platform that accepts cryptocurrency as a means of payment. E and F may not know that the origin of the funds from C and D was illegal so do not conduct client due diligence and then convert the cryptocurrency into fiat currency. As the transactions are all made on the public chain network, everybody mentioned here can be protected by anonymity and it would be difficult for law enforcement agencies to trace the identity of C and D.

Cryptocurrency can also be used for facilitating fraud and escaping trade sanctions.[70] For instance, A can use ransomware on B, an innocent party, and ask B to purchase cryptocurrency through a legitimate cryptocurrency exchange. B then sends the specified amount of cryptocurrency to A who uses it as payment for a legitimate trade to receive goods and services. Even if A has been tracked down through other means (e.g. tracing A's IP address), it might be difficult for law enforcement agencies to obtain evidence of the payment because only A has the private key to gain access to the fund. Without the private key, the law enforcement agencies may not be able to investigate and prove that the transaction took place.

Cryptocurrency systems can also be used to avoid trade sanctions. Some countries are subject to trade sanctions and trading with them would be either illegal or subject to stringent scrutiny. The anonymity in some unstable coin systems can facilitate trade with these countries when the system does not rely on financial intermediaries. Intermediaries might be subject to the jurisdiction or extra-territorial jurisdiction of a country that imposes such a sanction or is obliged to enforce the sanctions regime.

Stable coin systems

In a stable coin system based on a private chain infrastructure, the consortium acts as a trusted third party as well as an intermediary. Users must provide a real identity to make transactions, which are then traceable. Even though it is possible to use stable coins in money laundering transactions, activities on a private chain network are recorded and it would be difficult to tamper with information without the consensus of the nodes. As a result, network and law enforcement agencies are able to detect, investigate and identify perpetrators of crime and their illegal proceeds.

How would the Know Your Customer (KYC) requirement and other reporting obligations be carried out in a stable coin system? Although transactions are

---

70 John Taskinsoy, 'Bitcoin Mania: An End to the US Dollar's Hegemony or Another Cryptocurrency Experiment Destined to Fail?' 9 (2018). Available at SSRN: https://ssrn.com/abstract=3311989 or http://dx.doi.org/10.2139/ssrn.3311989.

transparent and immutable,[71] the consortium can decide how the KYC requirement should be carried out, who has the duty to report suspicious transactions and who has the right to view the transactions. If exchanges were to be created, similar to those in unstable coin systems that provide digital wallets, they would also need to carry out the KYC requirements and reporting obligations as they would have direct personal information about their clients. In addition, the merchants and service providers might also need to carry out these duties as they would have access to their clients' transaction information. Hence, there are potentially three categories of stakeholders in this system who may have to carry out anti-money laundering duties: system providers who can view the transactions on the network; cryptocurrency exchanges who hold personal information about their clients; and merchants who can access the transaction information. This means that the law should make clear who is responsible for carrying out anti-money laundering duties in stable coin systems.

State-backed cryptocurrency systems

In state-backed cryptocurrency, the state can view and monitor all transactions. Since this kind of private blockchain network requires its users to reveal their identity, the maintenance of market integrity against criminal transactions can be significantly strengthened because the state can use algorithms to detect suspicious transactions. Furthermore, the circumstantial data around the transactions enable law enforcement agencies to investigate in detail. If the state decides to allow banks to act as intermediaries in distributing currency to users at the retail level, the banks will then need to carry out the KYC requirements and reporting duties. In this scenario, a state-backed cryptocurrency system can be more effective at detecting crime than a fiat currency system, but there is a greater risk to individual privacy, data protection and human rights.

Consumer protection and fairness in trade

There are several issues that relate to consumer protection and fairness in trade. When users purchase cryptocurrency either as an investment asset or for payment purposes, they run the risk of value fluctuation, as discussed in the previous section, and if they are not sophisticated investors, their risk of losing the investment or the power of purchasing is all the greater. Investment protection law is therefore required to mitigate this risk. For example, when goods are purchased with cryptocurrency,[72] the contract made might not be covered by the UK Sale

---

71 Malcolm Campbell-Verduyn, *Bitcoin and Beyond: Cryptocurrencies, Blockchains, and Global Governance* (London: Routledge, Taylor & Francis Group, 2018) 33.

72 The LawTech Delivery Panel, 'Legal Statement on Cryptoassets and Smart Contracts' (2019). Available at: https://35z8e83m1ih83drye28oo9d1-wpengine.netdna-ssl.com/wp-content/uploads/2019/11/6056_JO_Cryptocurrencies_Statement_FINAL_WEB_111119-1.pdf; https://technation.io/about-us/lawtech-panel/ (accessed 20 January 2020); Miklós Király, 'The Vienna

of Goods Act 1979 because for consumers or contractors to be protected under that Act, payment must be made in cash, i.e. fiat currency.[73] But if cryptocurrency were to be considered a commodity rather than a means of payment, when it is used to purchase goods, some of the implied terms intended by the Act to protect the parties will not be in the contract. I will focus on this in more detail under the three different coin systems.

Unstable coin systems

As mentioned, unstable coin systems are not currently recognised as legal currency. The European Central Bank has clearly stated that unstable coins such as Bitcoin are crypto-assets but not currencies because they do not have a stable value. If this continues to be the regulatory approach to cryptocurrency systems, it creates a major confusion for both contract parties and consumers in sales contracts, especially cross-border ones.[74] For example, on a digital platform for selling goods, consumers may believe that they are protected under the consumer law of the jurisdiction in which they reside. It may then transpire that the law in which the platform is based, or the choice of law specified in the sales contract, recognises a particular type of cryptocurrency as a legal means of payment. However, the jurisdictional law of the platform may offer less protection than the law of the country in which the consumer resides. The law that offers most protection to the consumer ought to govern the contract but currently there is no guarantee that this is the case.

Even if unstable coins are recognised as legal tender and consumer protection law applies, consumers may suffer a loss when there is a breach of contract. For example, a consumer might purchase an electronic device on an e-commerce platform, paying with cryptocurrency coins to the value of £100. If the device is unsatisfactory and the consumer asks for a refund, by the time of the repayment the value of the cryptocurrency could have halved and the consumer's refunded coins are now only worth £50. The consumer is not then entitled to ask the merchant to make up the £50 loss of value.

If goods are paid for with cryptocurrency, there may be an incentive for the merchant to break the contract. For example, if the value of the cryptocurrency falls, there is an incentive for the merchant to return the cryptocurrency to the consumer rather than giving the contracted goods. Equally, there can be an incentive for the consumer not to fulfil the payment obligation if the value of the

Convention on International Sales of Goods and the Bitcoin' (2018) 16(5) *US–China Law Review* 179; Neil Tiwari, 'The Commodification of Cryptocurrency' (2018) 117(3) *Michigan Law Review* 611.

73 See Joseph Lee and Florian Lheureux, 'A Regulatory Framework for Cryptocurrency' (2020) 3(31) *European Business Law Review* 423.
74 See World Bank, 'Accelerated Remittances Growth to Low- and Middle-Income Countries in 2018' (Press Release, 8 December 2018) www.worldbank.org/en/news/press-release/2018/12 /08/accelerated-remittances-growth-to-low-and-middle-income-countries-in-2018. Accessed 23 December 2019.

cryptocurrency has risen. This is especially true when there is an open and ready market for the seller to sell the goods. In business-to-business (B2B) international trade, traders can use a currency exchange to hedge against value fluctuations. However, in a non-B2B trade, the parties may not be familiar with hedging strategies and may not have access to the currency swaps market. Fluctuations in value will affect the behaviour of the parties in trade and can give rise to claims based on "conscionability," "duress" and "public policy" in contract law.

Stable coin systems

Stable coin systems have less risk to their value than unstable systems, so may not affect the behaviour of contracting parties and consumers to the same extent. However, there is still a risk that the contracting parties and consumers may game on differences between stable coins and fiat currency, a common practice of arbitrage in trade. When such gaming is used extensively by consumers, both stable coins and fiat currencies are easily accessible and also in competition. If a fiat currency is unstable, parties may speculate on its price or use currency forwards to hedge against the risk of value fluctuation. For instance, in a hire-purchase agreement, a consumer may lack stable coins after the first instalment payment is made according to the contract. The consumer then needs to convert local fiat currency to cryptocurrency. In international trade, traders may take out instruments such as currency swaps to ensure that value is not lost in currency conversion. However, consumers may not have access to a derivatives market of this kind and may not understand the risk to value in currency conversion.

In a consumer market, when a range of currencies is available on the digital markets, consumers can compare prices of goods in different currencies, and then choose which currency to use. Arbitrage behaviour will be more prevalent in the consumer market where goods are listed in multiple currencies. The assumption is that currencies compete in the market, and that consumers will choose the most favourable so the most stable coin system is likely to be chosen as a means of payment. Goods may be bought in a local market using a stable coin system and then sold off to another local market or a black market to people who do not have access to the goods through lack of stable coins or local fiat currency. Such behaviour would encourage black markets and defeat cryptocurrency's aim to provide access to a stable means of payment. Unless people in poorer regions have consistent equal access to affordable stable coins, a stable coin system can create further inequality.

State-backed cryptocurrency systems

Pricing arbitrage in the consumer market may not be a major issue when a state-backed cryptocurrency is used in the state which issues it because it is likely to be linked to the state's fiat currency. This gives no opportunity for pricing arbitrage, and no chance of making an associated windfall. However, problems may arise when state-backed cryptocurrency is used for cross-border transactions.

The cryptocurrency issued by state A will be in competition with the fiat currency issued by state B and goods and services will be priced in both currencies. Assuming that both currencies can be legally used and are easily accessible, unless B's fiat currency is pegged to A's state-backed cryptocurrency, a pricing arbitrage can occur. In a competitive currency exchange market, exchange rates fluctuate and a state may even engage in currency manipulation to stabilise its own fiat currency. This can result in unfair practice especially when a state wishes to lower its exchange rate to make its goods more competitive. As an example, if the US Federal Reserve instigated quantitative easing, many countries' central banks would purchase their own currencies in order to maintain their exchange rate against the US dollar. There is then the risk of a currency war where countries impose tariffs on goods and services and consumers suffer.

Security against theft

Loss of cryptocurrency through theft or the loss of a private key is a major security risk to users.[75] The estimated amount lost from hacks and frauds between 2011 and 2018 was approximately US$2.3 billion, and most of these thefts occurred on exchanges, although some relate to offline storage wallets.[76]

Theft can happen when the digital wallet for safekeeping a cryptocurrency,[77] either maintained by a currency exchange[78] or a trusted third party,[79] is hacked or when the private key has been illegally obtained by someone other than the owner.[80] A wallet created by an exchange, especially an online wallet on the public chain, can be hacked and the hacker can transfer the cryptocurrency to another account and sell it to a third party who then converts it to another cryptocurrency or a fiat currency.[81] It would then be difficult to trace the lost asset. Another risk is when a user loses a private key – the password needed to access an account and make transfers. Once the password is lost, the user is not able to recover it because

75 Financial Inclusion Global Initiative – Security, Infrastructure and Trust Working Group, *Security Aspects of Distributed Ledger Technologies* (2019).
76 The New York Times Editorial Staff, *Cryptocurrencies: Bitcoin, Blockchain and Beyond* (The Rosen Publishing Group, Inc., 2018).
77 Neil Mathew, '$571 Million: Notorious North Korean Hacker Group Has Stolen a Fortune', www .ccn.com/571-million-notorious-north-korean-hacker-group-has-stolen-a-fortune-in-cryptocurrency (accessed 17 March 2019).
78 Robby Houben and Alexander Snyers, 'Study Requested by the TAX3 Committee: Cryptocurrencies and Blockchain – Legal Context and Implications for Financial Crime, Money Laundering and Tax Evasion' (2018). Available at: www.europarl.europa.eu/cmsdata/150761/TAX3%20Study %20on%20cryptocurrencies%20and%20blockchain.pdf.
79 Timothy G. Massad, *It's Time to Strengthen the Regulation of Crypto-Assets* (Economic Studies at Brookings, 2019).
80 A. Blandin et al., *Global Cryptoasset Regulatory Landscape Study* (Cambridge: Cambridge Centre for Alternative Finance, 2019).
81 Patrick McCorry, Malte Möser and Syed Taha Ali, 'Why Preventing a Cryptocurrency Exchange Heist Isn't Good Enough' (2018) *Security Protocols Workshop* 3.

on a public chain network there is no copy of the password and no trusted third party to safeguard private keys. This is a particular risk for unstable coin systems on the public chain network.

Unstable coin systems

In unstable coin systems on the public chain, loss is a major risk to users. This is especially the case for users who do not have great IT knowledge and find it difficult to recover lost assets on the public chain network. The way to mitigate this risk is to keep assets secure in an offline wallet provided by a third party, such as a cryptocurrency exchange. A digital wallet is an electronic system that stores users' payment information and passwords for a number of payment methods. With such wallets, users can complete purchases with computers or smartphones. There are several types of wallet that can manage the risk of loss: online digital wallets, desktop wallets, mobile wallets, paper wallets and hardware wallets. Online digital wallets operate on cloud technology and their providers are responsible for storing private keys. This kind of wallet can be hacked as happened when more than 25,000 Bitcoins were stolen in 2011. A desktop wallet is installed on a user's personal computer or laptop and is often referred to as an offline or cold wallet. The risk of hacking with desktop wallets is less than with online digital wallets but they do not give users the option of access when they do not have physical access to their PC or laptop.

When a digital wallet provides payment or asset custody services to users, the UK Payment Services Regulations of 2017 (PSR) could apply. PSR regulates payment services in the operation of payment accounts such as cash deposits and withdrawals from current accounts, execution of payment transactions, card issuing, merchant acquisition and money remittance.[82] If digital wallets also provided such payment services to their users, their software programmes could be classified as regulated payment services under the PSR. Yet the UK Financial Conduct Authority has stated that the use of crypto-assets is not covered by PSR because cryptocurrencies are not "banknotes and coins, scriptural money and electronic money."[83] In future, digital wallet services ought to be included within the remit of PSR.

Stable coin systems

In a stable coin system on the private chain network, wallets could be provided by the nodes in the network who can keep a copy of private keys so when they are lost, users can reclaim them. However, this would mean that users would lose their anonymity, and there is a risk of violating individual privacy and data

---

82 International Finance Corporation, 'Blockchain in Financial Services in Emerging Markets' (World Bank Group, 2017).
83 FCA, 'Guidance on Crypto-Assets' on 23 January 2019, 30.

protection rights because when a third party holds passwords to the system, hackers might obtain them. Once a hacker knows the system password, stable coins can be converted to a fiat currency or another cryptocurrency. In this situation, it would be difficult to trace assets once the transaction leaves the network. To make transactions traceable, the law should require networks to process transactions only with a regulated entity or network.

State-backed cryptocurrency systems

In a state-backed cryptocurrency system, it may be difficult for users to conceal their activity, especially if the system is centrally maintained and controlled because the state can view all the transactions on the network. If an account has been hacked and an amount of cryptocurrency moved to another account, it would be easy for law enforcement agencies to identify the accounts and the perpetrators involved in the theft. If retail banks were to join the network and provide account services for retail users, it would be similarly easy for them to identify the footprints of theft. However, when assets are stolen and then converted to another cryptocurrency on a different network which the law enforcement agencies have no control over, traceability is lost. For instance, if a criminal hacked into a system and moved an asset from a victim's account to a different account and, before the victim realised it, then converted the asset to Bitcoin through a regulated exchange, it would be difficult to identify the original owner since Bitcoin is an anonymous network.

Recommendations

Value maintenance

As discussed, value stability of a cryptocurrency is vital for users especially when the aim is to enhance access to finance. Financial instability contributes to users' reluctance to use cryptocurrency. Regulating the sector could promote value stability to protect users, and regulators may need to provide a clear legal status for cryptocurrency and regulate it accordingly.[84] As well as giving legal certainty, regulators should learn lessons from other markets about what affects value stability; much can be learnt from the way behaviour in the currencies and derivatives markets affects value stability.

Market integrity

Market integrity depends on the legality and legitimacy of a system and directly affects users' confidence. Even when a system is functional and effective, if it is

---

84 Hossein Nabilou, 'How to Regulate Bitcoin? Decentralized Regulation for a Decentralized Cryptocurrency' (2019) 27(3) *International Journal of Law and Information Technology* 271.

used for illegal purposes, users' confidence will be reduced. If a financial system is merely a space for speculation, users will not have confidence in it as a safe environment for investment, especially long-term investment. This is why insider dealing and market manipulation are criminalised, even if aspects of them might be seen as victimless behaviour and there is no evidence that they harm the overall functioning of the market. Even when trades such as arms trades are legitimate, moral justification must be established for the market to have a long-term confidence in them. Global arms trade markets are highly regulated in order to gain societal acceptance. Similarly, cryptocurrency markets have suffered from their use by criminals in drug trading, money laundering and tax evasion. These illegal and illicit activities have tainted the cryptocurrency market and threaten its legitimacy.[85] They also invite regulatory intervention that can defeat a cryptocurrency system's aim to provide better access to finance. It is true that all three types of cryptocurrency system, just like other financial systems, can act as intermediaries in facilitating crime. Some argue that transparency and immutability in a cryptocurrency system can record the digital footprints of criminal activity and lead to more effective detection and investigation. In this way, cryptocurrency systems can operate as legal technology to enhance market integrity. However, unstable coin systems on the public chain produce a major risk to market integrity so network participants must design protocols that prohibit criminal activity and make detection and investigation easier if the system is to be recognised as a legitimate space. It might be that participants' public and private keys should be forfeited if they engage in criminal activity. The network may need to work in partnership with law enforcement agencies to address market integrity issues.

Consumer protection and fairness in trade

Along with value stability, consumers need to be protected against manipulative behaviour in investment and trade when using cryptocurrency as a means of payment. Better financial education should be provided for consumers who purchase investments directly from cryptocurrency exchanges. Exchanges may need to be required to provide extra layers of protection, such as an entry knowledge test, and if investment advice is given, exchanges should assume a higher duty of care. When consumers use exchanges to trade, the law must provide clarity about terms in sales contracts that can be imposed under the current law. For example, the UK Sale of Goods Act 1979 only applies to a trade when payment is made in cash but not when it is a barter contract. There is also a potential risk that using cryptocurrency exchanges may alter consumer behaviour so that users become more like traders who engage in speculative activities to take advantage of price arbitrage. Trades on digital platforms are becoming more peer-to-peer, so both contracting parties may be consumers when they engage in a hire-purchase agreement and

---

85 Samantha Douma, 'Bitcoin: The Pros and Cons of Regulation' (2016) Universiteit Leiden 13; Joe Mont, 'Very Real Regulations Issued on Virtual Currencies' (2013) 10(112) *Compliance Week.*

one consumer can purchase goods while the other consumer (the counter party) provides the finance.

Security against theft

Clarifying the relevance of property law to cryptocurrency exchanges is essential when theft takes place on the network since property law needs to be infringed before enforcement agencies can launch an investigation or the court can provide remedies for victims such as re-vestment of property to its owner or issuing an injunction against a third party. There is also an important policy choice to be made here between anonymity and security. In an unstable coin system such as Bitcoin, there is an emphasis on individuals taking responsibility to safeguard their own assets. Sophisticated IT users may be more able to do so than those who have less IT knowledge. Regulated exchanges with digital wallet custodian services can provide security against theft but they may be unpopular with users unwilling to trade off their privacy rights against property security. When the state acts as a trusted third party for financial stability, digital money substantially enhances financial security for savers and the cashless world has increased security against petty theft. What cryptocurrencies such as Bitcoin offer is to replace the role of the state in these functions. Institutions such as cryptocurrency exchanges can offer retail services for protection against theft, yet paradoxically, their wallets also increase the opportunity of theft through hacking.

Further research is needed to understand participants' incentives in using cryptocurrency as an investment and a means of payment. There may be a need to see cryptocurrencies like Bitcoin not just as an instrument, a currency, a commodity, a digital payment service or a tokenised product, but as a system and an organisation. Bitcoin may be more than a remittance system but instead a decentralised autonomous organisation (DAO) that enables its stakeholders to fulfil their projects.[86] Bitcoin is currently subject to volatility because there is an uncertainty about it and there is an alternative system in the US dollar-based economy. When the Bitcoin system itself becomes an economy, there may be less need to focus on the value of its currency. But until that day comes, the problem is how to use the currency to stabilise the economy on this "Crypto-Republic." For instance, more products and services might be offered but there may not be enough coins available to match them. There might also be a case where there is a need to produce more coins in order to maintain consumer trust in the system, equivalent to the use of quantitative easing by some central banks. The question is who should have the ability to decide to make such changes designed to stabilise the economy and create confidence?

86 Y. Y. Hsieh, J. P. Vergne, P. Anderson et al. 'Bitcoin and the Rise of Decentralized Autonomous Organizations' (2018) 7(14) *Journal of Organization Design.* https://doi.org/10.1186/s41469-018 -0038-1.

The law does not yet recognise cryptocurrency as legal tender for trading or in sale of goods contracts, but this is an issue of policy rather than of law. Should it decide to, the state could recognise cryptocurrency as legal money and as a *sui generis* property. What is more problematic is how to maintain consumer confidence in the DAO economy if there are alternative systems in competition such as Euro-based or Dollar-based economies. This situation creates an arbitrage market and consumers may not have the know-how to hedge against the associated risks. More sophisticated players can exploit the opportunities in trade financing, but ordinary consumers or less sophisticated traders may suffer from pricing arbitrage.

Security against theft is less of a problem in the DAO system, but more problematic when a system that is not based on the blockchain participates in the network because it opens up opportunities for attack. For instance, a cold wallet that is not on the blockchain can be hacked and information altered. However, participating directly in the Bitcoin system to keep one's own property secure is not the same as keeping money in a physical wallet. A level of IT knowledge is required for users to keep their assets secure in a cold wallet that is maintained by third parties. There may be other technological solutions to ensure that individuals have secure access to their own assets without the need for a trusted third party. Hence, it is submitted that DAOs need to develop a new model and system to ensure that individuals have both autonomy and control over their assets. Further issues arise here when the state needs to have access to property, for example if it needs to freeze an individual's accounts and assets.

Conclusion

This chapter has discussed the use of cryptocurrency as an instrument for enhancing access to finance: as an investment and also as a means of payment. Three types of cryptocurrency systems are considered for their ability to promote access to finance: unstable coin systems such as Bitcoin, stable coin systems such as Facebook's Diem and state-backed coin systems. There are four regulatory objectives to ensure users' access to finance: value stability, market integrity, consumer protection and fairness in trade, and security against theft. These four objectives are useful in designing new technology and when considering future policy developments for the government of cryptocurrency systems.

6 Security token offering (STO) and investor protection

Introduction

This chapter investigates the legal and regulatory issues relating to security token offering (STO), a regulated form of initial coin offering (ICO).[1] A security token is a type of crypto-asset which is a cryptographically secured digital representation of contractual rights that uses distributed ledger technology (DLT) and can be transferred, stored or traded electronically.[2] ICO is a digital way of raising funds from the public using a crypto-asset, such as cryptocurrency, tokens representing shares in a firm, prepayment vouchers for future services or in some cases an offer of no discernible value.[3] After issuance, crypto-assets may be resold to others in a secondary market on digital exchanges or other platforms. With these features, ICO has been regarded as a financing mechanism similar to initial public offering (IPO) in which companies or firms issue shares to the investing public.[4] Despite burgeoning ICO activities, the ICO space has not received wide and positive support from the UK regulators, and as a result, many ICOs are not conducted in a regulated or organised market that is recognised by the law.[5] One of the reasons for this is that the legal nature of many ICO tokens cannot be securely defined in law,[6] and this causes difficulties in regulating the relationships between the token

---

1 World Bank and CCAF, 'Regulating Alternative Finance: Results from a Global Regulator Survey' (2019) www.jbs.cam.ac.uk/faculty-research/centres/alternative-finance/publications/regulating-alternative-finance/. Accessed 12 November 2020.
2 FCA, 'Distributed Ledger Technology to Define Potential Benefits and Challenges of the Underlying Technology that Facilitates ICOs' (2017) www.fca.org.uk/publication/discussion/dp17-03.pdf. Accessed 12 November 2020.
3 OECD, 'Initial Coin Offerings (ICOs) for SME Financing' (2019) www.oecd.org/finance/initial-coin-offerings-for-sme-financing.htm. Accessed 12 November 2020.
4 Securities and Markets Stakeholder Group, 'Advice to ESMA: Own Initiative Report on Initial Coin Offerings and Crypto-Assets' (2018) www.esma.europa.eu/sites/default/files/library/esma22-106-1338_smsg_advice_-_report_on_icos_and_crypto-assets.pdf. Accessed 12 November 2020.
5 FCA, 'Customer Warning about the Risks of Initial Coin Offerings' (2019) www.fca.org.uk/news/statements/initial-coin-offerings. Accessed 12 November 2020.
6 UK Jurisdiction Taskforce, 'Legal Statement on Cryptoassets and Smart Contracts' (2019). https://technation.io/about-us/lawtech-panel. Accessed 12 November 2020.

DOI: 10.4324/9780429023613-6

holders and issuers,[7] and in setting the regulatory parameters for their conduct with respect to ICO activities such as whether a prospectus is required or whether a white paper qualifies as a prospectus.[8] STO is a more legally secured ICO in that the security, which is legally defined, is digitally tokenised and is capable of being offered and issued to investors on the blockchain.[9] The law needs to provide the bedrock on which the STO market can build investor confidence and financial innovation, and thus increase access to the financial market.[10] Consequently, we need to know what benefits STO can bring, what safeguards are in place to ensure the STO market's safety and integrity, and what protection can be given to participants, especially token holders. To this end, I will assess whether the current securities law, which was designed for an IPO,[11] is suitable for an STO, and identify any deficiencies for the STO market. This discussion will be followed by an analysis of the protection of token holders within an organisation, using current UK company law as a framework to demonstrate the possible risk of harm to token holders posed by management and other controlling powers. In doing so, I will propose ways in which the law can maintain token holders' autonomy in negotiating the terms of their contracts, can reduce transaction costs and can mitigate other negative features. I will also reassess the monetary value of the tokens and the governance rights of token holders in the context of data economy and propose a new approach to this from the perspective of both securities and company law.

Recognising a security token as a financial instrument in law

Security tokens, as a type of crypto-asset, represent underlying assets such as shares, bonds (debt), commodities, units of investment and rights to deal in those assets, such as options and futures.[12] They may be issued by entities such as companies or firms, but also by an individual or an association of individuals or entities.[13] If security tokens were treated as securities,[14] it would bring them into the

---

7 Dirk Zetzsche et al., 'The ICO Gold Rush: It's a Scam, It's a Bubble, It's a Super Challenge for Regulators' (2019) 63(3) *Harvard International Law Journal* 267–315.
8 Hui Deng et al., 'The Regulation of Initial Coin Offerings in China: Problems, Prognoses and Prospectus' (2018) 19 *European Business Organization Law Review* 465–502.
9 FCA, 'Guidance on Cryptoassets: Feedback and Final Guidance to CP 19/3' (2019). www.fca.org.uk/publication/policy/ps19-22.pdf. Accessed 12 November 2020.
10 Shaanan Cohney et al., 'Coin-Operated Capitalism' (2019) 119(3) *Columbia Law Review* 591–676.
11 Moran Ofir and Ido Sadeh, 'ICO vs. IPO: Empirical Findings, Information Asymmetry, and the Appropriate Regulatory Framework' (2020) 53(2) *Vanderbilt Journal of Transnational Law* 525–614.
12 Deloitte, 'Are Token Assets the Securities of Tomorrow?' (2019) www2.deloitte.com/content/dam/Deloitte/lu/Documents/technology/lu-token-assets-securities-tomorrow.pdf. Accessed 08 July 2020.
13 Ibid.
14 Michaal Mendelson, 'From Initial Coin Offerings to Security Tokens: A U.S. Federal Securities Law Analysis' (2019) 22 *Stanford Technology Law Review* 1.

current legal and regulatory framework, and securities law would apply to the whole security trading cycle: issuing, trading, clearing and settlement.[15] The current securities law covers the entire operation of the securities market; it recognises primary and secondary markets, and divides market players into infrastructure providers, issuers, intermediaries, institutional and retail investors, domestic and foreign participants.[16] Securities law broadly divides into the prudential aspect of regulation with a focus on systemic risk issues, and the conduct aspect with a focus on market integrity, investor protection, consumer protection and market competitiveness.[17] In the UK, security tokens representing transferable securities or other financial instruments[18] are securities under the EU's Markets in Financial Instruments Directive II (MiFID II).

Can IPO market conduct rules be used as a template?

Prospectus regime

The UK Financial Conduct Authority (FCA) has issued a stark warning about the risks of ICOs because of the opaque process of this funding method.[19] Lack of governance and transparency in such an unregulated space affect investors' rights with respect to cash flow, liquidity and governance. What ICOs do not have, if they are to meet the same level of governance as IPOs, are: a prospectus issued for investors to make informed judgements about the issuers;[20] intermediaries to help issuers comply with the rules for safeguarding market integrity and safety;[21] and public and private enforcement proceedings available to sanction market participants and to provide redress to investors. Furthermore, there is no market surveillance infrastructure to ensure market integrity or investor protection against insider dealing and market manipulation.[22] For an STO market to develop suc-

---

15 Randy Priem, 'Distributed Ledger Technology for Securities Clearing and Settlement: Benefits, Risks, and Regulatory Implications' (2020) 6(11) *Financial Innovation* 1–25.
16 Baker McKenzie, 'Global Financial Services Regulatory Guide' (2016) www.bakermckenzie.com/-/media/files/insight/publications/2016/07/guide_global_fsrguide_2017.pdf?la=en. Accessed 07 July 2020.
17 FCA, 'Guidance on Cryptoassets' (2019) www.fca.org.uk/publications/consultation-papers/cp19-3-guidance-cryptoassets. Accessed 12 November 2020.
18 The Financial Services and Markets Act 2000 (Regulated Activities) Order 2001 (RAO) specifies that types of activities and investments for the purpose of clarifying the scope of the Financial Services and Markets Act 2000 (FSMA).
19 FCA, 'Consumer Warning about the Risks of ICOs' (2017) www.fca.org.uk/news/statements/initial-coin-offerings; FCA, 'Distributed Ledger Technology' (2017) www.fca.org.uk/publication/discussion/dp17-03.pdf. Accessed 12 November 2020.
20 The Prospectus Directive (PD) [2010] OJ L 327/1.
21 Markets in Financial Instruments Directive (MiFID II) [2014] OJ L 173/349; Alternative Investment Fund Managers and Amending Directives (AIFMD) [2011] OJ L 174/1.
22 FCA, 'Guidance on Cryptoassets' on 23 January 2019, p. 13. www.fca.org.uk/publications/consultation-papers/cp19-3-guidance-cryptoassets; The Fourth Anti-Money Laundering Directive [2015] OJ L 141/73.

cessfully, measures must be in place to prevent it becoming a fraudulent space where criminals can exploit investors through its opaqueness,[23] easy access to unsophisticated consumers, market volatility and lack of a regulatory and legal enforcement mechanism at domestic and cross-border levels.[24] Hence, to avoid the mistakes learnt from the ICO market, the STO market should not rely on the unregulated, unstandardised and unverified "white paper" system used in the ICO[25] as a way to show party autonomy, to demonstrate a more economical way to secure transparency or as a basis for a self-governing mechanism.

STOs have now been brought under the current legal and regulatory framework that applies to IPOs. Section 19 of the Financial Services and Markets Act (FSMA) 2000 provides that no person may carry on a regulated financial services activity in the UK unless they are authorised or exempt. Section 21 of FSMA 2000 further specifies that a person must not, in the course of business, communicate an invitation or inducement to engage in investment activity. Section 85 of FSMA 2000 also makes it a crime to offer transferable securities to the public in the UK or to request that they be admitted to trading on a regulated market situated or operating in the UK, unless an approved prospectus has been made available to the public before the offer. Hence, an STO is required to comply with the FCA Handbook's Prospectus Rules, Disclosure and Transparency Rules, and Listing Rules. An STO issuer is required to produce a prospectus that provides the necessary information to enable investors to make an informed judgement. Depending on the market segment that the STO falls into, different rules become relevant on the appointment of financial sponsors to guide the issuers[26] as well as for accounting[27] and codes of practice.[28]

Regulating the intermediaries

Issuers can also decide the method of offering an STO, which can be by direct subscription without intermediaries, or through intermediaries. It can also target

---

23 Alexander Torpey and Andrew Solomon, 'Tokenisation 2019: The Security Token Year Review' (2019) www.kingsleynapley.co.uk/insights/blogs/crypto-assets-blog/tokenisation-in-2019-the -security-token-year-in-review. Accessed 12 November 2020.

24 FCA, 'Guidance on Cryptoassets: Consultation Paper CP19/3' (2019) www.fca.org.uk/publication /consultation/cp19-03.pdf. Accessed 12 November 2020.

25 Paul Sinclair and Aaron Taylor, 'The English Law Rights of Investors in Initial Coin Offerings' (2018) 4 *Journal of International Banking and Financial Law* 214, 216.

26 FCA, 'The Sponsor Regime' (2020) www.fca.org.uk/markets/primary-markets/sponsor-regime. Accessed 12 November 2020.

27 Regulation (EC) 1606/2002 of the European Parliament and of the Council of 19 July 2002 on the application of international accounting standards.

28 Financial Reporting Council, 'Corporate Governance Code' (2018) www.frc.org.uk/getattachment /88bd8c45-50ea-4841-95b0-d2f4f48069a2/2018-UK-Corporate-Governance-Code-FINAL.pdf. Accessed 12 November 2020.

particular types of investor such as professional investors.[29] When an STO aims to access retail investors directly without the involvement of intermediaries,[30] it is similar to a direct listing on the exchange.[31] But if it is not offered directly, an STO would need to rely on financial intermediaries to connect with the investing public. This process can involve institutional investors who gauge investors' interest in the STO through market sounding.[32] A number of rules designed to protect market integrity through a wall-crossing regime apply to institutional investors.[33] Under the Market Abuse Regulation,[34] any investors who are wall-crossed are prohibited from dealing in the securities of the issuer, including their relevant securities (share, debt and other derivatives) currently traded on the regulated markets.[35]

One of the advantages of using STO on the blockchain is pricing transparency during the securities allocation.[36] This provides information necessary for end-investors to assess the reasonableness of the price paid for the tokens and the fees charged by their asset managers or broker-dealers.[37] Whether or not this function of transparency is used depends on the extent to which it reduces market competitiveness and on the willingness of financial intermediaries to underwrite the risks of the sale. It is also unclear if it is necessary to have market-makers in the STO's secondary market to provide liquidity. If the STO's secondary market is to be conducted by the end-investors themselves (probably retail investors), broker-dealers may become redundant in this supply chain. There may be a need for asset management to continue using security tokens in their structured investment portfolios

29 Partner Vine, 'LSE's Definition of Professional Investors under MiFID II' (2020) www.partnervine.com/blog/professional-investors-under-mifid. Accessed 12 November 2020.
30 David Donald, 'From Block Lords to Blockchain: How Securities Dealers Make Markets' (2018) 44 *Journal of Corporation Law* 29.
31 MemeryCrystal, 'Direct Listings – A Viable Alternative to the Traditional IPO?' (2018) www.memerycrystal.com/articles/direct-listings-viable-alternative-traditional-ipo/. Accessed 12 November 2020.
32 FCA, 'Market Abuse Regulation' (2020) www.fca.org.uk/markets/market-abuse/regulation. Accessed 12 November 2020.
33 FCA, 'Asset Management Firms and the Risk of Market Abuse' (2015) www.fca.org.uk/publications/thematic-reviews/tr15-1-asset-management-firms-and-risk-market-abuse. Accessed 12 November 2020.
34 FCA, 'Market Abuse Regulation' (2020) www.fca.org.uk/markets/market-abuse/regulation. Accessed 12 November 2020; FCA, 'Market Watch 63: Newsletter on Market Conduct and Transaction Reporting Issues' (2020) www.fca.org.uk/publication/newsletters/market-watch-63.pdf. Accessed 12 November 2020.
35 Norton Rose Fulbright, 'The Market Abuse Regulation: Key Considerations for UK Listed Issuers' (2016) www.nortonrosefulbright.com/en-gb/knowledge/publications/8d352a18/the-market-abuse-regulation-key-considerations-for-uk-listed-issuers. Accessed 12 November 2020.
36 FCA, 'Quid pro quo? What Factors Influence IPO Allocations to Investors?' (2016) www.fca.org.uk/publication/occasional-papers/occasional-paper-15.pdf. Accessed 12 November 2020.
37 Norton Rose Fulbright, 'MiFID II/MiFIR Series: Transparency and Reporting Obligations' (2014) www.nortonrosefulbright.com/en/knowledge/publications/abde0e6a/mifid-ii-mifir-series. Accessed 12 November 2020.

and if so, both the EU MiFIDII[38] and AIFMD[39] regimes would apply. Asset management funds would need to deposit security tokens with custodian banks to comply with client asset segregation rules (CASS).[40] A digital wallet provider or a digital exchange could act as a bank custodian and they would then need FCA registration for the money laundering law and to be authorised to conduct investment activities.[41] If they became significant within the system, they would also need to be approved and regulated by the Prudential Regulation Authority (PRA) of the Bank of England.[42] Since there may be no need for tokens to be cleared centrally, rules under EMIR may not be applicable.[43] Nevertheless, as tokens would be settled on the private blockchain, many provisions under CSDR would still need to be observed and the UK senior manager's regime would apply to key individuals within the asset management firms.[44] Under the FCA's new rules, asset managers are prohibited from offering derivatives of security tokens to retail clients.[45]

A professional investor market

A separate law and regulation has been designed for the professional investor market which does not provide access to retail investors. As a result, the disclosure requirement can be streamlined as in the Global Depository Receipts' professional investor market[46] and the London Stock Exchange's alternative investment market (AIM).[47] If AIM is to accommodate an STO market in which only professional investors are allowed to participate, the FCA's listing rules would not apply. Instead, AIM's rules would apply with the London Stock Exchange acting

38 Directive 2014/65/EU of the European Parliament and of the Council of 15 May 2014 on markets in financial instruments.
39 Directive 2011/61/EU of the European Parliament and of the Council of 8 June 2011 on Alternative Investment Fund Managers.
40 FCA Handbook: CASS 7.13: Segregation of Client Money.
41 FCA, 'The Money Laundering, Terrorist Financing and Transfer of Funds (Information on the Payer)' (2017) www.fca.org.uk/firms/financial-crime/cryptoassets-aml-ctf-regime. Accessed 12 November 2020.
42 Therese Chambers, 'Unstable Coins: Cryptoassets, Financial Regulation and Preventing Financial Crime in the Emerging Market for Digital Assets' (2020) www.fca.org.uk/news/speeches/unstable-coins. Accessed 12 November 2020.
43 Regulation (EU) No 648/2012 on OTC derivatives, central counterparties and trade repositories.
44 Regulation (EU) No 909/2014 of the European Parliament and of the Council of 23 July 2014 on improving securities settlement in the European Union and on central securities depositories; Deloitte (2019) Are Token Assets the Securities of Tomorrow? www2.deloitte.com/content/dam/Deloitte/lu/Documents/technology/lu-token-assets-securities-tomorrow.pdf. Accessed 12 November 2020.
45 PS20/10: Prohibiting the sale to retail clients of investment products that reference crypto-assets.
46 London Stock Exchange, 'Depositary Receipts: Guide to Depositary Receipts on London Stock Exchange' (2020) https://docs.londonstockexchange.com/sites/default/files/documents/dr-guide.pdf. Accessed 12 November 2020.
47 London Stock Exchange Group, 'Being an AIM' (2020) www.lseg.com/areas-expertise/our-markets/london-stock-exchange/equities-markets/raising-equity-finance/aim/being. Accessed 12 November 2020.

as the UK listing authority.[48] But this would limit the ability of the STO market to reach retail investors.

Using company law as a framework to identify the risks of STO

In addition to securities law, company law governs the internal affairs of a corporate organisation.[49] The major issues arising are: capital maintenance for investor protection, particularly minority shareholders and outside creditors, governance of the organisation such as the decision-making process and the right to obtain redress, re-organisation and dissolution of the organisation and dispute resolution.[50] Modern company law accommodates various types of company, from closely-held to publicly-listed companies. Specific regimes have been created within the company law framework to service companies with different objectives and functions.[51] The aim is to ensure, on the one hand, that capital can continue to be aggregated efficiently through the collective effort of promoters, directors, shareholders, employees and creditors, and, on the other hand, that benefits can be shared equitably among them.[52] New methods, processes, and markets, have been developed to facilitate the aggregation of capital, including private placement,[53] direct listing,[54] initial public offering,[55] private equity[56] and the newly emerged security token offering (STO).[57] To ensure that benefits are shared equitably, vari-

48 London Stock Exchange, 'AIM Rules for Companies' (2018) https://docs.londonstockexchange .com/sites/default/files/documents/aim-rules-for-companies-march-2018.pdf. Accessed 12 November 2020.

49 Deborah DeMott, 'Perspectives on Choice of Law for Corporate Internal Affairs' (1985) 48 *Law and Contemporary Problems* 161–198.

50 Neal Watson and Beliz McKenzie, 'Shareholders' Right in Private and Public Companies in the UK (England and Wales)' (2019) https://uk.practicallaw.thomsonreuters.com/5-613-3685?transitionType=Default&contextData=(sc.Default)&firstPage=true. Accessed 07 Jul 2020.

51 Harvard Law School Forum on Corporate Governance, (2016) 'Principles of Corporate Governance'. https://corpgov.law.harvard.edu/2016/09/08/principles-of-corporate-governance/. Accessed 07 Jul 2020.

52 Paul Davies, 'The Board of Directors: Composition, Structure, Duties and Powers' (2000) (Company Law Reform in OECD Countries: A Comparative Outlook of Current Trends).

53 Andrew Baum, 'The Future of Real Estate Initiative' (2020) www.sbs.ox.ac.uk/sites/default/files /2020-01/Tokenisation%20Report.pdf. Accessed 07 Jul 2020.

54 Ran Ben-Tzur and James Evans, 'The Rise of Direct Listings: Understanding the Trend, Separating Fact from Fiction' (2019) https://ncfacanada.org/the-rise-of-direct-listings-understanding-the -trend-separating-fact-from-fiction/. Accessed 07 Jul 2020.

55 Ryan Zullo, 'Can Tokenisation Fix the Secondary IPO Market?' (2020) www.eisneramper.com/ tokenization-secondary-ipo-catalyst-0420/. Accessed 07 Jul 2020.

56 'The Tokenisation of Financial Market Securities – What's Next?', (in Research Report by Greenwich Associates: 'Security Tokens: Cryptonite for Stock Certificates' (2019)) www.r3.com/wp -content/uploads/2019/10/R3.Tokenization.Financial.Market.Securities.Oct2019.pdf. Accessed 07 Jul 2020.

57 Deloitte, 'Are Token Assets the Securities of Tomorrow?' (2019) www2.deloitte.com/content/ dam/Deloitte/lu/Documents/technology/lu-token-assets-securities-tomorrow.pdf. Accessed 07 Jul 2020.

ous mechanisms have been introduced such as minority shareholder protection in closely-held companies, or corporate governance of listed and quoted companies. As well as these mechanisms, the takeover market has been developed as a way to monitor corporate performance rather than as a way to share the benefits of a company, mainly through the sale of the control premium to bidders.[58]

Including security tokens under the company law framework poses a manageable legal risk of uncertainty, but the problem is whether it would defeat the prime purpose of issuing asset tokens,[59] namely to ensure efficient capital aggregation and equitable sharing of benefits. In many STO projects, security tokens are offered on the open market to anyone who can access the internet; issue and purchase do not need the traditional financial intermediaries.[60] However, under the current company law framework, only certain companies can issue securities to the general public,[61] needing, for example, a clean three-year trading record.[62] Furthermore, the corporate governance rules in company law and the Corporate Governance Code place additional requirements on issuers who are often not able to afford the expense of governance services such as legal, compliance and auditing costs.[63] Although "code-as-law" seems to be able to mitigate some of these costs through automation,[64] many areas would still require human intervention, especially where cognitive judgement is required to interpret rules that are based on policy objectives, or where there are different acts to be balanced against one another.[65] The reason that STO is attractive to legitimate businesses is its ability to reach the entire internet community without infrastructure obstacles or national boundaries.[66] Bringing them under the current company law framework would compromise this benefit. As an example, the US's Howey test when applied

58 David Kershaw, *Principles of Takeover Regulation* (1st edn, Oxford University Press 2018) 44.
59 'Initial Coin Offerings: Issues of Legal Uncertainty Report' (2019) www.comsuregroup.com/ news/initial-coin-offerings-issues-of-legal-uncertainty-report-initial-coin-offerings-30-july-2019/. Accessed 09 Jul 2020; Ross Buckley et al., 'TechRisk' (2020) 1 *Singapore Journal of Legal Studies* 35.
60 Jovan Ilic, 'Security Token Offerings: What are They, and where are They Going in 2019?' (2019) https://medium.com/mvp-workshop/security-token-offerings-sto-what-are-they-and-where-are -they-going-in-2019-cc075aea6313. Accessed 07 Jul 2020.
61 Section 755 of Companies Act 2006 provides that 'a private company limited by shares or limited by guarantee and having a share capital must not; (a) offer to the public any securities of the company, or (b) allot or agree to allot any securities of the company with a view to their being offered to the public.'
62 Listing Rules 6.3.1R, FCA.
63 OECD, 'Risk Management and Corporate Governance' (2014) www.oecd.org/daf/ca/risk-management-corporate-governance.pdf. Accessed 07 July 2020.
64 Gabrielle Patrick and Anurag Bana 'Rule of Law Versus Rule of Code: A Blockchain-Driven Legal World' (IBA Legal Policy & Research Unit Legal Paper 2017).
65 Smart Contract Alliance, 'Smart Contracts: Is the Law Ready?' (2018) https://lowellmilkenins titute.law.ucla.edu/wp-content/uploads/2018/08/Smart-Contracts-Whitepaper.pdf. Accessed 07 July 2020.
66 Deloitte, 'Are Token Assets the Securities of Tomorrow?' (2019) www2.deloitte.com/content/dam/ Deloitte/lu/Documents/technology/lu-token-assets-securities-tomorrow.pdf. Accessed 07 July 2020.

to DAO (an STO project)[67] hinders development in security token finance, and encourages underground STO markets.[68] While many countries have created a specific legal and regulatory regime for STO and have provided trading platforms for the investment community, none has been successful.

Par value and no-discount rule

Under the UK Companies Act 2006, each share must have a face value, the so-called par value.[69] A share cannot be issued below its face value and cannot be issued at a discount. This no-discount rule is to ensure that both shareholders and creditors are protected as capital providers.[70] The amount raised must be kept in a separate account and be treated as capital in the balance sheet.

In an STO, a token can be issued without a face value and its value is determined purely through negotiation between the parties in the market i.e. the issuer of the token and the buyer. The capital raised, whether cash or another type of cryptocurrency or crypto-asset, does not need to be put in a special account or to be treated as a non-distributable asset. This substantially reduces the protection offered to shareholders or creditors when a business becomes insolvent and there is no reserve available to investors.[71] Without this protection, any capital raised can also be more easily returned to the investors, thus creating a major risk of asset stripping. As there is no value attached to tokens and repurchase can be through a one-to-one negotiation, the repurchase price can be higher than the issuing price, at the expense of other investors. There are jurisdictions, e.g. Delaware in the US, that do not require par value on a share,[72] but in this case shareholders are protected by stronger statutory claims against boards of directors.[73] As will be discussed later, there are no clear legal claims, procedures or appropriate forums for token holders to hold the agents of an organisation legally accountable.[74] Par value and the no-discount rule reduce the likelihood of management malpractice, reduce agency costs and provide a benchmark for other safeguards on capital maintenance and investor protection.

---

67 *SEC v W.J. Howey Co* 328 U.S. 293 (1946).
68 Lennart Ante and Ingo Fiedler, 'Cheap Signals in Security Token Offerings' (Blockchain Research Lab Working Paper Series No 1, 2019) www.blockchainresearchlab.org/wp-content/uploads/2019/07/Cheap-Signals-in-Security-Token-Offerings-BRL-Series-No.-1-update3.pdf. Accessed 07 July 2020.
69 Section 540, Chapter 1 of Companies Act 2006.
70 Section 580, Chapter 1 of Companies Act 2006.
71 OECD, 'Initial Coin Offerings (ICOs) for SME Financing' (2019) www.oecd.org/finance/initial-coin-offerings-for-sme-financing.htm. Accessed 12 November 2020.
72 James Bonbright, 'The Danger of Shares Without Par Value' (1924) 24(5) *Columbia Law Review* 449–468.
73 Peter Atkins et al., 'Directors' Fiduciary Duties: Back to Delaware Law Basics' (2020) www.skadden.com/insights/publications/2020/02/directors-fiduciary-duties. Accessed 12 November 2020.
74 Nevena Jevremovic, '2018 In Review: Blockchain Technology and Arbitration' (2019) Kluwer Arbitration Blog. http://arbitrationblog.kluwerarbitration.com/2019/01/27/2018-in-review-blockchain-technology-and-arbitration/. Accessed 12 November 2020.

Valid consideration for the token's issues

The UK Companies Act 2006 also provides detailed rules on the considerations for shares issued by the companies.[75] For public companies, shares must be paid for with cash, while non-cash consideration, such as contract performance, must be evaluated and certified by auditors.[76]

In an STO, the organisation may argue that it is not a public company so the rules on consideration do not apply. It may argue that cryptocurrency is a cash consideration, and hence require no further evaluation or certified report by auditors.[77] This increases the risk of fraud, market manipulation and misrepresentation in an STO. Investors could mistakenly believe that the process is transparent on the blockchain without knowing what is required of the issuers. Since the issuers can continue issuing more tokens on the blockchain, the participants could be misled into believing that the company has adequate assets, based on the capital raised through previous issuances. However, the participants cannot know whether the capital has been returned to the investors or whether the cash paid with a type of cryptocurrency such as Bitcoin (an unstable coin) is of the same value as the consideration requested for the new issuance. This can lead to unfair and unequal treatment among shareholders who should be able to bring a claim based on s 994 of the Unfair Prejudice claim. However, shareholders may encounter several problems in accessing the appropriate forum and its remedies. For the latter, since there is no benchmark provided for the consideration, the buyout right provided by s 996 (2)(e) CA 2006 is not adequate to address losses.

Allotment of tokens (s 517)

Directors need powers to allot shares when authorised by shareholders at a general meeting. In UK companies, these powers must be renewed every year. In addition to the requirement of shareholder authorisation, directors must use their power of allotment solely for proper purposes.[78]

These property rights mean that shareholders are protected against share dilution that can affect their control rights (voting rights and economic right to receiving dividends) and residual rights if the company becomes insolvent. In some cases, company directors may allot shares to friends or family members who will support management moves to introduce measures that harm other existing shareholders, notably by reducing majority shareholders' control in the general meeting, entrenching management's position or squeezing out minority shareholders.

---

75 Sections 593–597, Chapter 1 of Companies Act 2006.
76 Sections 580–592, Chapter 1 of Companies Act 2006.
77 Cristina Farras and Adria Salmeron 'From Barter to Cryptocurrency: A Brief History of Exchange' (2018) www.caixabankresearch.com/en/economics-markets/monetary-policy/barter-cryptocurrency-brief-history-exchange. Accessed 12 November 2020.
78 Bloomsbury Professional, 'Directors' Duties: Scope of the Proper Purpose Doctrine' (2015) https://law.bloomsburyprofessional.com/blog/directors-duties-scope-of-the-proper-purpose-doctrine. Accessed 12 November 2020.

Hence, the power to allot shares must be specifically authorised by the existing shareholders, must be renewed with specifically authorised conditions and must be exercised for a proper purpose that is subject to court scrutiny.

In an STO, businesses can issue tokens without these restrictions thus removing both the *ex ante* (shareholder authorisation) and *ex post* (court scrutiny) protection given to existing token holders. The business can issue tokens to specific persons or groups without existing token holders controlling the amount and timing of the issuance. Furthermore, the management can issue tokens merely to gain more support in the consensus voting structure or to increase the demand for an asset class such as the cryptocurrency that is the required consideration for the issuance of the tokens.

Token buyback

Under the UK Companies Act 2006, companies cannot buy back shares unless authorised to do so by the shareholders through a special resolution of a general meeting.[79]

These regulations make sure that there is no return of capital to shareholders and that companies do not use buyback to manipulate their market share price. There are also a number of safeguards in place against price manipulation and insider dealing in share buybacks that protect issuing companies, investors and the integrity of the market.

In an STO, the business can use buyback to return capital raised to investors. This can amount to unfair treatment of token holders who have not been offered the same chance to realise gains through the pre-emption right and it can also reduce the protection to creditors by decreasing the capital available to them if the business becomes insolvent. A buyback can also send the wrong signal to the market, especially to unsophisticated investors who may believe there is a demand for tokens issued by the business. A buyback programme can even be automated without adequate legal scrutiny of its procedures and purposes and, if its code is inaccessible to network participants, there is a real risk of fraud since funds raised by a new issuance can be used to buy back tokens of a previous issuance at no consideration or at a much reduced one.

Pre-emption right (s 561)

A further protection mechanism for existing shareholders is contained in section 561 of the UK Companies Act 2006. Before a company may allocate new shares, it must first offer shares on the same or more favourable terms to each shareholder who holds ordinary shares in the company, in an equivalent proportion to the shares already held in the company. Without such a right, shareholders' effective shareholding in the company would be reduced by the issue of the new

---

79 Sections 658–659, Chapter 1 of Companies Act 2006.

shares. The intention is to protect existing shareholders against dilution of their holdings.[80] Irrespective of any dilution of the asset substance, a capital increase can also reduce the chance of making a profit if the new shares do not lead to an increase in profit, and a profit that is the same or only slightly higher is distributed among more shareholders. This right gives existing shareholders priority in benefitting from the company's IPO through any subsequent sale in the secondary market to realise gains. Without such a right, investors would be less willing to take the initial risk involved in the early stages of the business. In addition, investors would have no *ex ante* protection against a deliberate dilution of their control rights in the company by the management.

In an STO, existing tokens do not have such a right to purchase newly issued tokens, either to take advantage of any demand for tokens in the secondary market or against a potential abuse of power by the management. However, the pre-emption right can increase the cost of finance, particularly when a company needs immediate finance to take up a business opportunity, and also that its application can be time-consuming and costly. This increases the investment costs and risks to the initial token holders. Hence, under UK law there is new guidance on how such a right can be disapplied for public companies, along with restrictions on the frequency of disapplication and the number of new tokens that can be issued.

Do the benefits of disapplying a pre-emption right in an STO outweigh any additional costs and risks to existing token holders that the right may incur?[81] A pre-emption right enhances business transparency and empowers token holders to scrutinise and challenge the rationale of the issuance, and to take advantage of it, if outside investors benefitted at the expense of existing shareholders. For this reason, a right of first refusal should also apply to an STO and this benefit would be lost if the right were to be disapplied. However, it would be possible to integrate pre-emption rights into a smart contract which could speed up the current procedure since it would not be necessary to contact all the existing shareholders within a time limit. This would make offering pre-emption rights to existing shareholders more efficient, cheaper and less time-consuming.

Voting right

One of the most important protection mechanisms for shareholders is their voting right because it involves them in important corporate decisions.[82] These rights significantly affect the value of the shares issued as well as the value of the company

---

80 Amal Awwad, 'Shareholders' Preemptive Rights in Listed and Closely Held Corporations and Shareholders' Protection Methods' (2013) https://papers.ssrn.com/sol3/papers.cfm?abstract_id =2739375. Accessed 12 November 2020.

81 Ibid.

82 As a right of membership, the right to vote forms an ancillary component of the membership and cannot be separated from it, Karsten Heider, *Münchener Kommentar zum Aktienrecht* (2019, 45th Edition, Verlag C.H. BECK München) § 12 Rn. 6.

and its corporate governance rating. A block of controlling shares is worth more than the aggregate of the fractional minority shares. When there is a transfer of corporate control, the purchaser needs, usually through negotiation, to pay for a control premium, rather than for the aggregate value of the number of shares based on the current market price of each share. This explains why bidders in a takeover incrementally purchase shares in the target in order to reduce the cost of the purchase.

However, in an ICO, voting rights may not be attached to the tokens, and if they are attached, they can be modified after issuance, with the knowledge and agreement of the token holders. It can happen that the "white paper" did not clearly state what voting rights could be exercised for, for example authorising a derivative claim, or how the rights are to be exercised and whether a quorum is required. The lack of rules poses a major risk to investors who can mistakenly believe that they have the same level of protection in an ICO as they do under current company law, and that the business they have invested in operates under the normal corporate governance framework. Token holders may not have the proper forum to challenge management decisions or the validity of decisions taken by consensus. Even if it is assumed that voting rights would be automated according to a pre-determined code,[83] there is also the possibility of faults in the design of the code and this means that token holders may wish to challenge the validity of decisions reached under the consensus rules.

Removal of management

The removal of directors is a corporate governance tool designed to ensure shareholder democracy and investor protection in a corporate business by giving shareholders the means to remove the management. The UK Companies Act 2006 provides a statutory regime through which shareholders can remove their board of directors.[84] For listed companies, further protection is given to shareholders by the requirement that the appointment of directors must be renewed annually.[85] This increases board accountability and reduces the agency costs incurred by mismanagement, board malpractice or illegal behaviour by the board.

An STO company needs clear rules on how its management can be held accountable and can be replaced. While some STO organisations emphasise a democratic and autonomous mechanism of governance,[86] exactly how their man-

---

83 Karen Yeung 'Regulation by Blockchain: The Emerging Battle for Supremacy between the Code of Law and Code as Law' (2019) 82(2) *Modern Law Review.* https://doi.org/10.1111/1468-2230 .12399. Accessed 12 November 2020.
84 Section 168 of Companies Act 2006.
85 Neal Watson and Beliz McKenzie 'Shareholders' Right in Private and Public Companies in the UK (England and Wales)' (2019) https://uk.practicallaw.thomsonreuters.com/5-613-3685?transition-Type=Default&contextData=(sc.Default)&firstPage=true. Accessed 12 November 2020.
86 Robbie Morrison, Natasha Mazey and Stephen Wingreen 'The DAO Controversy: The Case for a New Species of Corporate Governance?' (2020) https://doi.org/10.3389/fbloc.2020.00025. Accessed 12 November 2020.

agement will be brought to account or replaced remains unclear. Hence, the claim that the autonomous mechanism of governance is value-enhancing is in reality a regulatory vacuum. Without an effective mechanism to enable removal of those who act as agents of the token holders, there is a high risk of incurring agency costs by the organisation. The only option then left to token holders is the exit right – selling their tokens in the network. In the less transparent market of the blockchain network and without the support of trustworthy financial intermediaries to discover the price of the tokens, there might not be ready buyers who will offer a fair price to the token holders. Token holders may find themselves selling to the management and those in control at a value substantially below what they originally paid, either because the value of the organisation has gone down or, worse, through fraud.

Derivative action (ss 260–264)

Derivative action is a procedural regime provided by the UK Companies Act 2006 to empower shareholders, particularly non-controlling shareholders, to hold the board to account and to obtain redress for the company through judicial assistance.[87] Shareholders can bring a derivative claim for breach of duties against the board of directors or against a third party implicated in the breach, or both.[88] However, in order to do so, shareholders must pass a resolution at a general meeting or make a claim on the basis that there is a fraud on the minority if a general resolution of a shareholder meeting cannot be secured.

In an STO, since there is no clear structure for initiating such an action, minority token holders are at grave risk of investment loss because judicial assistance is not available to them to hold the board to account and obtain redress such as compensation, account of profits and other injunctive reliefs. There might not even be a legal person on whose behalf the token holders can bring claims against the board of directors. Whereas a shareholder resolution is one of the pre-requisites to initiating a claim under the Companies Act 2006, there is no forum for STO token holders to discuss and pass a resolution to bring such a claim. Even if this might have been pre-determined in the STO programme under the code-as-law, token holders may not have the knowledge or know-how to initiate it on the blockchain network or networks. The accountability of the board relies solely on the market as a monitoring mechanism. This gives opportunities for the board to extract rent for themselves through misuse of business opportunities or insider dealing at the expense of investors.

---

87 Section 260 of Companies Act 2006.
88 Carsten A. Paul, 'Derivative Actions under English and German Corporate Law – Shareholder Participation between the Tension Filled Areas of Corporate Governance and Malicious Shareholder Interference' (2010) 7 *European Company and Financial Law Review* 81, 87.

Insider dealing

Company directors have constant contact with price sensitive information that is not disclosed to investors or the public, and they can profit from trading in the company's securities using such information.[89] For this reason, insider dealing is deemed a criminal offence under UK law as it harms both the company and the market. It is also immoral to engage in insider dealing behaviour such as dealing, encouraging others to deal and disclosing insider information without authority. There are also compliance requirements in place to prevent management from misusing corporate information for its own benefit in an IPO, a share buyback,[90] a takeover or a merger.[91]

In an STO, there is a greater risk that the management or insiders can profit from price sensitive information that is not known to other investors or the public. Unless dealing in tokens with inside information is made a criminal offence, and unless systems and controls to prevent such an offence are introduced, the STO market will be tainted.[92] To increase the level of market integrity and investor confidence, it is imperative that insider dealing is eliminated from STO markets.[93] However, in the decentralised business structure proposed in DAO, it would be difficult to implement traditional systems and controls that have been designed for a centralised organisational system. It would also be difficult to identify a non-public inside source within a de-centralised/distributed organisation.

Shareholder transparency and data protection

Transparency of shareholder ownership aims to combat money laundering,[94] and can be achieved more effectively in an STO market that relies on a private or hybrid blockchain. With distributed ledger technology, shareholder ownership data can be recorded, allowing those with permission to access the information. The information is both current (almost real time) and historical, and is immutable

---

89 Nick Gibbon et al., 'Corporate Governance and Directors' Duties in the UK' (2017) www.dac-beachcroft.com/media/902386/uk_corporate-governance-and-directors-duties_3-597-4626.pdf. Accessed 12 November 2020.

90 In-MuHaw et al. 'Insider Trading Restrictions and Share Repurchase Decisions: International Evidence' (2015) www.fmaconferences.org/Orlando/Papers/Insider_trading_and_repurchase.pdf. Accessed 12 November 2020.

91 Anup Agrawal and Tareque Nasser, 'Insider Trading in Takeover Targets' (2012) 18 *Journal of Corporate Finance* 598–625.

92 Dirk Andreas Zetzsche et al., 'The Distributed Liability of Distributed Ledgers: Legal Risks of Blockchain' (2017) *University of Illinois Law Review* 1361.

93 John Anderson 'Insider Trading and the Myth of Market Confidence' (2018) 56 *Washington University Journal of Law and Policy* 1–16.

94 Transparency International UK, 'Beneficial Ownership Transparency' (2019) www.wiltonpark.org.uk/wp-content/uploads/WP1654-Beneficial-Ownership-Transparency.pdf. Accessed 12 November 2020; Department for Business Innovation & Skills, 'Transparency & Trust: Enhancing the Transparency of UK Company Ownership and Increasing Trust in UK Business' (Government response, April 2014).

once input into the system. Even if it is not tamper-proof, it is tamper-evident. This enhances compliance with anti-money laundering law that requires companies to maintain a register of information about persons with significant control (PSC)[95] – i.e. who own 25 per cent of the shares or votes[96] – or who can exercise real and actual control in the company.[97] In addition to fulfilling this legal requirement, the blockchain and smart contract technology can also facilitate effective e-voting.[98] This enables a company to collect information on investors' voting patterns on issues such as the election and re-election of directors, directors' remuneration, issuance of new security tokens, approval of dividends to be distributed or the acquisition and sale of major businesses assets.[99] Investors' behaviour on corporate governance issues will also be evident and this can reveal whether institutional investors are fulfilling their stewardship obligations to clients,[100] or if they are consistent in their commitment to corporate governance. Such information can be important for existing and future investors when deciding to purchase tokens, exercise their governance rights or deciding to exit the company.

Personal information stored on the blockchain, be it personal or behavioural data, can be of value to data companies, public authorities, researchers, market competitors, tech companies and the issuing companies' management. Although personal data should belong to the data subject according to the General Data Protection Regulation (GDPR)[101] which gives data subjects a number of rights in relation to their data, securities law and company law have not yet systemically recognised the data right of investors. For instance, platform providers can process data to provide further algorithm-based products and services which might be discriminatory to investors,[102] prejudicial to STO issuers or damaging to market integrity. Even though there are FCA rules regulating algorithm trading,[103] the current laws do not address the issues of Big Data which aggregates different types of personal information. Trading data used to develop algorithms often does not give rise to personal data protection issues because the current member-based trading

95 Section 21A of Companies Act 2006.
96 PCS schedule 1A Part 1 and 2, Companies Act 2006.
97 PCS schedule 1A Part 1 and 2, Companies Act 2006; S 790K, Companies Act 2006.
98 Spencer Nord, 'Blockchain Plumbing: A Potential Solution for Shareholder Voting' (2019) 29 *University of Pennsylvania Journal of Business Law* 706–710; Section 333 of Companies Act 2006.
99 Donald Pierce, 'Protecting the Voice of Retail Investors: Implementation of a Blockchain Proxy Voting Platform' (2019) 14(1) *Rutgers Business Law Journal* 9.
100 David Yermack, 'Corporate Governance and Blockchains' (2017) 21(1) *Review of Finance* 7, 23.
101 Regulation (EU) 2016/679 of the European Parliament and of the Council of 27 April 2016 on the protection of natural persons with regard to the processing of personal data and on the free movement of such data.
102 Article 21 of Charter of Fundamental Rights.
103 Article 17 of MiFID II; FCA 'Algorithmic Trading Compliance in Wholesale Markets' (2018) www.fca.org.uk/publication/multi-firm-reviews/algorithmic-trading-compliance-wholesale-markets.pdf. Accessed 09 June 2020.

and intermediated securities market structure enables privacy protection.[104] In a disintermediated STO market, data becomes not only an asset in itself[105] but its protection is relevant to investors' political and governance rights. Investors, as data subjects, should be able to decide who can control and process their data, and how. In law, the company, as a legal person, can hold investors' data. But, it may only do so with the consent of the investors and only process the data for legitimate purposes. It may not use data to gain profits or other benefits without the investors' consent. Internally, the management cannot use the data to manipulate the voting process and should not disclose information about individual shareholders' voting behaviour to majority shareholders without their consent.[106] If the management gives advice to specific shareholders based on their past corporate governance activities, e.g. voting behaviour, they would owe a number of fiduciary duties to them such as the duty to act in their best interests, the duty to avoid conflicts of interest and the duty to act in good faith.[107] By using their data, the management also owes a duty to exercise reasonable care, skill and diligence.[108] How should such duties be translated into law for the protection of token holders in the STO market? Investors' data should be treated as an economic right (like a dividend) if the company benefits from the dataset (making profits or reducing cost). And, in addition, the governance code for STO issuers should specifically include investors' data-based governance rights.

Recommendations

Protection of the new market space

As discussed, the current securities law can be made to apply to the STO market by extending the scope of "security" to include security tokens. And if so, securities market law that was designed to protect investors and to ensure market integrity

---

104 Thomas Keijser and Charles Mooney (2019), *Intermediated Securities Holding Systems Revisited: A View Through the Prism of Transparency.* In *Intermediation and Beyond* (L. Gullifer & J. Payne eds., Hart Publishing, 2019, Forthcoming), University of Pennsylvania, Institute for Law & Economics Research Paper No. 19-13. https://ssrn.com/abstract=3376873; Parliament and Council Directive (EU) 2017/828 of 17 May 2017 amending Directive 2007/36/EC as regards the encouragement of long-term shareholder engagement [2017] OJ L 132.

105 World Economic Forum, 'Personal Data: The Emergence of a New Asset Class' (2011) https://iapp.org/media/pdf/knowledge_center/WEF_ITTC_PersonalDataNewAsset_Report_2011.pdf; Jack Martin (2020), 'AI-Blockchain Platform Creates Digital Assets From Personal Data (JUL 17, 2020)'. https://cointelegraph.com/news/ai-blockchain-platform-creates-digital-assets-from-personal-data. Accessed 12 November 2020.

106 Article 6 (1) (a) of GDPR.

107 Bernard Black, 'The Principal Fiduciary Duty of Boards of Directors. Presentation at Third Asian Roundtable on Corporate Governance' (2001) www.oecd.org/corporate/ca/corporategovernance principles/1872746.pdf. Accessed 12 November 2020.

108 ICO, 'Guide to the General Data Protection Regulation' (2017) https://ico.org.uk/media/for -organisations/guide-to-the-general-data-protection-regulation-gdpr-1-0.pdf. Accessed 12 November 2020.

must also be made to apply to the STO market. The Prospectus regime and the continuing disclosure obligations, that are designed to address asymmetric information, should also apply to the STO market. As security tokens are recognised as a security under both UK and EU laws, there is no major difficulty in applying market conduct rules to the STO market but the question is whether bringing STO into a regulatory framework that has been designed for an intermediated securities market and which relies on financial intermediaries to perform the market gate-keeping role, would still serve the objective of access to finance that the STO market wishes to achieve. Financial intermediaries provide advice on the processes of the IPO, recommend the price of the securities issued after exercises such as "market sounding" and are involved in the wholesale underwriting and retail broker-dealing markets. Because the structure of the current securities law has been shaped by this intermediated market space, the law emphasises the function of intermediaries as market gatekeepers for liquidity, safety, integrity and functionality. In addition to regulating issuers, the conduct of intermediaries is the focus of regulation through detailed rules in MiFIDII,[109] AIFMD,[110] EMIR,[111] CSDR[112] and MAR.[113] These rules are necessary to protect clients' interests as well as the interests of the market intermediaries. The cost of compliance with these rules makes it less likely for smaller businesses to be able to access the investing public. While the disclosure regime is aimed at protecting end-investors, the involvement of financial intermediaries in the wholesale market means that some costs would fall on the end-investors.

Whether the disclosure regime should be aimed at protecting end-investors or issuers, or at covering the costs of financial intermediaries, needs to be investigated further. But, for an STO on the blockchain aiming at accessing the investing public directly, the current securities market law and regulation are inappropriate. Current law is adequate to protect the investing public, but an unintended consequence of the cost of compliance is that it hinders the financial inclusion of issuers and the investing public. Start-up companies do not have the means to go through the IPO process, and the majority of the investing public (retail investors) cannot afford shares in the IPO. STO issuers should comply with a disclosure regime in order to address the asymmetric information problem, but they should do so through a specific enabling regime that allows them access to a

109 Directive 2014/65/EU of the European Parliament and of the Council of 15 May 2014 on Markets in Financial Instruments Directive 2002/92/EC and Directive 2011/61/EU.
110 Directive 2011/61/EU of the European Parliament and of the Council on Alternative Investment Fund Managers.
111 Regulation (EU) No 648/2012 of the European Parliament and of the Council of 4 July 2012 on OTC Derivatives, Central Counterparties and Trade Repositories.
112 Regulation (EU) No 909/2014 of the European Parliament and of the Council of 23 July 2014 on Improving Securities Settlement in the European Union and on Central Securities Depositories.
113 Regulation (EU) No 596/2014 of the European Parliament and of the Council of 16 April 2014 on Market Abuse (Market Abuse Regulation) and Repealing Directive 2003/6/EU of the European Parliament and of the Council Commission Directives 2003/124/EC, 2003/125/EC and 2004/72/EC.

public who can invest with confidence. This does not imply that no intermediary could act as a trusted third party to facilitate the processes and provide safeguards because trusted third parties are able to provide a more streamlined process using the available technologies such as smart contract, blockchain, algorithms analytics and automation in order to reduce transaction costs. Market supervision could also be included, using technology to guard against market manipulation.

Governance right

Current company law protects investors against potential risks to their economic (monetary) and political rights, and security token holders need to be given equivalent protection if the STO market is to develop successfully. In devising such protection, we need to be clear about the purpose of these legal interventions. Is it to provide an organisational structure that reduces the time of negotiation between token holders and management? Is it to provide a structure that encourages innovation so that the STO market can compete with more traditional markets? Is it to reduce the negative way other stakeholders can be affected by dealings in the STO market? Is it to create a power balance within organisations and associations to reflect a political ethos? Or do we see STO issuers as state sanctioned entities, carrying with them a wider state responsibility? The answers to these questions must be decided if the law is to provide the default position for parties to develop their own structure and to stipulate what laws should be mandatory, and what enforcement mechanisms and consequential remedies to breaches of the laws are suitable for protecting token holders' interests.

The analysis given here suggests that current company law should not apply to STO entities, even though a company wishing to issue tokenised securities on the blockchain may find it easy to do so in terms of compliance. The technology available should make compliance more cost-effective and should have a transformative effect on the legal model. Corporate law scholars have been debating the legal nature of the corporation and of shares, and STO provides us with an opportunity to think anew about connecting with the disconnected and the excluded. This is reminiscent of the time when the corporate limited liability principle was introduced into the UK, enabling capital to be amassed in a way that broke the trade monopoly of the land-owning class. The fourth industrial revolution that we are now experiencing allows new types of entity to re-create capital and distribute wealth in a way that competes with multinational companies who use mergers and acquisitions to drive out market competition. Is it desirable to see merger and acquisition activities in the STO market similar to those that modern company law has been facilitating? This forces us to re-think the relationship between token holders and the issuing entity. Should token holders be the legal owners of the entity and should the management owe duties directly to them? What is the process for dissolving the entity? There is also the opportunity to make the issuing entity a nexus of contracts, bringing excluded stakeholders such as the employees, consumers and interested community stakeholders into the network.

New value and governance rights

Traditionally, data protection law stands outside capital markets regulation and company law. Capital markets law focuses on investor protection, market integrity and market safety to ensure market confidence, while company law focuses on economic rights (liquidity rights, credit rights and dividend rights) and political rights (the right to vote, the right to information and the right to redress). Data protection law relates to an individual investor's personal information and the issuers' responsibility with respect to information about investors and former investors. Personal information is not to be treated as a company asset and is protected by the duty of confidentiality that is owed by a company to individual investors. Software has been developed that identifies beneficial shareholders in a company using publicly available data. This can help achieve the objective of transparency about shareholder ownership and is able to combat money laundering. STO on the blockchain can make such data readily available not only to companies, but also to other participants such as token holders in the same entity or to third parties. However, although personal data is an asset belonging to individuals, when aggregated impersonally it can create valuable Big Data. Individual identity information and behavioural data can be useful for developing analytics that allow an issuing entity or its management to target particular kinds of people in order to raise capital, to understand their voting behaviour and to know when they are likely to exit an organisation or project. This means that data rendition, data surplus, surveillance capitalism and behavioural manipulation constitute risks in the STO market. Yet, the current capital markets law and company law do not focus on data issues because, under the current intermediated financial market structure, personal data rests with the intermediaries at different layers. Issuing companies do not necessarily have full knowledge of the identity of their shareholders, while intermediaries, such as trust banks or asset managers, often hold securities (shares) as legal owners on behalf of their immediate clients who, in turn, may also hold securities as an intermediary for their clients. Hence, data is not considered to be an asset and an investor's data is not included within investor protection in securities market law. Since a personal data right is not attached to a share as recognised by company law, investors cannot take dividends derived from it. It is also conceivable that voting information could be used to analyse investor behaviour and to provide proxy advisory services. If so, misuse of that data can amount to an interference with the investors' governance right. This is an area that company law needs to address.

Conclusion

This chapter discusses the importance of embedding security tokens in the law in order to provide investor confidence. However, current law and regulation should not apply to the STO market if it is to achieve its intended purpose of increasing access to finance. An STO is not an IPO on a smaller scale. To have a transformative effect, the STO market needs to emphasise its decentralised and disintermediated market structure that distinguishes it from the IPO market. Despite this, the current law and regulation regime for IPOs remains a useful tool to examine market structure, to identify market risks involved and the ways in which those risks can be mitigated. Company law helps to identify risks to investors' economic and political rights, and the discussion of UK company law given here provides benchmarks for the development of smart contracts in self-governing organisations. Finally, an investor's data rights should be recognised as both economic and political rights. Data dividends should be distributed to security token holders and data governance should consider the power aspect of the decision-making process. Centralised management should no longer be allowed to monopolise information.

7 Access to finance and artificial intelligence on blockchain network

Introduction

Access to finance

In the previous chapters, I have discussed how smart contracts can assist automation of various trading activities and corporate actions on the DLT-based capital market. The blockchain-based platforms, such as crowdfunding platforms, and operations of smart contracts, such as individual portfolio management of loans, can potentially perform the intermediary functions without human intervention, including trading execution, portfolio investment analysis and know-your-client risk management. This chapter investigates the relationship between artificial intelligence (AI) and the crypto-market. Transactions on the blockchain generate data (Big Data) which can be used to develop AI that enhances access to finance and financial inclusion. However, this can bring risk as well as benefit to the financial services sector. Market safety, investor protection and market integrity should continue to guide the regulation of AI to ensure continuity. In addition to these, access to finance should be a fundamental regulatory objective so that AI can be used to benefit not only financial intermediaries but also those previously excluded from financial opportunities.

Artificial intelligence (AI) is seen as a threat to employment, as it will take away manual jobs.[1] This threat is also true for financial services.[2] Nutmeg Review in 2017 revealed that a large proportion of the traditional business of financial advisers is threatened by automated services.[3] Despite this, the uncertainty that AI brings to incumbent operators, consumers and financial regulators has not stopped investment in AI Fintech. To strengthen its legitimacy in the financial

---

1 Hamza Ahmed, 'Online Social Networks Threats' (2014) 5(11) *International Journal of Scientific and Engineering Research* 986, 988.
2 Vishal Marria, 'Is Artificial Intelligence Replacing Jobs in Banking?' (2018) www.forbes.com/sites/vishalmarria/2018/09/26/is-artificial-intelligence-replacing-jobs-in-banking/#2b0d81343c55. Accessed 07 March 2021.
3 Andrew Meola, 'Nutmeg Review 2017: Fees, Returns, Investing Services and Competitors' (2017) www.businessinsider.com/nutmeg-review?r=US&IR=T. Accessed 07 March 2021.

DOI: 10.4324/9780429023613-7

services sector and to gain public acceptance, AI must provide some social benefits. Therefore, access to finance,[4] also referred to as financial inclusion, should be set as the policy priority in the regulation of the design, development and deployment of AI. According to the definition given by the Financial Inclusion Report 2018/19, "financial inclusion means that individuals, regardless of their background or income, have access to useful and affordable financial products and services. This includes products and services, as well as transactions and payment systems, and the use of financial technology."[5] The provision of access to finance should aim to enable those currently excluded by the existing systems to participate in the financial markets. To benefit from economic growth, these individuals should have access to capital pools for personal or business finance, access to real-time information with the aid of data analytics and have access to a range of investment providers. In this chapter, I will focus on three aspects of how AI can enhance financial inclusion: 1) increasing participation in Peer-to-Peer (P2P) platforms by providing security for them; 2) closing the advisory gap in investment services; and 3) allowing more financial outlets to be operated in the financial services sector by reducing their operational costs, such as compliance costs.

The chapter will discuss the regulatory objectives and methods of regulation in these three areas by looking at three close parallels. The first is the use of AI in the trading platforms for capital optimisation, such as an increase in efficiency, accuracy and the speed of capital optimisation through the foundations of computing capabilities, big data and mathematical concepts built by AI and machine learning (ML).[6] The second is the use of robo-advisers to provide investment services, such as identifying wider sources of available funds for Fintech, lending to small and medium-sized enterprises and clients through AI and ML's advanced credit scoring.[7] And the third is the use of AI in RegTech services to streamline compliance costs,[8] such as the costs involved in the Know Your Consumer (KYC) processes. In this way, I will examine how AI-facilitated access to finance can align with current regulatory objectives and methods of regulation. Whether the provision of this access will conflict with other values, such as privacy, data protection and ethics will also be examined.

---

4 Business, Energy and Industrial Strategy Committee, 'Access to Finance' (2016) https://committees.parliament.uk/committee/365/business-energy-and-industrial-strategy-committee/. Accessed 07 March 2021.
5 HM Treasury and Department for Work and Pensions, 'Financial Inclusion' (2019) www.gov.uk/government/publications/financial-inclusion-report-2018-to-2019. Accessed 07 March 2021.
6 FSB, 'Artificial Intelligence and Machine Learning in Financial Services: Market Developments and Financial Stability Implications' (2017).
7 Ibid.
8 Dunnly, 'Learn How Banks and Finance House Use AI for Regulatory Compliance' (2017) https://dunnly.com/learn-how-banks-and-finance-houses-use-ai-for-regulatory-compliance/. Accessed 07 March 2021.

Applications of AI in finance

Algorithmic trading on regulated platforms

The UK authorities regard financial technology as an efficient tool to tackle financial exclusion and also as a way to encourage firms to develop innovative processes and thus increase consumer access to the financial services.[9] P2P platforms have been regarded as providing a more economical way of bringing businesses and investors together. Compared with bank saving, P2P platforms offer higher interest rates.[10] In addition, investments through P2P platforms offer higher liquidity than traditional property investments.[11] Most importantly, P2P platforms normally split capital into several parts for multiple borrowers, thus lowering the risk of incurring major losses. Algorithmic trading can be used in P2P platforms to increase access to finance, particularly in capital allocation. The tightening of bank lending policies followed the financial crisis and p2p lending has become a major player in global financial markets. For instance, LendingClub Inc. developed its own platform, relying on sophisticated algorithms to pair borrowers and investors and also to evaluate the attributes of both sides.[12] Not only on the P2P lending platforms, it is envisaged that algorithms may also be used for secondary securities trading on blockchain-based trading platforms such as initial coin offerings (ICOs). For instance, in early 2019 the London Stock Exchange (LSE) invested 20 million dollars in Nivaura, a blockchain start-up that specialises in fully-automated tokenised bonds recorded on a blockchain.[13] In April 2019, LSE and Nivaura issued shares with £3 million on LSE's test network.[14] While traders in the financial markets are using algorithms to make gains, the author argues that similar tools and opportunities should also be given to investors and consumers. This is a way to provide access to financial markets. Therefore, algorithms should be made available through market competition. Real-time data should also be

9 HM Treasury and Department for Work and Pensions 'Financial Inclusion Report 2018/19' (2019) https://assets.publishing.service.gov.uk/government/uploads/system/uploads/attachment_data/file/789070/financial_inclusion_report_2018-19_web.pdf. Accessed 07 March 2021.

10 Sebastian Anthony, 'Peer to Peer Lending and Investments' (2019) www.bankrate.com/uk/savings-accounts/peer-to-peer-savings/. Accessed 07 March 2021.

11 Yann Murciano, 'P2P Lending Offers an Attractive Entry Point into Property Investment' (2019) www.mortgageintroducer.com/p2p-lending-offers-attractive-entry-point-property-investment/. Accessed 07 March 2021.

12 Mark Albertson, 'The Sophisticated Algorithms behind Peer-to-peer Money Lending' (2018) https://siliconangle.com/2018/08/24/%E2%80%8Bthe-sophisticated-algorithms-behind-peer-peer-money-lending-guestoftheweek/. Accessed 07 March 2021.

13 Hayley McDowell, 'LSEG Leads $20 Million Funding Round in Blockchain Startup' (2021) www.thetradenews.com/lseg-leads-20-million-funding-round-blockchain-startup/. Accessed 07 March 2021.

14 The Telegraph, 'London Stock Exchange Collaborates on First Issue of Blockchain "Token" Shares' (2019) www.telegraph.co.uk/technology/2019/04/15/london-stock-exchange-accepts-first-listing-blockchain-token/.

made available to consumers and investors, rather than being an expensive commodity only available to those who can afford it.

However, users need to feel confident that the platforms on which algorithms are used are not likely to cause a market crash or to manipulate the market. Market crashes due to human behaviour have occurred in modern capital markets[15] such as the "Dotcom Bubble" in the 1990s and the 1998 "Asian Crash." AI does not reduce the risk of a market crash and may even increase the chances of it happening.[16] This can be seen in the market crash in 2008 for which high frequency trading (HFT) was considered the cause, or at least a contributing factor.[17] Hence, the regulation of HFT can provide a blueprint for regulating algorithmic trading on a P2P platform.[18] HFT is a type of algorithmic trading that has been used for more than a decade on trading platforms.[19] The reason for its emergence was the market liberalisation and market competition that substantially reduced the trading revenues of the trading platforms.[20] HFT allows trading venues to raise trading fees. It is not yet clear if HFT will be used on other trading platforms, such as P2P platforms,[21] to provide the same benefit. The business model on P2P trading platforms may not be the same as that on securities trading platforms. Technical obstacles may need to be overcome; for instance, the speed on a blockchain-based P2P platform may not be sufficient to support HFT.[22] However, the lessons learned regarding the risks in algorithmic trading provide a good regulatory framework that can be applied to provide security for users on the platform.[23]

HFT, computerised trading controlled by algorithms, is a subset of the broader

---

15 Jennifer Jhun, Patricia Palacios and James Owen Weatherall, 'Market Crashes as Critical Phenomena? Explanation, Idealization, and Universality in Econophysics' (2018) 195 *Synthese* 4477, 4505.

16 Bank of England and FCA, 'Machine Learning in UK Financial Services' (2019) www.bankofengland.co.uk/report/2019/machine-learning-in-uk-financial-services. Accessed 07 March 2021.

17 D. Sornette and S. von der Becke, 'Crashes and High Frequency Trading: An Evaluation of Risks by High-Speed Algorithmic Trading' (2011) https://assets.publishing.service.gov.uk/government/uploads/system/uploads/attachment_data/file/289016/11-1226-dr7-crashes-and-high-frequency-trading.pdf. Accessed 07 March 2021.

18 Michael Morelli, 'Implementing High Frequency Trading Regulation: A Critical Analysis of Current Reforms' (2017) 6 *Michigan Business and Entrepreneurial Law Review* 201, 229; *also see* Megan Woodward, 'The Need for Speed: Regulatory Approaches to High Frequency Trading in the United States and the European Union' (2017) 50 *Vanderbilt Journal of Transnational Law* 2, 44.

19 Ibid.

20 Johannes Breckenfelder, 'Competition among High-Frequency Traders, and Market Quality' (European Central Bank, Working Paper No 2290, 2019).

21 Jaksa Cvitanic and Andrei Kirilenko, 'High Frequency Traders and Asset Prices' (2018) www.ft.com/content/0f18ea78-293f-11e8-b27e-cc62a39d57a0. Accessed 07 March 2021.

22 Merlinda Andoni et al., 'Blockchain Technology in the Energy Sector: A Systematic Review of Challenges and Opportunities' (2019) 100 *Renewable and Sustainable Energy Review* 143, 174.

23 Edgar Ortega Barrales, 'Lessons from the Flash Crash for the Regulation of High-Frequency Traders' (2012) 17 *Fordham Journal of Corporate and Financial Law* 1195, 1262; *also see* Steven R. McNamara, 'The Law and Ethics of High-Frequency Trading' (2016) 17 *Minnesota Journal of Law, Science and Technology* 71, 150.

(and older) phenomenon of algorithmic trading.[24] In essence, algorithmic trading is simply the use of specialised software to implement predetermined decision-making rules for the evaluation of market conditions and other data in order to make trading decisions without human involvement.[25] Hence, in algorithmic trading, the traders' computers directly interface with trading platforms, placing orders without immediate human intervention. The computers observe, at very high frequency, market data and possibly other information. Based on a built-in algorithm, trading instructions are sent to the platform, often within milliseconds. A variety of algorithms are used for identifying arbitrage opportunities; for seeking the optimal execution of large orders at a minimum cost; and for seeking to implement longer-term trading strategies.[26]

Market safety regulation

The main focus of the regulation of algorithmic trading is market safety to address systemic risks caused by algorithmic trading. These include flash crashes, reduced liquidity and herding behaviour.[27]

Flash crash

A market crash, predating the involvement of AI, has happened in the capital markets and the regulations put in place to avoid a recurrence focus primarily on human conduct. When machines are involved, systemic risk becomes the main concern, so market safety regulation needs to be introduced to provide security. The EU and UK regulators have introduced measures to mitigate the risk of a flash crash caused by AI. Algorithmic trading can result in a flash crash, for example, when the withdrawal of stock orders rapidly amplifies, price declines.[28] After the flash crash in 2010,[29] the UK's Financial Conduct Authority (FCA), alongside the Prudential Regulation Authority, started closely monitoring HFT. HFT firms

---

24 Government Office for Science, 'High Frequency Trading – Assessing the Impact on Market Efficiency and Integrity' (part of the UK Government's Foresight Project, 2012).
25 Charlotte Szostek et al., 'Studies of Interactions between Human Traders and Algorithmic Trading Systems' (2011) https://pdfs.semanticscholar.org/711e/f95dfa873e06274df93fd12c2b766078a837 .pdf. Accessed 07 March 2021.
26 Virginia Dignum, *Responsible Artificial Intelligence: How to Develop and use AI in a Responsible Way* (Springer, Cham 2019) 130–136.
27 M. Laboure and J. Turner, 'The Emergence of the Robo-Advisor' University of Pennsylvania Scholarly Commons (2018) https://repository.upenn.edu/prc_papers/10/. Accessed 28 October 2020; Proinsias O'Mahony, 'Could High-Frequency Traders Cause Another Flash Crash?' (2015) www.irishtimes.com/business/personal-finance/could-high-frequency-traders-cause-another-flash -crash-1.2233576. Accessed 07 March 2021.
28 Ibid.
29 Andrew Trotman, 'What Happened during the Flash Crash' The Telegraph (2010) www.telegraph .co.uk/finance/financial-crime/11553696/What-happened-during-the-Flash-Crash.html. Accessed 07 March 2021.

were considered to have contributed to market instability and to the overall lack of investors' trust in the market.[30] In the same effort, the EU regulates HFT activities under the "Markets in Financial Instruments Directive II"[31] and the "Markets in Financial Instruments Regulation,"[32] known together as "MiFID II and MiFIR."[33] MiFID II has three main strands. First, it provides for a new operational regime governing algorithmic trading by investment firms.[34] Second, it extends its scope to encompass all firms engaging in algorithmic trading, in particular, specialist firms that undertake HFT. Third, it imposes operational requirements on trading venues, such as exchanges e.g. platforms.[35] For instance, circuit breakers, also called shock absorbers, are required for trading venues such as exchanges to temporarily halt trading when market prices, as indicated by a benchmark index, fall by a certain percentage during a specific period.[36]

Under the first strand, investment firms that engage in algorithmic trading are subject to a "targeted operational regime."[37] They are required to have in place effective systems and risk controls to ensure that trading systems are resilient and maintain the appropriate thresholds and limits to prevent incorrect or erroneous orders which may create or contribute to a disorderly market.[38] In the UK, these algorithmic trading requirements were implemented through Chapter 7A of the Market Conduct Sourcebook.[39] The second strand requires that firms must have "effective business continuity arrangements" to handle any trading system failure and must ensure that systems are fully tested and continuously monitored.[40] Third, HFT firms must have an emergency "kill functionality," which allows them to cancel all unexecuted orders with immediate effect.[41] In addition to this organisational requirement, all firms must notify the Financial Conduct Authority and the

---

30 Edgar Ortega Barrales, 'Lesson from the Flash Crash for the Regulation of High-Frequency Traders' (2018) 17 *Fordham Journal of Corporate & Financial Law* 1197.
31 Directive 2014/65/EU of the European Parliament and of the Council of 15 May 2014 on markets in financial instruments and amending Directive 2002/92/EC and Directive 2011/61/EU [2014] OJ L 173/349.
32 Regulation (EU) No. 600/2014 of the European Parliament and of the Council of 15 May 2014 on markets in financial instruments and amending Regulation (EU) No 648/2012 [2014] OJ L 173/84.
33 Danny Busch, 'MiFID II: Regulating High Frequency Trading, Other Forms of Algorithmic Trading and Direct Electronic Market Access' (2016) 10 *Law and Financial Market Review* 72–82.
34 Niamh Moloney, *EU Securities and Financial Markets Regulation* (Oxford University Press, 2014) 528.
35 Ibid at 529.
36 Definition given by Financial Times Lexicon.
37 Niamh Moloney, *EU Securities and Financial Markets Regulation* (Oxford University Press, 2014) 528.
38 Art. 17 of MIFID II; Niamh Moloney, *EU Securities and Financial Markets Regulation* (Oxford University Press, 2014) 528.
39 FCA, 'Algorithmic Trading Compliance in Wholesale Markets – Financial Conduct Authority' (2018) www.fca.org.uk/publication/multi-firm-reviews/algorithmic-trading-compliance-whole-sale-markets.pdf. Accessed 07 March 2021.
40 Ibid at 5.
41 Ibid.

venue's competent authority if the firms engage in any HFT on any EU trading venue.[42] Last, firms must carry out an annual self-assessment and issue a validation report covering such elements as governance, the control framework, and overall compliance with the other MiFID II requirements.[43] Firms are required to identify the algorithm ownership, establish testing processes and identify relevant environmental factors, such as the counterparties that use algo-trade.[44] They are also required to identify risks and provide risk mitigation measures. The Prudential Regulatory Authority has also published a consultation paper to accompany these current regulations which focus on the proposed expectations of a firm's policies for the "governance and risk management of algorithmic trading."[45] Some countries go further than the EU regulations and have adopted measures such as a requirement to hold a licence to operate HFT. In Germany, under section 32 of the German Banking Act, HFT firms need to hold a licence issued by the German Federal Financial Supervisory Authority.[46]

Liquidity risk and procyclical behaviour

To address liquidity risk, HFTs are required to register as market makers.[47] A market maker is a market participant that buys and sells large amounts of a particular asset in order to facilitate liquidity and ensure the smooth running of financial markets.[48] Market makers are obliged to continually quote bid and offer prices, and to guarantee the full sale or absorption of the security at a certain price.[49] When the market becomes stressed,[50] an HFT has an additional duty to ensure liquidity. Market makers have to protect proposals to purchase and sell stocks at levels corresponding to different price and size thresholds. They have to comply with four different elements: to quote at the best price in a specified period of time; to quote at prices within the specified period of time from the National Best Bid or Proposal; to quote with a minimum dimension and various prices; and to

---

42 Section 17(2), MiFID II.
43 FCA, 'Algorithmic Trading Compliance in Wholesale Markets – Financial Conduct Authority' (2018) www.fca.org.uk/publication/multi-firm-reviews/algorithmic-trading-compliance-whole-sale-markets.pdf. Accessed 07 March 2021.
44 Bank of England, 'Algorithmic Trading' (Supervisory Statement 2018) www.bankofengland .co.uk/-/media/boe/files/prudential-regulation/supervisory-statement/2018/ss518. Accessed 07 March 2021.
45 FCA, 'Report on the Supervision of Algorithmic Trading' www.fca.org.uk/news/press-releases/fca -publishes-report-supervision-algorithmic-trading. Accessed 07 March 2021.
46 Ibid at 245.
47 FCA, 'Algorithmic and High Frequency Trading Requirements' (2018) www.fca.org.uk/mifid-ii/8 -algorithmic-and-high-frequency-trading-hft-requirements. Accessed 07 March 2021.
48 Pu Shen and Ross Starr, 'Market-Makers' Supply and Pricing of Financial Market Liquidity' (2002) 76 *Economics Letters* 53, 58.
49 Evangelos Benos and Anne Wetherilt, 'The Role of Designated Market Makers in the New Trading Landscape' (Bank of England Quarterly Bulletin, 2014 Q4).
50 Chairman Mary Scharpiro, 'Strengthening Our Equity Market Structure' (2018) www.sec.gov/ news/speech/2010/spch090710mls.htm. Accessed 07 March 2021.

build markets for a minimum amount of stocks.[51] Market makers take the highest trading risk to comply with the four elements, and are therefore required to maintain the necessary amount of capital.[52] Additionally, if market prices escalate or decrease more than a certain amount, exchanges have the authority to limit the usage of specific trading tactics.[53]

There is also a risk of procyclical behaviour when market participants begin to use similar AI and ML programmes.[54] The consequent correlated risks may bring about financial stability risks.[55] If an ML-based trader outperforms others, this could in the future result in many more traders adopting similar ML strategies, even if this reduces the profitability of such strategies.[56] While there is no evidence to date of this having occurred, it could become relevant as such trading strategies are increasingly adopted. As with any herding behaviour in the market, this has the potential to amplify financial shocks. The main risk is the creation of procyclical behaviour that is harmful to financial stability.[57] If regulators develop a preference for a robo-adviser design that is understood by firms, it could result in a convergence of models that would increase the probability of a systemic crisis.[58]

The same approach to Peer-to-Peer Trading Platforms

Market safety and soundness regulations are aimed at providing financial stability and security to the users. In this section, I will use the example of HFT to identify some of the risks to market stability of using AI. The main approaches to regulating activities and risks are internal systems and controls, self-assessment and the reporting by both firms and trading venues.[59] There are also specific requirements to deal with market crashes, liquidity risk and correlated losses. In addition, traders using AI will need to fulfil their duties as market makers. To avoid similar losses, brokers and investor advisers using similar AI technology will need to be

51 Edgar Ortega Barrales, 'Lessons from The Flash Crash for The Regulation of High-Frequency Traders' (2012) 17 *Fordham Journal of Corporate & Finance Law* 1246.
52 Ibid at 1248.
53 Ibid at 1247.
54 Jon Danielsson, Robert Macrae and Andreas Uthemann, 'Artificial Intelligence, Financial Risk Management and Systemic Risk' (Special Paper No 13, Systemic Risk Centre at LSE 2017) www.systemicrisk.ac.uk/sites/default/files/downloads/publications/SP13.pdf. Accessed 07 March 2021.
55 Jon Danielsson, Robert Macrae and Andreas Uthemann, 'Artificial Intelligence and Systemic Risk' (Special Paper No 16, Systemic Risk Centre of London School of Economics and Political Science 2019).
56 Jahanzaib Shabbir and Tarique Anwer, 'Artificial Intelligence and Its Role in Near Future' (2018) 7 *International Journal of Science and Research* 893–897.
57 Michael Papaioannou, Joonkyu Park, Jukka Pihlman and Han van der Hoorn, 'Procyclical Behavior of Institutional Investors during the Recent Financial Crisis: Causes, Impacts, and Challenges' (IMF Working Paper 13/193, 2013).
58 Tom Baker and Benedict Dellaert, 'Regulating Robo Advice across the Financial Services Industry' (2018) 103 *Iowa Law Review* 746.
59 Danny Busch, 'MiFID II: Regulating High Frequency Trading, Other Forms of Algorithmic Trading and Direct Electronic Market Access' (2016) 2 *Law and Financial Markets Review* 72–82.

subject to the same systems and controls as those used for HFT. In the application of regulations for the use of AI on P2P trading platforms, market safety and market integrity, alongside the access to finance, should continue to be the regulatory objectives. The risks, such as systemic risk, liquidity risk and correlated risk, are the same as those on the capital markets trading platforms. The difference lies in the methods of regulation. On the P2P platforms, organisational regulation is unlikely to be implemented for individual participants on the platforms. Instead, the regulatory emphasis will be on requiring the trading platforms to vet individuals who use algorithms to make transactions,[60] to maintain the capacity to absorb the liquidity risk and to have surveillance to control market manipulation. In fulfilling the objective of providing access to finance, the cost of maintaining the system should not be transferred to the users. If the cost of addressing these risks is too high, fewer platforms will operate. Hence, there should be ways to implement the systems of risks and control (organisational requirement) in a more economical way, such as by using certification systems to allow algorithmic uses on the platforms (an alternative way to submitting source code) and using RegTech solutions to monitor market manipulation.[61] In addition, the regulators can regulate the financial instruments (through product intervention power[62]) that could be used on the trading platforms.

Investor protection

AI should give more freedom of choice to investors as well as security. It can enable access to finance by providing more economical investment advice to consumers who are excluded from accessing investment opportunities through a lack of information. This presents an opportunity for the use of AI to provide services to consumers for both execution or investment advice through, for example, robo-advisers.[63] When AI is consumer facing, such as in the use of robo-advisers or the use of AI by intermediaries for stock and fund selections, the focus of regulation is on both the *ex ante* (including reviewing the algorithmic models, Customer Due Diligence (CDD) and algorithm explication[64]) and the *ex post* protection of investors (compensation and liability for AI[65]), especially retail investors. Hence,

---

60 European Commission, 'White Paper on Artificial Intelligence: A European Approach to Excellence and Trust' (2020) https://ec.europa.eu/info/sites/info/files/commission-white-paper-artificial-intelligence-feb2020_en.pdf. Accessed 05 October 2020.

61 *See* 2.1 Technical methods in EU Ethics Guidelines for Trustworthy AI. *Also see* 'Algorithms in Decision-Making' (Fourth Report of Session 2017–19, Science and Technology Committee, House of Commons 2018).

62 Section 137D, Financial Services and Markets Act 2000.

63 Megan Ji, 'Are Robots Good Fiduciaries? Regulating Robo-Advisors under the Investment Advisors Act of 1940' (2017) 6 *Columbia Law Review* 1543, 1583.

64 Panel for the Future of Science and Technology, European Parliament, 'A Governance Framework for Algorithmic Accountability and Transparency' (2019).

65 John Kingston, 'Artificial Intelligence and Legal Liability' (published in SGAI International Conference on Artificial Intelligence, 2019).

the main issues are the consumers' understanding of the nature of AI (through algorithm explicability[66]), the risk of using AI, and the liability associated with AI. Investors should also be protected in a fiduciary context: the providers of AI services have an obligation to act in the best interests of the customers and to present no conflict of interest.[67]

Using robo-advisers to close the investment advice gap

There is no consensus on the definition of the financial advice gap.[68] According to the definition given by the Financial Advice Market Review (FAMR), the financial advice gap refers to "situations in which consumers are unable to get advice and guidance on a need they have at a price they are willing to pay."[69] Cost is not the only factor causing this gap, and the financial advice gap should be defined as "the difference between the number of people who currently seek advice, and those who would seek advice if a cheaper and less intensive process existed."[70] However, there is a common view that a gap exists for (potential) customers who have lower incomes or a lower level of assets and could either not afford the advisory fee or find it hard to access.[71] The conclusion of the FAMR is that the underlying reason for the existence of the financial advice gap is that there are not sufficient financial advisers since too many advisers are serving wealthy clients.[72] According to the survey conducted by OpenMoney and YouGov, an increasing number of clients are falling into the financial advice gap.[73] OpenMoney's survey indicates that there are more than 400,000 people who believe they could not afford financial advice and over five million people who are not aware that there is free financial advice that could benefit them.[74] There are six million Britons who would be willing to pay for financial advice if the fee for that advice were lower.[75]

66 Margot Kaminski, 'The Right to Explanation, Explained' (2019) 1 *Berkeley Technology Law Journal*, available at SSRN: https://papers.ssrn.com/sol3/papers.cfm?abstract_id=3196985. Accessed 05 October 2020

67 John Lightbourne, 'Algorithms & Fiduciaries: Existing and Proposed Regulatory Approaches to Artificially Intelligent Financial Planners' (2017) 67 *Duke Law Review* 651, 679.

68 Kathryn Petrie, 'Informed Decision-Making: An Evaluation of the Advice Gap' (2017) www.smf.co.uk/wp-content/uploads/2017/06/5599-SMF-Financial-Advice-Gap-Report-WEB.pdf. Accessed 05 October 2020.

69 HM Treasury and FCA, 'Financial Advice Market Review' (Final report 2016) www.fca.org.uk/publication/corporate/famr-final-report.pdf. Accessed 05 October 2020.

70 Ibid.

71 Ibid.

72 Ibid.

73 Sonia Rach, 'Robo-Advisers Blow Advice Gap Further Apart' (2019) https://portfolio-adviser.com/robo-advisers-blow-advice-gap-further-apart/. Accessed 05 October 2020.

74 Ibid.

75 Financial Planning Today, '6 Million Britons would Pay for Cheaper Financial Advice' (2019) www.financialplanningtoday.co.uk/news/item/10261-6m-britons-would-pay-for-cheaper-financial-advice. Accessed 05 October 2020.

The role of robo-advisers such as Nutmeg and Wealthify is to fill this financial advice gap.[76] Robo-advisers are a type of financial adviser that provides financial advice "in person" or enables investment management online, with moderate to minimal human intervention. "Robo-advice" is an umbrella term that refers to a broad spectrum of online automated tools and algorithms to determine financial or investment decisions for an individual's portfolio. This process is based on financial analysis algorithms derived from mathematical rules. Progress through economic modelling and AI is the cornerstone of this technology. These algorithms are executed by software and thus, taken to extremes, human intervention is not required.[77] Robo-advisers aim at reducing the cost of financial advisory services, increasing consumer protection by reducing conflicts of interest,[78] providing better rational investment choices[79] and enabling more access to real-time information.[80] Hence, robo-advisers can enhance access to finance and reduce the cost of financial access that leads to more affordable financial services.[81] This effect would be highly beneficial for average savers who could access services that were previously inaccessible due to high commission fees.[82]

Risks of a conflict of interest, unsuitable products and design errors

The use of robo-advisers may put an end to two related problems in the financial markets. Financial advisers tend to sell high commission-fee products because the advisers draw their income from their sale.[83] Consequently, there is a conflict of interest between the investor and the adviser, who is also the broker.[84]

76 Financial Times, 'Financial Advice Gap has Widened since 2015, Says Report' www.ft.com/content/1b931788-7be1-11e9-81d2-f785092ab560. Accessed 05 October 2020.
77 Ron Lieber, 'Financial Advice for People who aren't Rich (2014) www.nytimes.com/2014/04/12/your-money/start-ups-offer-financial-advice-to-people-who-arent-rich.html. Accessed 05 October 2020.
78 Financial Times, 'Watchdog Probes Financial Advice Gap' (2019) www.ft.com/content/f675a6e2-6bf4-11e9-80c7-60ee53e6681d. Accessed 05 October 2020.
79 Marion Laboure and John Turner, 'The Emergence of the Robo-Advisor' (University of Pennsylvania Scholarly Commons 2018).
80 Empirica, 'Reasons for Asset Managers to Implement Robo Advisor Software' (2016) http://empirica-software.com/reasons-for-asset-managers-to-implement-robo-advisor-software/. Accessed 05 October 2020.
81 Thomas Philippon, 'On Fintech and Financial Inclusion' (The National Bureau of Economic Research Working Paper No. 26330, 2019).
82 Financial Times, 'Financial Advice Gap has Widened since 2015, Says Report' www.ft.com/content/1b931788-7be1-11e9-81d2-f785092ab560. Accessed 05 October 2020.
83 HM Treasury, 'Financial Advice Market Review (Final Report 2016) www.fca.org.uk/publication/corporate/famr-final-report.pdf; *also see* European Insurance and Occupational Pensions Authority, 'Final Report on Public Consultation on the Draft Technical Advice on Conflict of Interest in Direct and Intermediated Sales of Insurance-Based Investment Products' (2015) https://eiopa.europa.eu/Publications/Opinions/7%201%20_EIOPA-BoS-15-006_Final_Report_on_conflicts_of_interest_version_for_publication.pdf. Accessed 05 October 2020.
84 Benjamin P. Edwards, 'The Rise of Automated Investment Advice: Can Robo-Advisers Rescue the Retail Market?' (2018) 93 *Chicago-Kent Law Review* 97.

However, it is possible for the algorithms to be designed to avoid such a conflict.[85] There is also a risk that robo-advisers may promote products that are not suitable for the particular investor. In addition, there is a risk that there may be algorithm design errors that can cause investor losses.[86] There is clearly potential tension between the broker's interests and the client's interests.[87] Robo-advisers may only be used to provide advice or recommendations, without performing the executions, although the users in these situations are likely to be guided to place orders through a specific product provider. For instance, Scalable Capital, an online robo-advice company, launched over-the-phone and face-to-face consultations for clients to select their investment portfolios based on their level of risk tolerance from a range of suggested advice.[88] Although financial institutions are responsible for damages caused to investors by their using or relying on robo-advisers, there are some situations in which financial institutions are not responsible. These are the following: first, when financial institutions become insolvent and there is insufficient cover to compensate investors; and second, when advice given was regarded merely as "guidance" and the investor has autonomy to decide whether or not to accept it.[89]

Legal framework for protecting investors

Access to finance requires a legal and regulatory framework to protect investors who use robo-advisers for personal or business finance. There are various legal tools that govern the relationship between financial institutions and investors, as well as between developers of AI and investors.

In the UK, investors are protected by common law, statutory law and the regulators' rules. Under common law, investors are protected through contract law, the duty of care under tort law and the fiduciary duty provisions under the law of equity.

Contract

In contract law, investors are protected by the terms under the contract as well as by the various principles including mistake, misrepresentation, duress, undue influence and legality.[90] Under the Unfair Contract Terms Act 1977, they are also

---

85 Bank of England and FCA, 'Machine Learning in UK Financial Services: AI can Reduce Risks' (2019).

86 Deloitte, 'Managing Algorithmic Risks: Safeguarding the Use of Complex Algorithms and Machine Learning' www2.deloitte.com/content/dam/Deloitte/lu/Documents/risk/lu-risk-algorithmic-machine-learning-risk-management.pdf. Accessed 05 October 2020.

87 Ibid.

88 Financial Times, 'Robo Advisors Recognise the Need for Human Touch' (2019) www.ft.com/content/f9b8fda4-e1c1-11e7-a8a4-0a1e63a52f9c. Accessed 05 October 2020.

89 Oscar A. Stolper and Andreas Walter, 'Financial Literacy, Financial Advice, and Financial Behavior' (2017) 87 *Journal of Business Economics* 581, 643.

90 John Cartwright, 'Protecting Legitimate Expectations and Estoppel in English Law' (Reported to the XVIIth International Congress of Comparative Law 2006).

protected against unfair terms.[91] Therefore, the use of AI devices by advisers should not violate these principles. Furthermore, if the investors are consumers, they will also be protected by consumer protection law. However, contract law is unlikely to be an effective tool in providing protection to investors who do not have the capacity to appreciate the nature of AI, the performance of it and whether AI is a suitable device for them to use for making investments.[92] Increasingly, a contract will appear merely as evidence of the existence of an agreement for the conduct between financial advisers and their clients. Prior to investors' use of AI, the terms of a contract between them and their advisers are unlikely to be negotiated between the parties. Investors are unlikely to be sophisticated enough to ask the financial advisers to disclose relevant information before they agree to accept the advice derived from the algorithms. Clients may not even be able to negotiate a specific term that requires their advisers to explain how particular products were selected for them.

Tort

In tort, the advisers should owe a duty of care to the investors,[93] which entails ensuring that in deploying AI for providing advice or even execution services, the advisers' behaviour does not fall short of a standard of care. The difficulty lies in how to identify an appropriate standard of care when using AI. There is currently no such standard set by either the financial services regulators or the industry.[94] Even if the regulators have set out rules with which the investment advisers must comply, these rules do not necessarily form the standard of care that the court will apply in determining whether there is a breach.[95] Relevant questions in setting the standard include: which AI devices are suitable for the client? what kind of data should be fed into an AI device to produce investment advice? what kind of warning should be given to investors? what kind of assistance should be given to investors? what kind of explanation should be given to investors about the outcome of the algorithms?

Fiduciary duty

The core of the fiduciary duty is both the duty of loyalty and the duty of good faith.[96] Under the duty of loyalty, investor advisers should not put their interests

---

91 Art. 2 (Negligence Liability), Unfair Contract Terms Act 1977.
92 Bryce Goodman, Seth Flaxman, 'European Union Regulations on Algorithmic Decision-Making and a "Right to Explanation"' (2017) 3 *AI Magazine* 6.
93 Seth Lipner and Lisa Catalano, 'The Tort of Giving Negligent Investment Advice' (2009) 36 *University of Memphis Law Review* 663.
94 Matthew Scherer, 'Regulating Artificial Intelligence Systems: Risks, Challenges, Competencies, and Strategies' (2016) 2 *Harvard Journal of Law and Technology* 353, 400.
95 Ibid.
96 *Bristol & West Building Society v Mothew* [1998] Ch 1 at 18.

in conflict with those of their clients.[97] This duty should not be removed by contract,[98] as fiduciary duties may generally be altered or restricted by agreement between the parties.[99] In practical terms, advisers need to use their best endeavours to find a suitable investment product for their clients[100] rather than offering products that will reward themselves with a commission. Compared with the duty of care, the fiduciary duty applies in more limited circumstances. The fiduciary duty prohibits financial advisers from acting in a disloyal or improper way, i.e. it is a negative obligation.[101] However, the duty of care requires financial advisers to act competently and not recklessly, i.e. it is a positive obligation compared with the fiduciary duty.[102] When used in executing the clients' request, AI should be used to fulfil the advisers' duty of best execution.[103] While price discrimination is a common practice in market transactions, the fiduciary duty is insufficient to remove such a risk.

Consumer protection is key

Access to finance will require stronger consumer protection to increase consumers' willingness to use robo-advisers. Relying on an *ex post* regime based on common law is ineffective in providing protection to investors. The FCA stated[104] that if robo-advisers filter products and propose them based upon specific factors relating to a customer's life and/or situation, this amounts to a personal recommendation. Therefore, the entire set of laws related to consumer protection would apply. Consumers are usually deemed to be vulnerable, as they do not understand the mechanisms working in financial markets and also because they cannot fully understand the advice provided.[105] As an experimentation space, a "sandbox" would provide a more suitable environment for the emerging technologies.[106] Firms could then test a new business model built on Fintech without fearing the

---

97 Ibid.
98 John Kay, 'The Kay Review of UK Equity Markets and Long-Term Decision Making' (Final Report 2012) Recommendation 7.
99 FCA, 'Discussion Paper on a Duty of Care and Potential Alternative Approaches' (FCA DP 18/5, 2018).
100 Law Commission, 'Fiduciary Duties of Investment Intermediaries' (No. 350, 2014).
101 Law Commission, 'Fiduciary Duties of Investment Intermediaries' (Law Commission CP No 215, 2013).
102 Ibid.
103 John Lightbourne, 'Algorithms & Fiduciaries: Existing and Proposed Regulatory Approaches to Artificially Intelligent Financial Planners' (2017) 67 *Duke Law Review* 651, 679.
104 Tom Baker and Benedict G. C. Dellaert, 'Regulating Robo Advice Across the Financial Services Industry' (2018), Faculty Scholarship 1740, available at http://scholarship.law.upenn.edu/faculty _scholarship/1740. Accessed 05 October 2020.
105 Benjamin P. Edwards, 'The Rise of Automated Investment Advice: Can Robo-Advisers Rescue the Retail Market?' (2018) 93 *Chicago-Kent Law Review* 97.
106 FCA, 'Regulatory Sandbox Lessons Learned Report' (2017).

demanding scrutiny of the FCA.[107] However, it would not be sufficient to use a sandbox to protect consumers. In the US, the Securities Exchange Commission (SEC) charged two robo-advisers with making false disclosures.[108]

Product liability

The institutions, i.e. investment firms, are responsible for damages caused to, or profits gained from, investors. As the institutions will be deploying the AI devices, the current law specifies that they are responsible for damages caused to investors,[109] even though the AI devices have been developed by third parties, i.e. a tech company. In line with the approaches taken in the area of algorithmic trading, institutions using algorithmic trading are responsible for the effects caused and for the initial and continued testing of the algorithms.[110] However, the extent of the investor liability that the third parties should assume is not simply a matter for debate. The financial institutions could be insolvent, and there might be inadequate funding to compensate investors, whether provided through insurance or the government's scheme of compensation. There might be an issue of how investors may hold the third-party developers responsible for losses.[111] In the realm of product liability, third parties are strictly liable for consumer losses.[112] However, AI is not a product and may not be used or operated by the consumers themselves. More often than not, AI devices are a set of algorithms (software) used by financial institutions to provide advice or execution for clients. Should the computer scientists and tech developers be responsible for mistakes in the design of the algorithms? The general answer lies in the product liability of the software.[113] The more specific question is whether AI developers should be responsible for any damages caused by the design of AI. The same question also arises in automated

107 Wolf-Georg Ringe and Christopher Ruof, 'A Regulatory Sandbox for Robo Advice' (EBI Working Paper Series, May 2018).
108 SEC, 'SEC Charges Two Robo-Advisers with False Disclosures' (2018) www.sec.gov/news/press-release/2018-300. Accessed 05 October 2020.
109 Paulius Cerka, Jurgita Griginene and Gintare Sirbikyte, 'Liability for Damages Caused by Artificial Intelligence' (2015) 31 *Computer Law and Security Review* 376–389.
110 FCA, 'Algorithmic and High Frequency Trading Requirements' (Chapter Eight in MiFID II – Policy Statement I by FCA 2018) www.fca.org.uk/mifid-ii/8-algorithmic-and-high-frequency-trading-hft-requirements. Accessed 05 October 2020.
111 John Kingston, 'Artificial Intelligence and Legal Liability' (published in SGAI International Conference on Artificial Intelligence, 2019).
112 Section 2(1), Consumer Protection Act 1987.
113 European Commission, 'White Paper on Artificial Intelligence: A European Approach to Excellence and Trust' (2020) https://ec.europa.eu/info/sites/info/files/commission-white-paper-artificial-intelligence-feb2020_en.pdf. Accessed 05 October 2020.

vehicles[114] and defence software.[115] The EU Directive 1985[116] imposes strict liability on all parties in the supply chain for defective products, whether or not the defect arose from negligence. The UK law[117] that embodies this directive is not clear on whether software is a product: the application of this law to software might cause a floodgate risk, and due to the widespread use of software, a legal finding that software providers are at fault could lead to unlimited liability.

Regulating robo-advisers to achieve access to finance

To enhance financial inclusion through the use of robo-advisers, the AI solutions used must not be inferior to those used by wealth management providers to offer services to wealthier clients.[118] The major challenge of retail investors is to make informed decisions based on market information, such as fundamental aspects of companies, the industry specificities, market competition and macro-economic conditions. Average investors are not normally equipped with professional expertise or the time to collect and analyse these data. By contrast, the wealthier investors with the help of professional financial advisers could make better data-driven investment decisions. In the UK, after a free introductory session, typical independent financial advisers' fees are £450 for advice in an £11,000 investment asset scale; and £1,500 for investment strategy advice for a £50,000 inheritance.[119] AI should be used to level the playing field.[120] The World Bank's research indicates that the asset amount under the management of robo-advisers will be tripled in the US from 426 billion US dollars in 2018 to 1,486 billion in 2023.[121] For retail investors, robo-advisers are in place to reduce minimum investment requirements, even to no minimum investment criteria at all, as in the case of Betterment, and to charge lower fees, normally 0.25 per cent of managed assets for robo-advisers and 0.75 to 1.5 per cent of managed assets for human advisers. This is because robo-advisers save on fixed costs, such as the salaries of financial advisers, and reduce behavioural biases, such as limited capacity to manage and

114 Sunghyo Kim, 'Crashed Software: Assessing Product Liability for Software Defects in Automated Vehicles' (2018) 16 *Duke Law & Technology Review* 300–317.
115 Liis Vihul, 'The Liability of Software Manufacturers for Defective Products' Tallinn Paper No. 2. 2014. https://ccdcoe.org/uploads/2018/10/TP_02.pdf. Accessed 05 October 2020.
116 EU Directive 85/374/EEC on liability for defective products (Product Liability Directive) [1985] OJ L 210/29.
117 Part 1, Consumer Protection Act 1987.
118 Louise Langridge, 'How AI Levels the Playing Field for SMEs' (2018) www.morganmckinley.com.au/article/how-ai-levels-playing-field-smes. Accessed 05 October 2020.
119 Ibid.
120 Ibid.
121 Facundo Abraham, Abraham Schmukler and Jose Tessada, 'Robo-Advisors: Investing through Machines' (Research and Policy Briefs No 21, The World Bank 2019) http://documents.worldbank.org/curated/en/275041551196836758/pdf/Robo-Advisors-Investing-through-Machines.pdf. Accessed 05 October 2020.

invest in various categories of assets.[122] The Bank of America requires $25,000 US to create an account with private financial advisers, compared with $5,000 US to create an account with robo-advisers.[123] In addition, robo-advisers can easily be accessed at any time and from anywhere.[124]

In terms of redress, consumers are less likely to bargain for their terms and are less likely to bring lawsuits to recover compensation, due to the excessive costs of doing so.[125] Therefore, there must be more *ex ante* control in the design, development and deployment of the robo-advisers used, and a more robust complaint or compensation scheme for consumers.[126]

AI as RegTech

RegTech and SupTech in financial markets

Since AI can streamline KYC/CDD processes to reduce the compliance costs of financial intermediaries,[127] more investment firms could be set up to provide services to investors. This would increase market competition and allow more financial innovation, thereby providing better access to finance for consumers and investors. AI devices can be used to detect conduct that violates market integrity, such as market manipulation, price fixing, disinformation, insider dealing and money laundering. They can be used by financial institutions, regulators, policymakers or even private market watchdogs to detect and prevent such misconduct. When devices are used for this purpose, they are dubbed "regulatory technology" (RegTech).[128] RegTech will also include SupTech that is mainly used for the purpose of market supervision.[129] When RegTech is used to detect market misconduct, it involves elements of market surveillance that include the collection

---

122 Ibid.
123 Ibid.
124 Ibid.
125 Mitchell Polinsky and Steven Shavell, 'The Uneasy Case for Product Liability' (2010) 123 *Harvard Law Review* 1437 https://pdfs.semanticscholar.org/bc7a/62029d2eb48719140b1e32f2b71 41473a88e.pdf?_ga=2.52763693.481831465.1565280574-211989861.1563719626.   Accessed 05 October 2020.
126 Matthew Scherer, 'Regulating Artificial Intelligence Systems: Risks, Challenges, Competencies, and Strategies' (2016) 2 *Harvard Journal of Law and Technology* 353–400; *also see* 'Who's to Blame When Artificial Intelligence Systems Go Wrong?', available at https://theconversation .com/whos-to-blame-when-artificial-intelligence-systems-go-wrong-45771. Accessed 05 October 2020.
127 John Kingston, 'Using Artificial Intelligence to Support Compliance with The General Data Protection Regulation' (2017) 25 *Artificial Intelligence and Law* 429–443.
128 According to the definition given by FCA, 'RegTech applies to new technologies developed to help overcome regulatory challenges in financial services' www.fca.org.uk/firms/regtech. Accessed 05 October 2020.
129 Patrick Armstrong, 'Developments in RegTech and SubTech', available at www.esma.europa.eu /sites/default/files/library/esma71-99-1070_speech_on_regtech.pdf. Accessed 05 October 2020.

of individual data.[130] In this situation, the value of protecting individual rights and dignity may conflict with market integrity and public interest. For instance, an anti-money laundering regime requires financial intermediaries to screen personal data. However, this may be in contravention of the spirit of the General Data Protection Regulation (GDPR).[131] The main objective of RegTech is to protect market integrity. AI has been used as a SupTech service by exchanges,[132] in providing supervision and as a RegTech service by financial institutions,[133] for compliance purposes. In addition to ensuring the previously mentioned appropriate design modes in investor protection, another emerging concern is the need for data governance that ensures privacy protection and data protection.[134] In this case, to ensure market integrity, data on individuals can be collected that relates to law enforcement-related activities, such as insider dealing, market manipulation and money laundering.[135] Personal data, transaction/order book data, communications, and suspicious transaction and order reports (STORs) are collected for market oversight.[136]

The collection of personal data for RegTech may violate data protection rules and privacy rights.[137] While consent is required for controlling and processing data, data collected for market integrity can be processed and transferred without the consent of the individual.[138] That is to say, individuals may not have the right to prevent the unauthorised sharing of their personal information in accordance

130 Dirk Broeders and Jermy Prenio, 'Innovative Technology in Financial Supervision (SubTech) – The Experience of Early Users' (FSI Insights on Policy Implementation No 9, 2018).
131 Regulation (EU) 2016/679 of the European Parliament and of the Council of 27 April 2016 on the protection of natural persons with regard to the processing of personal data and on the free movement of such data, and repealing Directive 95/46/EC (General Data Protection Regulation) [2016] OJ L 119/1.
132 Mitchell Polinsky and Steven Shavell, 'The Uneasy Case for Product Liability' (2010) 123 *Harvard Law Review* 1437–1492.
133 Information Commissioner's Office, 'Big Data, Artificial Intelligence, Machine Learning and Data Protection' Information Commissioner's Office, available at https://ico.org.uk/media/for-organisations/documents/2013559/big-data-ai-ml-and-data-protection.pdf. Accessed 05 October 2020.
134 European Commission, High-Level Expert Group on Artificial Intelligence (2018) https://ec.europa.eu/digital-single-market/en/high-level-expert-group-artificial-intelligence. Accessed 05 October 2020.
135 FCA, 'Personal Data and Market Oversight' (2018) www.fca.org.uk/privacy/personal-data-and-market-oversight. Accessed 05 October 2020.
136 Ibid.
137 Information Commissioner's Office, 'Data Protection by Design and Default' Information Commissioner's Office (2019) https://ico.org.uk/for-organisations/guide-to-data-protection/guide-to-the-general-data-protection-regulation-gdpr/accountability-and-governance/data-protection-by-design-and-default/. Accessed 05 October 2020.
138 Information Commissioner's Office, 'Lawful Basis for Processing' (2019) https://ico.org.uk/for-organisations/guide-to-data-protection/guide-to-the-general-data-protection-regulation-gdpr/lawful-basis-for-processing/. Accessed 05 October 2020.

with the GDPR and Data Protection Act 2018.[139] The right of privacy can be violated when personal data are collected for the development and deployment of RegTech.

AI and anti-money laundering (AML)

Some regulators are using AI for fraud and anti-money laundering and countering the financing of terrorism (AML/CFT) detection.[140] It is possible, for example, that machine learning (ML) algorithms could detect suspicious transactions and provide a risk score for such transactions through supervised learning.[141] In addition, ML could be applied in order to screen known criminals, individuals and institutions who are on the global "black-list" and to forecast the likelihood of money laundering.[142] Furthermore, unsupervised ML can summarise the characteristics of variables and tag them based on certain criteria established by unsupervised learning.[143] That is to say, through unsupervised ML, financial institutions and regulatory authorities could identify the behavioural characteristics of financial crimes, including money laundering. The Australian Securities and Investments Commission (ASIC) has been exploring the quality of results and the potential use of natural language processing (NLP) technology to identify and extract entities of interest from evidentiary documents.[144] ASIC is using NLP and other technology to visualise and explore the extracted entities and their relationships. To fight criminal activities carried out through the banking system (such as money laundering), detailed information on bank transfers is collected and this information is correlated with information from newspaper articles.[145] Similarly, the Monetary Authority of Singapore (MAS) is exploring the use of AI and ML in the analysis of suspicious transactions to identify those transactions that warrant further attention,[146] allowing supervisors to focus their resources on higher risk transactions. Investigating suspicious transactions is time-consuming. Regulated

139 FCA, 'Personal Data and Market Oversight' (2018) www.fca.org.uk/privacy/personal-data-and-market-oversight. Accessed 05 October 2020.
140 FSB, 'Artificial Intelligence and Machine Learning in Financial Services: Market Developments and Financial Stability Implications' www.fsb.org/wp-content/uploads/P011117.pdf. Accessed 05 October 2020.
141 Deloitte, 'The Case for Artificial Intelligence in Combating Money Laundering and Terrorist Financing: A Deep Dive into the Application of Machine Learning Technology' www2.deloitte.com/content/dam/Deloitte/sg/Documents/finance/sea-fas-deloitte-uob-whitepaper-digital.pdf. Accessed 05 October 2020.
142 Ibid.
143 Ibid.
144 FSB, 'Artificial Intelligence and Machine Learning in Financial Services: Market Developments and Financial Stability Implications' (2017) www.fsb.org/wp-content/uploads/P011117.pdf. Accessed 05 October 2020.
145 Medici, 'Risk Management – The Most Important Application of AI in the Financial Sector' (2018) https://gomedici.com/risk-management-most-important-application-of-ai-in-financial-sector.
146 Ibid.

entities use defensive filings to protect themselves,[147] and this leads to a high rate of false positives.[148] ML is being used to identify complex patterns and highlight suspicious transactions that are potentially more serious and warrant closer investigation.[149] Coupled with ML methods to analyse the granular data from transactions, client profiles and a variety of unstructured data, ML is being explored to uncover non-linear relationships among different entities and to detect potentially complicated behaviour patterns of money laundering and terrorism financing that are not directly observable through suspicious transaction filings from individual entities.[150]

KYC of fund and asset management

Funds and other methods of investment, such as AIFs (alternative investment funds), attract a large number of organisations and individuals to invest. When individual investors or corporations make investments, they may also be requested to provide their personal information – including their name, address, date of birth, contact information, related anti-money laundering information, documents of income certification, payment details for dividend and redemption proceeds, and tax residence information. They are collected for different purposes, such as identification or to guarantee an obligation.[151] Thus, personal information is being controlled, processed and stored not only by investment fund companies, management companies or transfer agencies but also by the directors of these companies or other third-party agencies working for them.

To guarantee the security of fund transactions, MiFID II requires fund companies to reinforce six aspects of data collection.[152] For example, to prevent money laundering, customers may be asked to provide a certification of income. Furthermore, the Money Laundering, Terrorist Financing and Transfer of Funds Regulations 2017 require firms to maintain the safe custody of assets belonging to

---

147 Dunnly, 'Learn How Banks and Finance Houses Use AI for Regulatory Compliance' (2018) https://dunnly.com/learn-how-banks-and-finance-houses-use-ai-for-regulatory-compliance/. Accessed 05 October 2020.
148 Financial Action Task Force and Asia/Pacific Group on Money Laundering, 'Anti-Money Laundering and Counter-Terrorist Financing Measures' (Mutual Evaluation Report 2016) www.fatf-gafi.org/media/fatf/documents/reports/mer4/MER-Singapore-2016.pdf. Accessed 05 October 2020.
149 Ibid.
150 Ibid.
151 Deloitte, 'GDPR for Funds' (2019) www2.deloitte.com/content/dam/Deloitte/ie/Documents/FinancialServices/investmentmanagement/GDPR%20for%20Funds%20FINAL.pdf. Accessed 22 November 2018.
152 ESMA, 'Technical Advice to the Commission on MiFID II and MiFIR', (ESMA/2014/1569, 2014) https://www.esma.europa.eu/sites/default/files/library/2015/11/2014-1569_final_report_-_esmas_technical_advice_to_the_commission_on_mifid_ii_and_mifir.pdf. Accessed 22 November 2018.

their clients.[153] Under these regulations, firms should establish and keep records for at least five years with as much detail as possible.[154] This includes personal information regarding relationships, order handlings, reports, assets and so forth.[155] However, GDPR authorises data subjects to have their personal data erased without delay.[156] The data subject has the right to demand the information controller to erase personal data concerning them without undue delay and the information controller has an obligation to do so.[157] This principle conflicts with the MiFID II principle that requires a firm to retain all records kept by it in relation to its MiFID business for a period of at least five years.[158] The purpose of the information collected is paramount. Is it being collected for law enforcement purposes, for guarantee obligations, for developing new products or for research purposes such as developing RegTech?

Streamlining compliance processes

The KYC process is often costly, laborious and highly duplicative, covering many services and institutions.[159] According to Thomson Reuters, some major financial institutions spend 500 million US dollars on KYC and CDD annually; the annual spending of 10 per cent of the world's top financial institutions is at least 100 million dollars and the average is 48 million dollars globally.[160] ML is increasingly used in the remote KYC processes of financial services firms to perform identity and background pre-checks. For example, applying AI in the process of KYC could detect any attempt to use fake documents to perform KYC in real time. AI could complete the facial, documentary and any other verifications in real time in a single cycle. Hence, AI helps financial institutions to perform AML background checks in real time to avoid unwanted regulatory scrutiny and monetary fines.[161] ML is predominantly used in two ways: 1) evaluating whether images in identifying documents match one another, and 2) calculating the risk scores on which firms determine which individuals or applications need to receive

---

153 FCA, 'Safe Custody Services and Money Laundering' (2018) www.fca.org.uk/firms/money-laundering/safe-custody-services. Accessed 22 November 2018.
154 Ibid.
155 David Varney and Gareth Malna, 'How to Align MiFID II and GDPR when Processing Client Data: Actions for Regulated Firms' (2018) www.burges-salmon.com/news-and-insight/legal-updates/how-to-align-mifid-ii-and-gdpr-when-processing-client-data/. Accessed 22 November 2018.
156 Art. 17, GDPR.
157 Art. 17(1), GDPR.
158 FCA's Systems and Control Sourcebook 9.1.2.
159 John Callahan, 'Know Your Customer (KYC) will be a Great Thing When It Works' (2018) www.forbes.com/sites/forbestechcouncil/2018/07/10/know-your-customer-kyc-will-be-a-great-thing-when-it-works/#1f3fe9a98dbb. Accessed 22 November 2018.
160 Ibid.
161 Muhammad Imran, 'Use Case: AI and the KYC Industry' (2018) https://dzone.com/articles/how-artificial-intelligence-can-revolutionise-kyc. Accessed 22 November 2018.

additional scrutiny. ML-based risk scores are also used in ongoing periodic checks based on public and other data sources, such as police registers of offenders and social media services.[162] The use of these sources may enable risk and trust to be assessed quickly and cheaply.[163] Firms can use risk scores on the probability of customers raising "red flags" on KYC checks to help make decisions about whether to proceed with the time and expense of a full background check. Nonetheless, concerns about the tools' accuracy have kept some financial services from incorporating them. Research is needed to discover how regulators accept this kind of approach and what their worries are.

Public interest and individual rights

For public enforcement agencies, such as the National Crime Agency, the Serious Fraud Office, the FCA and policing agencies, current data protection law aimed at protecting individual sensitive data does not prevent them from collecting that information for the purpose of law enforcement, such as ensuring the security of citizens.[164] Furthermore, the current law does not prevent public agencies or financial institutions from collecting individual data in the public domain, and that can help them construct an individual profile for the purpose of KYC, as well as for the detection of suspicious transactions.[165] However, the ethical foundations of individual profiling for market surveillance have not yet been robustly established.[166] The identification of the parameters for agencies – either public or private – to carry out individual profiling will need to be built on human rights and human

---

162 FSB, 'Artificial Intelligence and Machine Learning in Financial Services: Market Developments and Financial Stability Implications' (2017) www.fsb.org/wp-content/uploads/P011117.pdf. Accessed 05 October 2020.

163 Ibid.

164 Art. 6.1(c and f), GDPR; Information Commissioner's Office, 'Guide to Law Enforcement Processing' (2019) https://ico.org.uk/for-organisations/guide-to-data-protection/guide-to-law -enforcement-processing/. Accessed 05 October 2020.

165 Art. 6.1(e), GDPR; also see PWC, 'Anti-Money Laundering: Understanding Global KYC Differences' (2014) www.pwc.com/gx/en/financial-services/publications/assets/pwc-anti-money-laun dering-know-your-customer-quick-reference-guide.pdf. Accessed 05 October 2020.

166 Information Commissioner's Office, 'Information Commissioner's Report to Parliament on the State of Surveillance' (2010) https://ico.org.uk/media/about-the-ico/documents/1042386/surveil lance-report-for-home-select-committee.pdf. Accessed 05 October 2020.

dignity principles[167] to ensure not only individual safety but also societal safety.[168] Such information could fall into the wrong hands and be used maliciously.[169]

Individual consent is inadequate in protecting the individual for the following reasons: first, a person, as a general principle, cannot consent to be harmed;[170] second, the individual may not appreciate the risk;[171] and third, the individual may not know to what they are consenting.[172] Hence, there is also a need to redefine individual consent: the method of consent, the purpose of consent and the possible revision and withdrawal of consent.[173]

Even for KYC processes conducted for the purpose of protecting the individual, such as assessing the clients' risk appetite in accordance with the clients' suitability rules,[174] the consent to individual profiling is also problematic. The problem can arise in data quality and accuracy that can affect the quality and accuracy of profiling.[175] The data could be collected via social media and smart devices. These integrated datasets containing information about an individual, possibly with extended information, can easily be seized by third parties through a legal request, e.g. a request from a foreign government.[176] Since clients did not consent to the sharing of their datasets with third-party government agencies, transferring these data or providing government agencies with access may have prejudicial effects on the individuals' rights in the legal process. For instance, the original data collector, even if fully complying with statutory obligations initially, will still breach its legal obligations if it shares data with the next public authority to

167 Paul Bernal, 'Data Gathering, Surveillance and Human Rights: Recasting the Debate' (2016) 1 *Journal of Cyber Policy* 243, 264.

168 Jerogen Hoven, 'The Use of Normative Theories in Computer Ethics' in Luciano Floridi (ed), *The Cambridge Handbook of Information and Computer Ethics* (Cambridge University Press, Cambridge 2012) 59–76; 'EU Ethics Guidelines for Trustworthy AI' (High-Level Expert Group on Artificial Intelligence 2019). See Respect for Democracy, Justice and the Rule of Law; and the Principle of Prevention of Harm.

169 Hamza Ahmed, 'Online Social Networks Threats' (2014) 5 *International Journal of Scientific and Engineering Research* 986, 988.

170 Victor Tadros, 'Consent to Harm' (2011) 1 *Current Legal Problems* 23–49; 'The Principle of Prevention of Harm under EU Ethics Guidelines for Trustworthy AI' (High-Level Expert Group on Artificial Intelligence 2019). The validity of consent to harm depends on the content of what is consented to and it is valid in some circumstances.

171 Matthew Humerick, 'Taking AI Personally: How the EU Must Learn to Balance the Interests of Personal Data Privacy and Artificial Intelligence' (2018) 34 *Santa Clara High Technology Law Journal* 405.

172 Ibid at 405–406.

173 Ibid at 407.

174 Victor Tadros, 'Consent to Harm' (2011) 1 *Current Legal Problems* 23–49.

175 Rick Sherman, 'Data Integration Processes', in *Business Intelligence Guidebook* (Morgan Kaufmann, 2015) Part V.

176 European Commission, 'Data Sharing between Public Bodies' (Consultation Paper No 214, 2013) 18. Intrusive surveillance technologies would be considered 'high risk'.

process the data further, unless the first collector provided a detailed explanation of the further sharing of the data and obtained consent at the time of collection.[177]

Policy recommendation

In this chapter, I have looked at the regulatory objectives and regulatory methods associated with management systems and processes where AI has been deployed in securities trading and investment services. The author uses HFT as an example to examine how AI is regulated on a trading platform that is not consumer facing. The primary regulatory objective is to deal with systemic risk – flash crashes, liquidity risks and procyclical behaviour. The secondary objective is investor protection (fairness) against market manipulation. The main regulatory approach is the requirement that operators – HFT specialist firms, securities firms, proprietary traders and trading venues – have internal risk management systems and processes. In this way, these operators are also required to consider market safety and market integrity. Whether HFTs should disclose algorithms to the regulators remains a contentious issue, and the UK regulators do not require such disclosure. The regulatory objective of market safety is appropriate as the basis for continuing the regulation of AI for trading platforms. However, HFT firms, securities firms and trading venues are all being subjected to a higher degree of control by regulators. These methods of regulation may not be appropriate for newcomers in the development of AI Fintech services provided on P2P trading platforms. The new P2P trading platforms, either on a distributed ledger technology (DLT) network or on Amazon-like ones, will need more consumer protection including price discrimination and the protection of privacy rights. In a P2P trading platform where consumers trade securities, the same regulatory objectives of market safety and market integrity should apply. The platform providers who use algorithms to execute client transactions, such as distributing their portfolios, need to ensure the protection of clients. To ensure there is no market manipulation behaviour, including price manipulation and price discrimination, the platform providers will also need to bear the burden of identifying those who use algorithms to trade or allocate securities. Unlike regulated trading platforms, the users of P2P platforms are likely to be individuals who rely on algorithms developed for interactions on the platforms. It is unlikely that individuals will have the capacity to implement risk management systems and controls. Therefore, to increase financial inclusion, the onus will be on the trading platform to monitor operations and to set the parameters of where these algorithms will operate. There should be an effective mechanism to exclude anybody from participating in the platforms who is found to be using algorithms to cause systemic problems or to manipulate the market.

---

177 Fleur O'Shea, 'Data Sharing in the Public Sector' (2015) https://byrnewallace.com/assets/components/uploads/Data%20Sharing%20in%20the%20Public%20Sector.pdf. Accessed 05 October 2020.

More detailed discussion on investor protection on the DLT-based crowdfunding platforms will be given in Chapter 8.

Section 3 discussed the protection of investors from asset managers and investment advisers who are using AI. Since asset managers and investment advisers (even online ones) are more consumer facing, more protection should be given to investors, particularly retail and consumer investors, to increase their willingness to use robo-advisers to manage their assets. It is unlikely that investors will be able to negotiate contractual terms that serve to protect them against potential harm such as misleading information and price discrimination. The standard of care under tort law in financial services is an unstable concept for investors to use to claim redress. Furthermore, it is not clear whether a fiduciary duty can be assumed by robo-advisers or by advisers using algorithms.[178] Fiduciary duties can also be altered and restricted by parties. A fiduciary duty concerns what a fiduciary (investment adviser) cannot do (conflict of interest) rather than should do (act in the best interests of the client).

Therefore, using common law principles to provide protection to consumer investors would be inadequate, particularly if AI aims to provide access to finance and to close the advice gap where less wealthy investors do not have access to the same advice services as the wealthier ones. Wealthier investors are not only able to rely on common law principles to control the level of their protection but are also more likely to make complaints and bring lawsuits. It is more likely that statutory protection based on policy will balance the need for closing the advice gap with that of financial innovation. For instance, the "best interests" principle and the suitability principle should continue to apply to the use of AI for providing advice on execution and investment. Detriments to consumers' welfare such as price discrimination – wealthier clients' investments are sold at a higher price – should also be factored in. In terms of user protection, the more problematic situation is the one in which an AI investment advice tool is provided online – freely downloadable – and can be used on the providers' platform or other platforms. These tools may not have been developed in-house by the investment firms. The advice may simply provide free guidance. In this situation, it is difficult to argue that there is a fiduciary relationship between a firm using robo-advisers and consumers/investors. There can also be a question about whether a contract is formed if the robo-advisers provide free investment guidance. Furthermore, it is likely that the software will continue to be treated as a "non-product," hence product liability rules do not apply. These factors could leave investors relying on robo-advisers without adequate protection.

Rather than traditional investment services, consumers may use online robo-advisers to purchase financial products that might otherwise be unavailable to them, because they do not have access to the information that wealth management

---

178 Simone Degeling and Jessica Hudson, 'Financial Robots as Instruments of Fiduciary Loyalty' (2018) 40 *Sydney Law Review* 63. http://classic.austlii.edu.au/au/journals/SydLawRw/2018/3 .html. Accessed 28 October 2020.

advisers provide. With open data and the development of more sophisticated algorithms, users may select online advisers that provide more economical services for advice and investment portfolio management. Consumers should be protected against poorly developed algorithms that do not act in their best interests, that are prejudiced against them or that cause damage through errors.[179] In Section 4, the focus was on using AI in RegTech or SupTech solutions for preventing, detecting and controlling financial crime, such as money laundering. Due to the cost of compliance, many online financial firms are prohibited from giving financial advice, especially if they process transactions on behalf of clients or if they provide P2P investment platforms. RegTech will streamline the KYC/CDD processes and hence reduce their compliance costs. This, in turn, will allow more firms to come to the market to offer services. The regulatory objective of market integrity directly conflicts with the privacy rights of individuals and data protection laws. It is submitted that data governance will need to be established to protect individual rights but also societal safety.

Conclusion

AI will bring benefits and risks to the financial services sector. Market safety, investor protection and market integrity should continue to guide the regulation of AI to ensure continuity. In addition to these, access to finance should be a regulatory objective so that AI can be used not only to benefit financial intermediaries but also to provide a larger social benefit to those previously excluded from financial opportunities. Access to finance will help the use and regulation of AI to gain wider public acceptance. For this objective, AI can be used to help the optimisation of capital on p2p platforms, to help consumers to have cheaper access to more information through robo-advisers and through the use of RegTech services to streamline KYC/CDD processes, hence reducing compliance costs. More detailed rules need to be developed to certify good algorithms and good platforms, to strengthen *ex ante* and increase *ex post* the protection of individuals who use robo-advisers, and to address how individual rights, such as privacy rights and data rights, can be protected to allow more efficient KYC processes to be conducted.

---

179 European Commission, 'White Paper on Artificial Intelligence: A European Approach to Excellence and Trust' (2020) https://ec.europa.eu/info/sites/info/files/commission-white-paper-artificial-intelligence-feb2020_en.pdf. Accessed 05 October 2020.

8 DLT-based crowdfunding platforms and investor protection

Introduction

In Chapter 7, I discussed how AI can be used in trading execution, in providing investment advice and in providing risk management solutions against fraud and money laundering. I have touched on how AI can augment these functions on a p2p platform. In this chapter, I will focus on how a crypto-market based on the blockchain technology can be used to facilitate a crowdfunding platform, and on the aspect of investor protection. The EU Crowdfunding Regulation will be used as a benchmark to identify legal risks and further opportunities for innovation. Although there are many provisions in the Regulation that protect investors, this chapter concentrates specifically on those included under the heading of "investor protection." Conflicts of interest,[1] marketing communications[2] and the investor complaints regime[3] are dealt with in other chapters.

Investor protection is a cornerstone of the financial market and is a key regulatory objective upon which many principles have been established.[4] It provides market confidence and has become an accepted universal moral principle in financial transactions.[5] It has also become a guiding principle for peer-to-peer

1 Article 8, Council Regulation (EC) 2020/1503 of 7 October 2020 European Crowdfunding Service Providers for Business, and Amending Regulation (EU) 2017/1129 and Directive (EU) 2019/1937 [2020] OJ L 347/1 (Council Regulation (EC) 2020/1503).
2 Chapter 5, Council Regulation (EC) 2020/1503.
3 Art 7, Council Regulation (EC) 2020/1503.
4 Niamh Moloney et al., *The Oxford Handbook of Financial Regulation* (1st edn, Oxford University Press 2015) 160; Dirk Zetzsche and Christina Preiner, 'Cross-Border Crowdfunding: Towards a Single Crowdlending and Crowdinvesting Market for Europe' (2018) 19 *European Business Organization Law Review* 217.
5 Edward Schoen, 'The 2007–2009 Financial Crisis: An Erosion of Ethics: A Case Study' (2017) 146 *Journal of Business Ethics* 805, 830.

DOI: 10.4324/9780429023613-8

crowdfunding platforms[6] which aim to increase access to finance,[7] access to a shared economy[8] and access to justice[9] when disputes occur. To what extent do the provisions of the Regulation provide effective protection to investors while at the same time giving entrepreneurs access to finance and investors access to the shared economy? Crowdfunding platform providers are also important stakeholders in this marketplace as they intermediate between investors and project owners,[10] between access to finance and access to a growing economy,[11] and between market competition and innovation.[12] Hence, when examining how investors are protected, other performance indicators such as the choices provided by the market (competition) or the quality of services given by platform providers (innovation) should not be overlooked.[13]

Crowdfunding platforms are an innovation in digital finance whose novelty lies in the application of technology to peer-to-peer financing. The innovation is not the crowdfunding itself, but the way that technology facilitates peer-to-peer transactions.[14] The role of the technology is to allow a broader spectrum of the crowd to interact, to promote trust between participants and to increase the returns. The blockchain-based crowdfunding platforms will allow the participants to have better access to the information and transaction costs can be substantially reduced due to the features of disintermediation and decentralisation.

6 Maximilian Goethner et al., 'Protecting Investors in Equity Crowdfunding: An Empirical Analysis of the Small Investor Protection Act' (2021) 162 *Technological Forecasting and Social Change* 1, 5. DOI: https://doi.org/10.1016/j.techfore.2020.120352.

7 Joseph Lee, 'Access to Finance for Artificial Intelligence Regulation in the Financial Services Industry' (2020) 21 *European Business Organisation Law Review* 731, 757; Araz Taeihagh, 'Crowdsourcing, Sharing Economies and Development' (2017) 33 *Journal of Developing Societies* 191, 222; Steven Schwarcz, 'Empowering the Poor: Turning De Facto Rights into Collateralized Credit' (2018) 8 *Duke Law School, Public Law & Legal Theory Series* 2018/38. DOI: http://doi.org/10.2139/ssrn.3167507.

8 Jochen Wirtz et al., 'Platforms in the Peer-to-Peer Sharing Economy' (2019) 30 *Journal of Service Management* 452, 483.

9 Columbia Centre on Sustainable Investment, 'Impacts of the International Investment Regime on Access to Justice' (Roundtable Outcome Document 2018) www.ohchr.org/Documents/Issues/Business/CCSI_UNWGBHR_InternationalInvestmentRegime.pdf. Accessed 24 April 2021.

10 European Commission, 'Proposal for Regulations of the European Parliament and of the Council on European Crowdfunding Service Providers for Business' (2018) https://ec.europa.eu/transparency/regdoc/rep/1/2018/EN/COM-2018-113-F1-EN-MAIN-PART-1.PDF. Accessed 24 April 2021.

11 Kurt Stanberry, 'Crowdfunding and the Expansion of Access to Start-up Capital' (2014) 5 *International Research Journal of Applied Finance* 1382, 1391.

12 Anton Miglo, 'Crowdfunding in a Competitive Environment' (2018) 13 *Journal of Risk and Financial Management* 1, 38.

13 Dan Awrey and Kathryn Judge, 'Why Financial Regulation Keeps Falling Short' (2020) 61 *Boston College Law Review* 2295. https://lawdigitalcommons.bc.edu/bclr/vol61/iss7/2. Accessed 24 April 2021.

14 Joseph Lee, 'Embedding Cryptoassets in the Law to Transform the Financial Market: Security Token Offering in the UK' in Philipp Maume et al. (eds) *Law of Crypto Assets* (1st edn, Beck/Hart/Nomos 2021) Forthcoming.

The objectives of technology on the platforms

Reaching out

Technology in the form of social media has played a significant role in connecting people across geographical boundaries[15] and in enabling strangers to interact by matching their interests. It can be used to reach people in every corner of the world who have access to the internet. Traditional village crowdfunding did not have the technological infrastructure to enable it to reach a larger spectrum of the population outside the village. As a result, legal innovations such as company law and secured transactions were invented to allow investors and savers to participate in ventures that they could not normally access through their limited monetary and physical capabilities, and to transact with people outside their geographical vicinity or social circle. However, stock exchanges only allow professional members to participate directly in raising capital and this makes the initial public offering process exclusive to a closed circle of professionals.[16] The technological ability to reach anyone and everybody through a crowdfunding platform means that such platforms are different in nature from modern stock exchanges.[17] As shown in Chapter 6 on the securities token offering (STO), crowdfunding platforms can facilitate the issuance of the STOs – bringing the project owners who issue STOs and the investors outside the constraints of the geographical boundaries.

Closing the trust gap

Crowdfunding relies on mutual trust between the participants,[18] traditionally village neighbours or clients of respected institutions, but such trust needs to be created among participants on a crowdfunding platform as they are strangers to one another. In traditional village crowdfunding, participants were familiar with the background of both the fund raisers and the contributors. The project seeking funding was often sanctioned by a person of prominence in the village such as a religious leader, a wealthy family, a politically influential clan or a government official. The church was often the place for fund-raising for projects to be carried out for the welfare of people in the parish or for a mission abroad. When members of a social circle know and trust one another, a robust credit assessment

---

15 Jenna Clark et al., 'Social Network Sites and Well-Being: The Role of Social Connection' (2017) 12 *Current Directions in Psychological Science* 32, 37. DOI: https://doi.org/10.1177/0963721417730833.

16 Benn Steil, 'Changes in the Ownership and Governance of Securities Exchanges: Causes and Consequences' (2015) https://core.ac.uk/download/pdf/6649711.pdf. Accessed 24 April 2021.

17 Joseph Lee, 'Law and Regulation for a Crypto-Market: Perpetuation or Innovation?' In Iris Chiu and Gudula Deipenbrock (eds) *Routledge Handbook on FinTech and Law – Regulatory, Supervisory, Policy and Other Legal Challenges* (1st edn, Routledge 2021) Chapter 20.

18 Krystallia Moysidou and Piet Hausberg, 'In Crowdfunding We Trust: A Trust-Building Model in Lending Crowdfunding' (2019) 11 *Journal of Small Business Management* 32, 37. DOI: https://doi.org/10.1080/00472778.2019.1661682.

or disclosure of information regime is unnecessary. But this is not the case on a technology-based crowdfunding platform, so the technology needs to play a role in closing the trust gap.[19] It is, therefore, important to decide what information should be made available to crowdfunding investors, what information should be retained by project owners and what information platforms can use to enhance innovation, services or their own returns. The blockchain-based crowdfunding platform can ensure information transparency and immutability. Information that can increase mutual trust between the project owners and investors can be shared on the platform to avoid misleading information and fraudulent activities.

Increasing returns

Investors look for a return on their investment, and technology can play a role in meeting their expectations with investor-driven financial innovation.[20] Even though a financial return may not be the only reason for their investment, it is so far unlikely that investors, either retail or professional, would use crowdfunding platforms for hedging purposes. As the number and activity of trading venues and market makers grows, market liquidity increases, and investors are able to realise their returns more quickly than they would have if they had to wait for dividends or interest to be paid. At the secondary market level (trading), trading by algorithms increases liquidity and reduces price arbitrage, while a central match-engine enables faster trading.[21] Technology also allows the development of products, such as exchange traded funds (ETFs).[22] Although the design of business models and the way returns are made on investments are under human control, technology has already demonstrated its ability to yield higher returns for investors and it has similar potential in the crowdfunding market. For instance, it can be used to manage individual loan portfolios when rates of return and default need to be precisely indicated.[23] Technology can also be used to match investors' offers in the secondary marketplace. In this regard, as discussed in Chapter 2, a blockchain-based secondary market can reduce transaction costs where trading activities can be both bilateral or multilateral without the intermediaries. The transactional information could be made public to the network participants. With the assistance of the algorithms, the participants are able to set the parameters for

19 Ryan Randy Suryono et al., 'Challenges and Trends of Financial Technology (Fintech): A Systematic Literature Review' (2020) 11 *Information* 1, 20. https://doi.org/10.3390/info11120590.
20 Kathryn Judge, 'Investor-Driven Financial Innovation' (2018) 8 *Harvard Business Law Review* 296, 438.
21 Michael Morelli, 'Regulating Secondary Markets in the High Frequency Age: A Principled and Coordinated Approach' (2016) 6 *Michigan Business and Entrepreneurial Law Review* 79, 107.
22 EY, 'Achieving Sustainable Growth through Exchange-Traded Fund (ETF) Product Innovation' (2020) https://assets.ey.com/content/dam/ey-sites/ey-com/en_gl/topics/emeia-financial-services/ey-etf-innovation-pov-6.pdf. Accessed 24 April 2021.
23 Hyeongjun Kim et al., 'Corporate Default Predictions Using Machine Learning: Literature Review' (2020) 12 *Sustainability* 1, 11. DOI: 10.3390/su12166325.

matching their trade orders and executing the token transfers without the need for having a central counterparty (CCP) and a settlement facility such as a central securities depository (CSD).

Enhancing value

Investors increasingly look for something beyond monetary returns and today, social media is used to connect with others who have common interests. Common value is increasingly seen as a reason for investment rather than simply maximisation of returns. For example, crowdfunding has been used to combat climate change[24] and to support performance art[25] that promotes diversity, and it can be used to raise capital for political causes.[26] Although value-related investment funds are already offered in the financial market, crowdfunding platforms can give more direct access to investors and entrepreneurs to match their values with an investment, without incurring excessive agency costs. This is what the UK Stewardship Code is aimed at achieving.[27] The advantage of the blockchain-based crowdfunding platform is that the audit trail can be made transparent and immutable. This aspect can help the investors monitor the project against the value statement produced by the project owners and the tokens issued can be redeemed by the investors if certain conditions have been breached, such as failure to reach a CO_2 emission target.

The scope

There are several types of crowdfunding, each giving different investment returns and having a different relationship between project owners and investors. There are four main types: lending-based, investment-based, rewards-based and donation-based.[28] There are also hybrid forms so that, for instance, lending-based crowdfunding includes raising capital through loans and through individual portfolio management of loans,[29] but if the platform facilitates issuance and trading of

---

24 Konrad von Ritter and Diann Black-Layne, 'Crowdfunding for Climate Change: A New Source of Finance for Climate Action at the Local Level?' (ECBI Working Paper 2013) https://unfccc.int/files/cooperation_and_support/financial_mechanism/standing_committee/application/pdf/paper_-_microfinancing_.pdf. Accessed 24 April 2021.

25 Benjamin Boeuf et al., 'Financing Creativity: Crowdfunding as a New Approach for Theatre Projects' (2014) 16 *International Journal of Arts Management* 33, 48.

26 Crowdfunder, 'Crowdfunding for Political Change on Crowdfunder' (2019) www.crowdfunder.co.uk/general-election/political-change. Accessed 27 April 2021.

27 Arad Reisberg, 'The UK Stewardship Code: On the Road to Nowhere' (2015) 15 *Journal of Corporate Law Studies* 217, 253.

28 Mokter Hossain and Gospel Onyema Oparaocha, 'Crowdfunding: Motives, Definitions, Typology and Ethical Challenges' (2017) 1 *Entrepreneurship Research Journal* 1, 14. www.degruyter.com/document/doi/10.1515/erj-2015-0045/html. Accessed 28 April 2021.

29 Burze Yasar, 'The New Investment Landscape: Equity Crowdfunding' (2021) 21 *Central Bank Review* 1, 16.

bonds it is categorised as investment-based crowdfunding. In investment-based crowdfunding, transferable securities such as shares are issued to investors by the project owner, who is normally a legal entity rather than an individual. Rewards-based crowdfunding gives investors access to goods to be produced or services that will be rendered by the project owners in the future. In donation-based crowd-funding, donors do not require any monetary return, but demand that any finance raised should be used solely for the purpose stated by the project owner. Donors are unlikely to reclaim their money if it is not used for the stated purpose. The role that technology plays in these four areas is primarily to digitise documents that show the state of the project, the relationship between the stakeholders and the property in issue. Digitisation not only streamlines the process,[30] but also facilitates any subsequent actions such as corporate actions, distribution of benefits and tax collection. Secondarily, the technology automates transactions on the platforms and provides guidance to participants on them.[31]

The Regulation only covers the first two types of crowdfunding (lending-based and investment-based) which are similar to the current capital markets where loans, bonds, funds and shares are issued as a means of evidencing the relationship between project owners and investors. Omission of the other two types from the Regulation can reduce potential legal risks in the crowdfunding markets but these types of crowdfunding are likely to become mainstream if properly supported. For example, rewards-based crowdfunding can become a stakeholder-based investment[32] that combines the interests of investors and consumers in the behaviour of the investment. The split between investors and consumers has been seen as a problem in the finances of modern corporations when management focuses on the maximisation of returns to investors[33] at the expense of the interest of other major stakeholders, for instance in consumer surplus. Donation-based crowdfunding is a way for citizens to invest in projects that deliver social good in a private, individual way. This is a potential model for the way government raises taxes and uses them for social benefit and public infrastructure. Even though citizens do not require monetary returns from the project owners, benchmarks can be set by which donors are able to monitor spending.[34] It is possible to specify consequences for a failure to meet the targets set, such as by reducing the salaries of,

30 Brennan IT, 'Process Automation and Digitisation' (2021) www.brennanit.com.au/digital-work-place-solutions/process-automation-and-digitisation/. Accessed 24 April 2021.
31 McKinsey Global Institute, 'A Future that Works: Automation, Employment, and Productivity' (Executive Summary 2017) www.mckinsey.com/~/media/mckinsey/featured%20insights/Digital%20Disruption/Harnessing%20automation%20for%20a%20future%20that%20works/MGI-A-future-that-works-Executive-summary.ashx. Accessed 24 April 2021.
32 Liang Zhao and Sunghan Ryu, 'Reward-Based Crowdfunding Research and Practice' in Rotem Shneor et al. (eds) *Advances in Crowdfunding* (Palgrave Macmillan, Cham 2020) 119, 143.
33 Michael Jensen and William Meckling, 'Theory of the Firm: Managerial Behaviour, Agency Costs and Ownership Structure' (1976) 3 *Journal of Financial Economics* 305, 360.
34 Lili Liu et al., 'Donation Behavior in Online Micro Charities: An Investigation of Charitable Crowdfunding Projects' (Proceedings of the 50th Hawaii International Conference on System Sciences 2017) https://core.ac.uk/download/pdf/77239562.pdf. Accessed 24 April 2021.

or benefits to, the project owners. As well as the advantage of reducing the legal risk, excluding the latter two types of crowdfunding may be a strategic decision to test the market sentiment on crowdfunding. Once the Regulation has been shown to support the crowdfunding market, rewards- and donation-based crowdfunding can be brought under its aegis or a similar regime can be created to support them, based on the lessons learnt. Already, there are examples of how these two types can operate to increase access to finance and the shared economy as well as matching stakeholders' common values.

Lending- and investment-based crowdfunding operate like a smaller scale of bank lending and IPO without the involvement of banks and other intermediaries.[35] The innovation is not the business model but the role of technology as an alternative to professional intermediaries. The question is how technology can act as an honest broker, as an information gatekeeper, as a value enhancer and as a social transformer.[36]

On a blockchain-based crowdfunding platform, the first two types can be easily tokenised with the underlying assets of bonds and shares. What can be more problematic is the reward-based and donation-based crowdfunding projects. The problem has been discussed in Chapter 3. It is therefore sensible that the Regulation should leave out the latter two types of crowdfunding.

Categorisation of investors: sophisticated and non-sophisticated

Categorising investors into sophisticated and non-sophisticated in order to assess whether a product or service is suitable for them has long been a way to protect investors against fraud and mis-selling. This *ex ante* approach, which might be seen as paternalistic,[37] has also shown how differentiating between investors can serve the legitimate function of promoting investor confidence. However, it can also result in over-protection that produces discrimination. The approach would be discriminatory if non-sophisticated investors are denied access to products or services that are only available to people who have the experience, the money and the information that allows them to analyse the risks and benefits of products, and the ability to share or spread any risks through packaging products further and selling them on the market. Non-sophisticated investors do not have this ability. Any requirement for assessing the suitability of products for particular categories of investors may protect the non-sophisticated, but it risks denying them access to a shared economy and thereby extending the wealth gap in society. Digital

35 Joseph Lee and Doreen Geidel, 'Mapping an Investor Protection Framework for the Security Token Offering Market: A Comparative Analysis of UK and German Law' (2021) http://doi.org/10.2139/ssrn.3765581. Accessed 28 April 2021.
36 European Commission, 'Study on the Role of Digitalisation and Innovation in Creating a True Single Market for Retail Financial Services and Insurance' (Final Report of the Centre for European Policy Studies Luxembourg Institute of Science and Technology, University College Cork 2016).
37 Cass Sunstein, 'The Storrs Lectures: Behavioural Economics and Paternalism' (2013) 122 *Yale Law Journal* 1826, 1899.

technology could remove this disadvantage by informing investors better and by using indicators to assess the risks that they might be exposed to. This approach would not make all investors equally sophisticated, but it could help to give better access to the non-sophisticated. What the technology should aim to achieve is to remove discriminatory barriers.

Start-ups have been considered risky investments[38] and have been reserved for venture capital firms.[39] This means that start-ups are experienced at pitching their projects to venture capital firms but may need to change their approach when making an offer to "crowds" of people who they do not normally deal with. The crowds are not necessarily less sophisticated in terms of the amount of money they have to invest or their ability to process information and assess risk, but they lack experience because they have previously been excluded from the market by the regulatory criteria. The role of technology deployed by the platforms is therefore to increase the level of "sophistication" of the crowds and to compensate for their lack of experience. There may be a temptation for platform providers to use Big Data and algorithms to increase the efficiency of confirming investors' level of sophistication and to fulfil the requirement of know-your-customer,[40] but the aim must always be to remove barriers so that technology does not result in denying access to the shared economy. It is submitted that blockchain-based platforms are able to record the behaviours of investors and can demonstrate if an investor is sophisticated or not. However, this function must be used with the objective of providing more access to the shared economy. For instance, if a record has shown that an investor has had a previous investment experience, more projects and services should be offered without imposing a requirement for more knowledge.

It is not only investors who may be categorised; there is an equivalent variety among projects. Platform providers may attach a risk score to a project and only allow certain investors to be involved in high-risk projects. However, it might be that these projects would benefit from longer term commitment whereas non-sophisticated investors are considered to be more likely to switch between projects. In this case, it is the preference of the project owners that discriminates rather than the riskiness of the project. Categorising investors can become discriminatory especially if project owners prefer not to associate their projects with a particular type of investor based on their geography, nationality, social class, gender or race. This is where platforms need to respect equality laws to prevent discrimination and technology can play a part by detecting and preventing it.

---

38 Jumpstart, 'Risky Business: All Startup Investments Come with Risk, but that doesn't Erase the Need for Storing Founder Fundamentals' (2017) www.jumpstartinc.org/risky-business/. Accessed 24 April 2021.
39 Jihye Jeong et al., 'The Role of Venture Capital Investment in Startups' Sustainable Growth and Performance: Focusing on Absorptive Capacity and Venture Capitalists' Reputation' (2020) 12 *Sustainability* 1, 13. DOI: 10.3390/su12083447.
40 Deloitte, 'How can Fintech Facilitate Fund Distribution?' (2016) www2.deloitte.com/content/dam/Deloitte/lu/Documents/technology/lu_how-can-fintech-facilitate-fund-distribution.pdf. Accessed 24 April 2021.

Hence, when applying the blockchain technology to the crowdfunding platforms, not only is the compliance with data protection law paramount, but how the investor's data can be used to profile an investor must adhere to good policy objectives.

Characteristically, crowdfunding platforms deal with large numbers of interactions and it is possible for categorisation to give rise to unfair and manipulative practices.[41] For instance, the investment strategy of sophisticated investors can be easily followed by the non-sophisticated who wish to capitalise on experience, but the existence of large numbers of non-sophisticated investors in a project may discourage further investment. This provides an opportunity for sophisticated investors to manipulate the behaviour of non-sophisticated investors. Categorisation can bring benefits in certain defined situations but the effects of categorisation, or profiling on open platforms where the behaviour of investors can be tracked, should be re-considered. There can be a dark side to transparency on crowdfunding platforms. It is therefore important for the platform providers to set the parameters on what information can be revealed.

Another more functional point is to decide whether borrowers on lending-based platforms should be treated as consumers. In the consumer credit market, a consumer who borrows is protected by consumer protection law and this should also be applied to borrowers on peer-to-peer lending platforms. It may be that transactions take place between consumers and investors, both of whom are considered non-sophisticated. The natural instinct is then to ask the platform provider to act as a guarantor against a consumer's default for the benefit of the investor, as well as acting as protector against unreasonable terms set by investors for the benefit of consumers. This implies that investors are unlikely to set their own lending terms and are merely contract-takers. Equally, consumers are unlikely to set the terms of loans and platform providers would set the terms to match the assumed interests of both investors and borrowers. In consumer-to-consumer lending cases,[42] more burdens would be put on platform providers because it is difficult to assess whether a borrower is a consumer or a business. For instance, crowdfunding may be used to finance a study as part of a business project and this may lead to a benefit such as a music album or attendance at a performance art work. Traditionally, this would be classified as personal finance, but in a blended economy, it can cut across business and personal finance and as a result it would be difficult to categorise a borrower as either a business or a consumer.

41 European Bank for Research and Development and Clifford Chance, 'Regulating Investment and Lending-Based Crowdfunding: Best Practices' (2018) www.ebrd.com/news/publications/guides /best-practices-for-regulating-investment-and-lendingbased-crowdfunding.html. Accessed 27 April 2021.

42 Christy M. K. Cheung et al., 'Customer Loyalty to C2C Online Shopping Platforms: An Exploration of the Role of Customer Engagement' (Proceedings of the 2014 47th Hawaii International Conference on System Sciences) DOI: 10.1109/HICSS.2014.382.

Information to clients

The theory of market transparency to ensure market confidence continues to apply to the crowdfunding market. The burden is on platform providers to ensure that clients are properly informed so they can make rational choices. A platform provider acts not only as a broker for the parties but also as a trusted third party of the information gatekeeper. Without such a role, platform providers would fail in their duty to provide critical market infrastructure. There have been cases where social media and search engines have provided platform services without ensuring the accuracy of their information and this has led to a greater problem than asymmetric information: disinformation.[43] In the financial markets, financial intermediaries safeguard the accuracy, quality and dissemination of information and platform providers need to play a similar role in order to safeguard investor confidence but also to ensure market safety and democratic values. They need to ensure that project owners and investors on the platforms are safe and honest players which means that they need to create their own rules to evaluate project owners and investors. On the one hand, they need to ensure that the projects are safe for investment, but on the other, that the investors are of integrity and do not intend to use the platform to launder illegally obtained money or to manipulate the market in a way that harms the projects. Platform providers must conduct their own due diligence to know their clients before they can offer their products or services or broker deals between project owners and investors. Platform providers may need to rely on third-party services to conduct their "known your consumers" duty.[44] They will need first to conduct due diligence to ensure that projects are genuine and not fraudulent and to conduct credit checks on the individuals behind the projects. This will also apply to investors. The data about an investor generated on the platforms can also be used for authenticating an investor. A blockchain-based database can be shared among regulated platform providers to ensure market integrity.

Adhering to the theory of transparency that aims to protect the investor, the Regulation requires that all information given by providers should be fair, clear and not misleading.[45] This includes information about the selection criteria for crowdfunding projects, and about the nature of, and risks associated with, crowdfunding services. They should also inform investors that providers' services are not covered by the deposit guarantee scheme or the investor compensation scheme.[46] Non-sophisticated investors should also be informed of the reflection period.[47] If credit scores or pricing suggestions are given, the provider must make

---

43 European Commission, 'Tackling Online Disinformation' (2021) https://digital-strategy.ec.europa.eu/en/policies/online-disinformation. Accessed 24 April 2021.

44 Geraint Howells, 'Protecting Consumer Protection Values in the Fourth Industrial Revolution' (2020) 43 *Journal of Consumer Policy* 145, 175.

45 Art 19(1), Council Regulation (EC) 2020/1503.

46 Art 19(2), Council Regulation (EC) 2020/1503.

47 Art 19(3), Council Regulation (EC) 2020/1503.

available a description of the method used to calculate them.[48] The blockchain-based platforms can gather more information about projects and are able to develop algorithms to provide credit scores and price guidance. This aspect has been discussed in Chapter 7.

Default rate disclosure

The default rate information on borrowers is a key indicator of their creditworthiness.[49] However, borrowers who are likely to be consumers or small businesses often have an unhealthy cash flow which may be the reason they came to the crowdfunding platform. While business lenders may understand how businesses may face cash flow problems, less sophisticated investors may easily be scared off by a default on the part of the borrower and react less rationally than a business lender would. Although the default rate is important information for investors, the key to increasing access to finance and a shared economy is the way platforms can help investors understand whether a default has been caused by a cyclical issue,[50] by an unavoidable event or simply due to borrowers' carelessness. There could be indicators that show what has contributed to a default rate so as to differentiate one default from another.

Because of this, the Regulation requires providers to disclose annually the default rates of the products they have offered over at least the preceeding 36 months[51] and an outcome statement for each financial year indicating the expected and actual default rates of all loans,[52] a summary of the assumptions used in determining expected default rates[53] and the actual return achieved through the individual portfolio management of loans.[54] The European Securities and Markets Authority (ESMA) will develop regulatory standards to specify the methodology for calculating default rates. This is similar to the principle of algorithms' expandability that a financial institution uses to provide investment advice to consumers and investors. The implications have been discussed in Chapter 7.

---

48 Art 19(6), Council Regulation (EC) 2020/1503.
49 Adair Morse, 'Peer-To-Peer Crowdfunding Information and the Potential for Disruption in Consumer Lending' (National Bureau of Economic Research Working Paper Series 20899, 2015) www.nber.org/papers/w20899. Accessed 27 April 2021.
50 Nanko Nemoto et al., 'Optimal Regulation of P2P Lending for Small and Medium-Sized Enterprises' (Asian Development Bank Institute Working Paper Series 2019) www.adb.org/sites/default/files/publication/478611/adbi-wp912.pdf. Accessed 27 April 2021.
51 Art 20(1)(a), Council Regulation (EC) 2020/1503.
52 Art 20(1)(b)(i), Council Regulation (EC) 2020/1503.
53 Art 20(1)(b)(ii), Council Regulation (EC) 2020/1503.
54 Art 20(1)(b)(iii), Council Regulation (EC) 2020/1503.

Entry knowledge test and stimulation of the ability to bear loss

The entry knowledge test has been a way to differentiate between investors for the purpose of protecting them.[55] In essence, it is a good way to test investor's knowledge but also to educate them about the potential risks of their investment. However, when the "knowledge" can also be learnt by repeating the test set by the platform providers, such a test would not reveal much about the real investment ability of the investors. The assumption is that they would be more careful with their own investment than an investment intermediary such as an agent might be. It is implicit that a professional agent needs a more thorough knowledge of the investment market and also of the investment knowledge of their clients. But when investors select their own products and services on crowdfunding platforms and agents are not involved, the entry knowledge test and simulation is intended to warn investors about the risks they are taking before they act. When they design the test questions, the platform providers make sure that they are not so difficult that they prevent investors from engaging in the market. But once non-sophisticated investors have passed the entry knowledge test, there is no further test to examine their knowledge and ability. There is no equivalent test of the supposedly greater investment knowledge of more sophisticated investors. This kind of risk warning is also used in other retail markets such as when buying cigarettes and tests can be used to make sure that consumers are fully aware of risks.

To this end, the Regulation requires providers to assess how appropriate any crowdfunding services offered might be for prospective non-sophisticated investors.[56] Under this requirement, they should request information about the prospective investor's experience, investment objectives, financial situation and basic understanding of the risks involved in investing.[57] This might include their past investments in transferable securities or past acquisitions of admitted instruments for crowdfunding purposes.[58] When investors fail to provide this information, or when providers consider them to have insufficient knowledge, skills or experience, providers must inform them that the services offered by the platforms may be inappropriate and issue them with a risk warning that states clearly the risk of losing the entirety of the money invested.[59] Investors should also estimate their ability to bear loss, calculated as 10 per cent of their net worth.[60] Furthermore, when an investor invests more than either EUR1,000 or 5 per cent of their net worth,[61] the provider must give the investor a risk warning, provide explicit consent to the crowdfunding service provider and demonstrate to the provider that the

---

55 Art 21, Council Regulation (EC) 2020/1503.
56 Art 21(1), Council Regulation (EC) 2020/1503.
57 Art 21(2), Council Regulation (EC) 2020/1503.
58 Art 21(2)(a), Council Regulation (EC) 2020/1503.
59 Art 21(4), Council Regulation (EC) 2020/1503.
60 Art 21(5), Council Regulation (EC) 2020/1503.
61 Art 21(7), Council Regulation (EC) 2020/1503.

investor understands the investment and its risks.[62] However, investors should not be prevented from investing in a crowdfunding project even if they show that they do not have sufficient knowledge or the ability to bear the risk. The responsibility of the provider is to make clear the risks of the investment, to help investors understand what they are investing in and the risks involved. The ESMA provides technical standards on how providers should assess whether their services are appropriate for investors, how to carry out the test of ability to bear loss and what information investors need to provide for the entry knowledge test.[63] There is the possibility for a trusted third party to provide data based on the investor's investment experience and financial ability. Currently, this is done by self-assessment and there is a possibility that an investor may not provide accurate information about themselves. A blockchain-enabled database shared by the providers may enhance this regulatory tool.

Pre-contractual reflection period

The pre-contractual reflection period is designed to protect investors from over-hasty action when investments can be made simply at the click of a button.[64] It is also important to ensure that consumers can retract investment decisions made in error, through misinformation or on perceived market pressure, after considered reflection. Platform providers cannot be expected to read the minds of investors and to know whether they have made conscious and rational decisions. On a crowdfunding platform, once the reflection period is past and investors can no longer cancel an investment without legal consequences, their contractual commitment is not a bilateral matter but one that affects the whole investment community. If someone decides to withdraw their investment, especially a large amount, other investors or potential investors may question the reason behind such a cancellation and draw negative inferences about the project. The reflection period can also prevent people from making a claim of mistake in contract law,[65] an excuse to vitiate the contract and thereby manipulate the market sentiment.[66] Interactive discussion in a chat room[67] on the platform can even prompt committed investors to worry and cause the project fundraising to fail. The Regulation requires providers to give a reflection period of four calendar days[68] from the moment the

---

62 Art 21(7), Council Regulation (EC) 2020/1503.
63 Art 21(8), Council Regulation (EC) 2020/1503.
64 Art 22, Council Regulation (EC) 2020/1503.
65 Duncan Sheehan, 'Vitiation of Contracts for Mistake and Misrepresentation of Law' (2003) 11 *Restitution Law Review* 26, 45.
66 Michele Meoli and Silvio Vismara, 'Information Manipulation in Equity Crowdfunding Markets' (2021) 67 *Journal of Corporate Finance* 1, 17.
67 Swindon, 'How Online Platforms Have Implemented Chat Rooms for Users' (2021) www.swindon24.co.uk/lifestyle/how-online-platforms-have-implemented-chat-rooms-for-users/. Accessed 24 April 2021.
68 Art 22(3), Council Regulation (EC) 2020/1503.

offer to invest, or an expression of interest by a prospective non-sophisticated investor, has been made. During this period, no reason needs to be given if the investors decide to revoke their offer. Platform providers must inform investors of this reflection period and the way in which their offer or expression of interest can be revoked.[69]

Publishing the offer

Some questions are left unanswered by the Regulation. First, when an offer or expression of interest is made, should it be made public during the reflection period? This may have a critical impact on the start of a campaign, especially if it is on a "first-come-first-served" basis. Some apparently impressive projects that have the backing of sophisticated investors can herd the non-sophisticated into investing. When a campaign fails to reach a critical momentum at the beginning, it may not impress non-sophisticated investors. Equally, if information is made public about the number and amount of investment offers (and expressions of interest), would the sudden withdrawal by non-sophisticated investors cause a market shock? Further study is needed on the behaviour of platform investors, and the subsequent regulations or rules designed by the ESMA should take account of potential market abuse and irrational investor behaviour. Providers may need to take remedial action to address market failures such as by publishing information about market dynamics – offers made and cancelled – during the reflection period.

The second question is whether a reflection period needs to be given to sophisticated investors, allowing them to withdraw without giving reasons. Since, according to the Regulation, a sophisticated investor may simply be someone who has invested in non-listed companies over the past two years, it does not necessarily mean that they are significantly less likely to make an oversight mistake. This is especially true when a person, whether sophisticated or not, is self-certified. Further studies are needed to observe the dynamics of sophisticated investors during the four-day reflection period,[70] in order to decide whether offers should be made public and if the reflection period should be lengthened.

The third question is how technology can help minimise the impact of the reflection period on market dynamics. Currently, the Regulation does not require investors to disclose reasons for their withdrawal. However, it may in future require providers to publish information about why investors have withdrawn offers or cancelled expressions of interest. It may be that investors will be required to state why they have withdrawn, but without the information being immediately disclosed to the investor community, or early statistics only being published later, perhaps after a delay of 12 months. Furthermore, in order to protect investors, providers must anonymise the responses and should have systems in place to protect

---

69 Art 22(6), Council Regulation (EC) 2020/1503.
70 Paul Belleflamme et al., 'Crowdfunding Dynamics' (CESifo Working Paper No. 7797, 2019). Available at SSRN: https://ssrn.com/abstract=3468029. Accessed 27 April 2021.

investors' privacy and personal data. Blockchain-based platforms can gather the information and set the timeframe for such information to be made public without revealing personal data about the investors. This information can also be used by the platforms to monitor potential market abuse behaviours.

Key investment information sheet

The key investment information sheet[71] is similar to a prospectus produced by a company seeking to raise capital. It sets out the information to be disclosed to clients in an investment fund,[72] and also that to be disclosed to borrowing clients. The former is to protect investors and the latter to protect consumer-borrowers. This information is critical to anyone who needs to make an investment or a borrowing decision, but what information needs to be disclosed depends on who will be relying on it. In a p2p lending case, even though the information should be disclosed to consumer-borrowers before they take out a loan, the people who will make the ultimate investment decisions to finance the borrower are the investors. This means that platform providers have information duties[73] to both consumer-borrowers and investors. They have a duty to warn investors and consumers on the platform about risks, and the mandatory disclaimer must be shown to investors. Platform providers act as an information gatekeeper[74] and therefore need to have procedures in place through which they can verify the completeness, correctness and clarity of the information[75] and to signal any defaults in the information sheet to project owners so that they can complete or correct it. Platform providers should suspend an offer if its project owner does not complete and correct the information and they should inform the investors of any irregularities. If the project owner does not rectify the irregularities, the provider must cancel the offer.[76]

Platform providers may act as more than simply brokers and can provide products for investors, acting like an investment advisor.[77] In this case, they would

---

71 Art 23, Council Regulation (EC) 2020/1503.
72 Council Regulation (EU) 1286/2014 of 26 November 2014 key information documents for packaged retail and insurance-based investment products [2014] OJ L 352/1.
73 Nanko Nemoto et al., 'Optimal Regulation of P2P Lending for Small and Medium-Sized Enterprises' (Asian Development Bank Institute Working Paper Series 2019) www.adb.org/sites/default/files/publication/478611/adbi-wp912.pdf. Accessed 27 April 2021.
74 John Armour and Luca Enriques, 'The Promise and Perils of Crowdfunding: Between Corporate Finance and Consumer Contracts' (2018) 81 *Modern Law Review* 51, 84.
75 Art 11, Council Regulation (EC) 2020/1503.
76 Art 12, Council Regulation (EC) 2020/1503.
77 Council Directive 2014/65/EU of 15 May 2014 Market in Financial Instruments and Amending Directive 2002/92/EC and Directive 2011/61/EU [2014] OJ L 173/34 (Council Directive 2014/65/EU); See also ESMA, EBA and EIOPA, 'Joint Committee Report on the Results of the Monitoring Exercise on "Automation in Financial Advice"' (2018) https://esas-joint-committee.europa.eu/Publications/Reports/JC%202018%2029%20-%20JC%20Report%20on%20automation%20in%20financial%20advice.pdf; ESMA, EBA and EIOPA, 'Report on Automation in Financial Advice (2016) https://esas-joint-committee.europa.eu/Publications/Reports/EBA%20BS

assume a higher duty to disclose information to investors since they are not sim-ply an information gatekeeper, but also give out investment specific advice.[78]

Providers also need to produce a key investment information sheet for inves-tors at the platform level when they provide individual portfolio management of loans.[79] This is when providers use algorithms to allocate investors' funds (auto-mated processes or auto-bid) to projects according to set parameters and at a level of risk predetermined by the investors. Providers must inform investors who have made an offer to invest, or expressed an interest in a crowdfunding offer, about any material change to the information and must rectify any omissions, mistakes or inaccuracies in the key information sheet if they could have a material impact on the expected return of the individual portfolio of loans.[80] The information sheet at platform level has to be fair, clear and not misleading,[81] and it must be updated by the providers throughout the duration of the crowdfunding offer.[82]

In neither of these two types of information sheet do the competent authori-ties exercise screening control. In other words, the sheets do not need to be pre-approved by the regulator. The platform provider acts as the sole information gatekeeper and needs to have procedures in place by which it verifies the accuracy of the information. For the key investment information sheet provided by a project owner, the provider is clearly an information gatekeeper. But in the individual portfolio management of loans, there is no equivalent entity that can verify the information provided by the platform provider, so the platform must itself verify the information it provides. One solution is, therefore, to put more emphasis on the procedure in place and on its application to verify the information. There may be a need to require the provider to have a separate and independent department within its institution to provide the risk management function.

The key role that technology can play here is to extract information about pro-jects and to provide comparisons for investors on the investment platforms, based on benchmarks. For instance, a benchmark can be designed for a project to show the risk, investment return, governance rating and ESG rating and to indicate its prospects. Platform providers are also obliged to disclose their methodology.[83] Blockchain technology can be used to more effectively extract information and

%202016%20422%20(JC%20SC%20CPFI%20Final%20Report%20on%20automated%20 advice%20tools).pdf. Accessed 27 April 2021.

78 Council Directive 2014/65/EU; See also Wolf-Georg Ringe and Christopher Ruof, 'Robo Advice – Legal and Regulatory Challenges' In Iris Chiu and Gudela Deipenbrock (eds) *Routledge Hand-book on FinTech and Law – Regulatory, Supervisory, Policy and other Legal Challenges* (1st edn, Routledge 2021) Chapter 11.

79 Art 24(1), Council Regulation (EC) 2020/1503.

80 Art 24(7), Council Regulation (EC) 2020/1503.

81 Art 24(3), Council Regulation (EC) 2020/1503.

82 Eversheds Sutherland, 'EU Regulation on European Crowdfunding Service Providers - A New Dawn for Crowdfunding' (2020) www.eversheds-sutherland.com/global/en/what/articles/index .page?ArticleID=en/global/ireland/eu-regulation-on-european-crowdfunding-service-providers_a -new-dawn-for-crowdfunding. Accessed 24 April 2021.

83 Art 24(2), Council Regulation (EC) 2020/1503.

benchmarks can be more fairly applied to the projects to deliver scores. With the functions of transparency and immutability of the blockchain technology, the platform providers can explain the methodology and the outcomes of rating activities more effectively.

Bulletin board

Some platforms allow investors to purchase or sell their investment after the primary market has raised the capital. In this secondary market,[84] investors can sell their investment at a premium, at par or at a discount. There are also buyers who might have missed the primary market sale for reasons such as lack of funds, but are later able to make an offer to purchase in the secondary market. To facilitate this, platforms can provide a bulletin board for buyers and sellers to advertise their interest.[85] However, unlike the secondary market provided by an exchange or a financial institution, platforms do not act as a central counterparty or a firm offering a systematic internaliser.[86] This ensures that a platform provider does not take on excessive risks of default and can continue to act as a broker without using the technology of an internal matching system which may cause default risk as well as legal risk. There are four main reasons why technology should not be allowed to speed up the process in the secondary market offered by providers. First, because it is difficult to control the trading behaviour of investors. Stock exchanges have the market-maker regime to ensure liquidity, but no equivalent system exists for crowdfunding platforms. Second, it is difficult to control the information flow on the platform, so companies do not have the continuing obligation of disclosure that allows investors to gauge the appropriate price of shares. Third, there is no regime in place that requires investors, especially block investors, to disclose reasons for their sales. And fourth, there is no appropriate regime to prevent market abuse and insider dealing on the platforms.

Hence, the Regulation's main focus on the bulletin board is to ensure that participants have access to the information they need to make decisions. This includes information disclosed for the purpose of raising capital in the primary market as well as information about the current state of the company or project in question.[87] Providers should require clients who advertise the sale of a loan,

---

84 Devasis Chakma, 'Objectives and Functions of Secondary Market' (2019) https://onlinenotebank .wordpress.com/2019/12/29/objectives-and-functions-of-secondary-market/. Accessed 24 April 2021.

85 Rasmus Jensen and Christian Uhlig, 'European Crowdfunding Platforms – New Opportunities for Alternative Financing for Start-ups and SMEs' (2020) www.plesner.com/insights/artikler/2020/10 /european-crowdfunding-platforms?sc_lang=da-DK. Accessed 24 April 2021.

86 Art 25(2), Council Regulation (EC) 2020/1503; Elizabeth Brooks Callaghan, 'MiFID II Implementation: The Systematic Internaliser Regime' (2017) www.icmagroup.org/assets/documents/ Regulatory/MiFID-Review/MIFIDII-the-SystematicInternaliserRegime-060417.pdf. Accessed 24 April 2021.

87 Art 25(3), Council Regulation (EC) 2020/1503.

security or instrument to make available the key investment information sheet about the project. If it is a loan sale, providers should provide prospective clients with information on the performance of the loan such as whether there has been any default or late repayment of interest. Furthermore, warning about the risk of loss of an investment, which is not covered by the deposit guarantee scheme[88] or the investment compensation scheme,[89] should be given to non-sophisticated investors. If a reference price is suggested, providers need to inform their clients that the price is non-binding and they must show how they arrived at the suggested price by disclosing the key elements of their methodology.[90] The blockchain-enabled platform can help project owners and investors fulfil their reporting duties on the secondary market. The information can then be shared by the participants on the network. There can also be a cross-platform sharing database to increase innovation and governance.

Access to finance, access to the shared economy and access to justice

The Regulation's focus on investor protection is grounded in the theory of market transparency whereby investors should be able to make their own decisions based on disclosed information. The role of the provider is to act as a trusted information gatekeeper. Furthermore, the provider has a duty to educate non-sophisticated investors about the generic risks of investment on crowdfunding platforms, rather than any specific risks to a particular project. In this regard, blockchain technology can be utilised to enhance market transparency by extracting more accurate data for investors,[91] by verifying the accuracy of the information provided by the project,[92] by compiling an index based on benchmarks to highlight aspects of the project,[93] by indicating the risks related to the project[94] and by providing guidance on the price of the investment.[95] Auto-investment, where providers

88 Council Directive 2014/49/EU of 16 April 2014 Deposit Guarantee Schemes [2014] OJ L 173/149.
89 Art 19(2), Council Regulation (EC) 2020/1503; European Directive 1997/9/EC of 3 March 1997 Investor-Compensation Schemes [2014] OJ L 84/22.
90 Art 25(5), Council Regulation (EC) 2020/1503.
91 Jannik Podlesny et al., 'The Power of Emerging Technologies: Finding Value through Data' (2020) www.mckinsey.com/business-functions/mckinsey-digital/our-insights/tech-forward/the-power-of-emerging-technologies-finding-value-through-data#. Accessed 24 April 2021.
92 Robert Klaschka, 'Construction Verification – A Revolution in Accuracy' (2020) www.thenbs.com/knowledge/construction-verification-a-revolution-in-accuracy. Accessed 24 April 2021.
93 Project MI, 'Improving Project Performance through Leadership and Technology' (Paper Presented at PMI Research Conference: New Directions in Project Management 2006) www.pmi.org/learning/library/project-performance-through-leadership-technology-8105. Accessed 27 April 2021.
94 Amine Nehari Talet, 'Risk Management and Information Technology Projects' (2014) 4 *International Journal of Digital Information and Wireless Communications* 1, 9.
95 PwC, 'Beyond Automated Advice: How FinTech is Shaping Asset & Wealth Management' (Global FinTech Survey 2016) www.pwc.com/gx/en/financial-services/pdf/fin-tech-asset-and-wealth-management.pdf. Accessed 24 April 2021.

use algorithmic technology to match projects and investors, is more problematic because it involves assessing investors' risk appetite. The entry knowledge test does not provide this information as it merely warns about the general risks associated with the crowdfunding platform. In addition to different degrees of risk tolerance, investors may have preferences for their investment and algorithmic technology can be used to match investments to such preferences. In this case, clients would need to disclose their preferences. There are no rules relating to investors' preferences, and collecting information about them may expose providers to the legal risk of violating privacy rights and data protection law. Matching investors' preferences with projects may raise questions around equalities law, for instance if an investor were to indicate a preference for investment in projects managed exclusively by a certain race and gender.

As the ESMA develops further technical rules, they need to bear in mind how the regulatory objectives can be achieved.[96] Smart technology can be used to extract more data from projects, for instance through the digital regulatory reporting system, and this would substantially reduce the project owners' burden.[97] Yet, the information generated would need to be further processed to make it useful to investors.[98] What information might be useful to investors would depend on their background, their risk tolerance and their preferences.[99] While standardised information disclosure can be simple for investors to understand, individuals may want additional information to be disclosed to them for their consideration. The significant factors are not the quantity or quality of data disclosed through the digital regulatory reporting system[100] but rather the processed information that investors have available to them as they make their investment decisions. Such processed information would include ratings of the expected default rate, the ESG

96 ESMA Consultation Paper, 'Draft Technical Standards under the ECSP Regulation' (2021). www.esma.europa.eu/sites/default/files/library/esma35-36-2201_cp_-_ecspr_technical_standards.pdf. Accessed 27 April 2021.
97 Lawrence Lessig, *Code and Other Laws of Cyberspace* (New York: Basic Books 1999); Eva Micheler and Anna Whaley, 'Regulatory Technology: Replacing Law with Computer Code' (2020) 21 *European Business Organisation Law Review* 349, 377; Karen Yeung, 'Regulation by Blockchain: The Emerging Battle for Supremacy between the Code of Law and Code as Law' (2019) 82 *Modern Law Review* 207, 239.
98 Mannesh Samatani, 'UK Digital Regulatory Reporting Pilot Completes Phase Two' (2020) www.regulationasia.com/uk-digital-regulatory-reporting-pilot-completes-phase-two/. Accessed 24 February 2021.
99 Fennie Wang and Primavera De Filippi, 'Self-Sovereign Identity in a Globalized World: Credentials-Based Identity Systems as a Driver for Economic Inclusion' (2020) 2 *Frontiers in Blockchain* www.frontiersin.org/articles/10.3389/fbloc.2019.00028/full?field=&id=496586&journalName=Frontiers_in_Blockchain&utm_campaign=Email_publication&utm_content=T1_11.5e1_author&utm_medium=Email&utm_source=Email_to_authors_. Accessed 27 April 2021.
100 Johan Von Solms, 'Integrating Regulatory Technology (RegTech) into the Digital Transformation of a Bank Treasury' (2020) 1 *Journal of Banking Regulation* 1, 17. DOI: https://doi.org/10.1057/s41261-020-00134-0; PA, 'Digital Regulatory Reporting: A Review of Phases 1 and 2 of the Digital Regulatory Reporting Initiative' (2020) www2.paconsulting.com/rs/526-HZE-833/images/DRR-Report-Sept-2020.pdf. Accessed 24 April 2021.

rating[101] and various other indicators. The Regulation requires providers to disclose how they calculate such ratings, even though it is questionable whether the methodology, and especially its implications, can be properly understood by nonsophisticated investors. Chapter 11 of this book has a more detailed discussion on the concept and implementation of a digital regulatory reporting system based on the DLT infrastructure.

This chapter focuses on the *ex ante* approach to investor protection based on the disclosure regime in which the provider acts as an information gatekeeper. An *ex post* approach would rely more on investors bringing their claims to tribunals to seek redress, and thereby correcting poor behaviour. Such an *ex post* approach relies on investors having the time, the know-how and the finance to initiate claims to obtain justice, not merely for themselves but also for the market as a whole. It therefore puts the onus on investors to ensure market confidence and justice, and if they lack the time, the expertise or the finance, access to justice may be denied them. What blockchain technology can do is to identify any gaps between the project owner's original hopes about the outcome of the project, and what actually happened.[102] This does not necessarily mean that the project owner produces unfair, unclear and misleading information, but it is natural for project owners to be optimistic about their enterprises and the before-and-after comparison can help investors identify differences easily, without the need to scrutinise project owners' and platform owners' documentation. It can also be easier for investors to detect if an originally genuine project became fraudulent during the investment period. If the supply chain of a project is based on other crowdfunded projects, it would be easier for investors to monitor a project and discover faults. This can give investors an informational advantage that might have needed financial forensic and legal experts to discover in a normal financial misinformation claim.

Conclusion

This chapter discusses how blockchain-based crowdfunding platforms can enhance investors' protection under the EU Crowdfunding Regulation, in particular in respect of the information disclosure regime. Such protection is based on the theory of market transparency in which investors are enabled to make rational decisions based on available information. Even though crowdfunding may be similar to other professional fundraising markets, the fact that investor profiles vary and that an aim of crowdfunding is to increase participation by non-sophisticated savers means that more research is needed to achieve access to a

---

101 Elena Escrig-Olmedo et al., 'Rating the Raters: Evaluating How ESG Rating Agencies Integrate Sustainability Principles' (2019) 11 *Sustainability* 1, 16. DOI: https://doi.org/10.3390/SU11030915.

102 Michael Becker et al., 'RegTech – The Application of Modern Information Technology in Regulatory Affairs: Areas of Interest in Research and Practice' (2020) 27 *Intelligent Systems in Accounting, Finance and Management* 161, 167.

shared economy by platform providers. Although technology already puts crowds of investors in touch with entrepreneurs, there is much that technology can do to increase investors' ability to make informed choices. More information does not necessary translate into more informed judgment by investors, so as well as the information gatekeeping role that providers can play, there is more that they can do through technology to help investors digest information and make choices. Algorithms may help investors choose products, yet auto-invest facilitated by smart contracts needs to increase access to finance rather than foreclose it by discrimination. While it is right that non-sophisticated investors should not be prevented from investing in projects and products, it is equally important to ensure that project owners should not be unjustly denied access to investors based on investors' preferences. Providers need to have procedures in place, and to apply them, to test their methodology and algorithms for extracting information, for providing indication, for giving guidance on pricing and for auto-bid/auto-invest. Blockchain-based platforms can enhance providers' abilities in achieving these tasks. The regulator should also devise regimes to determine when provisions apply to ensure the fairness and safety of the technology used, taking into account how blockchain technology may offer some regulatory solutions. Any provisions should also adhere to the objectives of access to finance, access to a shared economy and access to justice.

9 The economics and politics of data and its legal protection in cryptocurrencies

Introduction – breakdown of the old social contract: access to finance and equal economic opportunity

The rise of cryptocurrency is a response to dissatisfaction with the current financial markets which are dominated by a few powerful currencies, financial institutions and advanced economies.[1] As a consequence, the creation and distribution of wealth have favoured individuals holding these international currencies and the shareholders of financial institutions. The rise of cryptocurrency carries some clear messages: financial inclusion, wider access to finance and disruption of the current global financial system.[2] This potential attracts a lot of attention from both private and public entities as they decide how to respond to the demands of a new global financial system that could close gaps between advanced and underdeveloped economies and societies.[3] How can cryptocurrency empower people who have been deprived of their economic rights by not being able to participate in a centralised and intermediated global financial system?

Many virtual, mobile, digital currencies can empower users, particularly those who are unable to create wealth due to lack of access to finance for project funding, or to receive wealth due to them because of financial instability, corruption or the high cost of currency exchange.[4] In today's increasingly IT-based world, by providing access to finance, welfare, public services and justice through technology such as blockchain, cryptocurrency can provide not only better access

1 Marek Dabrowski and Lukasz Janikowski, 'Virtual Currencies and Central Banks Monetary Policy: Challenges Ahead' (Monetary Dialogue, Policy Department for Economic, Scientific and Quality of Life Policies of European Parliament, July 2018).
2 Peter Gomber, Robert Kauffman, Chris Parker and Bruce Weber, 'On the FinTech Revolution: Interpreting the Forces of Innovation, Disruption and Transformation in Financial Services' (2018) 35(1) *Journal of Management Information Systems* 220, 265.
3 Lieve Fransen, Gino Del Bufalo and Edoardo Reviglio, 'Boosting Investment in Social Infrastructure in Europe' (Report of the High-Level Task Force on Investing in Social Infrastructure in Europe, European Commission and European Association ELTI Long-Term Investors, 2018).
4 Vrajlal Sapovadia, 'Financial Inclusion, Digital Currency, and Mobile Technology' in David Lee Kuo Chuen and Robert H. Deng (eds), *Handbook of Blockchain, Digital Finance and Inclusion: ChinaTech, Mobile Security, and Distributed Ledger* (Academic Press 2018) 361, 385.

DOI: 10.4324/9780429023613-9

to finance but also access to other public services such as justice,[5] thus enabling developmental "leapfrog" for the poorer regions and nations.[6] Private entities, government agencies and other consortia all have launched programmes that create cryptocurrencies that are virtual, cross-border, peer-to-peer, global, algorithmic and data-based.

As in many smart technology-based spaces, data protection and violations of privacy rights are major risks to users,[7] particularly to vulnerable and marginalised people who lack effective access to finance, services and justice. Cryptocurrency is no exception, despite any reassurance that cryptography and encryption technologies can be embedded in the system to provide adequate safeguards. In this chapter, I intend to show how issues of personal data and privacy are major risks to the users of cryptocurrency, which, despite potential benefits, can exacerbate exclusion through discriminatory user profiling, state surveillance[8] and data rendition practices (so-called surveillance capitalism).[9] I will use three policy goals – personal autonomy, the development of digital economy and crime prevention – to measure the effectiveness of data protection law and privacy rights under different types of cryptocurrency: unstable coins on the public chain (Bitcoin[10]); stable coins on the private chain created by private entities such as LIBRA;[11] and state-backed cryptocurrency created by the state such as a central bank, e.g. the Chinese digital currency electronic payment (DCEP).[12] I will then discuss the extent to which information generated by cryptocurrency will enhance economic rights, such as access, or whether in addition it is likely to diminish or transform political rights. In particular, how will the development of cryptocurrencies affect and be affected by international relations?

5 Robby Houben, 'Cryptocurrencies and Blockchain: Legal Context and Implications for Financial Crime, Money Laundering and Tax Evasion' (Policy Department for Economic, Scientific and Quality of Life Policies, July 2018).
6 Douglas Arner, Janos Nathan Barberis and Ross Buckley, 'The Evolution of FinTech: A New Post-Crisis Paradigm?' (University of Hong Kong Faculty of Law Research Paper No. 2015/0467, 2019).
7 Gilad Rosner and Erin Kenneally, 'Privacy and the Internet of Things' (Centre for Long-Term Cybersecurity White Paper, 2018).
8 Jules Polonetsky and Omer Tene, 'Privacy and Big Data: Making Ends Meet' (2013) 66(25) *Stanford Law Review* Online. https://fpf.org/wp-content/uploads/Big-Data-and-Privacy-Paper-Collection.pdf. Accessed 18 October 2020.
9 Shoshana Zuboff, *The Age of Surveillance Capitalism: The Future at the New Frontier of Power* (Profile Books, Main Edition, January 2019).
10 Joseph Lee and Florian Lheureux, 'A Regulatory Framework for Cryptocurrency' (2020) 31(3) *European Business Law Review* 423, 446.
11 Bruhl Volker, 'LIBRA – A Differentiated View on Facebook's Virtual Currency Project' (CFS Working Paper Series No. 633, 2019).
12 Jemma Xu and Dan Prudhomme, 'China's Digital Currency Revolution and Implications for Global Business Strategy' 2020 *London School of Economics Business Review*. DOI: https://doi.org/10.13140/RG.2.2.18819.94240.

Risk of data violation and privacy right violation through cryptocurrency

Does privacy benefit the public?

The rise of unstable coins on the public chain is both a political movement and an economic response to dissatisfaction with the current global financial system. It is also a preferred method of transaction by users who need privacy (or secrecy) in their transactions. Anonymity[13] is essential for those who require or prefer their identity to be unknown to the world or even to the counterparty in a transaction. Detailed information about the transactions remains confidential to third parties, secret to the world and, more significantly, untraceable by anyone, including the parties themselves. Criminals have been exploring anonymity to engage in illicit and illegal activities,[14] thereby tainting the reputation of cryptocurrency as a legitimate way of disrupting the established economic and political governance. Anonymity is now seen as a "public bad." These criminal activities are often associated with market manipulation, fraud, money laundering, tax evasion and the drug trade.

One of the public goods of fiat currency (cash) is to protect the privacy of users through anonymity in transactions. Users do not need to reveal their identity when using fiat currency to make a transaction, unless required by law or mutual agreement. Once the transaction is concluded, it cannot be traced unless the parties keep a record e.g. a contract or a receipt. With the invention of the credit card (third-party payment systems) and digital money (PayPal and the like), both anonymity and privacy have been greatly eroded. An array of information such as name, age, gender, nationality and address can be revealed. In addition, third-party intermediaries – such as the credit card companies and merchant acquirers – can also access information related to transactions,[15] including the price, the subject matter, the location of the transactions and the financial intermediaries (banks or third-party payment systems) used. Whether or not the transaction information is a public good must be assessed against different policy goals: personal autonomy,[16] the development of the digital economy or crime prevention.[17] These

---

13 'FATF Report to the G20 Finance Ministers and Central Bank Governors on So-Called Stable-coins' (The Financial Action Task Force, 2020).
14 Joseph Lee, 'Law and Regulation for a Crypto-Market: Perpetuation or Innovation?' In Chiu Iris and Deipenbrock Gudula (eds) *Routledge Handbook on FinTech and Law – Regulatory, Supervisory, Policy and other Legal Challenges* (1st edn, Routledge 2021).
15 Susan Herbst-Murphy, 'Clearing and Settlement of Interbank Card Transactions: A MasterCard Tutorial for Federal Reserve Payments Analysts' (Discussion Paper of Payment Card Centre, 2013).
16 Arjen Mulder, 'Government Dilemmas in the Private Provision of Public Goods' (Erasmus Research Institute of Management Research Paper 2004).
17 'The Age of Digital Interdependence' (Report of the United Nations Secretary-General's High-Level Panel on Digital Cooperation), www.un.org/en/pdfs/DigitalCooperation-report-for%20web.pdf. Accessed 18 October 2020.

policy goals will affect users' understanding of public good and their implementation through law and regulation can establish trust in the cryptocurrency system.

Over the course of history, fiat currency has replaced the barter system in trade and replaced the use of treasury stone such as gold and silver as means of payment.[18] In the same way, central banks have replaced private institutions or associations as trusted third parties in issuing currency and have performed the economic and political functions of monetary control that had not previously been taken on.[19] Unstable coins on the public chain, such as Bitcoin, now resemble another form of financial system and governance that facilitates the exchange of goods and services. They allow users to transact the provision of goods and services in the virtual world more cheaply, while protecting the privacy of the users who exercise their autonomy in the virtual economic and social spaces. The unanswered question is what form of democratised governance[20] should be adopted in this new virtual space and how should users be able to exercise their political rights in terms of monetary control for market stability, currency manipulation for market integrity and fiscal transparency?[21]

Information as a public good?

Information is the foundation of the modern financial system,[22] and its infrastructure needs to perform a monetary function, to supervise the market, to allow innovation of products and services and to support financial aid. Its infrastructure controls the way information can be gathered, stored, processed, utilised and shared.[23] The information infrastructure of unstable coins on the public chain, such as Bitcoin using open source technology, is a consensus system, in which a consortium or a group of people or entities can take collective decisions to deliver transparency and immutability of any transactions that are recorded.[24] However, many aspects of this consensus-based information infrastructure remain opaque.[25]

---

18 Ross Starr, 'Money: In Transactions and Finance' (University of California Working Paper), https://econweb.ucsd.edu/~rstarr/Money%20in%20Transactions%20and%20Finance.pdf. Accessed 18 October 2020.

19 Stefano Ugolini, 'The Historical Evolution of Central Banking' (*Handbook of the History of Money and Currency*, Springer Nature 2018).

20 Yan Chen, 'Blockchain Tokens and the Potential Democratisation of Entrepreneurship and Innovation' (2018) 61(4) *Business Horizons* 567, 575.

21 Huw Van Steenis, 'Future of Finance – Review on the Outlook for the UK Financial System: What It Means for The Bank of England' (June 2019) www.bankofengland.co.uk/-/media/boe/files/report/2019/future-of-finance-report. Accessed 20 October 2020.

22 Mario Strassberger, 'Thoughts on Foundations of the Modern Theory of Finance' (2015) https://papers.ssrn.com/sol3/papers.cfm?abstract_id=2648520. Accessed 18 October 2020.

23 'The Future of Financial Infrastructure: An Ambitious Look at How Blockchain Can Reshape Financial Services' (An Industry Project of the Financial Services Community, World Economic Forum 2016).

24 Ibid.

25 Marcella Atzori, 'Blockchain Technology and Decentralised Governance: Is the State Still Necessary?' (2017) 6(1) *Journal of Governance and Regulation* 45, 62.

It is difficult to know if the information collected through it is beneficial or detrimental to the public. It is difficult to assess how privacy is guaranteed, how information will be used to increase the system's digital capability or how the risk of crime will be mitigated.[26] On the one hand, unstable coins on the public blockchain promises total anonymity and privacy protection; but on the other, it also promotes transparency and immutability as a unique selling point.[27] This contradiction has caused not only developers, but also regulators, to take a "wait and see" approach. Developers want to see what information can be legally collected and processed on the chain in order to develop the technology, and regulators want to see what the industry develops and to construct laws to mitigate any risks. However, the "regulatory sandbox" provided by regulators[28] as a safe space to test the functionality of cryptocurrency does not contribute to the discussion of how privacy and data can be for or against the public good. The answer lies in the policy goals of cryptocurrency. If cryptocurrency is going to be developed as a digital payment system which is able to collect transaction information, the existing legal and regulatory treatment for information management by digital payment operators can easily be applied to it.[29] Digital payment operators such as debit and credit card operators or third-party payment operators are already able to obtain personal information and are required to protect data subjects under the data protection law and privacy law. These operators are able to monetise information, through creating ownership in the information, and are able to share information with third parties under legal obligations such as law enforcement agencies.[30] By using digital payment services, large amounts of personal information are in the hands of the operators. As more digital transactions are carried out, more information can be generated through the systems. However, each operator has its own system to manage the information and, by default, cannot share information without the data subject's consent. "Big Data" can be created through the information collected and processed without the possibility of revealing personal data.[31] The operator may not even share such a valuable "Big Data" asset (a private good) with others, including government agencies, unless required by the law for regulatory reporting or law enforcement purposes (a public good). But cryptocurrency is more than

26 'Privacy and Information Technology' (Stanford Encyclopedia of Philosophy, 2019) https://plato.stanford.edu/entries/it-privacy/. Accessed 18 October 2020.
27 Andrej Zwitter and Mathilde Boisse-Despiaux, 'Blockchain for Humanitarian Action and Development Aid' (2018) 3(16) *Journal of International Humanitarian Action* 1, 7.
28 Jayound James Goo and Joo-Yeun Heo, 'The Impact of the Regulatory Sandbox on the FinTech Industry, with a Discussion on the Relation between Regulatory Sandboxes and Open Innovation' (2020) 6(43) *Journal of Open Innovation: Technology, Market, and Complexity* 1, 18.
29 'Digital Financial Services: Regulating for Financial Inclusion – An ICT Perspective' (Working Paper of the International Telecommunication Union, 2016) www.itu.int/dms_pub/itu-d/opb/pref/D-PREF-BB.REG_OUT02-2016-PDF-E.pdf. Accessed 18 October 2020.
30 Heiko Richter and Peter Slowinski, 'The Data Sharing Economy: On the Emergence of New Intermediaries' (2019) 50 *International Review of Intellectual Property and Competition Law* 4, 29.
31 Priyank Jain, Manasi Gyanchandani and Kilay Khare, 'Big Data Privacy: A Technological Perspective and Review' (2016) 3(25) *Journal of Big Data* 1, 25.

just a digital payment system like a credit card company, third-party payment system (PayPal) or a merchant acquirer.

Unstable coins' public chain operations – opaque information infrastructure and space for criminality

Unstable coins on the public chain such as Bitcoin claim that users or participants are able to view all the transactions on the blockchain network (information as a public good), however, personal identity (a private good) is encrypted to safeguard personal autonomy. In this way, access to information can be achieved while protecting individual data and privacy. Whether it is technologically or legally possible is yet to be seen. There is a risk that the encryption technology is not secure. With time, computing power will be able to decrypt the information.[32] Hence, personal data and privacy are only temporarily safe, and cannot be protected in the long term. On the other hand, even if the encryption is secure, the government would lose its ability to supervise the system, to prevent criminality and to act as a trusted party to adjudicate disputes and enforce promises. Nor would it be able to understand the social and economic exchanges in order to devise the monetary and fiscal policies that are important for providing access to finance, public services and justice. Cryptocurrency developers and regulators need to resolve this informational dilemma. They need to have clear policy goals for cryptocurrency development and policy goals are needed to guide how information will be managed: who has access to what information between operators, developers and regulators? what information is of private good and of public good? what measures should be in place to mitigate the risks? While international standards are being formed for cryptocurrency,[33] what the technology is capable of doing is linked to what it is legally able to do. Policy goals must be the basis for such international standards but there can be conflicting and competing goals among the various international actors.

Information as a market power for stable coin operators and surveillance capitalism

The risks associated with unstable coins, such as value fluctuation and complete anonymity, are said to be able to be mitigated by stable coins issued by private consortia such as LIBRA, a known network operator registered in Switzerland.[34] LIBRA differs from Bitcoin's opaque system in that the identity of the operators

32 Christopher Mims, 'The Day When Computers Can Break All Encryption Is Coming' (2019) *The Wall Street Journal* www.wsj.com/articles/the-race-to-save-encryption-11559646737. Accessed 18 October 2020.
33 Sandra Maguire, 'International Crypto Standards: Who will Define Them?' (2019) https://irishtechnews.ie/international-crypto-standards-who-defines-them/. Accessed 18 October 2020.
34 'Public or Private? The Future of Money' (Monetary Dialogue Papers of Policy Department for Economics, Scientific and Quality of Life Policies, December 2019).

and the design of the information infrastructure are known.[35] A private consortium issuer of stable coins aims to act as a trusted third party, an intermediary, that issues stable coins based on known methodology, as opposed to the opaque "mining" process[36] used by unstable coins on the public chain such as Bitcoin. A private issuer acts not only as a digital payment operator, like credit cards or PayPal, and as a bank custodian, but also as a central bank that can issue money as a means of payment and investment. On the network, the operator will be able to collect, store, process, use and monetise information, including personal and transaction information so it will be able to obtain a broad view of transaction information recorded across the private blockchain network.[37] In addition, it will be able to gain access to personal information if it is on a private blockchain network. In the current digital payment systems, such as credit cards or PayPal, operators usually know only part of the transaction data but not the entirety or the whole chain of information related to transactions. For instance, credit card companies only know about transactions made through their system, but not the amount of money that users have in their bank accounts. Banks know the amount of money in clients' accounts but may not know the details of each transaction made, such as the object of the transaction or even the counterparty. In a private chain network of stable coins, detailed information such as the specific goods and services purchased, the price paid or "coins" exchanged, the details of the counterparty and their respective locations, can all be collected and stored on the network.

This raises three issues: 1) security; 2) consumer protection; and 3) market competition.[38] There is a higher risk of security breaches as information is more centralised, hence prone to cyber-attacks.[39] Second, the network operators control the behavioural data of the users (particular individuals), and there is a risk that this information can be used to herd or manipulate users' behaviour,[40] particularly the consumers, the vulnerable and the disadvantaged. Third, as operators can claim ownership of the data, there is a risk of foreclosing the market at the expense of other payment operators,[41] especially if data portability or Big Data

35 Peter Van Valkenburgh, 'The Differences between Bitcoin and Libra Should Matter to Policymakers' (2019) www.coincenter.org/the-differences-between-bitcoin-and-libra-should-matter-to-policymakers/. Accessed 18 October 2020.

36 'Investgating the Impact of Global Stablecoins' (G7 Working Group on Stablecoins, October 2019).

37 'Blockchain in Trade Facilitation' (White Paper of the United Nations Centre for Trade Facilitation and Electronic Business) www.unece.org/fileadmin/DAM/cefact/GuidanceMaterials/WhitePaperBlockchain.pdf. Accessed 18 October 2020.

38 'Regulatory Guidance on Virtual Currencies' (The Commonwealth Working Group on Virtual Currencies, October 2019).

39 Julian Jang-Jaccard and Surya Nepal, 'A Survey of Emerging Threats in Cybersecurity' (2014) 80(5) *Journal of Computer and System Science* 973, 993.

40 Ryan Calo, 'Digital Market Manipulation' (2014) 82(4) *The George Washington Law Review* 995, 1051.

41 'Digital Disruption in Banking and Its Impact on Competition' (OECD, 2020).

sharing becomes more difficult. There is a risk that individuals do not obtain a fair exchange for the data rendered to the operators.[42]

Information by state-backed currency used for a "paternal" economy and social surveillance

State-backed cryptocurrency represents a major risk to democratic values. Currently, central banks do not have access to individual data or individual transaction data which are distributed among different layers of the financial markets: banks, payment operators, trusts and custodian banks. If individual users use cash and keep their money in their own possession, only they have the transaction information. This coincides with the liberal view of a modern state in which the role of a central bank is to act as lender of last resort and monetary policy is used to maintain financial and monetary stability. In a state-backed currency, central banks can exercise greater monetary control and provide more targeted access to finance for individuals or entities perceived as being in need.[43] Central banks are not usually designated as law enforcement agencies against tax evasion, fraud, money laundering, terrorist financing or market manipulation. They can set rules and guidelines for the internal or organisational risk management of the financial institutions under their supervision but do not target individuals or entities that are not under their supervision. However, state-backed cryptocurrency on the blockchain network gives the potential for state surveillance[44] under which personal data and privacy will be at risk. Because of the centralised character of the private chain, there is also a greater security risk through hacking and other types of cyber-attack. As state-backed cryptocurrency aims at reaching beyond national borders, the risks associated with it, in terms of individual autonomy and safety, are raised to a transnational level. It becomes easier for the state to collect, store, process and share information for the legitimate purpose of managing the cryptocurrency system, and to prevent crime. The capacity for state surveillance is even greater than in cryptocurrency networks operated by private institutions. It is also easier for the state to exercise extra-territorial jurisdiction over transactions on the network and it can more easily obtain information belonging to foreign parties.[45] Because of this, national authorities may begin to impose a data location requirement in order to block links with the state issuing the cryptocurrency,

42 Ben Williamson, 'Learning from Surveillance Capitalism' (2019) https://codeactsineducation .wordpress.com/2019/04/30/learning-from-surveillance-capitalism/. Accessed 18 October 2020.
43 'Guidance for a Risk-Based Approach: Virtual Currencies' (A Working Paper of the Financial Action Task Force, 2015).
44 Per Aarvik, 'Blockchain as an Anti-Corruption Tool: Case Examples and Introduction to the Technology' (2020) www.u4.no/publications/are-blockchain-technologies-efficient-in-combatting-corruption. Accessed 18 October 2020.
45 Matthew Kohen and Justin Walse, 'State Regulations on Virtual Currency and Blockchain Technologies' (2019) www.carltonfields.com/insights/publications/2018/state-regulations-on-virtual -currency-and-blockchain-technologies. Accessed 18 October 2020.

or to use other laws to stop foreign issuing states exercising jurisdiction over its citizens or entities.[46]

Policy goals for information management on cryptocurrency space

Personal autonomy

The purpose of data protection rights and privacy rights is to protect personal autonomy but these two aspects overlap and differ in several respects.[47] Both can be based on fundamental human rights[48] although some jurisdictions have different legal bases for privacy and data protection. For instance, at English common law, privacy is based on the duty of confidentiality in the law of tort,[49] whereas data protection law gives a stronger proprietary claim to the data subject, as well as a personal claim against discrimination, market manipulation, and market and state surveillance.[50] Data protection law is particularly aimed at abuse by tech companies, whereas privacy rights, as a social contract between the state and the individual, focus on abuses by the state.[51] This distinction is becoming blurred, as tech companies increasingly provide public services on behalf of the state through which they obtain personal information about individuals.

The anonymity of unstable coins on the public chain, if it is effective, gives the best level of privacy and data protection. However, personal autonomy also affects the way individuals can control their data, and exercise proprietary ownership in it. Unstable coins on the public chain do not provide individuals with the power to negotiate with operators about how their data should be used, or at what price, or to decide when data can be withdrawn and erased from the system.[52] This personal autonomy is both economic and social. Since the information infrastructure of unstable coins is opaque, it is difficult for an individual who wishes to exercise personal autonomy to identify the data controllers and processors. Personal autonomy also needs legal guarantee and although unstable coins use the argument of "code as law" to minimise the requirement of a conventional

---

46 Tom Tobin, 'GDPR and EU Data Location Requirements' (2018) www.twilio.com/blog/2018/05/gdpr-and-eu-data-location-requirements.html. Accessed 18 October 2020.
47 'Ethics and Data Protection' (European Commission, 2018) https://ec.europa.eu/info/sites/info/files/5._h2020_ethics_and_data_protection_0.pdf. Accessed 18 October 2020.
48 Juliane Kokott and Chirstoph Sobotta, 'The Distinction between Privacy and Data Protection in Jurisprudence of the CJEU and the ECtHR' (2013) 3(4) *International Data Privacy Law* 222, 228.
49 Robert Walker, 'The English Law of Privacy – An Evolving Human Right' (The Supreme Court, UK) www.supremecourt.uk/docs/speech_100825.pdf. Accessed 18 October 2020.
50 'Guide to the General Data Protection Regulation (GDPR)' (Information Commissioner's Office, 2018) https://ico.org.uk/media/for-organisations/guide-to-the-general-data-protection-regulation-gdpr-1-0.pdf. Accessed 18 October 2020.
51 Alan Charles Raul, *The Privacy, Data Protection and Cybersecurity Law Review* (6th edn, The LawReviews 2019) 5, 40.
52 Orna Rabinovich-Einy and Ethan Katsch, 'Blockchain and the Inevitability of Disputes: The Role for Online Dispute Resolution' (2019) 1 *Journal of Dispute Resolution* 47, 75.

legal institution to protect personal autonomy, there is a strong risk that systems can be hacked and individual information obtained illegally.[53] Furthermore, without a system of identification, this personal autonomy is at risk due to the lack of a trusted third-party dispute resolution mechanism to provide redress to harmed individuals. An automated online dispute resolution mechanism[54] will not be able to guarantee such protection without a credible digital identification system. Privacy, once breached, is difficult to restore and data obtained by others cannot be "forgotten" by returning data to the owners. In economics, individuals are free to exchange goods and services, and a legal institution is required to safeguard this market space so that individuals can enforce their economic rights (i.e. contractual rights) when goods or services are not of good quality. Without the identification system,[55] there will be higher transaction costs and personal autonomy to transact will be compromised. Stable coins can potentially address enforcement issues by installing a legal institution to resolve disputes. Its private network system would be able to identify users and the transactions.

The use of data by operators can lead to discrimination, behavioural manipulation, surveillance capitalism and surveillance for the state. When this takes place, personal autonomy will be taken away. It is, therefore, important to know what data the operators will collect and process, and what and how they will share it with third parties. In a private consortium such as LIBRA, there are social media companies, retail companies, payment system operators such as credit or card companies and banks. Personal information can easily be shared among these organisations whose common objective is to increase business margins.[56] Even though users may find using stable coins convenient and cheaper due to lower currency exchange costs, their personal autonomy to select products and services can be distorted by algorithms that give preferential treatment according to users' profiles. Biased algorithms generated by transaction data can affect credit ratings and change how individuals might be treated by financial institutions.[57] Users with more spending power will find that the product ranges offered to them are limited to the higher price bracket.[58] At a macro-market level, Big Data can be created by gathering personal and transaction data allowing network operators to gain a

53 Gabrielle Patrick and Anurag Bana, 'Rule of Law Versus Rule of Code: A Blockchain-Driven Legal World' (IBA Legal Policy & Research Unit Legal Paper, 2017).

54 Orna Rabinovich-Einy and Ethan Katsch, 'Blockchain and the Inevitability of Disputes: The Role for Online Dispute Resolution' (2019) 1 *Journal of Dispute Resolution* 47, 75.

55 'Next Steps Outlined for UK's Use of Digital Identity' (Matt Warman MP and Department for Digital, Culture, Media and Sport, 2020) www.gov.uk/government/news/next-steps-outlined-for-uks-use-of-digital-identity. Accessed 18 October 2020.

56 Luke Irwin, 'The GDPR: What Exactly is Personal Data?' (2020) www.itgovernance.eu/blog/en/the-gdpr-what-exactly-is-personal-data. Accessed 18 October 2020.

57 Nicol Turner Lee, Paul Resnick and Genie Barton, 'Algorithmic Bias Detection and Mitigation: Best Practices and Policies to Reduce Consumer Harms' (2019) www.brookings.edu/research/algorithmic-bias-detection-and-mitigation-best-practices-and-policies-to-reduce-consumer-harms/. Accessed 18 October 2020.

58 'When Algorithms Set Prices: Winners and Losers' (Discussion Paper of Oxera, 2017).

market advantage and to develop more effective algorithms. When Big Data is not shared with other networks, participants in the network, particularly operators and their business associates, are able to foreclose the market, leading the users to have fewer market choices. If users wish to leave the network, they would need to convert their currency into another fiat currency, thus incurring extra costs which, if too high, become a disincentive to switching.

A state-backed cryptocurrency can potentially enhance access to finance.[59] With personal information and Big Data, the state can target disadvantaged regions, businesses, households and individuals.[60] It can inject money into the regions and businesses that need finance through giving aid or zero-interest credit to households and individuals for living expenses and personal development. However, this will also allow the state to monitor more closely how users manage their finances. The state is then able to set spending parameters, limiting the amount that can be spent and what it can be spent on. The state can also decide whether an individual should spend or save by using stricter monetary control. For instance, it can impose a negative interest rate on cryptocurrency saved in the digital wallet,[61] encouraging the users to spend. Furthermore, the state will have access to personal finance information and can exercise fiscal enforcement on entities and individuals. The state will be able to collect tax more easily; however, entities and individuals would lose their tax planning autonomy. While the state can also participate in the market by offering goods and services, state-run businesses would have an information advantage over private businesses. This asymmetric information will concentrate social and market powers among state entities at the expense of personal autonomy.

Development of digital economy

Digital economy is a common vision of many governments and private entities.[62] But for the relevant hardware to be developed, companies need to be convinced of a promising future before making the necessary investment. Software companies play an important part here in driving market demand for intensive hardware R&D. A smart economy and a smart society encourage this market demand and it is unlikely that law in the advanced economies and some emerging powers will reverse this trend. Intensive investment in data centre technology will need to find a market for these products to provide yields, and cryptocurrency will need just such data centres,[63] with super computing power, to maintain its ecosystem

59 'Investing the Impact of Global Stablecoins' (G7 Working Group on Stablecoins, October 2019).
60 Ibid; 'Financial Inclusion Overview' (The World Bank, 2018) www.worldbank.org/en/topic/financialinclusion/overview. Accessed 18 October 2020.
61 Amber Wadsworth, 'The Pros and Cons of Issuing a Central Bank Digital Currency' (Reserve Bank of New Zealand Bulletin, 2018).
62 'Digital Economy Report 2019 – Value Creation and Capture: Implications for Developing Countries' (United Nations Conference on Trade and Development, 2019).
63 'The Tokenisation of Assets and Potential Implications for Financial Markets' (OECD, 2020).

sustainably. The transactional data recorded will also provide unprecedented social and market information in a more efficient way. Currently, transactional data is fragmented and it is difficult for smaller entities and private individuals to benefit from data intensive economy. Data companies have the infrastructure to aggregate data along with greater market power to provide data streams to users who can afford them. This data space is currently not available to ordinary individuals because they lack sufficient computing power to process the data and lack finance to purchase the data streaming services.[64] Cryptocurrency can potentially remedy these problems and provide a data facility for the users. As data protection only covers personal data, corporate transaction data, both current and historical, can be made available. This can allow individuals or other smaller entities to design their own algorithms with the available data sets thus opening up the data streaming markets that have been dominated by major players.[65] While data protection law does not protect corporate data, companies are able to claim privacy rights.[66] It is, therefore, important to continue to protect corporate entities' privacy rights and the ability of users to benefit from the data streaming services. In order to enable this to happen, data sharing is the key. Legal issues pertinent to this include: 1) how personal data can be exchanged; 2) how personal data can be portable to increase competition within networks or between the different networks; and 3) how Big Data can be transferred to different countries.

Unstable coins

In an unstable coin space, there is limited opportunity to manage personal data as it is an anonymous system on the public chain. However, it is claimed that an overall view can be obtained. For instance, it is possible to know how many users are transacting Bitcoins, when, and in what amount. However, without specific information, this is not useful data for the users, even for the algorithm developers. With regards to illicit transactions using Bitcoins as payment, the trading data is of little use to law enforcement agencies in developing anti-money laundering algorithms to detect such activities.

64 'Guide to the General Data Protection Regulation (GDPR)' (Information Commissioner's Office, 2018) https://ico.org.uk/media/for-organisations/guide-to-the-general-data-protection-regulation -gdpr-1-0.pdf. Accessed 18 October 2020.

65 Jens Prufer and Patricia Prufer, 'Data Science for Entrepreneurship Research: Studying Demand Dynamics for Entrepreneurial Skills in the Netherlands' (2020) 55 *Small Business Economics* 651, 672.

66 'Data Protection Under GDPR', (European Commission, 2020) https://europa.eu/youreurope/ business/dealing-with-customers/data-protection/data-protection-gdpr/index_en.htm. Accessed 18 October 2020.

Stable coins

In a stable coin space on the private chain, transactional data is available to the operators. It is not clear how individuals, as data subjects, could monetise personal data as a commodity, but a plug-and-play mechanism could allow data subjects to provide and withdraw data from the system. In such a system, they would be able to exercise consent, withdraw data and erase their personal data. The problem is whether such a plug-and-play mechanism can also deliver the function of Big Data. Even if personal data is erased from the system, data subjects can continue to claim part ownership of the Big Data and claim entitlements to benefits through the monetisation of Big Data by the operators. This is an area that data protection law has yet to address. In addition to this, data portability gives data subjects the right to choose another service that requires personal data.[67] How such a private consortium can enable data portability is questionable; it would require the operators to provide interoperable systems. In other words, the data, such as on the LIBRA blockchain, would need to be made interoperable to another private blockchain network so that the data are "readable."[68] Otherwise, the data would only be readable on LIBRA's own machine and would defeat the aim of data portability to achieve more competition and provide more choices to users.

This also raises the question of transfer of mass data. If data is to be transferred to another entity to increase digital capability, both transferor and transferee entities would need to comply with rules to safeguard the data subject's rights and privacy rights. The participants in the network may not be able to share data freely unless they are within the same entity. They will need to comply with additional data protection safeguards such as binding corporate rules.[69] This will make the original transferor of data and the transferees both liable if there are data breaches. In the case of LIBRA, they will need to make sure that participants in the network, who have access to the data, also comply with the additional safeguards. This can make it difficult to share data with parties outside the network. The difficulties of data portability and transferability may, however, be an advantage to networks which do not share data with outsiders.

State-backed cryptocurrency

In a state-backed currency network, the state has all the data. The mass data allows the state to provide better, targeted public services through more sophisticated algorithms.[70] As mentioned, since the state has access to all the data, it can

67 Lachlan Urquhar, Neelima Sailaja and Derek McAuley, 'Realising the Right to Data Portability for the Domestic Internet of Things' (2018) 22 *Personal and Ubiquitous Computing* 317, 332.
68 'Blockchain and Interoperability: Key to Mass Adoption' (2020) www.finextra.com/blogposting /18972/blockchain-and-interoperability-key-to-mass-adoption. Accessed 18 October 2020.
69 'Personal Data Transfers: Binding Corporate Rules (BCRs) under the GDPR' (2017) www.i-scoop .eu/gdpr/binding-corporate-rules-bcrs-gdpr/. Accessed 18 October 2020.
70 'Data Driven Innovation for Growth and Well-Being' (Interim Synthesis Report of OECD, 2014).

also come up with better monetary tools, better fiscal control and can provide aid to those in need. There is, however, a risk that the state may be less efficient in providing public services through the lack of incentives, lack of expertise, bureaucratic processes and corruption. The question then is, who owns the data? Should the state share the data? What governance is required? The exceptions granted to the state to control and process data are based on the legitimate functions it carries out, the public interest it relies on and its public policy.[71] The state could claim ownership of the data and sell it to create revenue. The state could share data among its various departments under these exceptions without additional safeguards such as the binding corporate rules. They can refuse to share data with non-state entities or charge them fees for sharing them. The state can decide how they want to control and process the data, and their right to do so would not be subject to the data subject's right to data portability and right to erasure. The state has the power to require other network entities to disclose data and can then integrate the data sets. These powers and exceptions can lead to a state holding a data monopoly[72] in which private entities cannot compete.

In the conventional banking sphere with several layers in the market, the state does not have full access to transaction data and would, according to law, need to request such data.[73] But the data sets generated by state-backed cryptocurrency could lead to the foreclosure of the data market and the formation of a monopoly in the development of technology for data centres. Since the state can claim ownership in the data, it is difficult to require the state to share it as a "public good." Even if the data is treated as a public good, the state would be able to impose conditions on its use and increase the state's power over private entities.

Crime prevention

Many technologies can generate both positive and negative results but it is up to both policy and law to make them fulfil our objectives. Smart technology is multifaceted when it comes to crime and crime prevention. It can facilitate crime through complete anonymity while at the same time making crime easy to detect and prosecute. Unstable coins on the public chain with their complete anonymity have shown how the public chain network can become a hotbed for criminal activities. State-backed cryptocurrency significantly reduces the opportunity for theft, welfare fraud, money laundering, tax evasion and terrorist financing. This is not only because transactions can be linked with identified users, but also because the surrounding data of the transactions can contextualise them, i.e. where they took place and why the goods were purchased. The data can also create user

---

71 'Processing Personal Data on the Basis of Legitimate Interests under the GDPR: Practical Cases' (Research Paper of the Future of Privacy Forum) www.ejtn.eu/PageFiles/17861/Deciphering _Legitimate_Interests_Under_the_GDPR%20(1).pdf. Accessed 18 October 2020.
72 Joe Kennedy, 'The Myth of Data Monopoly: Why Antitrust Concerns about Data are Overblown' (2017) www2.itif.org/2017-data-competition.pdf. Accessed 18 October 2020.
73 'Digital Disruption in Banking and Its Impact on Competition' (OECD, 2020).

180 The economics and politics of data

profiles, showing the pattern of behaviour of individuals and their associates.[74] This helps the state to develop algorithms to detect the behavioural pattern of fraud, tax evasion and money laundering.[75] What is more, since the state is watching the users of the network, users would be less inclined to commit crime. With the sophisticated algorithms, users may not even need to file a tax return since every transaction is recorded on the network and tax can be collected by the tax authorities at the click of a button. This raises the question of how many people would use a state-backed cryptocurrency when there are effective alternatives. How many of us would use emails if the state has easy access to our email inbox? The state may rely on its legitimate public function, public interest and public policy around crime prevention to justify its surveillance capability but it is unlikely that any democratic state would allow these principles to be used to stretch the state powers. The doctrine of proportionality and the principle of reasonableness are the safeguards against such omnipotent state power.[76] There are cases in the EU showing a clear stance on human rights against state surveillance.[77] There may be exceptional circumstances where state surveillance is required to protect public health but it is unlikely that a liberal and democratic state would be given the power to hack into a data system for the purpose of law enforcement without concern about human rights violations. The current financial market multilayer infrastructure is designed to safeguard financial privacy even though it may also facilitate (or not be able to prevent) tax fraud and criminal activity.

The more problematic area is the stable coins issued by private consortia and private entities such as LIBRA: what are their obligations in crime prevention, should they provide access to their data to the state and should they allow others to have access to the data for the purpose of developing anti-crime tools? For anti-money laundering purposes, financial institutions such as banks, brokers and payment companies are under a legal duty to prevent money laundering through detecting and reporting suspicious transactions. However, financial institutions have no legal duty to do so if they do not have sufficient data and information to identify suspicious transactions. For instance, central banks, trading venues, clearing houses and some custodian banks only process information about large institutional members[78] and do not have the details of individual users' transactions

---

74 McKinsey, 'Capturing Value from Your Customer Data' (2017) www.mckinsey.com/business-functions/mckinsey-analytics/our-insights/capturing-value-from-your-customer-data#. Accessed 18 October 2020.
75 Suhaib Alzoubi, Haitham Alshibly and Mohammad Al-Maaitah, 'Artificial Intelligence in Law Enforcement, A Review' (2014) 4(4) *International Journal of Advanced Information Technology* 1, 9.
76 Alice Ristroph, 'Proportionality as A Principle of Limited Government' (2005) 55 *Duke Law Journal* 263, 265.
77 Such as *Big Brother Watch and Others v. The United Kingdom* (Application nos: 58170/13, 62322/14 and 24960/15).
78 Ben Norman, Rachel Shaw and George Speight, 'The History of Interbank Settlement Arrangements: Exploring Central Banks' Role in the Payment System' (Working Paper No. 412, Bank of England, 2011).

revealing money laundering activities. This means that it is entities that have a client-facing entry point that should act as gatekeeper as they collect detailed information under the "Know-Your-Customer" (KYC) requirement.[79] The KYC requirement in private chains will be made easier through digital identification. If, however, a consortium such as LIBRA that issues stable coins does have access to detailed individual information – fund transfers, trade financing and retail purchasing – and has the capability to identify suspicious transactions through its algorithms, it then has an obligation to report its suspicions to the authorities. This obliges LIBRA and similar network operators to act as a surveillance mechanism for the state, rather than the state directly monitoring its citizens. States need to follow the legal procedure to obtain data, either for reasons of monetary policy or for law enforcement purposes and this provides an additional layer of safeguarding of civil liberty. To provide further safeguards, the law should be able to specify only certain participants, such as wallet providers and cryptocurrency exchanges, that can access detailed information. This would prohibit network operators from providing a back-door facility[80] to the state authorities. Even if the network operators have the data, the obligation to provide information to the state, through reporting or at the state's legal request, rests with the wallet providers[81] and trade financiers.

The data that network operators have access to can be used for the purpose of research, such as understanding the pattern of criminal activities. This would require operators to have a robust data governance mechanism to ensure data security, accuracy and quality, along with other internal cyber security measures. Algorithms that are developed from data sets generated by the network for the purpose of crime prevention would need to be tested in a safe environment and should be free of discrimination. In this way, data generated for the public good can be used for the public interest of crime prevention while safeguarding personal liberty.

Politics of information in cryptocurrency

From economic to political

The fourth industrial revolution may disrupt the financial system and socio-economic transformation as well as threaten humanity,[82] job security and democratic values. Cryptocurrency's disintermediation is intended to reduce transaction costs

79 Emily Lee, 'Financial Inclusion, FinTech, RegTech and Anti-Money Laundering' (2017) 6 *Journal of Business Law* 473, 498.
80 Cynthia Dion-Schwarz, David Manheim and Patrick Johnston, 'Terrorist Use of Cryptocurrencies' (2019) www.rand.org/content/dam/rand/pubs/research_reports/RR3000/RR3026/RAND _RR3026.pdf. Accessed 18 October 2020.
81 Robby Houben, 'Cryptocurrencies and Blockchain: Legal Context and Implications for Financial Crime, Money Laundering and Tax Evasion' (Policy Department for Economic, Scientific and Quality of Life Policies, July 2018).
82 'Regulation for the Fourth Industrial Revolution' (Policy Paper, Department for Business, Energy & Industrial Strategy, 2019).

for users and its decentralisation aims to create more distributive justice by giving back powers of wealth creation. The data aspect of cryptocurrency is at the centre of the debate about how one should own data, who has the right to manage it in the collective interest and who has the right to use data in the public interest. Transparency and accountability have been key in democratic politics. In a representative democracy, we put the emphasis on transparency and accountability of the politicians and government agencies (intermediaries) to make the political system function. In a direct democracy, such as by referendum, more emphasis is placed on the individual's right to information and the power of vote to show the centralised, collective sovereignty. It is still difficult to know what disintermediation and decentralisation of cryptocurrency are intended to achieve in the political space. These intentions will affect the design of such an operating system. Who operates the system and for whose benefit are questions still to be answered. There should be different requirements, in terms of privacy and data protection, for private and public entities who, in turn, have different political powers. For whose benefit is even harder to answer, as users are not monolithic individuals (high net-wealth or low income) or corporations (consortium or state). These differences would affect the understanding and applications of legitimate interest and public interest under privacy law and data protection law. Just as technology has shown its power of increasing inequality, disintermediation can cause job losses in the payment services sector.[83] Furthermore, there are potential discriminatory effects of the use of smart technology. In a decentralised system, there is a risk of reduced transparency due to data and privacy protection; and reduced accountability due to the lack of a centralised power to respond to instability. To make cryptocurrency legal and technologically interoperable, we will need to define the purpose of such mobile currency. When the Euro was introduced, its purpose was to bring unity to the single market; there are reasons why one currency is pegged to another:[84] for preventing market manipulation of the weaker currency.

To make such cryptocurrency compliant with fundamental rights and innovation, one would need to enquire again about the fundamental rights that are to be achieved and what priority is to be given to each right. Decisions are needed about the kind of governance that cryptocurrency should be linked to and, in addition to the expectation of privacy, the need for cyber security, the agreeable level of surveillance and who controls the computing power i.e. the nodes on the cryptocurrency network. The nodes can have the power to decide what to register on the blockchain, how to revise the protocol, how to manage the split of the system i.e. the hard fork problem[85] and how to manage the data obtained from users. In

83 Carla Hobbs, 'Europe's Digital Sovereignty: From Rulemaker to Superpower in the Age of US-China Rivalry' (Essay Collection of the European Council on Foreign Relations, 2020).
84 Virginie Coudert, Cecile Couharde and Valerie Mignon, 'Pegging Emerging Currencies in the Face of Dollar Swings' (2013) 45(36) *Applied Economics* 1, 28.
85 Tae Wan Kim and Ariel Zetlin-Jones, 'The Ethics of Contentious Hard Forks in Blockchain Networks with Fixed Features' (2019) https://doi.org/10.3389/fbloc.2019.00009. Accessed 18 October 2020.

other words, the nodes are the intermediaries for processing transactions for users and for possessing distributive decision-making powers in cryptocurrency operations, such as controlling the level of liquidity. No country currently allows its citizens to decide monetary policy through direct democracy such as the referendum. Many central banks are independent of the government so that their policies are not made on the basis of short-term political appeal to win votes. However, in practice, central bankers also face political pressure from governments when making their decisions, and in some countries central banks are subject to parliamentary scrutiny. At a more local level, we have also witnessed how interest rates are being made by private consortia in a market-based manner, such as LIBOR, rather than by a centralised mechanism. The issue is whether we are ready to trust the nodes, assuming each node makes an independent decision, to make monetary decisions on behalf of the community. This would resemble a representative democracy where politicians and agencies make decisions for its people. However, the emphasis in this representative democratic system is transparency and accountability. How can the users hold the nodes in the distributed power system accountable? The users do not elect nodes, unless they can and there are agreements between the nodes and the users on how decision-making power is to be exercised on the network. Yet, how should voting secrecy be preserved? The function of the nodes is to process the transactions for users and, at the same time, to make monetary decisions for them. Will nodes act on the instructions given by the users who elect or choose them? It may also be the case that the nodes refuse to follow users' instructions and refuse users' participation in the network through its node. Rather than empowering the users, the system could operate to exclude.

Data location and international relations

The data location requirement demands that data of a particular type is situated in a jurisdiction or a region. For instance, EU law requires its citizens' data to be situated in the EU.[86] Data location gives rise to jurisdiction competition.[87] A country or region's legal requirement of data location can affect data transferability and data portability. The restriction on data transferability through the location requirement can affect regulatory capability, law enforcement, competition in the tech sector and transnational cooperation. In other words, this requirement affects how personal autonomy is guaranteed, how the digital economy can be developed further to compete and how the risk of crime can be effectively managed. In some countries, data location law requires data generated from that country to

86 Lokke Moerel, 'The Long Arm of EU Data Protection Law: Does the Data Protection Directive Apply to Processing of Personal Data of EU Citizens by Websites Worldwide?' (2011) 1(1) *International Data Privacy Law* 28, 46.
87 Jacques Cremer, Yves-Alexandre de Montjoye and Heike Schweitzer, 'Competition Policy for the Digital Era' (Research Report of European Commission, 2019).

be situated in its jurisdiction with or without data transferability.[88] Even with data transferability, the law may demand a copy or replica to be kept within the jurisdiction. In some countries, such a data location requirement has different applications according to the type of data. For instance, in the Trans-Pacific Partnership, the US demands that US financial data is located in the US and is not subject to the principle of free data flow. This is because, in the opinion of the US government, there is a strong policy reason to keep financial data in the region. The recent Court of Justice of the European Union (CJEU) decision invalidating the EU–US Privacy Shield[89] has shown that data transfers may not be easily carried out even for the purpose of law enforcement of the requesting state. This case shows how human rights law and other constitutional and fundamental safeguards require European data controllers and processors to protect the EU's data subjects from a third country's state power. Even though individual consent could be the basis, it is unlikely that a blanket consent of an individual would allow such cross-border data transfers. The problem is that when data needs to be transferred for legitimate purposes,[90] once the transfer to the third country for processing has taken place, it would be difficult for the data controllers in the EU and the data subjects in the EU to prevent data being seized by the third country authorities. The challenge for cryptocurrency is how to protect individual data against state power as conferred by criminal law or by national security law. This case shows how the EU can use the equivalence regime[91] to control the flow of data to third countries. In some countries, such as China, data transferability is subject to cyber security law. China's Cyber Security Law came into force on 1 June 2017 with an array of supporting regulations to facilitate the interpretation and implementation of this law. The Cyber Security Law emphasised the issues in relation to the data localisation and cross-border data transfers. For instance, in accordance with the Cyber Security Law, personal information[92] and important data[93] collected and generated by entities designated as Key Information Infrastructure Operators (KII) must be stored domestically within China.[94]

Data on the cryptocurrency network will show specific local dynamics, geographic, demographic and temporal. This will reveal the sentiment in a particular location – train tickets showing if workers are returning to work, mask sales

---

88 The GDPR restricts the transfer of personal data to countries outside the EEA. For more details, see https://ico.org.uk/for-organisations/guide-to-data-protection/guide-to-the-general-data-protection-regulation-gdpr/international-transfers/. Accessed 18 October 2020.
89 *Data Protection Commissioner v. Facebook Ireland Limited, Maximillian Schrems* (Case C311/1).
90 Morgan, Lewis & Bockius LLP, 'Transfer of Data in the GDPR: The Definition of Legitimate Interest' (2020) www.lexology.com/library/detail.aspx?g=bbd12b14-79c8-4141-a585-7b7eb-0ca59e2. Accessed 18 October 2020.
91 Data Protection Commission, 'Transfers of Personal Data to Third Countries or International Organisations' (2020) www.dataprotection.ie/en/organisations/international-transfers. Accessed 18 October 2020.
92 Article 76(5), Cyber Security Law of China.
93 The Cyber Security Law of China does not provide the definition of important data.
94 Article 37, Cyber Security Law of China.

showing the rise of the pandemic, energy sales showing population behaviour in a particular time. Such data can be of strategic importance both economically and politically. Smart contracts on the network with detailed terms and conditions can further contextualise the data. This no longer just provides the broad picture of what Big Data can show, but very specific dynamics in a sector (e.g. pharmacy), in a region (e.g. around government buildings) and a particular retail establishment such as bars and pubs showing the level of risk of Covid-19 infection. Hence, data is not just financial, but can be about medical well-being, educational capabilities, entertainment provisions, social media activities, and small and medium enterprises' moves. In terms of personal autonomy, the citizens of a state would be less willing to engage in the network if they knew that they were being watched by their state, let alone a foreign state. Such restricted personal autonomy will not only affect political freedom but also the economic activities in the space. Citizens may feel inhibited from spending, fearing that it would attract tax authorities' attentions. The unwillingness to engage in the crypto-space will affect the level of data generated to feed into the development of the digital economy and society. This will substantially reduce the competitiveness of the tech industry in the jurisdiction and the region. This will have a long-term digital capability issue and can directly affect regional security. In terms of crime prevention, prosecuting crime is a national sovereign power.[95] This power can be exercised on an extra-territorial basis.[96] We have witnessed how long-arm jurisdiction[97] has been exercised against entities and individuals for fraud, money laundering, tax evasion, terrorism and security breaches. In *R (KBR Inc) v Director of the Serious Fraud Office* [2018] EWHC 2368 (Admin) the High Court concluded that section 2 of the Criminal Justice Act 1987 permits the Serious Fraud Office to compel the production of documents held by a foreign person, even where those documents are outside the jurisdiction, provided that the foreign person has a "sufficient connection" to the jurisdiction and that the section 2 notice is validly served on the foreign person. The court also concluded that the implied intention behind the SFO's section 2 regime created sufficient justification to permit extra-territorial application.

Giving away data will mean giving away a jurisdiction's legal power and technological capability to understand, detect and prosecute crime. Cryptocurrency space, i.e. on the private chain, also allows national law enforcement agencies to impose sanctions more easily, both in law and in technology. This is the reason why certain states, including the USA in the Trans-Pacific Partnership,[98] require

95 Mireille Caruana, 'The Reform of the EU Data Protection Framework in the Context of the Police and Criminal Justice Sector: Harmonisation, Scope, Oversight and Enforcement' (2017) 30(3) *International Review of Law, Computers & Technology* 249, 270.

96 Danielle Ireland-Piper, 'Extraterritorial Criminal Jurisdiction: Does the Long Arm of the Law Undermine the Rule of Law?' (2012) 13 *Melbourne Journal of International Law* 2, 35.

97 'Global Money Laundering & Terrorist Financing Threat Assessment' (FATF Report, July 2010).

98 Michael Geist, 'Data Rules in Modern Trade Agreements: Toward Reconciling an Open Internet with Privacy and Security Safeguards' (2018) www.cigionline.org/articles/data-rules-modern-trade -agreements-toward-reconciling-open-internet-privacy-and-security. Accessed 18 October 2020.

data to be located in their jurisdiction so that they retain law enforcement powers. Any request for this data by a state power would need to be done at inter- or intra-governmental level,[99] reaffirming national sovereignty. This is the rationale behind the ECJ's ruling on the EU–US Privacy Shield; any request of personal data for the purpose of law enforcement would need to be done at inter-governmental level.

The data location requirement has the potential to create regional data barriers, data nationalism and data protectionism.[100] The possible effect is the creation of a data silo.[101] Data flows would be subject to a number of legal safeguards, such as the third country equivalence regime. In a virtual space, smaller jurisdictions would need to form alliances with each other, or with a larger regime, to operate in the digital space. In terms of cryptocurrency, the countries using the data would need to form a silo in order to achieve the said benefits of cryptocurrency at the cross-border level. There will need to be inter-governmental agreement to decide on data governance.[102] A cryptocurrency network without such a data silo would substantially reduce the effectiveness of it. An EU citizen using a Chinese state-backed cryptocurrency can request its data in the EU to be erased. This will affect the operations of the Chinese DCEP. Equally, a UK citizen can request the same action to be carried out to LIBRA based in Switzerland. It is likely that such a data silo will be formed based on the locations of the users, i.e. EU and EU–Japan.[103] It will be cross-border but the alliances would be formed. The defunct US-led TPP[104] was aimed at forming such an alliance. Data fortress might be an inevitable outcome, albeit different from data nationalism and data protectionism.

Conclusion

In this chapter, I have discussed how the policy goals of personal autonomy, development of the digital economy and crime prevention can be enhanced or damaged in three different types of cryptocurrency. Current data protection law and privacy law can only address some of these issues, and the discussion of their propriety and effectiveness needs to be made against the policy goals. I have

---

99 'International Co-Operation against Tax Crimes and Other Financial Crimes: A Catalogue of the Main Instruments' (2nd Annual Forum on Tax and Crime, June 2012).

100 Nigel Cory, 'Cross-Border Data Flows: Where Are the Barriers, and What Do They Cost?' (2017) www2.itif.org/2017-cross-border-data-flows.pdf. Accessed 18 October 2020.

101 Edd Wilder-James, 'Breaking Down Data Silos' (2016) *Harvard Business Review* https://hbr.org/2016/12/breaking-down-data-silos. Accessed 18 October 2020.

102 'Data Governance and Data Policies' (European Commission, 2020) https://ec.europa.eu/info/sites/info/files/summary-data-governance-data-policies_en.pdf. Accessed 18 October 2020.

103 'European Commission Adopts Adequacy Decision on Japan, Creating the World's Largest Area of Safe Data Flows' (2019) https://ec.europa.eu/commission/presscorner/detail/en/IP_19_421. Accessed 18 October 2020.

104 Xiaobai Ji and Pradumna Rana, 'The United States and the Rise, Fall and Future Prospects of the (Comprehensive and Progressive Agreement for) Trans-Pacific Partnership' (SWP Working Paper No. 5, October 2018).

shown that cryptocurrency is not just a financial tool, but also a political space. It is for governments to implement effective monetary and fiscal policy, for the tech companies of the region to obtain future technological capability and for sovereign states to exercise sovereign powers individually or collectively. There is scope for users and citizens to exercise their political power in the crypto-space. The question is, how desirable is direct democracy and how can such a political power of users be written into the new social contract with the state or the network provider? How data artefacts are to be generated on the crypto-space and how they are to be used will depend on the political ideology of the day in the particular country.

10 The Peer-to-Peer Energy Trading Platform

Introduction

As mentioned in Chapter 3 when analysing the legal taxonomy of tokens on the blockchain, I argued that there should be a new approach, a new social contract, for the users in the emerging Crypto-Republic to allow more innovative social projects. I have also discussed the possibility of a more autonomous organisation with the help of STO in Chapter 6 and smart contract in automating rights benefits and governance in Chapter 4. In this chapter, I intend to explore the possibility of realising a sustainable social project based on the trading system on the blockchain as a climate change solution. Combating climate change is at the top of the international political agenda, and many economic initiatives have been developed to alleviate this global problem. Climate change has been attributed to fast economic development that has hugely increased CO_2 emissions causing massive damage to the environment across the world, especially in poorer regions. Climate change increases the disparity in the level of development between rich and poor countries, but it is a collective problem that everyone faces, both rich and poor; no one is immune from its consequences. Sustainable development has been the motor for changing both institutional and individual behaviour, not only for reducing carbon footprints but also for actively seeking sources of renewable energy. There have been several sustainable development initiatives, including using technology to reduce CO_2 emissions, developing green financing programmes to provide incentives for using renewable sources and putting in place governance infrastructure to support these initiatives. The CO_2 emission-trading scheme is one example. DLT has shown its potential in trading commodities, and using its infrastructure to enable sustainable development in, for example, communal energy trading, experiments have been carried out to demonstrate how smart technology can facilitate localised, self-sufficient energy projects. In this chapter, I will discuss how the crypto-market – a blockchain-based trading system – can also contribute to sustainable development through the Peer-to-Peer Energy Trading Platform (P2P ETP). I will first discuss the potential benefits of the P2P ETP and whether its rationale coincides with the objectives of blockchain-based financial markets: a disintermediation and decentralisation of the network. Second, I will map out the components required by this model (the blockchain, smart meters,

DOI: 10.4324/9780429023613-10

smart grids, smart contracts and the trading platform) to show how they can assist local, communal energy trading systems. Third, the legal risks of this model will be highlighted and I will make some recommendations. Finally, I will assess the potential transformative effects of the model.

Why do we need a P2P ETP?

The rationale behind this P2P ETP model is to encourage householders to use sustainable energy systems such as solar, wind or biofuel through waste, to reduce their reliance on traditional energy sources such as coal, nuclear and petroleum. It aims to give them control over how they produce energy and how they allocate the energy they have produced. Hence, P2P ETP can be regarded as part of the "smart city" initiative that aims to use smart technology to provide sustainable solutions to climate change with a bottom-up approach.

There are numerous academic assessments of the potential beneficial attributes of P2P ETPs, which promotes sustainability by removing the intermediaries and allowing consumers to trade energy on their own terms in their community. It satisfies many of the United Nations Sustainable Development Goals (SDGs) for the 2030 Agenda for Sustainable Development.[1] Most notably, SDGs 7, 9, 11 and 13, which all touch on access to affordable sustainable energy and building infrastructure that combats climate change.[2] These goals are also reflected in the Third Energy Package for the European Union (EU) and the Smart Meter Act 2018 in the United Kingdom. The P2P ETP system thus can encourage consumers to create their own renewable energy, such as solar energy, using installed solar panels.[3] Smart meters, which can track and observe the exact amount of energy produced and spent, would promote greater consumer consciousness while ensuring control over the energy they directly produce, consume and trade. This model also empowers consumers by using smart contracts to facilitate bilateral energy transactions within specific demand periods. In order to empower consumers, it must be acknowledged that energy consumers are unique individuals with different preferences in terms of environmental concerns, financial burdens and levels of trust towards emerging technology. Therefore, smart contracts can introduce a

---

1 United Nations, 'Transforming Our World: The 2030 Agenda For Sustainable Development' (United Nations General Assembly 2015) www.un.org/ga/search/view_doc.asp?symbol=A/RES/70 /1&Lang=E. Accessed 13 March 2021.

2 United Nations, 'Transforming Our World: The 2030 Agenda For Sustainable Development' (United Nations General Assembly 2015). SDG 7 reads: to "[e]nsure access to affordable, reliable, sustainable and modern energy for all." SDG 9 reads: to "[b]uild resilient infrastructure, promote inclusive and sustainable industrialization and foster innovation." SDG 11 reads: to "[m]ake cities and human settlements inclusive, safe, resilient and sustainable." SDG 13 reads: to "[t]ake urgent action to combat climate change and its impact."

3 Rafael Leal-Arcas et al., 'Smart Grids in The European Union: Assessing Energy Security, Regulation & Social and Ethical Considerations' (2018) 24 *Columbia Journal of European Law* 291, 389.

market mechanism suited to the individual consumers' concerns that are within their control.

The P2P ETP system gives consumers the ability to negotiate prices through supply and demand models. In embedding smart contracts within P2P ETPs, the pricing would be flexible and trading can also be automated based on pre-set conditions and demand. Consumers would be able to personalise their own ceiling cap for purchasing, and therefore, avoid potential overcharge or overconsumption of energy. This dynamic style would assist the energy consumer's ability to negotiate in conjunction with complex tariff structures. Consequently, by enabling energy trading throughout a period of fluctuating pricing, demand at peak times could be lowered as energy will be purchased at will by the individual consumer prior to use or when necessary.[4]

As a result of these dynamics, P2P ETPs facilitate the management of energy supply through this shared economy model with the facilities of smart grids and smart meters.[5] Energy consumers can actively manage their household energy usage and cost through accessing their data.[6] The UK Government has also issued a research paper analysing the cost and benefit of this application. One of the benefits is that the real-time awareness of usage and cost will encourage consumers to reduce demand and contribute to lower energy bills.[7] A real-world example of this structure is the Brooklyn Microgrid Project[8] in the United States, where participants generate their own energy and resell to consumers who need it, at a cheaper rate.[9] This model would allow the consumers of energy to be prosumers who produce, control and consume the energy in a disintermediated and decentralised system.

What is the infrastructure?

Blockchain

The P2P ETP is built on the blockchain technology and utilises a number of smart technology elements such as smart grid, smart meters, smart contract and artificial intelligence to provide its functions. The blockchain technology allows the participants to add information to the database and for them to view the information

---

4 Claire Henly et al., 'Energizing the Future with Blockchain' (2019) 39 *The Energy Bar Association Energy Law Journal* 197–232.
5 Hilary Brown et al., 'Some Characteristics of Emerging Distribution Systems Considering the Smart Grid Initiative' (2010) 23 *Electricity Journal* 64, 75.
6 Sonia McNeil, 'Privacy and the Modern Grid' (2011) 25 *Harvard Journal of Law and Technology* 199, 224.
7 Department of Business, 'Energy and Industry Strategy, Smart Meter Roll-Out Cost-Benefit Analysis' (2019) www.gov.uk/government/publications/smart-meter-roll-out-cost-benefit-analysis-2019. Accessed 17 May 2021.
8 Merlinda Andoni et al., 'Blockchain Technology in the Energy Sector: A Systematic Review of Challenges and Opportunities' (2019) 100 *Renewable and Sustainable Energy Reviews* 155–156.
9 Brooklyn Microgrid (2019) www.brooklyn.energy/bmg-101. Accessed 17 May 2021.

added by other participants on the network. The information is hence transparent and immutable (at least it is tamper-proof). As mentioned in the previous chapters, there are three types of blockchain: the public chain, the private chain and the hybrid chain. In the public chain, everyone can simply download the software and participate in the network without permission. In the private chain, it is maintained by an individual, an entity or a consortium, and permission to join the network is required. Once the participants join the network and become a node, they will be able to add information and view it on the network database. As the network can decide the rules of participation, the participants may only have the authority to add information but not view it. In a hybrid chain, it is a mixture of some features of the public chain and the private chain, in which permission would be required on certain aspects of the operation. For instance, the participants may not be able to revise the protocols and can only participate in certain aspects such as providing information but not adding to it; trading the tokenised energy units but not recording the transactions; viewing their own transactions but not those of others. It is recommended that private chain should be used for this model. However, some parts could potentially be made interoperable with other private or public chains in order to take part in larger green financing markets at an international level. Within the P2P ETP ecosystem, users interact with the blockchain via private or public keys depending on the accessibility of the chain itself. Private keys give access solely to the individual's personal transactions, while public keys create access to the network transactions. The dual system works as an "asymmetric cryptography,"[10] which brings authentication and integrity to the dealings on the network. Each block is identified by its cryptographic lock and references the block that came before it.[11] This creates the immutability of the technology because the data and prior blocks cannot be deleted, but only copied – while more information can be added to the following blocks. Blockchain blends several existing technologies alongside P2p networking.

Smart contract

Smart contract can embody the rights attached to the energy produced through the process of tokenisation. It also has the function of automating the whole or certain parts of the transactions, for example through the use of algorithms trading. It can also be used to allocate risks and responsibilities in the governance of this model. A smart contract can also be used as a digital agreement which executes automated instructions, such as an order to buy or to sell at a certain price based on pre-set

10 Elias Leake Quinn, 'Smart Metering and Privacy: Existing Laws and Competing Policies' 18 (May 9, 2009) (unpublished manuscript), https://papers.ssrn.com/sol3/papers.cfm?abstract_id =1462285.
11 Primaver De Filippi and Aaron Wright, 'Blockchain and the Law: The Rule of Code' (2018) 78 *The Cambridge Law Journal* <sc>213, 217. Accessed</sc> *Reuteurs.com* (London, December 7 2020), www.reuters.com/article/g7-digital/g7-finance-officials-backneed-to-regulate-digital-currencies-treasury-idUSKBN28H1Y6. Accessed 03 January 2021.

conditions.[12] Smart contracts have been known for the trading of cryptocurrencies such as Bitcoin and Ethereum. In the proposed P2P ETP, smart contracts shall be used to trade units of energy represented by tokens ("tokenisation"). Judge Steven Morris QC specified in *Armstrong DLW GmbH v. Winnington Networks Ltd*[13] that tradable carbon emission credits constitute an intangible property[14] in English law. This forms the legal basis for trading "tokenised energy" as an intangible property via smart contracts on P2P ETP. These tokens will be stored in digital wallets as dematerialised certificates representing the energy commodity on the P2P ETP to be traded with the smart contracts. Digital wallets are software applications that facilitate the storing and safe-keeping of these energy tokens.[15] These tokens are subsequently assigned value based on the context of trading and stored within the digital wallet of the consumer. For example, a single token can represent one kilowatt, or an hour of power, and consumers can use these tokens to trade energy[16] along smart grids via the smart meters installed in their households.

A basic smart contract process as a trading agreement on the P2P ETP has three steps. First, parties must agree upon a transaction with terms and conditions for energy. Second, once the requirements are met for the transaction to proceed, the first "block" unlocks and distributes energy via the encoded instructions. Third, if these requirements are not met, the block will remain locked and nothing will be distributed. To execute a smart contract, the parties must negotiate terms until a "meeting of the minds"[17] occurs and the parties enter a legally binding contract. After this relationship is established, the smart contract is subsequently encoded to contain the requirements and instructions following the agreed upon terms and conditions of the legal contract. If an energy consumer does not pay, as required by their contractual obligations, the smart contract will not transfer the energy to that consumer.

Smart meters

Smart meters are the initial step towards smart electricity grids and lay the foundation for further implementation of renewable energy production and

---

12 Florian Möslein, 'Legal Boundaries of Blockchain Technologies: Smart Contracts as Self-Help' (2019) www.law.ox.ac.uk/business-law-blog/blog/2019/01/legal-boundaries-blockchain-technologies-smart-contracts-self-help. Accessed 17 May 2021.

13 *Armstrong DLW GmbH v. Winnington Networks Ltd* [2012] EWHC (Ch) 10 [52]-[54], [2013] Ch 156.

14 *Official Receiver (as liquidator of Celtic Extraction Ltd and Bluestone Chemicals Ltd) v. Environment Agency* [2001] Ch 475.

15 Adam Levitin, 'Pandora's Digital Box: The Promise and Perils of Digital Wallets' (2018) 166 *University of Pennsylvania Law Review* 305, 307.

16 Merlinda Andoni et al.<sc>, '</sc>Blockchain Technology in The Energy Sector: A Systematic Review of Challenges and Opportunities' (2019) 100 *Renewable and Sustainable Energy Review* 143, 174.

17 *Carlill v. Carbolic Smoke Ball Co.* [1893] 1 QB 256, 266.

consumption.[18] Smart meters will also be used to record the energy a household has produced and consumed, which will provide information to the individual household about how their individual behaviour should alter in response to the climate change crisis. Some information in the smart meters, if agreed by the network, can then be added onto the blockchain network for managing and trading purposes. They are communication devices, similar to a messaging service, which correspond to the electricity usage of in-house appliances of the consumer and external providers. Smart meters provide a detailed breakdown of usage, including peak consumption and other relevant energy regulatory data.[19] A crucial difference between smart meters and traditional meters is the smart meter's ability to communicate immediately with the household and energy providers – who may also be the consumer if renewable energy appliances are installed in the house. Traditional meters only give the current usage of the household, and an accurate breakdown of usage is inaccessible to the individual consumer. Smart meters can communicate usage to consumers and other parties, such as utility companies, in real time.[20] In P2P ETP applications, smart meters are vital to the tracking, trading and allocating of energy of the participants in the network.

Smart grids

Smart grids allow access to detailed information on electricity production (with renewable energy appliances) and consumption to improve the reliability of the service, reduce costs and introduce renewable energy sources into a nation's energy portfolio.[21] The purpose of a smart grid is to ensure that consumers can establish real-time situational awareness over vast stretches of energy systems, as well as their production and consumption. In doing so, these smart technologies collect, aggregate and report detailed energy production and consumption data from individual households.[22] Smart grids rely on the installation of smart meters to achieve these goals of greater consumer awareness and participation – producing, consuming and trading energy. Traditional energy trading is mostly unilateral, as it flows from producers to consumers through a centralised grid. P2P ETP disrupts this model by promoting multi-directional trading without a central body

18 Nancy King and Pernille Jessen, 'Smart Metering Systems and Data Sharing: Why Getting a Smart Meter Should Also Mean Getting Strong Information Privacy Controls to Manage Data Sharing' (2014) 22 *International Journal of Law and Information Technology* 215, 253.

19 Kevin Doran, 'Climate Change and The Future of Energy: Privacy and Smart Grid: When Progress and Privacy Collide' (2011) 41 *The University of Toledo Law Review* 909, 910.

20 N. King and P. Jenssen, 'For Privacy's Sake: Consumer "Opt-Outs" for Smart Meters' (2014) 30(5) *Computer Law and Security Review* 222.

21 A. Brown, et al., 'Smart Grid Issues in State law and Regulations' <sc>(2010),</sc> http://galvin-power.org/sites/default/files/SmartGridIssuesInStateLawAndRegulation_Whitepaper_Final(1). pdf Accessed 17 May 2021.

22 Elias Leake Quinn, 'Smart Metering and Privacy: Existing Laws and Competing Policies 18' (2009) (unpublished manuscript), https://papers.ssrn.com/sol3/papers.cfm?abstract_id=1462285. Accessed on 17 May 2021.

transmitting energy unilaterally.[23] Hence, it removes the role of a monopolist grid. Within this decentralised system, smart contracts serve as the digital medium and form a reliable and secure foundation for peer-to-peer energy trading.

The P2P ETP system allows individual householders to understand how much energy they have produced and consumed in terms of both units and price. As they have access to information about energy consumption across the network, they are also able to trade any surplus they may have with others who have a shortage. This removes the grid company's role as information intermediary (or information monopoly) and allows householders to manage their energy production and to supply any surplus energy to others on a peer-to-peer basis. They may also use the project to engage with larger emission-trading platforms.

Tokenisation of assets

One very important component of this model is the ability to use the blockchain platform to trade energy units produced by renewable sources. Energy trading is a type of commodity trading, and is a common commercial trading platform at the wholesale level. In CO_2 emission trading, the system digitises CO_2 emission allowances which are then traded on an exchange. The concept of trading digitised assets is not new, and commodity trading markets have operated to stabilise commodity prices in the energy market. Traders also use commodity trading markets to hedge against associated risks in derivatives markets by trading energy commodity options and futures. In the P2P ETP system, energy produced by households through renewable sources is tokenised into commodity tokens which specify the rights of the token holder. These include the right to obtain energy stored in communal batteries, the right to sell the tokens and any governance rights that the tokens may have such as voting rights. The following sections explain the function of these tokens (mainly utility tokens and commodity tokens) and how they can be given legal recognition to achieve the reduction of CO_2 emissions through collective exchange. I will also discuss how payment tokens can be used by community projects to engage with other sustainable markets.

Utility tokens

Utility tokens allow their holders to access products and services either currently or in the future.[24] They are issued by an individual, an entity or an association, and in this, they differ from payment tokens that have their origin in the "mining" process according to a pre-designed protocol. Payment tokens have no fixed face value, but utility tokens have a value that is linked to particular products (two meals or three smart technology applications, for example) or services (three

---

23 Ning Wang, et al., 'Peer-To-Peer Energy Trading Among Microgrids with Multidimensional Willingness' (2018) https://doi.org/10.3390/en11123312. Accessed 17 May 2021.
24 FCA, 'Guidance on Cryptoassets' (FCA Consultation Paper 19/3, 2019).

hours of legal services, a training course or purchase of clean energy). In the P2P ETP, it can represent a unit of energy produced by the household through solar panels, for example. They are similar to vouchers or membership cards. A voucher can be redeemed for goods (a book) and for services (seeing a film or using the gym) in the P2P ETP, the units of energy stored in the communal batteries. The terms and conditions of these vouchers usually make their transferability restricted and time limited. When issuers become defunct due to bankruptcy, insolvency or project failure, voucher holders do not have access to asset pools and are unlikely to have any significant monetary claim.[25] However, some vouchers can be transferable,[26] lack a time limit and are even redeemable for multiple goods and services provided by people other than the issuers.

Some membership cards allow their holders to access goods and services.[27] For example, members might access unlimited film viewings at home, gym facilities or benefits provided by golf clubs. When these membership cards are tokenised, they become utility tokens that enable the token holders – individuals or entities – to have access to the utilities provided by the issuer or other third-party partners. Some systems allow membership cards to be sold, even on the open market, and some even allow participation in the decision-making process of the associated business, for example, a golf club. Some membership cards only allow membership to pass to the next-of-kin, others give cardholders priority in the purchase of goods or services at favourable rates, and with further cumulative benefits (the more you use, the more benefits you get).

In a P2P ETP, the utility tokens can be made transferable within the community in which each household is a member. This can be made as a specific condition that is coded in the smart contract. The tokens enable the household to access energy stored, such as in the communal batteries. There may be limitations on the tokens in terms of when and how the tokens can be redeemed for units of energy. For instance, the tokens cannot be redeemed after a certain period of time, such as one year. Furthermore, if the project is to be on a larger market, members should also consider some of the measures about dissolution. For instance, if the project takes the form of a corporation, how should the dissolution process work in order to protect the members of the network?

25 Gareth Malna and Sarah Kenshall, Chapter 25, in Thomas Frick (ed) *The Financial Technology Law Review* (2nd edn, The LawReviews 2019).

26 Michael Junemann and Johannes Wirtz, 'ICO: Legal Classification of Tokens: Part 4 – Utility Tokens' (2019) www.twobirds.com/en/news/articles/2019/global/ico-legal-classification-of-tokens-utility-token. Accessed on 07 July 2020.

27 FCA, 'Guidance on Cryptoassets', (FCA Consultation Paper 19/3, 2019).

Commodity tokens

Commodity tokens represent underlying commodities, such as raw materials, agricultural products or clean energy.[28] In some commodity trades the underlying commodities are securitised with the securities mostly being options and futures – contractual instruments that represent a right to purchase or sell the underlying commodities at a pre-determined price and at a specific time in the future. They do not involve directly securitising a particular asset or an identifiable quantity of asset.[29] Trade, in other types of commodity, involves setting up funds such as Exchange-Traded-Funds,[30] Hedge Funds or Private Equity Funds.[31] When tokenised, the units of investment in these funds can be classified as asset tokens which may be traded in the same way as other security tokens.[32] This means that commodity tokens are not tokenised titles in the underlying asset or commodity and do not represent the title in the goods both for the market and in law. Currently, commodity markets are organised as multilateral trading platforms with their own specific market rules.[33] They are only accessible to institutional investors through trading market members; retail investors do not participate directly. Commodity trades are used not only to purchase the underlying commodity goods but also to hedge against the risk of market volatility.[34] In addition, traders, clearing houses and settlement entities may be involved in trading in order to mitigate default risk, enhance legal certainty and provide liquidity. For instance, default in a settlement would be covered by clearing houses. The types of market described above for trading title tokens are mostly bilateral rather than multilateral and even an auction house, which could be seen as an organised market, is not a multilateral trading platform in the way that commodity markets operate. Failure to deliver goods could result in the award of damages or other remedies by a court or by some other dispute settlement mechanisms.

In law, commodity tokens do not represent the specific titles of goods nor a specifically defined bulk of goods, unlike title tokens. Commodity tokens do not

---

28 AAX Academy, 'Tokenising Commodities: It's Possible, But Should We?' (2020) https://academy.aax.com/en/tokenizing-commodities-its-possible-but-should-we/. Accessed 08 July 2020.

29 OECD, 'The Tokenisation of Assets and Potential Implications for Financial Markets' (2020) www.oecd.org/finance/The-Tokenisation-of-Assets-and-Potential-Implications-for-Financial-Markets.pdf. Accessed 08 July 2020.

30 Adam Marszk and Ewa Lechman, *Exchange-Traded Funds in Europe* (1st edn, Academic Press 2019).

31 Anne Jansen, et al., 'Hedge Funds and Financial Market Dynamics' (Occasional Papers of the IMF 1998).

32 Deloitte, 'Are Token Assets the Securities of Tomorrow?' (2019) www2.deloitte.com/content/dam/Deloitte/lu/Documents/technology/lu-token-assets-securities-tomorrow.pdf. Accessed 08 July 2020.

33 European Commission, 'Review of the Markets in Financial Instruments Directive' (2011) https://ec.europa.eu/commission/presscorner/detail/en/MEMO_11_716. Accessed 08 July 2020.

34 Deloitte, 'Commodity Price Risk Management: A Manual of Helping Commodity Price Risk for Corporates' (2018) www2.deloitte.com/content/dam/Deloitte/in/Documents/risk/in-risk-overview-of-commodity-noexp.PDF. Accessed 08 July 2020.

confer ownership of goods or goods in bulk to their holders. This affects contractual claims where there has been default in the delivery of the underlying goods, and also claims in priority in insolvency proceedings,[35] as well as other market rules attached to the tokens. The current commodity trades regulators are likely to continue to oversee tokenised commodity trades, but whether the commodity markets regulator should also have jurisdiction over inter-exchangeable tokenised commodities such as computing power or electricity should be examined further.

In a P2P ETP, if the tokens are not simply to be purchased but also traded, then it might be useful to recognise it as a commodity token that represents an interest such as a unit of energy. In this way, the commodity token can be traded both in a bilateral setting and in a multilateral trading platform.

Payment tokens

Payment tokens can be used to pay for energy units or as a reward for any energy produced. In a P2P ETP system, a community can decide to use cryptocurrency such as stable coins to purchase utility or commodity tokens on the platform in a similar way to using cash to settle securities transactions. In this way, a community can use cryptocurrency to access other goods and services either within the community or outside it. Alternatively, the community or the network can issue its own cryptocurrency as a reward for units of energy produced. In such a case, the currency can only be used within the community and the network and the community can decide how to set the conditions for the reward-coins.

What is the use of a smart contract?

A smart contract has two main primary functions: first, it can embody the rights of token holders and second, it can automate some aspects of transactions, for instance trading and distributing rights attached to the tokens. It must be borne in mind that a smart contract is a technical rather than a legal term so a smart contract may not be a legal contract but a legal contract can be coded in a smart contract. At the trading level of P2P ETP, householders can decide when, at what price and with whom they would like to trade. When they are away from home and energy continues to be produced through the household's solar panel or other green energy generator, they can decide when they would like to sell surplus energy through the platform. The community can decide if there should be a cap on the selling price to avoid price inflation and may decide to suspend trading at a particular time such as when there is an energy shortage in other parts of the community. This would avoid knowledge of a shortage causing panic buying in the community. Smart contracts can also be used to process aspects of dispute

35 INSOL International, 'Cryptocurrency and Its Impact on Insolvency and Restructuring' (Special Report, 2019).

resolution, supported by Online Dispute Resolution operated on the blockchain infrastructure.

Legal issue a smart contract

Scholars have been attempting to fit smart contracts into traditional contract law principles.[36] A smart contract, that is a set of computer codes, may contain more than one contract.[37] For instance, a smart contract can encode a debt instrument (bond) as well as a contract to purchase the debt instrument; smart contracts are used in online commercial activities such booking train tickets;[38] they have also been used by traders on stock exchanges to buy and sell securities; high frequency traders (HFTs) use smart contracts (computer codes) to "negotiate" (placing and cancelling orders) and execute transactions.[39] The emerging legal issue with using smart contracts to trade is that the DLT network (i.e. blockchain network) is potentially open to the general public.[40] While stock exchanges are membership-based centralised trading platforms, the decentralised and disintermediated DLT platforms can potentially be accessed by anyone.[41] Hence, the risk of default in the chain of transactions in automated DLT platforms cannot be mitigated as they would be by clearing institutions which are only accessible to professional members.[42] Therefore, it is recommended that a private chain should be used for smart contract trading to limit the risk of default. Membership can be limited to the households in the community for the P2P ETP.

Furthermore, there are a number of legal factors that can cause a contract to be null and void, to be rescinded and to be unenforceable, but these outcomes

36 Amelia Rawls, 'Contract Formation in an Internet Age' (2009) 10 *The Columbia Science and Technology Law Review* 200, 231; Kevin Werbach and Nicolas Cornell, 'Contracts Ex Machina' (2017) 67 *Duke Law Review* 368; Larry Dimatteo and Cristina Poncibó, 'Quandary of Smart Contracts and Remedies: The Role of Contract Law and Self-Help Remedies' (2018) 26 *European Review of Private Law* 813.

37 Primavera De Filippi and Aaron Wright, *Blockchain and the Law: The Rule of Code*, (1st edn, Harvard University Press 2018) 23; Mark Giancaspro, 'Is a "Smart Contract" Really a Smart Idea? Insights from A Legal Perspective' (2017) 33 *Computer Law and Security Review* 825, 835.

38 *Thornton v. Shoe Lane Parking Ltd* [1971] 2 QB 163; *Software Solutions Partners Ltd, R (on the application of) v. HM Customs & Excise* [2007] EWHC 971.

39 AFM, 'High Frequency Trading: The Application of Advanced Trading Technology in the European Market Place' (2010).

40 Peter Cartwright, 'Understanding and Protecting Vulnerable Financial Consumers' (2014) 38 *Journal of Consumer Policy* 119, 138.

41 'Distributed Ledger Technology (DLT) and Blockchain' (Fin Tech Note No. 1, World Bank Group, 2017), available at http://documents.worldbank.org/curated/en/177911513714062215/pdf/122140 -WP-PUBLIC-Distributed-Ledger-Technology-and-Blockchain-Fintech-Notes.pdf. Accessed 17 May 2021.

42 Louise Gullifer and Roy Good, *Good on Legal Problems of Credit and Security* (5th edn, Sweet & Maxwell 2013) 607.

are difficult to implement by smart contracts on the DLT platform.[43] A breach of term might not entitle the innocent party to repudiate the contract – terminating his or her side of the obligation – if the smart contract automatically transfers the tokenised interest to a third party.[44] Even if the consequences of a breach of such a term can be properly encoded into the smart contract, for example by a liquidated damage clause, other consequences of stopping the transfer of the securities in question could cause serious traction in the trading system. This can happen when a household purchases utility vouchers from another household, but the selling household failed to install the panel properly, so energy cannot be produced or the household used up the units of energy. This could cause the buying household to default the subsequent contracts it may have with another household.

There are legal factors that can cause a default in the chain of transactions. On a DLT platform, an underage person, such as a child in the household, who does not have the legal capacity (capacity) to execute transactions,[45] may have access to the trading platform and begin dealing in tokenised securities or interests.[46] Besides, if material information was not properly presented to the user, as a result of such a misrepresentation, the user is entitled to rescind the contract (misrepresentation). There is also a great risk that people using a smart contract do not have a good understanding of what it entails. For instance, they may not appreciate that pressing the "click" button on the screen will trigger a transfer of interest to a third party at a particular price with reference to a benchmark and this may give rise to a mistake in contract where there is no meeting of minds (mistake).[47] When the validity of the contract is successfully challenged, the smart contract may cause the energy tokens transferred (if not fungible) to third parties to be re-vested to innocent parties.

Computer science is not capable of producing smart contracts that transpose the legal terms accurately, without mistakes (no bugs) into a set of computer codes (errors in coding).[48] When contract terms are wrongly interpreted, or mistakenly drafted with grammatical or spelling mistakes,[49] judges or arbitrators can

---

43 Global Legal Insights, 'Blockchain and Cryptocurrency Regulation 2020: 13 Legal Issues Surrounding the Use of Smart Contracts' (2019) www.globallegalinsights.com/practice-areas/blockchain-laws-and-regulations/13-legal-issues-surrounding-the-use-of-smart-contracts. Accessed 17 May 2021.

44 Kevin Werbach and Nicolas Cornell, 'Contracts Ex Machina' (2017) 67 *Duke Law Review* 340.

45 *Chapple v. Cooper* (1844) 13 M & W 252; 153 ER 105.

46 Ewan McKendrick, *Contract Law* (12th edn, Palgrave 2017) 311; Unless there is a digital identification system to ensure the capacity of the person, the automation of the smart contracts can render the trading system unworkable.

47 Ewan McKendrick, *Contract Law: Text, Cases and Materials* (6th edn, OUP 2014) ch 16; *Cundy v. Lindsay* (1878) 3 App Cas 459; *Shogun Finance Ltd v. Hudson* [2003] UKHL 62.

48 Phoebus Athanassiou, 'Impact of Digital Innovation on the Processing of Electronic Payments and Contracting: An Overview of Legal Risks' (European Central Bank Legal Working Paper Series, No. 16, October 2017).

49 Jeremy Sklaroff, 'Smart Contracts and the Cost of Inflexibility' (2017) 166 *University of Pennsylvania Law Review* 292.

correct the terms and attempt to interpret them in such a way that they meet the original intentions of the parties.[50] However, in a DLT trading platform facilitated by smart contracts, parties may not be able to rely on judges or other human beings in tribunals to remedy human mistakes.[51] The computer programmes will not be able to "correct" the mistakes in coding, and the effect can be both systematic (causing a computer glitch in the transaction)[52] and systemic (causing a serious traction in the chain of transactions).[53] The risk of mistake is amplified when vague terms such as "reasonable," "good faith" or "frustrating event" are coded into a smart contract.[54] Even when using advanced natural language processing (NLP) to define these terms based on legal precedents,[55] there is a substantial risk that parties may not agree with an outcome delivered by algorithms. The codes in smart contracts would need to be able to suspend the automation function until the parties decide how such disputes will be resolved. It is not possible in a contract for parties to waive their right to have the disputes resolved through a dispute mechanism.[56] It is also questionable whether the outcome of an NLP "decision" would be legally recognised as dispute resolution.[57]

Therefore, the autonomous nature of smart contracts makes them potentially riskier than traditional legal agreements in terms of consumer protection. To make a smart contract legally enforceable, it is feasible to have a hybrid system of contracts. For example, context-sensitive legal prose, such as good faith or warranty provisions, can be governed by traditional written contracts, while more time-dependent actions, such as payment dates, can be governed by smart contracts. This hybrid system of contract is achievable as most coding programmes allow clauses, also known as DocStrings, to explain the purpose of the code. DocStrings exist between the lines of code to allow the programmer or readers to understand the functions of the programme. Smart contracts operate on similar coding platforms backed by typical computer programming. DocStrings allow for written

---

50　Kristian Lauslahti, et al., 'Expanding the Platform: Smart Contracts as Boundary Resources', in Anssi Smedlund et al. (eds), *Collaborative Value Co-Creation in the Platform Economy* (Transnational Systems Sciences 2018) 65, 90.

51　Steffen Wettig and Eberhard Zehendner, *A Legal Analysis of Human and Electronic Agents* (1st edn, Springer 2004) 111, 135.

52　European Securities and Markets Authority (ESMA), 'The Distributed Ledger Technology Applied to Securities Markets' (2017) para 5.36.

53　Philipp Maume and Mathias Fromberger, 'Regulations of Initial Coin Offerings: Reconciling U.S. and E.U. Securities Laws' (2019) 19 *Chicago Journal of International Law* 548, 585.

54　Wulf Kaal and Craig Calcaterra, 'Crypto Transaction Dispute Resolution' (2017) 73 *Business Lawyer* 109, 152.

55　J. G. Allen, 'Wrapped and Stacked: "Smart Contracts" and the Interaction of Natural and Formal Language' (2018) 14 *European Review of Contract Law* 307, 343.

56　Kevin Webach, 'Trust, But Verify: Why the Blockchain Needs the Law' (2019) 33 *Berkeley Technology Law Journal* 487, 550; But also see Charles Clark, 'The Answer to The Machine Is the Machine', in Bernt Hugenholtz (ed) *The Future of Copyright in a Digital Environment: Proceedings of the Royal Academy Colloquium* (The Hague: Kluwer Law International 1996) 139, 145.

57　Joseph Raz, *The Authority of Law: Essays on Law and Morality,* (Oxford University Press, 2011) 164; John Finnis, *Natural Law and Natural Rights* (2nd edn, Oxford University Press 2011) 6, 8.

explanations of the functions of the code in the interests of applying them alongside traditional legal contracts. This system creates the foundation for a hybrid style smart contract that accommodates both smart contract developers and lawyers. Consequently, in the P2P ETP models that would utilise smart contracts, the contractual agreements between the parties would be enforced through the transparency of the automated smart contract, while they would also be legally protected through the terms and applicable body of law governing the traditional contract. Therefore, when parties are in dispute, they may either renegotiate or seek traditional legal routes, such as court ordered compensation, to resolve the dispute.

Errors in coding

A systematic chain reaction stemming from errors within the smart contract would severely impact both parties involved with the contract. For example, an error in the contract's application and execution would create a crisis of time-restricted consequences. The contract's intricate system of immutability to editing and retracting on the blockchain would be a negative characteristic. There is a risk of using niche languages with smart contract coding, and even if there is an error within the code of the smart contract, the programme itself could potentially still run without indication of error. However, it would run incorrectly. For example, errors in the execution of smart contracts could lead to incorrect billing, malfunctions between transactions and loss of potential or purchased energy units. Smart contracts rely on trusting the computer programmers behind them. This trust also depends on the resilience to tampering once adequately coded. Due to the difficulty of changing the underlying blockchain code, the narrow opportunities for anyone to access or change the contract without preceding agreements can also represent a risk of errors in coding.

Blockchain technology and smart contracts should assist households, in this case the consumer, in understanding the risks and terms better before agreeing. Trust can be reinforced by requiring them to digitally check marked terms and clauses indicating acceptance, or by enabling a feature that tracks how long someone spends on a page to guarantee that the household has properly read all the terms and conditions. It is also symbiotically beneficial to companies, such as the controllers of the private blockchain network, that rely on consumer acknowledgement for their legal protection. Clauses should be drafted in the traditional contract to include legal accountability through the consumer protection legislation for any breach or errors in service.

Consumer knowledge, trust and understanding are vital to the contractual agreements between consumers and energy producers. However, 60 per cent of domestic consumers within the United Kingdom, who are on default tariffs, are not currently benefitting from this model. This indicates that most domestic consumers in the energy market fail to meet their needs. An example of this was demonstrated by OVO Energy in January 2020, where consumers were extraordinarily overcharged and issued incorrect energy usage information. It is submitted that the implementation of P2P ETPs would ensure greater consumer protection and company compliance through transparency and accountability. P2P ETPs would enable consumers to access their own energy data (produced, consumed, purchased, stored in the custody of the wallet and traded) and avoid a disastrous billing system. The platform can also ensure a cap on energy expenditure based on the amount of energy produced and used within the household. With the collected data from smart meters, consumers would know the precise amount of energy produced and used while utilising smart contracts for their legal protection and billing.

The P2P ETP smart contract trading for energy detailed above is exemplified through a cyclical ecosystem. Smart meters are the medium to regulate energy consumption and production. As discussed, the consumer has agreed to energy tariffs and contracts, and the smart contract enforces accountability and price arrangement. When the terms and conditions of trading have been agreed to, the information is encoded into the smart contract as an automated system. To avoid overbilling, a cap can be introduced into the smart contract transaction to ensure that the consumer does not consume or pay for more than stipulated. Options for additional purchases may be presented if the consumer is reaching their limit. The consumer can use the smart meter to enforce their smart contract with the energy company. The smart meter requires no direct regulation and functions autonomously using its own data, ensuring that the consumer is receiving the agreed amount of energy. In turn, the smart contract also ensures that the energy company is receiving payment at the specified time and date, as agreed in the hybrid contract. This limits the potential of energy being cut off during colder times of the year and protects vulnerable consumers from sudden heating cuts. Therefore, this example of a smart contract in the P2P ETP would not require any additional regulation outside of traditional contract law and application, as it utilises predetermined conditions in a traditional contract as protection.

What is the function of the trading platform?

The trading platform is the most important mechanism through which householders can take control by setting the rules that define how trading can take place. Energy units produced are tokenised and can then be traded peer-to-peer on the platform. The trading platform is modelled on an exchange trading venue where participants can make offers (submissions) to buy or sell, and algorithms match their submissions with those of other participants. For example, householders might trade surplus energy they produce, or those who want to use more energy than they produce can purchase the shortfall on the platform. As the blockchain platform provides information transparently and immutably, householders can view historical transaction records, allowing them to manage their energy consumption and price their energy units more efficiently. In a community, it is likely that participants will use algorithms to engage in the trade so it would be efficient for there to be a clearing system that allows participants to net their positions at the end of the trading day. There may also need to be a delivery mechanism, such as a smart grid, that allows token holders to have access to energy units produced by others.

As discussed in the previous chapter, there is a need to have a central counterparty (CCP) that stands in the middle of all the transactions to ensure the safety of tokenised securities traded on a DLT.[58] This can also apply to the P2P ETP. This central counterparty would perform the function of contractual guarantee to mitigate risks.[59] It can act to certify that the smart contracts used are securely coded and that they are compliant with relevant laws and regulations. When the CCP acts as a guarantor to the transactions, transfers of the tokens and the corresponding funds would continue uninterrupted. Any dispute among the households, such as a contractual dispute or a dispute over the smart contract, can be raised with the CCP which would then act as a mediator or adjudicator. Any compensation for damages can be made outside the trading system. For instance, the users could claim mistaken transactions because of the problem of "fat fingers."[60] The parties may not allow the transactions of the tokens to be rewound, but the fund could be returned.[61] The CCP needs to design a system where household consumers can be protected from mistakes caused by "fat fingers." It might be that margins should be collected from the users and used to cover mistakes of this kind. This would also allow the CCP to vet users and assess their risks based on their attributes and previous behaviour on the blockchain.[62] The CCP could provide risk scores on the users which will affect the collateral and margins to be required of users.[63]

The legal risk

Black box smart contract

On P2P ETPs, smart contracts are considered to function as intended by the developer.[64] Thus, the smart contract, if not properly executed, can result in malfunctions. For example, an attack on the DAO, a digital decentralised autonomous organisation that operated as an investor-directed venture capital fund on the Ethereum blockchain, led to over 60 million US dollars being moved into an

---

58 Andrea Pinna and Wiebe Rettenberg, 'Distributed Ledger Technologies in Securities Post-Trading: Revolution or Evalution?' (European Central Bank Occasional Paper Series No. 172, April 2016).
59 Steven Schwarcz and Joanna Benjamin, 'Intermediary Risk in the Indirect Holding System for Securities' (2002) 12 *Duke Journal of Company and International Law* 309, 310.
60 Government Office for Science, The Future of Computer Trading in Financial Markets: An International Perspective (Final Project Report, 2012).
61 Scott McKinney, et al., 'Smart Contracts, Blockchain, and the Next Frontier of Transactional Law' (2018) 13 *Washington Journal of Law, Technology and Arts* 329.
62 IFC, 'Blockchain: Opportunities for Private Enterprises in Emerging Markets' (Working Paper, Second and Expanded Edition, January 2019).
63 Marc Pilkington, 'Blockchain Technology: Principles and Applications' in F. Xavier Olleros and Majlinda Zhegu (eds) *Research Handbook on Digital Transformations* (Edward Elgar 2016) 228.
64 Maher Alharby and Aad van Moorsel, 'A Systematic Mapping Study on Current Research Topics in Smart Contracts' (2017) 9 *International Journal of Consumer Science and Information Technology* 151, 164.

incorrect account.[65] This resulted in a legal controversy regarding the automation and ownership of these tokenised funds on the blockchain. To avoid this risk with P2P ETP systems, an established and accredited standard for trustworthy professionals at the back end of the technology is necessary. Consumer contracts must be clearly and unambiguously understood[66] in relation to what they are binding to; therefore, the development of smart contracts as legal contracts would create a hurdle for those who are not technologically inclined. Placing trust in a contract that an average person cannot read or understand opens a technological "Pandora's box" of litigation and misunderstanding.

Consumer protection

Consumers are empowered through P2P ETPs by having more control over their energy usage. However, technological infrastructure should be regulated in the interests of consumers and there is evidence that this is beginning to take shape. For example, for P2P ETPs, the Renewable Energy Directive states that the infrastructure of smart technology and regulatory instruments should embed consumer protection. The Directive indicates that an applicable regulatory framework should be established to empower renewables for self-consumers (consumers and prosumers) without disproportionate burdens.[67] Thus, the foundation for consumer protection, while consuming and generating energy, has been enshrined in this legislation for the encouragement of P2P ETPs. Discussions throughout this chapter indicates that smart contract obligations on the P2P ETP can be regulated through traditional contract law via hybrid contractual arrangements. Other legislative measures can also be applied to blockchain-based smart contracts depending on the legal recognition of smart contracts. Furthermore, the transparent model also raises legal issues around security, individual privacy and data protection.[68]

Data protection

Information privacy is a major concern with regard to DLT, and therefore, P2P ETPs. The primary purpose of using smart meter data is to ensure that consumers can take advantage of the opportunity to access their households' energy data (i.e. production and usage) and make smarter choices to conserve and trade energy while potentially saving money on their energy bills. Access to more detailed energy-use information, increased control over households' energy use and costs, the ability to transfer data to others and personal involvement in energy

---

65 Fan Zhang et al, 'Town Crier: An Authenticated Data Feed for Smart Contracts' (2016) http://doi .org/10.1145/2976749.2978326. Accessed 17 May 2021.
66 *WRM Group Ltd v. Wood* [1997] Lexis Citation 4581.
67 Directive 2018/2001 of the European Parliament and of the Council of 11 December 2018 on the promotion of the use of energy from renewable sources, recital 66.
68 Nancy King and Perlline Jessen, 'For Privacy's Sake: Consumer "Opt-Outs" for Smart Meters' (2014) 30 *Computer Law and Security Review* 530, 539.

conservation are all potential benefits for consumers with access to P2P ETPs. These considerations justify treating consumers' access to smart meter data as a primary purpose of P2P ETP.[69] However, there are privacy risks in terms of transferring such important data to third parties. For example, energy usage patterns and profiles based on smart meter data can be used for many secondary purposes. Such purposes include generating targeted and personalised advertising in online and mobile frameworks.[70] Under the Data Protection Act 2018, it is an offence to disclose personal data without consent.[71] It would be necessary to include such consents in the traditional contractual terms and obligations prior to enabling P2P-ETPs access to household data.

Another risk in terms of data sharing on a transparent model of P2P ETP is the fear of individual data tracking. Consumer interest includes an individual's legal right to be free of unreasonable surveillance[72] and other types of intrusions into their homes and personal lives.[73] There is potential to apply data-mining technologies to energy usage data produced by P2P ETPs and use the information for primary and secondary commercial purposes, including many purposes that have not yet been identified in the evolving digital economy.[74] Parties involved in data sharing with P2P ETPs include direct consumers, energy suppliers and other third parties.[75] These third parties would include energy service management companies with whom the consumer's energy data has been shared, or marketing entities that rely on consumer data for product advertising and profiling. Data sharing on P2P ETP may be carried out by the consumer or their energy supplier. Data that could potentially be shared by third parties includes the amount of automated transfers of smart meter data.[76]

Data sharing is often necessary to achieve the benefits of P2P ETPs, and that data can trickle down to secondary purposes. For example, energy companies may

---

69 N. King and P. Jenssen, 'For Privacy's Sake: Consumer "Opt-Outs" for Smart Meters' (2014) 30(5) *Computer Law and Security Review* 229.

70 The European Data Protection Supervisor, 'Opinion of the European Data Protection Supervisor on the Commission Recommendation on preparations for the Roll-out of Smart Metering Systems' (2012) https://edps.europa.eu/sites/edp/files/publication/12-06-08_smart_metering_en.pdf. Accessed 17 May 2021.

71 Data Protection Act 2018, c. 6, § 170(1).

72 N. King and P. Jenssen, 'For Privacy's Sake: Consumer "Opt-Outs" for Smart Meters' (2014) 30(5) *Computer Law and Security Review* 533.

73 D. Wright et al., 'Sorting Outsmarts Surveillance' (2010) 26(4) *Computer Law & Security Review* 3–4.

74 Omer Tene and Jules Polonetsky, 'Privacy in the Age of Big Data: A Time for Big Decisions' (2012) 64 *Stanford Law Review* 63.

75 N. King and P. Jenssen, 'For Privacy's Sake: Consumer "Opt-Outs" for Smart Meters' (2014) 30(5) *Computer Law and Security Review* 251.

76 Department for Business, Energy and Industry, 'Strategy, Smart Meeting Implementation Programme' <sc>(2018)</sc> https://assets.publishing.service.gov.uk/government/uploads/system /uploads/attachment_data/file/700382/SMETS1_maximising_interoperability_enrolment_mandate_consultation_.pdf. Accessed 17 May 2021. (Hereinafter smart metering implementation programme.)

utilise the consumer's smart meter data with a third-party advertising company to earn advertising revenue.[77] These distinctions about parties and purposes of sharing are the foundation of the transparent and accountable model of P2P ETP. An example can be taken from the United States, where significant progress has been made for consumer privacy concerns with regard to smart meter data. The US Department of Energy enacted a task force[78] specifically focussed on addressing the issue.[79] Currently, their key responsibility is to craft a voluntary smart grid code of conduct specific to privacy.[80] Another development is the construction of a voluntary "smart grid privacy seal program"[81] aimed at companies that utilise consumer energy data.[82] Policy and legislation play major roles in assisting consumer protection while implementing smart technologies in everyday life. For example, in the United Kingdom, consumer protection for privacy and personal data is included in the suppliers' licensing terms.[83] Under these terms, a P2P ETP supplier may collect monthly meter readings for billing and regulation purposes without the need for consumer consent. Furthermore, it would be possible to collect daily meter readings with an option of opting out at the consumer's consent, or half-hourly meter readings solely with consumer consent for opting in.

Market manipulation and insider dealing

Householders can trade their tokenised energy units on the distributed ledger technology network at a price determined by supply and demand, but, as in other trading venues, there is a risk that prices can be manipulated to make unjustifiable gains. Even though the purpose of the market is to give community users control through a collective trading system, if the price can be easily manipulated at the expense of others, users will quickly lose confidence in the market. Unlike a normal commodity market where there are regulations and governance in place, a community-based P2P ETP would need to be regulated to provide user confidence. Market transparency, safety and integrity as well as price stability should continue to be the regulatory objectives for a P2P ETP. This is especially

---

77 N. King and P. Jenssen, 'For Privacy's Sake: Consumer "Opt-Outs" for Smart Meters' (2014) 30(5) *Computer Law and Security Review* 235–236.

78 *See* 42 U.S.C. § 17336 (2018).

79 US Department of Energy, 'Voluntary Code of Conduct Final Concepts and Principles' (2015) www .energy.gov/sites/prod/files/2015/01/f19/VCC%20ConcETPs%20and%20Principles%202015_01 _08%20FINAL.pdf. Accessed 17 May 2021.

80 Angelique Carson, 'Stakeholders Aim to Craft Smart Grid Privacy Code of Conduct<sc>'</sc> (2013) https://iapp.org/news/a/2013-02-27-stakeholders-aim-to-craft-smart-grid-privacy-code-of -conduct/. Accessed 17 May 2021.

81 N. King and P. Jenssen, 'For Privacy's Sake: Consumer "Opt-Outs" for Smart Meters' (2014) 30(5) *Computer Law and Security Review* 537.

82 Eleanor, 'Privacy Risk Summit Preview: Privacy by Design for IoT' (2016) www.trustarc.com/ blog/2016/05/23/privacy-risk-summit-preview-privacy-design-iot/. Accessed 17 May 2021.

83 Office of Gas and Electricity, 'Supply License Guide: Smart Metering' (2017) www.ofgem.gov.uk /system/files/docs/2017/11/smart_metering.pdf. Accessed 17 May 2021.

true when members have to rely on smart contracts and some degree of artificial intelligence in automated trading. Regulation of algorithms is needed to ensure both the safety of the market system to provide consumer protection as well as to provide energy security. A P2P ETP trading venue is different from a normal commodity trading venue or securities trading platform where there are professional members who trade on behalf of clients and do not have a long-term stake in the invested companies. In P2P ETP, the "clients" are the householders themselves who do have a long-term stake in the enterprise. It is also important that the market should assist householders in making their decisions. For instance, any information about future forecasts should be made available to them and, in order to stabilise prices, no excessive betting based on the forecast information should be permitted. Some market trading strategies such as shorting should be avoided at the community level.

There is also a risk that a member who has privileged information might gain through its use. For instance, a member might become aware of a shortage of demand in a particular period due to some government planned activity, or there might be enhanced demand due to a planned compulsory lockdown. If this information is not disclosed to the household network, those who are privy to it could use this inside information to trade-in the tokens to make a gain or avoid a loss. In financial market regulation, this would amount to insider dealing. Therefore, to ensure the integrity of the market, there should be a system that encourages those with relevant information to disclose it, and to discourage them from using it to trade until it is made public.

Regulators may need to intervene to suspend the trading of tokens on the platform when necessary.[84] They may do so to prevent systematic risk, to protect investors and to maintain market integrity. For instance, regulators must be able to suspend securities trades to prevent a flash crash due to algorithm trading;[85] to suspend trades when householders are manipulated by discriminatory algorithms;[86] or to suspend trades when there are suspected insider dealings.

Will there be a transformative effect?

Empowering the local residents

This platform aims to give control to its users so that they can decide collectively on how energy will be produced, how it will be priced and how any surplus can be used. This coincides with the philosophy of a DLT system where there is a collective way of managing and sharing resources in a disintermediated

---

84 Chapter 5 (Suspending, Cancelling and Restoring Listing and Reverse Takeovers: All Securities) of the Listing Rules. www.handbook.fca.org.uk/handbook/LR/5.pdf. Accessed 17 May 2021.

85 Government Office for Science, 'The Future of Computer Trading in Financial Markets' (Working Paper 11/1276, 2011).

86 Danny Busch, 'MiFID II: Regulating High Frequency Trading, Other Forms of Algorithmic Trading and Direct Electronic Market Access' (2016) 10 *Law and Financial Market Review* 72, 84.

and decentralised way. From the energy perspective, the P2P ETP aims for sustainability to combat climate change as part of a global sustainable development project. What it can do is to bring about behavioural change, to install a shared management platform, to deliver both localised energy and energy security. These aims are all dependent on a market-based solution: the trading platform. Such a localised social enterprise demonstrates how the idea of cooperation can bring benefit to the community as a whole.

Previous chapters have shown how blockchain on the internet can allow people to participate in the platform beyond geographical boundaries. P2P ETP, by contrast, aims to empower local people to control their energy. The transformative effect it can bring is to stop householders from having to rely on non-renewable energy with little or no say on how they are charged. Since this is a localised trading platform, the objective is to change how householders produce and consume energy. For energy production, there would be incentives for householders to install facilities that can produce renewable energy such as solar panels, and for consumption, with real-time usage data, they have the incentive to use energy more responsibly. Even if the P2P ETP is a localised project, there is potential for its effects to reach beyond the local community when, for example, local communities join the green allowance scheme and participate internationally as an entity on the green certificate trading platform. Alternatively, crypto-exchanges can be set up to allow reward tokens to be exchanged for other stable coins or they can be used to purchase green certificates or allowance units. In this way, energy produced in a remote area such as Africa can be purchased as an allowance by companies in other regions. Energy produced by local householders can also be used to start other sustainable developments in the area. What P2P ETP can contribute to the larger global energy trading system is to show the origin of the energy produced. The existence of an audit trail of when and how energy has been produced reduces the risk of audit and energy trading fraud. Since the units of energy produced can be turned into non-fungible tokens, it is possible for locally produced energy to be purchased globally. Because the P2P ETP is linked to the global crypto-market, energy units can be purchased affordably by local householders in a way that gives global participants an incentive to support localised sustainable projects by exchanging other tokens. If tokens for locally produced energy can be converted into globally tradable green certificates and the price is supported by a more incentivised global green finance system, the project can enrich local initiatives. In this way, local community projects can be connected to the global crypto-market system. A local community project may be locally self-sufficient, but without a more global support system, it may lack other resources needed to initiate further sustainable development projects. A blockchain community may be able to exchange its reward tokens on global sustainable commodity platforms where goods and services can be exchanged. Since there is an audit trail enabled by the P2P ETP, there is less need for audit activities that can increase the cost of certification.

Would the global crypto-market affect local community projects?

There is a risk that local community projects could lose their original purpose of empowering local consumers in their energy use and turn them into rent-seeking investments on the global crypto-market. One way to prevent this is to enable a local community to form an association such as a corporation so that members can participate in decision making at the community level. If there is a proposal to convert tokens or to trade them on an interconnected global crypto-market, agreement could require a unanimous decision by the community. There could also be a corporate component to the P2P ETP where a householder is able to participate in the decision-making process. How they vote and how many votes they are able to cast can be a private arrangement between households. The resolutions adopted by the community can be exhibited on the global network so that the global crypto-market can see whether the community has obtained the householders' authority to participate in wider trading activities. If the community wishes, the global network may also view its requirement for sustainable goods and its intention to exchange goods and services for any green certificates it has produced.

While P2P ETP raises issues of privacy, its transparency can draw the attention of global policy makers and sustainable development commodities traders. Lack of knowledge and transparency have been a main barrier to investment as investors are not confident in investing in areas where they lack expertise and sufficient information. The P2P ETP with more standardised information can close this information gap and provide confidence to global investors. A community P2P ETP can also start a crowdfunding project to exchange green certificates for the commodities it requires. While the P2P ETP is essentially a community project for householders to produce and consume energy locally, through access to wider crowdfunding platforms, the community can begin to crowdfund for other commodities.

Conclusion

The aim of this chapter has been to show how a market solution such as a trading platform can help deliver sustainable goals. P2P ETP is a model operated by smart technology that demonstrates how a blockchain-enabled system can empower householders at the local level. There are, however, potential legal risks involved, relating to the failure of smart contracts and associated issues of contractual law, as well as errors in coding, consumer protection issues and the risk of data breaches. Market manipulation in the trading platform is another potential problem and interventions might be needed to ensure market safety, consumer protection and market integrity. It is possible to link a P2P ETP system with a wider blockchain-based community in a way that supports local community projects by allowing tokens to be exchanged for other goods or services on blockchain platforms. However, there should be a way of preventing local communities from losing their identity in a global trading system.

11 Code-as-law in financial markets: functions, risks and governance

Introduction

In the previous chapters, I have mentioned how "code-as-law" has been proposed as new governance for the financial market on the blockchain. Although in some parts I have argued that it might not be the best governance solution, there are areas where code-as-law can be used to realise a legal function or form some parts of a governance system. This chapter, therefore, has three principal aims. First, to examine the technology used in different financial markets in order to understand how code-as-law defines the nature of those markets, how it assigns functions and responsibilities to participants and how it increases compliance by regulating participants' behaviour. The second aim is to investigate whether machine learning can be incorporated into the concept of code-as-law in finance, looking in particular at the benefits and risks of implementation through RegTech, SupTech and LegalTech. The third aim is to discuss how code-as-law can be developed and applied to crypto-platforms in order to disintermediate and decentralise financial markets. How can code-as-law be adapted to the crypto-environment to enhance access to finance, to shared economy and to justice?

Code-as-law – shaping market structure

Code-as-law refers to the internal rules of computing systems which take the form of executable software code and technical protocols.[1] In the cyber space, code-as-law also denotes the internet's technical infrastructure and software code that regulates, constrains and enables online behaviour and interaction.[2] In this sense, I argue that code-as-law can define the structure of a market.[3] Computing systems

---

1 Karen Yeung, 'Regulation by Blockchain: The Emerging Battle for Supremacy between the Code of Law and Code as Law' (2019) 82(2) *Modern Law Review* 207–239.
2 L. Lessig, *Code and Other Laws of Cyberspace* (New York: Basic Books 1999).
3 Primavera De Filippi, *Blockchain and the Law: The Role of Code* (1st edn, Harvard University Press 2018) 193, 204; Tim Wu, 'Will Artificial Intelligence Eat the Law? The Rise of Hybrid Social-Ordering Systems' (2019) 119 *Columbia Law Review* 1, 29; Tim Wu, 'When Code Isn't Law' (2003) https://papers.ssrn.com/sol3/papers.cfm?abstract_id=413201. Accessed on 25 February 2021; Orin

DOI: 10.4324/9780429023613-11

have long been used in transactional and regulatory activities in the financial markets, especially the vibrant equity market and this section will use the example of that market to show how code-as-law is currently being applied to a computerised market space.

Stock exchanges, particularly their trading sections, have computerised their operations and the financial infrastructure industry, which is mostly operated by exchanges, has gradually followed suit.[4] NASDAQ was the first exchange to computerise its operations and has been at the forefront of expanding its operational technology into other markets to computerise market interconnection.[5] Today, all major stock exchanges rely on non-manual technology to systematise securities trading, particularly in the segment of the trade which matches buy and sell orders in a centralised, computerised system.[6] The law has been playing a particularly important role in catalysing this transformation by laying down the legal conditions for recognising digitised assets and governing relationships between participants such as traders. One crucial innovation is digitising share certificates so that equity securities no longer have a paper form.[7] The manual labour involved in safekeeping assets and recording transactions is now either redundant or substantially streamlined. The digitisation process enables equity securities to be transferred and transacted more quickly and securely through central securities depositories (CSDs) and the chain of intermediaries.[8] It also increases participation in equity investment by encouraging the asset management industry to become more active.[9] Digitising securities has prompted institutional developments in clearing houses and CSDs, including the international CSD, to enhance the efficiency of trading processes and increase internationalisation of the securities market where

Kerr, 'Enforcing Law Online' (2007) 74 *The University of Chicago Law Review* 745, 760; Lawrence Lessing, *Code and Other Laws of Cyberspace* (1st edn, Basic Books 1999) 1, 320.

4 FinTech in the Exchange Industry: Potential for Disruption (2017) 11 *Masaryk University Journal of Law and Technology* 245, 266; Government Office for Science, 'The Future of Computer Trading in Financial Markets: An International Perspective' (Working Paper, 2012) www.cftc.gov/sites/default/files/idc/groups/public/@aboutcftc/documents/file/tacfuturecomputertrading1012.pdf. Accessed 24 February 2021.

5 Finextra, 'Nasdaq Bids to Become One of the World's Leading Technology Organisations' (2013) www.finextra.com/newsarticle/24447/nasdaq-bids-to-become-one-of-the-worlds-leading-technology-organisations. Accessed 24 February 2021.

6 Daniel Lee, 'Stock Exchanges' Order Matching System' (2020) https://lee0118.medium.com/stock-exchanges-order-matching-system-96af1557e46e. Assessed 24 February 2021.

7 PWC, 'Dematerialisation of Securities -Unlisted Public Companies' (2018) www.pwc.in/assets/pdfs/news-alert-tax/2018/pwc_news_alert_14_september_2018_dematerialisation_of_securities.pdf. Accessed 24 February 2021.

8 OECD, 'The Tokenisation of Asset and Potential Implications for Financial Markets' (2020) www.oecd.org/finance/The-Tokenisation-of-Assets-and-Potential-Implications-for-Financial-Markets.pdf. Accessed 24 February 2021.

9 Amin Rajan, 'Digitisation of Asset and Wealth Management: Promise and 'Pitfalls' (2017) https://ifwe.3ds.com/sites/default/files/2017-12/fabs-whitepaper-digitisation-study-financial-services.pdf. Accessed 24 February 2021.

securities can be owned, traded, and settled across borders.[10] This innovation also enables algorithm trading and high frequency trading which can close the pricing gap caused by arbitrage trading,[11] as well as supporting indices-based exchange traded funds (ETFs)[12] by increasing the volume of trading. However, digitisation of equity securities through coding is mainly done at the quantitative level for quantitative management rather than at the qualitative level. Coding securities for quantitative management allows traders to submit orders electronically, and enables trading venues to match their trades via centralised matching engines and to record the volume of trade.[13] It can also use real-time trading data,[14] recorded on the platform to assess the risk that each trader exposes the market to, and to manage such risk through margin and collateral collection. The system for digitised recording of security transactions can calculate the net position of total trades by clearing houses for clearing trades, and for security depositaries to settle trades.[15]

The qualitative aspect of securities such as the rights and conditions attached to them are not coded and as a result do not function on a computerised capital market. Currently, rights, including the corporate actions of voting rights and dividends rights that are attached to securities, cannot be recognised by exchanges' computer systems. This means that the qualitative aspect of securities has to be managed separately by third-party entities such as corporate data management companies[16] and corporate actions advisors[17] in order to record corporate actions, process associated data and communicate with investors. This work incurs a fee. Although it is possible to automate corporate actions, it is rare for companies and investors to rely on code-as-law to process this aspect because securities are held in a chain of intermediaries and automation of corporate actions would make some functions of the intermediaries and corporate advisory firms redundant.

10 SWIFT, 'Cross-Border Securities Market Infrastructure Links: Lessons and Perspectives for Asia Pacific' (Information Paper, 2017).
11 Alain Chaboud et al., 'Rise of the Machines: Algorithmic Trading in the Foreign Exchange Market' (2013) 6 *Journal of Finance* 2045, 2084; Albert Menkveld, 'High Frequency Trading and the New Market Makers' (2013) 16 *Journal of Financial Markets* 712, 740.
12 Seungho Baek et al., 'Robo-Advisors: Machine Learning in Trend-Following ETF Investments' (2020) 12 *Sustainability* 1, 15.
13 Arsyad Aldyan et al., 'The Implication of Technological Development on Stock Trading in the Stock Markets of Indonesia Stock Exchange' (2019) 358 *Advances in Social Science, Education and Humanities Research* 123, 126.
14 OECD, 'Keeping Track of Global Trade in Real Time' (Economics Department Working Papers No. 1524, 2018) www.oecd.org/officialdocuments/publicdisplaydocumentpdf/?cote=ECO/WKP(2018)72&docLanguage=En. Accessed 25 February 2021.
15 David Mills et al., 'Distributed Ledger Technology in Payments, Clearing and Settlement' (2012) 6 *Journal of Financial Market Infrastructures* 207, 249.
16 Adriano Koshiyama, 'Towards Algorithm Auditing: A Survey on Managing Legal, Ethical and Technological Risks of AI, ML and Associated Algorithms' (2021) https://papers.ssrn.com/sol3/papers.cfm?abstract_id=3778998. Accessed 21 February 2021.
17 Department for Business Innovation & Skills, 'Exploring the Intermediated Shareholding Model' (BIS Research Paper, 2016) www.uksa.org.uk/sites/default/files/BIS_RP261.pdf. Accessed 24 February 2021.

Nevertheless, digitising securities and coding the corporate actions attached to them both are technically feasible and incorporating them through code-as-law to reflect agreed rights and conditions would be critical to a disintermediated crypto-market. This qualitative aspect of the code can reduce transaction costs and enhance investors' control of their companies or projects, but it must be designed effectively and securely to protect the rights of the parties.

Digitisation of securities also enables segmentation of the equity market and lays down the conditions for each segment to develop its own specialism. In this way, listing, trading, clearing and settlement segments have appeared in the securities cycle, each with their own specialist functions and arrangements through which participants engage with each other. Law and regulation have subsequently developed to govern these digitised markets and to enhance their market competitiveness. In trading, there are laws regulating algorithmic trading and high frequency trading in order to close the pricing arbitrage and to support the ETF market.[18] The role of code-as-law here is to provide a digital definition of the market and the behaviour of participants on the platform. The computerised trading platform only permits market members to participate,[19] and they must participate in accordance with the digitally defined computer programme. Traders must use specified computer technology, compatible with that of the trading platform, to communicate their trading activities as they submit or cancel orders.[20] Trading platforms can set the limits and conditions for submitting orders by traders digitally, whether manually or by algorithms. Traders are subject to technological control by the trading platform and are subject to audit and inspection by them. The use of hardware or software incompatible with that of the exchange denies access and the systems can authenticate orders and detect irregular orders originating from cyber attackers. Code-as-law defines the nature of the market (equity trading or currency clearing), the function of the market (trading or settlement) and controls who has access to the market, in a similar way to geo-blocking.[21] Finally, code-as-law can specify the conditions and limitations of trade contracts to ensure

---

18 Michael Morelli, 'Implementing High Frequency Trading Regulation: A Critical Analysis of Current Reform' (2017) 6 *Michigan Business & Entrepreneurial Law Review* 201, 229.

19 Jakob Arnoldi, 'Computer Algorithms, Market Manipulation and Institutionalisation High Frequency Trading' (2016) 33 *Theory, Culture and Society* 29, 52.

20 European Compliance & Ethics Institute, 'The Influence of Technology on Stock Trading' (2020) www.europeanbusinessreview.com/the-influence-of-technology-on-stock-trading/. Accessed 25 February 2021.

21 Georgios Dimitropoulos, 'The Law of Blockchain' 2020 Washington Law Review (Forthcoming) www.researchgate.net/publication/339998624_THE_LAW_OF_BLOCKCHAIN. Accessed 24 February 2021.

that they meet the conditions set by the trading platform's central match-engine,[22] and can monitor risk by using real-time data to collect margins and collateral.[23]

Code-as-law in trades and compliance

Code-as-law in contractual transactions

Code-as-law can be defined as computer codes that are able to perform all or some of the functions of the written law: creation, application, adjudication and enforcement.[24] The law here can include case law, statutory law, regulation, rules, standards, guidelines and other codes of best practice (softlaw). In this sense, code-as-law is already a reality and is being applied to many market spaces, such as data-trained algorithms that analyse legal documents. For instance, a vending machine is an example of executing and automating contract law where only one party is a human being and the other is a purely mechanical body.[25] Electronic toll collection uses a combination of a sensor mechanism and a payment system to automate motorway payment.[26] Purchasing flight tickets online is another example of the operation of code-as-law,[27] dubbed "smart contract" in commerce, whereby a flight contract can be concluded without human negotiation, without a written paper form, and automated when the code is scanned at the check-in counter and ID checks are carried out. In future, it is envisaged that compensation for flight delay or cancellation can be automated by code-as-law. In these three instances there is no human being on the other side of the contract, and it is the computer code that confirms, executes and enforces the contract terms when there is a breach of contract. In a more sophisticated usage, computer code can both match the terms of the contracts submitted by the parties and execute them. This is evidenced in the algorithm trading space where transactions are automated according to pre-set parameters by computer programmes, even though individual trades have not been negotiated by human parties, agreed by the meeting of human minds, or executed by human action.

---

22 Haim Bodek, 'A Case Study in Regulatory Arbitrage and Information Asymmetry' in Walter Mattli (ed) *Global Algorithmic Capital Markets: High Frequency Trading, Dark Pools, and Regulatory Challenges* (Oxford University Press 2018) 28, 44.

23 Citi, 'The Road to an Effective Collateral Management Program' (2020) www.citivelocity.com/insights/the-road-to-effective-collateral-management-program/. Accessed 24 February 2024.

24 Primavera De Filippi, *Blockchain and the Law: The Role of Code* (1st edn, Harvard University Press 2018) 193, 204; Mimi Zou, 'Code, and Other Laws of Blockchain' (2020) 4 *Oxford Journal of Legal Studies* 645, 665; Daniel Drummer and Dirk Neumann, 'Is Code Law? Current Legal and Technical Adoption Issues and Remedies for Blockchain-Enabled Smart Contracts' (2020) 35 *Journal of Information Technology* 337, 360.

25 Max Raskin, 'The Law and Legality of Smart Contracts' (2017) 304 *Georgetown Law Technology Review.* https://georgetownlawtechreview.org/the-law-and-legality-of-smart-contracts/GLTR-04 -2017/. Accessed 24 February 2021.

26 Wei-Hsun Lee, 'Design and Implementing of Electronic Toll Collection System Based Vehicle Positioning System Techniques' (2018) 31 *Computer Communication* 2925, 2933.

27 Orly Lobel, 'The Law of the Platform' (2016) 137 *Minnesota Law Review* 87, 110.

Having said that, there are two major functions of contract law that code-as-law does not perform: detailed negotiations such as those involving offers and counter-offers; and resolution of complex disputes. Code-as-law at this contractual law level merely executes orders set within the parameters strictly defined by the human designers of algorithms. The parameters incorporate the terms upon which the traders wish to trade and are subject to the rules imposed by the exchanges. Furthermore, the exchanges' circuit breaker mechanism is able to halt trading activities[28] if certain conditions defined by the exchanges have been triggered.[29] In this way, exchanges are able to intervene in contractual transactions between parties and can require them to cancel orders (offers) that they have submitted to the system. The circuit breaker is an example of the way code-as-law can be used to intervene in trade, based on public or collective market interest, in order to prevent systemic risk and to maintain market safety.[30]

Further research is currently being conducted to increase the capability of code-as-law to the level where codes can be designed to negotiate and to adjudicate disputes. However, it has not so far been possible to devise mechanisms to supervise these functions, and there are no credible legal and regulatory infrastructures to guide and support this level of operation by code-as-law in contract. The fact that algorithm trade was made possible and any risks mitigated is due to the development of institutional frameworks such as the central counterparty[31] and the regulatory framework of algorithm trading. Without this critical institutional and legal infrastructure in place, code-as-law cannot gain sufficient trust to be allowed to perform contractual negotiation and adjudication.

Regulatory compliance

Code-as-law can be used to achieve many aspects of regulatory compliance.[32] Based on the available quantitative data (corporate accounts) and qualitative data (corporate reports), code-as-law has been used to provide ratings of institutional or personal credit. It can also set benchmarks for institutional performance on, for

---

28 Aziza Kasumov, 'GameStop Shares Extend Surge in Early Trading' (2021) www.ft.com/content/50eaa1b5-d244-4b3e-b460-736828c049cd. Accessed 25 February 2021.
29 Government Office for Science, 'Stock Market Circuit Breakers' (Economic Impact Assessment, 2014) https://assets.publishing.service.gov.uk/government/uploads/system/uploads/attachment_data/file/289043/12-1066-eia4-stock-market-circuit-breakers.pdf. Accessed 24 February 2021.
30 Tanvi Patel, 'Potential Business Markets for the Digital Circuit Breaker: An Investigation of the Swedish Electricity Market' (2017) www.semanticscholar.org/paper/Potential-Business-Markets-for-the-Digital-Circuit-Patel-Hansson/3f5a1da53a6669bc30e9c8adc75c01cb32f539d7. Accessed 24 February 2021.
31 European Central Bank and Federal Reserve Bank of Chicago, 'The Role of Central Counterparties' (2007) www.ecb.europa.eu/pub/pdf/other/rolecentralcounterparties200707en.pdf. Accessed 24 February 2021.
32 Michael Becker et al., 'RegTech – The Application of Modern Information Technology in Regulatory Affairs: Areas of Interest in Research and Practice' (2020) 27 *Intelligent Systems in Accounting, Finance and Management* 161, 167.

example, contributions to combating climate change.[33] Scores against the benchmark can inform institutions, regulators and other stakeholders as they decide on future action or as they monitor the risks associated with particular securities or potential projects. Using code-as-law for regulatory compliance requires that the relevant data is transformed into machine readable format.[34] Currently, quantitative data such as trading behavioural data on the exchanges can be coded in this way and research now aims to turn qualitative data into machine readable code so that it can be scored against benchmarks such as the Environmental, Social and Governance benchmark (ESG).[35]

At the individual level, biometric information has also been used to authenticate people's identity,[36] and this technology has replaced written and other procedures of compliance, such as oral questionnaires or on paper with proof of signature. In the exchanges, there are equivalent authentication processes to ensure that orders have been sent by permitted traders rather than by impersonators or cyber attackers. Authentication here is carried out by computer codes rather than by humans.

Regulatory level

A higher grade of code-as-law than machine readable data is provided by machine readable regulation.[37] This turns written law into computer codes that can be read by natural language processing technology.[38] The main use of machine readable regulation is in the development of digital regulatory reporting systems to assist regulators,[39] institutions and even stakeholders to monitor risk and increase compliance efficiency. Technologies have been deployed to read financial regulations and translate the contents of financial regulations into computer programmes which eventually process data.[40] However, currently it is not possible for software to cope with the full spectrum of subtleties used in human language, and as a consequence a double translation process is needed.[41] At the first stage, the

---

33 Harrison Hong et al., 'Climate Change' (2020) 33 *The Review of Financial Studies* 1011, 1023.
34 Eva Micheler and Anna Whaley, 'Regulatory Technology: Replacing Law with Computer Code' (2020) 21 *European Business Organisation Law Review* 349, 377.
35 Natasha Condon and Jessica Cavalletto, 'Sustainable Financing: What Does the Rise of ESG Mean for Trade Finance?' (2019) www.citibank.com/tts/insights/assets/docs/articles/1928395_Sustainable_Finance_Article.pdf. Accessed 24 February 2021.
36 Vanitha Carmel, 'A Survey on Biometric Authentication Systems in Cloud to Combat Identity Theft' (2020) 7 *Journal of Critical Review* 540, 547.
37 Eva Micheler and Anna Whaley, 'Regulatory Technology: Replacing Law with Computer Code' (2020) 21 *European Business Organisation Law Review* 349, 377.
38 Ibid.
39 Johan Von Solms, 'Integrating Regulatory Technology (RegTech) into the Digital Transformation of a Bank Treasury' (2020) 1 *Journal of Banking Regulation.* DOI: https://doi.org/10.1057/s41261-020-00134-0.
40 Tom Butler and Leona O'Brien, 'Understanding RegTech for Digital Regulatory Compliance' in Lynn T. et al. (eds) *Disruptive Finance* (Palgrave Pivot Cham 2019) 85, 102.
41 Eva Micheler and Anna Whaley, 'Regulatory Technology: Replacing Law with Computer Code' (2020) 21 *European Business Organisation Law Review* 349, 377.

natural language should be translated into a machine readable version, which is then processed to create a programme that automatically executes certain regulatory objectives.[42]

The computer code can be designed to prohibit certain behaviours, for example to prevent directors purchasing securities of their company when a takeover bid has been announced.[43] Attempted transgression would result in directors' security accounts in the company being frozen by the code during the takeover period. The code can specify the period of prohibition when one or more events meet the conditions, such as when the board has been approached by the bidder, when the board was contemplating an imminent takeover bid or when a director has reason to believe there would be an imminent bid. When one of these events has been triggered, the director's security accounts would automatically be frozen. Converting terms that require the exercise of cognitive judgement into computer code is a major challenge to regulatory integrity and some existing interpretations are ambiguous, inconsistent or controversial.[44] Even if case law can indicate how terms such as "reasonable care," "acceptable risk" or "good faith" have been interpreted and applied in a given context, making them machine readable in an insensitive way can have a negative impact on regulatory integrity, as well as on access to justice. For instance, the subjective test which requires a decision as to whether a director has "reason to believe" that a bid is imminent is difficult to turn into effective computer code. If the code freezes the securities account of the director, and the director subsequently challenges a regulatory decision which was automated by the code, the regulator would need to explain how the algorithms operate and demonstrate the transparency, accuracy and fairness of the code.[45] The regulator's responsibility is not merely to show that he would have arrived at the same decision as the code, but also how the code arrived at such a decision in such a way that it adheres to the rule of law. As regulatory decisions are subject to appeal, the appeal body would need to examine not only the substantive question of the law but also the procedural aspects of the law. The substantive question would require the regulator to present not only how the code interprets the law but also how code-as-law accurately reflects this interpretation. This would remove the regulator's ability to make decisions on a case-by-case basis,[46] which is normal regulatory practice to ensure consistency and the delivery

---

42 Ibid.
43 Joseph Lee, 'Access to Finance for Artificial Intelligence Regulation in Financial Services Industry' (2020) 21 *European Business Organisation Law Review* 731, 757.
44 Jesus Rodriguez, 'Ambiguity in Natural Language Processing' (2017) https://jrodthoughts .medium.com/ambiguity-in-natural-language-processing-15f3e4706a9a. Accessed 24 February 2021; Carsten Schulz, 'The Law of AI and Machine Learning' (2020) https://iot.taylorwessing .com/the-laws-of-ai-and-machine-learning/. Accessed 24 February 2021.
45 The Harvard Gazette, 'Ethical Concerns Mount as AI Takes Bigger Decision-Making Role in More Industries' (2020) https://news.harvard.edu/gazette/story/2020/10/ethical-concerns-mount-as-ai -takes-bigger-decision-making-role/. Accessed 25 February 2020.
46 OECD, 'Regulatory Impact Analysis in OECD Challenges for Developing Countries' (2005) www .oecd.org/gov/regulatory-policy/35258511.pdf. Accessed 25 February 2021.

of regulatory objectives. As for procedure, the regulator would need to satisfy the requirements of "reasonableness" and "proportionality,"[47] as established by rule of law doctrine, to ensure regulatory integrity. In doing so, code-as-law would need to be designed to reflect past case law not only on the same concept but also in fields other than financial law, for example in competition law. It would also need to be able to digest the case law of other fields to apply similar concepts in the context of financial regulation in order to uphold the spirit of the rule of law expressed in other contexts.

Institutional level

At the institutional level, code-as-law can be used by financial institutions to code their internal rules and to use cloud computing technology to extract data necessary for risk monitoring and regulatory reporting.[48] When code-as-law is used internally, the risks mentioned above concerning regulatory integrity and access to justice are less significant; they apply mainly to public entities. Since each institution designs its own codes for internal risk management and to fulfil regulatory requirements, the emphasis is on how the management of internal risk, as based on code-as-law, satisfies regulatory requirements. Financial institutions must be able to explain to auditing regulators how they operate code-as-law and how they ensure the integrity of the code in terms of transparency, accuracy, fairness and non-discrimination.[49]

As the efficacy of internal risk management also depends on internal training courses, the whistle-blower mechanism,[50] and manual reporting systems, institutions need to know to what extent code-as-law replaces these functions and whether it reduces efficacy. For instance, should personnel be trained in the operation of code-as-law in order to detect when it goes wrong? Should the code be revised if it acts as a whistle-blower but is found to give a false result? How would staff be able to assess whether the code accurately conducts regulatory reporting? Various activities are required by the regulations without specifying how institutions should carry them out. For example, in the client due diligence exercise, would speech recognition[51] used to transcribe a client's information be adequate

47 Benedikt Pirker, *Proportionality Analysis and Models of Judicial Review: A Theoretical and Comparative Study* (Europa Law Publishing 2013) 235, 275.
48 Dirk Broeders and Jermy Prenio, 'Innovative Technology in Financial Supervision – The Experience of Early Users' (Bank for International Settlements Policy Implementation, 2018) www.bis.org/fsi/publ/insights9.pdf. Accessed 24 February 2021.
49 Adriano Koshiyama, 'Towards Algorithm Auditing: A Survey on Managing Legal, Ethical and Technological Risks of AI, ML and Associated Algorithms' (2021) https://papers.ssrn.com/sol3/papers.cfm?abstract_id=3778998. Accessed 21 February 2021.
50 Maria Krambia-Kapardis, 'An Exploratory Empirical Study of Whistleblowing and Whistleblowers' (2020) 27 *Journal of Financial Crime* 755, 770.
51 Rachel Vanni, 'How Artificial Intelligence is Transforming the Legal Profession' (2020) https://kirasystems.com/learn/how-artificial-intelligence-is-transforming-the-legal-profession/. Accessed 25 February 2021.

in the eyes of the regulator? Might human face-to-face contact reveal more than speech recognition could, in terms of nervousness, hesitation, or confidence? And if so, how should such a gap in efficacy be closed? Is it possible for encoded internal rules to extract all the information about clients necessary to detect suspicious activity?[52]

Market level – sustainable financing

Code-as-law can contribute to sustainable financing.[53] Index companies create their own algorithms to provide sustainability scores based on pre-set benchmarks and data they collect,[54] such as information disclosed directly by a company or provided by third parties. Index companies create indices, such as ESG indices,[55] which enable financial institutions to create index-based funds and promote index-based products to investors. Financial products based on ESG indices can be attractive to investors who have an interest in sustainable development and need to structure their portfolios to meet particular targets, or to invest in sustainable financial products.[56] The algorithms created by the index companies are computer codes, and data fed into the algorithms produces a score similar to the credit rating of companies or individuals. Code-as-law, through digitising benchmarks and available data, reinforces the value of ESG indices in the financial market. It is possible to turn ESG benchmarks into machine readable soft law that can access necessary data from a number of data pools. For instance, in a peer-to-peer energy trading platform supported by DLT,[57] data can show the extent to which a company utilises energy in a sustainable way, and this can be digitally compared with regulatory benchmarks set by the index providers. This then raises a legal question of whether the design of the algorithms guarantees a fair scoring,[58] and this requires the algorithms to be transparent. In addition, the index providers

52 Deloitte, 'The Case for Artificial Intelligence in Combating Money Laundering and Terrorist Financing – A Deep Dive into the Application of Machine Learning Technology' (2018) www2 .deloitte.com/content/dam/Deloitte/sg/Documents/finance/sea-fas-deloitte-uob-whitepaper-digital .pdf. Accessed 25 February 2021.
53 United Nations, 'Financing for Sustainable Development Report 2020' (Report of the Inter-Agency Task Force on Financing for Development 2020).
54 The Economist, 'The Stockmarket is Now Run by Computers, Algorithms and Passive Managers' (2019) www.economist.com/briefing/2019/10/05/the-stockmarket-is-now-run-by-computers -algorithms-and-passive-managers. Accessed 25 February 2021.
55 Guido Giese et al., 'Performance and Risk Analysis of Index-Based ESG Portfolios' (2019) 9 *The Journal of Index Investing* 46, 57.
56 Mario La, 'Does the ESG Index Affect Stock Return? Evidence from the Eurostoxx50' (2020) 12 *Sustainability* 1, 12.
57 Joseph Lee and Vere Marie Khan, 'Blockchain and Smart Contract for Peer-to-Peer Energy Trading Platform: Legal Obstacles and Regulatory Solutions' (2020) 19 *Review of Intellectual Property Law*. https://repository.law.uic.edu/ripl/vol19/iss4/1/. Accessed 25 February 2021.
58 Yash Raj Shrestha and Yongjie Yang, 'Fairness in Algorithmic Decision-Making: Applications in Multi-Winner Voting, Machine Learning, and Recommender Systems' (2019) 12 *Algorithms* 1, 28; Art Jahnke, 'Are Computer-Aided Decisions Actually Fair? – Researchers from BU and MIT are

should be able to explain how their models arrive at a particular decision and should provide a mechanism for companies to raise questions and challenge the scores they have received. Even though the index providers are not regulators nor performing the function of a public body, there should be rigorous checks on the algorithms used. What is needed to promote sustainability is a regulatory regime for benchmarks that covers code as soft law.[59]

Code-as-law and the rule of law

Interpreting ambiguous terms in law relies on detailed examination of laws in their context before they are introduced. This preparatory work[60] is a component of the statutory interpretation exercise. Code-as-law impairs this contextualising process[61] and can result in the execution of laws without the interpretation process having been undertaken. Under a code-as-law legal system, the law must be defined with utmost precision without ambiguity and the subsequent need for interpretation. This is because it is impossible to study the genesis of coded law in order to examine its historical trajectory, to take account of cases previously decided and to differentiate them based on various regulatory objectives and policies. Equally, it is not possible to take into consideration other binding laws in the legal hierarchy or to consider other international laws and practices. In financial law, there are major objectives to be expressed through law and regulation, including market stability, market integrity, consumer protection, market competitiveness, market competition, investor protection and access to finance.[62] Often, law and regulation serve multiple purposes in practice and however exhaustive the preparatory work, it cannot precisely define the eventual functioning of a particular law or regulation. Any primary and secondary purposes that arise can be the subject of fierce academic debate.[63] It is even possible for tribunal judgments and administrative decisions to obscure the original purpose of the law because tribunals, as they deliver a remedy to an aggrieved party, aim to keep their decisions consistent, to fill any gaps that were not considered by the original law-markers, and to align the law with other international standards as a matter of

---

Trying to Overcome Algorithmic Bias' (2018) www.bu.edu/articles/2018/algorithmic-fairness/. Accessed 24 February 2021.

59 Marcel Meyer et al., 'The EU Benchmark Regulation: Users be Cautious' 2018 (17) *Performance Magazine* https://www2.deloitte.com/content/dam/Deloitte/lu/Documents/financial-services/lu-eu -benchmark-regulation-users-be-cautious-092018.pdf. Accessed 24 February 2021.

60 Eric Engle, 'Legal Interpretation by Computer: A Survey of Interpretive Rules' (2011) 5 *Akron Law Journal* 71, 93.

61 Willem Salet and Jochem De Vries, 'Contextualisation of Policy and Law in Sustainable Urban Development' (2019) 62 *Journal of Environmental Planning and Management* 189, 204.

62 United Nations, 'Comparative Neutrality and Its Application in Selected Developing Countries' (UNCTAD Research Partnership Platform Publication Series 2014) https://unctad.org/system/files /official-document/ditcclpmisc2014d1_en.pdf. Accessed 25 February 2021.

63 Georges Ugeux, 'The Multiple Objectives of Financial Regulation' in International Finance Regulation: The Quest for Financial Stability (Wiley Online Library 2014) Chapter 1.

public interest. The law then develops in an autonomous way which may differ from its original purpose and intention.

In this regard, the challenge that code-as-law faces is how to embrace the value or the spirit of the law and whether it is required, in the interests of justice, to limit the autonomous nature of a law that enables it to adapt to changes in the market. It has been said that code-as-law can act as a trusted third party,[64] replacing the court as arbiter by becoming an outsourced party to fill gaps in the law and to enforce it. However, if automation is to take place, the designer of the law will need to decide whether the law should be limited to precisely defined situations or whether it can develop in parallel with changes in the market. Precisely defined law that is used to underpin automation, such as in a contractual transaction, can make the purpose of the law (the spirit of the rule) irrelevant if the context in which it operates changes. For instance, in UK takeover law, a mandatory bid is triggered when the ownership of shares in a company or the control of shares in it crosses the 30 per cent threshold.[65] Yet, the concept of "control"[66] is hard to define and needs to take account of newly developing markets such as the derivative market as well as other factors such as tacit shareholder agreement. Precisely-defined law results in the reduction of cognitive judgement in the regulatory and justice systems. This affects the function of the legal profession in which students are trained to understand the rationale behind a law, to appreciate circumstances in which it may need to be applied differently and to use critical judgement to analyse whether it is applied in a way that meets the concept of justice.[67]

Code-as-law that learns by itself

Risk to due process

Machine learning and deep learning are sophisticated forms of Artificial Intelligence and their application through code-as-law represents a higher level of risk to the technological, market, regulatory and justice systems than straightfor-ward automation. When the code is able to learn from its own experience and then to execute the law, it not only replaces the regulator in monitoring and regulating the market, but it also replaces the court in filling gaps in the legal system. What is more, code-as-law with machine learning capability would act as a legislative body in the law-making process. In these two respects, the court's role of filling the legal gap is done by the code itself through deep learning from past decisions. Traditionally, court decisions are subject to internal review, academic criticism

---

64 Martin Abadi, 'Trusted Computing, Trusted Third Parties, and Verified Communications' (1) https://users.soe.ucsc.edu/~abadi/Papers/verif.pdf. Accessed 24 February 2021.

65 Rule 9, The Takeover Code.

66 Umakanth Varottil, 'Comparative Takeover Regulation and the Concept of "Control"' (2015) 7 *Singapore Journal of Legal Studies* 208, 231.

67 Martijn Hesselink, 'Common Frame of Reference and Social Justice' in *Social Justice: Emerging Dimensions* (The Icfai University Press 2010) 1, 25.

222 *Code-as-law in financial markets*

and judicial appeal, but code-as-law bypasses this aspect of due process and lack of transparency becomes a major risk to access to justice.[68] Decisions made through the code would be increasingly difficult to justify and human supervision becomes more difficult. When decisions cannot be challenged and human control is impeded through lack of understanding of the way algorithms operate and how data is fed into the decision-making process, automation is, in effect, a "black box"[69] that cannot be challenged and would cause systematic damage to trust in code-as-law as a component of the regulatory and legal systems.

Code defines market function and participant behaviour

An automated circuit breaker with machine learning capability can prevent systemic risk caused by algorithm trading.[70] The circuit breaker is able to learn from digitised trading data of interactions, and then to predict risk and act to avoid it. Assuming the code is properly designed and accurate data is fed to the system, machine learning can augment the capability of the circuit breaker. An automated circuit breaker is even capable of learning whether it should apply to the whole market, a particular sector of the market or a particular stock.[71] However, it has proved difficult for current circuit breaker regimes to set standards,[72] and it would be dangerous to allow code-as-law to operate as a circuit breaker in a situation where humans are struggling to devise consistent policy and stable solutions.

Code-as-law in compliance

As discussed, code-as-law may not be able to perform the role of market risk regulator and enforcer of the law when regulatory discretion is needed to meet regulatory objectives and to perform an effective public role. Using code-as-law with machine learning technology can exacerbate the risk of violating regulatory integrity but also increase the risk to market safety because machine learning is much more difficult to control than code-as-law with simple automation. Taking algorithm governance as an example, code-as-law will need to act as a regulator for the code itself, to detect bugs in the code, to investigate abnormalities in

---

68 Vincent Samar, 'At the Intersection of Due Process and Equal Protection: Expanding the Range of Protected Interests' (2019) 68 *Catholic University Law Review* 87, 135.
69 Yavar Bathaee, 'The Artificial Intelligence Black Box and the Failure of Intent and Causation' (2018) 31 *Harvard Journal of Law & Technology* 890, 934.
70 Joshua Gerlick and Stephan Liozu, 'Ethical and Legal Considerations of Artificial Intelligence and Algorithmic Decision-Making in Personalised Pricing' (2020) 19 *Journal of Revenue and Pricing Management* 85, 98.
71 Yong Kim and Jimmy Yang, 'What Makes Circuit Breakers Attractive to Financial Markets? A Survey' (2004) 13 *Financial Markets Institutions & Instruments* 109, 146.
72 Dimensional, 'Circuit Breakers and Dimensional Approach to Trading' (2020) www.dimensional .com/us-en/insights/circuit-breakers-and-dimensionals-approach-to-trading. Accessed 24 February 2021.

application, to remedy unjust application of the algorithms and to align application with policy goals.

Code-as-law in internal compliance

Code-as-law can be used in internal compliance and risk management. Machine
learning must ensure that human values continue to oversee code-as-law by
checking whether humans would arrive at the same conclusions as the code, using
the same logic to arrive at these conclusions. This is because machine learning
learns from its past experience, and its conclusions may not be reached through
the same bases and reasons as human learning. In court decisions, different reasons can be used to arrive at the same decision; in comparative law, the differ-
ing bases in civil and common law systems can be used to arrive at the same
conclusions;[73] in the regulatory space, different regulations can be used to achieve
the same results; and in internal compliance, different internal policies and rules
may be used to deliver regulatory obligations of compliance. Internal rules can be
subject to change depending on management objectives, internal resources available, products developed and internal conflicts between marketing and compliance
divisions. Therefore, even if machine learning code can be precisely defined and
data is correctly extracted to meet the compliance duties, a code-as-law system
would take away the liberty, creativity, and practicality that institutions need to
use in developing their own self-regulatory systems and this limitation can impair
regulatory innovation.

Code-as-law for the market

Although code as soft law can be used to develop sustainable finance for the market, it creates the risk of benchmark manipulation.[74] The code is used to develop
benchmarks that reflect good ESG practice, but defective algorithms can produce
defective results that inaccurately indicate a company's ESG performance. There
are two main areas where code-as-law can lead to error. First, when it fails to
define an ESG activity correctly; and second, when it fails to extract ESG data
accurately. For instance, it may operate at close-range and identify rice farming as an environmentally damaging activity, based on the amount of water used
and thus cause small farming companies to appear unsustainable. Yet, at a wider
focus, it may be geographically essential to support rice farming in that region.
To take another example, code-as-law may collect data on the number of labour
protests that a company receives over a period of time and give it a poor social

---

73 Caslav Pejovic, 'Civil Law and Common Law: Two Different Paths Leading to the Same Goal'
(2001) 32 *Victoria University of Wellington Law Review* 817, 842.
74 Andrew Verstein, 'The Law and Economics of Benchmark Manipulation' (Columbia Law School's
Blog on Corporations and the Capital Market, 2014) https://clsbluesky.law.columbia.edu/2014/08
/27/9223/. Accessed 24 February 2021.

rating. But at the same time, it is possible that the company should have received a better social rating because it has provided a framework for the labour unions to exercise their right to protest.

Code-as-law in the crypto-market

Defining the market

Removal of intermediaries and decentralisation are the main features of the crypto-market set up as a reaction to the inequity of a financial market which is mainly controlled by a small number of advanced capital markets.[75] Concentration of capital in the current markets results in restricted access to finance, including restricted access to sharing economic profits, limitation in sources of finance and lack of choice in available financial services. Crypto-markets rely heavily on codes and computing power to define market functions,[76] and to provide favourable conditions for transactions, and support for legal and regulatory infrastructure. Some of the functions of code-as-law currently used in capital markets to define the markets and their function can continue to be used on crypto-markets, notably, its use to define who can access the markets in order to enhance market efficiency, stability and integrity. As the crypto-market's aim is to provide better access to finance,[77] codes can be defined in such a way that thresholds for entry are lowered, enabling more participation at the individual or even peer-to-peer level. Code-as-law in the form of smart contracts can also remedy the risk of default in trades by coding for the consequences of default.[78] Smart contracts can be designed by market infrastructure providers, either an association or an entity, in a way that allows participants to negotiate terms and then to trade on the conditions so defined. These terms can be designed by factoring in both the rules and the regulatory objectives of the market. Smart contracts can also be designed to interact with market infrastructure providers in a way that ensures systemic safety by implementing circuit breakers and killer functionality to suspend flawed market trades. As participation is at the individual level, risk to personal data becomes

---

75 Zayn Khamisa, 'An Analysis of the Factors Driving Performance in the Cryptocurrency Market. Do This Factors Vary Significantly between Cryptocurrencies?' (University of Cambridge Working Paper 2019) www.researchgate.net/publication/333967521_An_analysis_of_the_factors_driving_performance_in_the_cryptocurrency_market_Do_these_factors_vary_significantly_between_cryptocurrencies/link/5d0f9463a6fdcc2462a00ba5/download. Accessed 25 February 2021.

76 Primavera De Filippi and Samer Hassan, 'Blockchain Technology as a Regulatory Technology: From Code is Law to Law is Code' (2016) 21 *First Monday* https://firstmonday.org/ojs/index.php/fm/article/view/7113/5657. Accessed 25 February 2021.

77 Joseph Lee, 'Law and Regulation for a Crypto-Market: Perpetuation or Innovation?' (2020) www.law.ox.ac.uk/business-law-blog/blog/2020/09/law-and-regulation-crypto-market-perpetuation-or-innovation. Accessed 25 February 2021.

78 Joseph Lee, 'Smart Contracts for Securities Transactions on the DLT Network: Legal Obstacles and Regulatory Challenges' (2020) https://sites.law.duke.edu/thefinregblog/author/joseph-lee/. Accessed 25 February 2021.

a factor in the market and, to ensure investor confidence, code-as-law can play a part in data protection by using privacy enhancing technology.[79] In this way, Big Data can be shared without revealing personal information to the whole market and, at the same time, it can allow market infrastructure providers, as trusted third parties, to act as gatekeepers for market integrity against money laundering, market abuse and cyber-crime.[80]

Compliance – privacy enhancement by encryption

Compliance is a mechanism that allows financial institutions to gauge risks according to regulatory objectives and to design their own risk management systems. Financial market infrastructures need to comply with rules for market safety and stability, so trading venues need to ensure safety when participants use algorithms to trade, and trading firms need to ensure the security of their algorithms before they are used on the market. Firms can also use algorithms to scan data and identify a client's level of risk when they carry out suitability checks or screen for money laundering. In addition, firms need to have systems in place to protect clients' personal data and privacy.[81] In intermediated and centralised systems, it is for the market infrastructure providers and the intermediary firms to carry out compliance functions, but in a disintermediated and decentralised crypto-market, code-as-law will take on some of the functions of these intermediaries. In other words, codes become the agents for compliance functions. Codes can be designed to detect clients who are unsuited for a particular class of financial product or for a particular market and then restrict market access to them. Codes can also be designed to signal suspicious money laundering transactions.[82] But who should be held accountable for compliance and accountable to the regulators? In an STO market,[83] issuers of tokens may code securities which define the nature of the tokens as well as the conditions on which the securities are to be traded. Disintermediation makes issuers accountable for compliance and for carrying out client due diligence to ensure client suitability as well as checking for money laundering. However, placing this burden on issuers potentially negates the benefits of

79 Bert-Jaap Koops and Ronald Leenes, 'Code and the Slow Erosion of Privacy' (2005) 12 *Michigan Telecommunication and Technology Law Review* 117, 186.
80 Robby Houben and Alexander Snyers, 'Cryptocurrencies and Blockchain – Legal Context and Implications for Financial Crime , Money Laundering and Tax Evasion' (2018) www.europarl.europa.eu/cmsdata/150761/TAX3%20Study%20on%20cryptocurrencies%20and%20blockchain.pdf. Accessed 24 February 2021.
81 Kelly Martin et al., 'Data Privacy: Effects on Customer and Firm Performance' (2016) 81 *Journal of Marketing* 36, 59.
82 Zhiyuan Chen et al., 'Machine Learning Techniques for Anti-Money Laundering Solutions in Suspicious Transaction Detection: A Review' (2018) https://dl.acm.org/doi/abs/10.1007/s10115-017-1144-z. Accessed 25 February 2021.
83 Karen Hsu, 'Addressing Regulation and Trust in Security Token Offerings' (2019) https://karenhsu-mar.medium.com/addressing-regulation-and-trust-in-security-token-offerings-6585da4d40b7. Accessed 24 February 2021.

STO and it could be preferable for market infrastructure providers, such as trading venues or platform providers, to design the codes and to take responsibility for compliance, even though this concentrates risks on the platform providers.

Digital regulatory reporting ecosystem[84]

One of the features of crypto-markets that are based on distributed ledger technology (DLT) is the ability to store transaction data in the system in a way that is transparent and immutable. A company's transactions can be recorded on the DLT system,[85] including what assets they hold and what they have disposed of. Corporate behaviour is also recorded by the system according to the transactions recorded on the ledgers and reports, through the use of natural language processing technology. Push-data or pull-data systems can be used to assist regulatory reporting.[86] The former enables data controllers to decide what to reveal to the regulators; the latter allows regulators to extract whatever data they need. When data can be comprehensively stored on the DLT system, Big Data can be generated and used to enhance financial services. The benefits of this include using Big Data to detect and screen for criminal activity and also to assess the level of risk that a firm takes in the market. In this way, the crypto-market not only reduces the function of intermediaries by performing the gatekeeping role, but also gives control of information to the data subjects. By using an API with privacy enhanced encryption technology,[87] data subjects can use a "plug and play system" to control their own data.[88]

This level of control and the ability of investors to keep track of activity in real time, along with access to transparent and immutable data bases, can help increase investor confidence in the project financing market.[89] There is an advantage here over peer-to-peer and crowdfunding platforms which face problems of

84 Mannesh Samatani, 'UK Digital Regulatory Reporting Pilot Completes Phase Two' (2020) www .regulationasia.com/uk-digital-regulatory-reporting-pilot-completes-phase-two/. Accessed 24 February 2021.

85 Randy Priem, 'Distributed Ledger Technology for Securities Clearing and Settlement: Benefits, Risks, and Regulatory Implications' (2020) 6 *Financial Innovation*. DOI: https://doi.org/10.1186 /s40854-019-0169-6.

86 Yang Zhao, 'A Model of Computation with Push and Pull Processing' (Research Project, 2003) https://ptolemy.berkeley.edu/papers/03/PushPullProcessing/PushAndPull.pdf. Accessed 24 February 2021.

87 Taunsree Sharma and Masooda Bashir, 'Are PETs (Privacy Enhancing Technologies) Giving Protection for Smartphones? A Case Study' (2020) www.researchgate.net/publication/342821549 _Are_PETs_Privacy_Enhancing_Technologies_Giving_Protection_for_Smartphones_--_A_Case _Study/link/5f07bba092851c52d6252a8a/download. Accessed 24 February 2021.

88 Shanny Basar, 'Blockchain in Capital Markets "On the Cusp" of Acceleration' (2020) www.mar- ketsmedia.com/blockchain-use-in-capital-markets-on-the-cusp-of-acceleration/. Accessed 24 February 2021.

89 Randy Priem, 'Distributed Ledger Technology for Securities Clearing and Settlement: Benefits, Risks, and Regulatory Implications' (2020) 6 *Financial Innovation*. DOI: https://doi.org/10.1186 /s40854-019-0169-6.

investor trust due to lack of reliable and timely information.[90] Digital regulatory reporting systems allow investors access to more detailed financial information as well as non-financial information such as ESG data. Projects can report data to the regulators in a push system but can also allow investors to verify data in a pull system and this means that investors can see how money is being spent in a project and whether funds are being used in accordance with the project plan (the STO prospectus). This can help the investors assess the risks of a project and see how their returns are being realised. If securities can also be tokenised and issued on the blockchain, the real-time information available there can close the information gap[91] and allow investors to exercise more control over their investment. Automation of digital reporting can reduce time spent on collecting information and on reporting activity to the regulators via a regulated information system and this can transform the information gatekeeping mechanism that has up to now been performed by expensive professional intermediaries such as lawyers, accountants and financial analysts.

Conclusion

This chapter has investigated code-as-law by studying the effects of computerisation in financial markets. Code-as-law has already been used to define the functions of the market, to monitor the behaviour of participants and to enhance access. It has also been used to digitise securities in a quantitative way which allows centralised match-engines to process trades more efficiently, even at a speed of milliseconds. A crypto-market provides the opportunity to digitise securities in a qualitative way which can facilitate corporate action at a peer-to-peer level and even give the possibility of automation. Thus code-as-law, combined with a digital regulatory reporting system, allows investors to have control over their investments as well as indicating how governance should be structured and monitored.

Code-as-law can also increase the efficiency of the compliance regime, especially when the rules can be designed with quantitative and qualitative precision. However, defining rules with qualitative accuracy is not easy to achieve, either in technology or in law, because both regulators and tribunals need to exercise cognitive judgement as they make decisions case-by-case in response to a changing market environment. Furthermore, it is very difficult for regulators to implement code-as-law in compliance. Code-as-law can be used by financial institutions for internal compliance, but regulators need the ability to assess whether code-based algorithms and compliance mechanisms are fit for purpose.

---

90 Maximilian Goether et al., 'Protecting Investors in Equity Crowdfunding: An Empirical Analysis of the Small Investor Protection Act' (2021) 162 *Technological Forecasting and Social Change* 1, 15.

91 EY, 'Capital Markets: Innovation and the FinTech Landscape' (2016) https://assets.ey.com/content /dam/ey-sites/ey-com/en_gl/topics/emeia-financial-services/ey-capital-markets-innovation-and -the-fintech-landscape.pdf. Accessed 24 February 2021.

Code-as-law also brings other potential benefits. Market providers, such as index companies, can use it to promote social values such as sustainability by manually defining ESG benchmarks in machine readable format and collecting data to give sustainability scores. These scores can then be used by investors to engage in sustainable investment. However, a regime of benchmark regulation needs to be developed to cover the risk of manipulation. By moving code-as-law from a centralised and intermediated space to the decentralised and disintermediated crypto-environment, it can provide data subjects with more control over their information as well as closing the information gap between projects and their investors.

12 Conclusion

This book has explored the emergence of a decentralised and disintermediated crypto-market and investigated the way in which it can transform the financial markets. The fundamental reasons for the existence of financial markets, which form the objectives of any new development, include providing access to finance, bringing about a shared economy, granting access to justice and enhancing sustainable development at both domestic and cross-border levels. If those aims are to be achieved through crypto-finance, they must be defined with clarity and precision and appropriate regulation needs to be in place to support the development of the new markets. Thinking about crypto-finance in this way shows that outcome-based law and regulation are a significant part of any future development, along with risk-based regulation, which has been the dominant philosophy in recent decades. The spirit of de-regulation has promoted innovation and a general liberalisation in the financial world, especially across national borders, but has also resulted in the concentration of capital in a small number of financial hubs, and that has allowed the development of financial products which distribute profits and risks in a non-equitable way. As everyone is now well aware, when this was taken to extreme, the result was the financial crisis that shook the world of finance to its core. Even now, economies across the world are only slowly recovering from this crisis and internationally the wealth gap has been enlarged. The costs of correcting the economic disaster caused by gross irresponsibility in the financial market have been disproportionately absorbed by society as a whole, taxpayers and employees, rather than by those whose recklessness caused the problem. There is a salutary lesson here that must guide the direction of any future development in financial markets. In a system of concentrated capital, financial intermediaries and those who can afford to employ them have emerged from the crisis comparatively unscathed. Those most affected have been taxpayers, entrepreneurs looking to finance projects, and everyone living in regions of the world with less stable currencies.

The rise of products such as cryptocurrency and blockchain-based financial systems such as ICOs has been driven by an enthusiasm for self-help at a time of dissatisfaction with centralised global financial markets. In this sense, the rise of the crypto-market is an anti-establishment movement, or even a political movement, that aims to change the economic structure of society. It is regarded as a

DOI: 10.4324/9780429023613-12

way of democratising the financial market by changing how it is constituted, how power and resources are allocated, how profits and risks are distributed and how governance is agreed and embedded. But in order for such a transformation to come about, appropriate legal and regulatory conditions must be in place.

Bearing all this in mind, the findings of the examination of crypto-finance and its development described in this book can be summarised in the following five headings.

Crypto-technology may be unsuitable for some current financial market practices

Chapter 2 discusses how distributed ledger technologies (DLTs) can revolutionise the capital market by removing functions and costs that are no longer needed when the trust and transparency of DLTs become apparent. When DLTs are used to create virtual currencies such as Bitcoin and Ether, they create an alternative system of financial payment services. This new blockchain-based capital market facilitates peer-to-peer trading that can democratise the financial services markets. This vision is based on the assumption that DLTs will result in two changes: decentralisation and disintermediation. To this end, I investigated whether DLT can be applied to the entire life cycle of securities trading – listing (issuing), trading, clearing and settlement – which is currently operated by financial market infrastructure providers. However, this investigation revealed that decentralisation and disintermediation would not bring about the intended benefits to the current equity market. It would not lower the costs of securities trading, facilitate more peer-to-peer trade at the domestic or cross-border level or enable more access to capital for SMEs. But that is not to say that DLTs, in their current form, cannot be used to correct some market failures by making trades more transparent, the system more secure and the process more cost-efficient for participants by reducing settlement costs. DLTs can provide a Regulation Technology that uses software and protocols to assure compliance with legal code and to reduce the cost of legal compliance. However, this would still require trusted third parties to maintain the DLT's network in order to mitigate market and operational risks and to act as *de facto* regulators. Furthermore, although the term "distributed" is used to describe the working of the blockchain network, it does not mean that there is no overall controlling authority or owner. There are various distributed ledger models that have different degrees of centralisation and different types of access control designed to suit different business needs. The question is who should act as the trusted third parties – governments, incumbent financial market infrastructure operators, banks, technology companies or the new FinTech companies? As DLTs will operate at the cross-border level, how is the governance of such networks to be coordinated?

The objectives of the crypto-market must be precisely defined in order to generate appropriate laws and regulations

Chapter 3 discusses the nature of crypto-assets and argued that the development of a crypto-market needs both a technological and a legal and regulatory infrastructure because any market is a legal construct. Hence, private law is important because it provides legal certainty for crypto-market transactions, and regulatory intervention is also required to enhance legal certainty, mitigate legal and market risks and address market failures.

There are different types of crypto-asset on the market. Current private law and public regulation can help define crypto-assets by looking at the function, participants and operation of market structures. Legal doctrines such as in contract law and property law can help define, or clarify, rights and obligations, the appropriate methods for their transfer and assignment and the resulting implications. Statutory definitions of money, insurance, security and units of investment can also provide such a basis. Some crypto-assets are hard to define, so new approaches are needed to support their development. Using current legal and regulatory frameworks for crypto-finance will not transform the economy or the market because they have evolved as mechanisms to support the *status quo* in the financial markets. Extending existing systems to include crypto-assets would merely perpetuate the dominance of existing interests by another form of regulatory capture. A new crypto-asset market structure cannot be created without introducing new laws and rules and this requires the establishment of a social contract for governance based on new legal doctrines that transcend "contract" and "property." A new regulatory form, and a new ethos, should be devised because code-as-law, RegTech or LegalTech, based on current legal and regulatory frameworks, are unlikely to result in a true transformation of the market. This new legal infrastructure must be based on a newly defined purpose for the financial market. The current classification of crypto-assets into payment, utility, security, title, commodity and hybrid tokens is based on their function, the perceptions of market participants and regulatory attitudes towards them. If we focus more on what the crypto-market intends to deliver, in particular, benefits to socio-economic conditions, a more harmonised approach can result. A crypto-market using smart contracts will affect current market practices such as securities lending and proxy voting and, despite any potential problems, there are positive effects for individual investors. They can, for instance, share benefits from securities lending businesses. Individual voting decisions about corporate affairs can be more efficiently implemented if proxy advisory services can advise individual investors directly, and advisory services can provide oracle services to smart contracts (smart votes) in order to automate individual voting. Regulation should be outcome-based to increase such sharing.

Similarly, **Chapter 7** investigates the relationship between artificial intelligence (AI) and the crypto-market. Transactions on the blockchain generate data (Big Data) which can be used to develop AI that enhances access to finance and financial inclusion. However, this can bring risk as well as benefit to the financial services sector. To ensure continuity, the regulation of AI should continue to be guided by market safety, investor protection and market integrity. In addition to these, access to finance should be a fundamental regulatory objective so that AI can be used to benefit not only financial intermediaries but also those previously excluded from financial opportunities. Evident benefits of this kind will help the properly regulated use of AI to gain wider public acceptance. In this context, AI can promote the optimisation of capital on p2p platforms, as discussed also in **Chapter 8**, and give to consumers and investors low-cost access to information through robo-advisers, and, to RegTech, services that streamline KYC/CDD processes and reduce compliance costs. More detailed rules need to be developed to certify good algorithms and platforms, to increase *ex ante* and *ex post* protection of individuals who use robo-advisers, to protect individual rights, such as privacy rights and data rights and to increase the efficiency of KYC processes.

Chapter 10 goes further in demonstrating how a blockchain-based system can enhance sustainability and as an example it examines how the crypto-market can be applied to the consumer energy market to promote sustainable development. It explores the potential benefits and shortcomings of using peer-to-peer energy trading platforms (P2P EPTs) for energy trading in the United Kingdom and shows how P2P ETPs would allow new market models to emerge for self-sustainable energy trading. P2P ETPs can facilitate energy trading for renewables, while tracking the duration and location of energy production, storage and consumption. Green Tariffs for retail energy supply contracts have been introduced in the European Union and the United States to certify for consumers the percentage of renewable sources used. In a similar way, blockchain-based P2P EPTs can promote consumer responsibility in energy consumption and reduce carbon emissions by promoting renewable energy use. However, on this platform consumers would be taking on potential risks. Smart contracts bring with them legal uncertainty, potential violations of privacy and data protection rights, price manipulation and system failure due to coding deficiencies so they alone cannot be legally binding and a hybrid system including a traditional contract should continue to be used to mitigate these risks. Trust groups and cooperative groups should be established to serve as links between consumers through smart contracts and communication via p2p devices such as smart meters. With adequate legislation and institutional coordination, P2P ETPs can give consumers power to produce, consume and share (through trading) energy with greater knowledge, accountability, awareness and protection than traditional systems. While the P2P ETP system is still in its early stages, stability is essential for smaller-scale community projects so, to maintain consumer trust, such projects should be operated and maintained by an independent publicly-funded body.

Current law and regulation can be used to define some crypto-market instruments and practices and to identify their risks

Chapter 4 investigates the applications of "smart contract" technology in the crypto-market (particularly in the securities trading space) and its relationship with transactional law. Smart contract, a technical term rather than a legal one, denotes the automation of some elements of a transaction in a computerised crypto-market and various processes in securities trading may be involved. Crypto-assets can be incorporated into smart contracts and then used for securities transactions on the DLT network. Transfers of tokenised securities have contract law implications and there are several legal risks involved in such transfers which may lead to systematic failures if they are not mitigated. Errors in the way contracts are coded into smart contracts can cause both systemic and systematic failures. A central counterparty system is needed with the dual function of ensuring the safety of the smart contracts and managing default risks. It can also conduct risk assessments on participants and collect margins from them as part of its management of risk.

Because the crypto-market can, in every corner of the world, actively reach out to individuals and passively be reached by individuals, conflicts of laws can arise which may affect market safety on the platform as well as regulatory oversight. There are difficulties for both market surveillance and enforcement proceedings in cross-border trading of securities. It is likely that a legal seat will be required for platform operators, despite the fact that the platform is accessible to parties outside the jurisdiction of that seat. It must be possible to exercise jurisdiction against a person outside the jurisdiction and against the assets of that person. Smart contracts can be designed to reach out to particular individuals and also to allow jurisdictions to protect crypto-markets.

The cryptocurrency market is the most vibrant crypto-market and **Chapter 5** argues that regulation needs to be in place to control the risks of unstable coins and the outcome of stable coins. Public chain crypto-assets should not be recognised as legal tender if value stability cannot be achieved, but, nevertheless, money laundering law and tax law should apply to them to prevent their use for illegal purposes. Crypto-asset exchanges should comply with KYC and AML requirements for anti-money laundering and fraud prevention. In order to protect consumers, the market abuse regime should also apply to exchanges. Exchanges should have a system to protect consumers by safekeeping the "points/tokens" in their wallets. Furthermore, cryptocurrency should not be used as benchmark for retail investors if there is no reliable basis for valuing the underlying assets. Crypto-asset price movements are extremely volatile, there is frequent market abuse and financial crime in the secondary market for crypto-assets, and most retail investors have inadequate product knowledge. To promote the use of stable coins for the sale of goods, consumer protection law should apply to contracts in which crypto-assets have been used as a means of payment. If a merchant fails to deliver the goods, the consumer could then demand compensation with fiat money.

Existing laws and regulations should be carefully reviewed in the STO market and **Chapter 6** examines the initial coin offering market which is an emerging alternative financial market that has been subject to intensive regulatory scrutiny. Although it is possible to develop an STO market and to provide investor confidence by embedding security tokens in the law, current law and regulation on IPOs should not apply to the STO market if it is to achieve its intended purpose of increasing access to finance because an STO is not an IPO on a smaller scale. To have a transformative effect, the STO market needs to emphasise the decentralised and disintermediated structure that distinguishes it from the IPO market. Despite this, the current law and regulation regime for IPOs remains a useful tool to examine market structure, to identify market risks and to mitigate them. In governing the internal affairs of an STO project, company law helps identify risks to investors' economic and political rights, and UK company law provides benchmarks for the development of smart contracts in self-governing organisations. Similarly, the EU Crowdfunding Regulation can be used as a benchmark to identify risks in investor protection on the DLT-based crowdfunding platform as shown in **Chapter 8**.

Outcome-based regulation should apply to data governance to achieve the intended purpose of the crypto-market

Chapter 9 investigates the economics and politics of data in cryptocurrencies and its legal protection. The blockchain collects data to allow access to finance and the Big Data generated is used to develop AI that enhances financial inclusion. But in the process, this crypto-market puts data protection and individual privacy rights at risk.

Three policy goals are set out to cover information generated by the cryptocurrency network: personal autonomy, the development of a digital economy and the prevention of crime. When current data protection law and privacy rights are assessed against these goals in the context of cryptocurrency, analysis shows that unstable coins on the public chain, stable coins on the private chain and state-backed currency on the private chain can all benefit but also create risks. **Chapter 9** also assesses whether current data protection law and privacy law are able to address and mitigate any risks. There is a political dimension to cryptocurrency at the domestic level in terms of how citizens can participate in a more democratised space but also at the international level, for which the data location requirement is an example. While regulators focus on the economics of cryptocurrency, it is international politics that will set its standards, and decide how policy goals are to be fulfilled, what information can be shared by whom and with whom, and how data protection and privacy law will set the new international or regional standards.

Chapter 6 also argues that an investor's data rights should be recognised as both economic and political rights. Data dividends should be distributed to security token holders and data governance should consider the power aspect of the decision-making process. Centralised management should no longer be allowed to monopolise information.

Technology must comply with the concept of justice

Chapter 11 examines the concept of code-as-law in financial markets. Code-as-law is embedded in Regtech, SupTech, LegalTech and consequently in the crypto-market. It has already been used to define the functions of the market, to monitor the behaviour of participants, and enhance access, as well as to digitise securities quantitatively so that centralised match-engines can process trades instantaneously. But on a crypto-market, in addition to these features, securities can be digitised qualitatively to facilitate corporate action at a peer-to-peer level and even give the possibility of automation. Thus code-as-law, combined with a digital regulatory reporting system, gives investors control over their investments as well as indicating how governance should be structured and monitored. I have discussed some of the applications to enhance investor knowledge in **Chapter 8** on the DLT-based crowdfunding platforms.

In addition, code-as-law can increase the efficiency of the compliance regime, especially when rules can be set out with both quantitative and qualitative precision. However, defining rules with qualitative accuracy is challenging in technology and in law because both regulators and tribunals need to exercise judgement as they make decisions case-by-case in a changing market. Furthermore, it is very difficult for regulators to implement code-as-law in the field of compliance. Code-as-law can be used by financial institutions for internal compliance, but regulators need the ability to assess whether code-based algorithms and compliance mechanisms are fit for purpose.

Code-as-law also brings other potential benefits. Market providers can use it to promote social values such as sustainability by manually defining ESG benchmarks in machine-readable form and collecting data to give sustainability scores. These scores can then be used by investors to engage in sustainable investment. However, a regime of benchmark regulation needs to be developed to cover the risk of manipulation. By moving code-as-law from a centralised and intermediated space to the decentralised and disintermediated crypto-environment, it can provide data subjects with more control over their information as well as closing the information gap between project owners and their investors.

Final message

The basic principles of the crypto-market are that it should provide access to finance, promote a shared economy, allow access to justice and promote sustainability. Although current laws and rules can help identify risk, these four principles provide the foundation on which laws and rules that are appropriate for the new market can be developed. While *lex cryptographia* can be a component of the governance framework, it must adhere to the concept of justice in order to gain social acceptance.

Index